WHY OBSERVA
LEAVE JU

CW00557729

OFF THE
DERECH

How To Respond
To The Challenge

Faranak Margolese

DEVORA
PUBLISHING
JERUSALEM ◆ NEW YORK

Off the Derech

Published by DEVORA PUBLISHING COMPANY

Text Copyright © 2005 Faranak Margolese

Cover and Inside Design: David Yaphe

Cloth ISBN: 1-932687-40-8
Paper ISBN: 1-932687-43-2

Email: publisher@devorapublishing.com
Web Site: www.devorapublishing.com

Printed in Israel

More Acclaim for
Off the Derech

"Sobering and required reading for anyone involved in any aspect of Jewish education — whether parent, teacher, rabbi, or citizen-representative of the Torah community. We are indebted to Faranak Margolese for studying so thoroughly a crisis too disturbing and painful for most of us even to consider."

Lawrence Kelemen
Author of *To Kindle a Soul: Ancient Wisdom for Modern Parents and Teachers*

"This is a courageous and necessary book. If Orthodox life takes it seriously, it will change all of Jewish life for the better."

Dennis Prager
Best selling author and nationally syndicated radio talk show host

"*Off the Derech* is essential reading for every Jewish parent and educator concerned with the alienation of our young people. It is an invaluable source for understanding why observant Jewish youth leave the fold and a priceless tool for preventing them from doing so."

Natan Lopez Cardozo
Dean of The David Cardozo Academy

"A probing book about a sensitive and rarely discussed topic, why people leave religion. Faranak Margolese seems to have considered this problem from every angle, interviewed everyone, and offers answers that can affect the future of Jewish life."

Joseph Telushkin
Author of *Jewish Literacy*, and
The Book of Jewish Values.

Dear Friends,

I have read *Off the Derech* by Faranak Margolese. I found it eye opening, mind opening and heart opening. The author deals with a very urgent issue and does not rely on clichés or simplistic explanations of the causes and solutions to this many-sided and complex problem. The depth and breadth of her study encompasses many causes, emotional, intellectual and psychological and many solutions that encompass home, school, and Jewish community in general. Causes and solutions to this issue, or for that matter to any issue, are not monolithic as people are not monolithic. Although one can disagree with various points made in the book as to the causes or solutions to going off the derech, the discussion of the various points itself will lead to further understanding of the roots of this problem and engender further solutions on a long-term basis.

Much of the book focuses on making Judaism fulfilling to our youth which might seem at odds with the ideal of serving G-d to fulfill His will. But as the Rambam explains, we must approach people on their level and although altruistic love of Hashem is a precious ideal, our generation requires incentives of fulfillment in order to be properly inspired.

I recommend this work as a healthy forum to inform and sensitize one to this multi-faceted challenge of our generation and to open one's heart to realize how heartbreaking the problem is and how urgently we must seek and implement solutions. Every Jewish soul is a world to itself and saving that soul is tantamount to saving the world. Additionally, we are all inter-related and the loss of one individual soul to Torah is a loss to each and every one's own soul.

I commend the author for a job well done and may G-d grant her life and health to continue to benefit the community with further works such as this, and may He help us to return those who have defected from Judaism, which will be her greatest reward in having a part in that process.

Sincerely,

Rabbi Zev Leff
Rav, Moshav Matityahu
Rosh Yeshiva, Yeshiva Gedola Matityahu

FOR MY PARENTS

Your love and dedication

made me who I am,

taught me to love Judaism,

and showed me by example

what exceptional people and parents are like.

My greatest accomplishment would be

to follow in your footsteps.

Acknowledgements

The five-year journey of researching and writing this book would not have been possible without the invaluable help of numerous people:

Yaacov Peterseil, who enthusiastically agreed to publish this book and worked hard to do so; Elise Teitelbaum who helped to edit and refine this manuscript; and Stuart Schnee who has been a dedicated, passionate publicist.

Arthur Kurzweil who encouraged me to write this book (and offered to publish it before he ever saw a page). Without his encouragement, I never would have embarked on the journey in the first place.

The experts I interviewed (and the assistants who helped me get to them), who generously gave of their time, enlightened me, and trusted me with their thoughts on a delicate subject. Among them: David Berger, Rabbi Ephraim Buchwald, Rabbi Shaya Cohen, Yohanan Danziger, Sergio Della Pergola, former Chief Rabbi Mordechai Eliayhu, Debbie Greenblatt, Leah Kohn, Rabbi Dr. Norman Lamm, Dr. Jerry Lob, David Mandel, Rabbi Daniel Mechanic, Dennis Prager, Rabbi Moshe Prager, Chief Rabbi Jonathan Sacks, Rabbi Nota Schiller, Rabbi Yaakov Shapiro, Nate Siegal, Rabbi Adin Steinsaltz, Rabbi Joseph Telushkin, Rabbi Shlomo Riskin, Avi Rothenberg, Rabbi Berel Wein, Dr. Meir

Wikler, Judy Young, and Rabbi Yehuda Zakatinsky.

With a special thanks to Basy and Rabbi Raviv Shaked, and Rabbi Dr. Natan Lopes Cardozo for teaching me, guiding me, and going out of their way to help me refine and develop this book.

All those who have "gone off the derech" whom I interviewed and the hundreds who responded to the web survey. This book would not have been possible without their honesty and courage and the time it took for them to share their thoughts and feelings with me.

David Yaphe, who designed the book cover and content; Chani Hadad, who served as the proofreader; Yehudis Golshevsky, who located and researched sources for the book; Alys Yablon, who helped with editing this book; Rabbi Frances Nataf, who provided valuable feedback on the book; Mareleyn Schneider who generously gave of her time to analyze and verify the results of the web survey; Marc Belzberg and Margy Davis, who connected me with rabbis and other important contacts whom I otherwise would not have met; Cheryl Chronis, who designed and created the web site; Yogen Kapadia, who helped maintain it; and Kent Kroger, who ran initial statistics.

Rabbi Mordechai Prager, for being my rav and changing some of my perceptions about the observant world. If all observant Jews were like him, this book would be irrelevant. Dr. Bruce Powell for teaching me how to write, Rochelle Krich for teaching me how to conduct and organize effectively, and the Columbia School of the Arts for helping turn my hobby into a profession. All my teachers, who inspired me to question, to learn, and to love Judaism through their example.

Most importantly, my husband, David, who not only tirelessly edited and re-edited this book, but who inspired me to ask the question, helped me to find the answer, and patiently and lovingly supported me through every step of this journey. I couldn't have done it without him and wouldn't have wanted to.

And finally, God, who, in addition to giving me the ability to write, created a people like none other and made me a part of it.

Table of Contents

Introduction

"The best simile for what is happening today is Roman suicide: In ancient Rome, people would enter into a warm bath and slice their wrists. The blood would slowly, slowly flow out of their bodies and they would die a gradual, enjoyable death. Something like this is happening to the Jewish people... For every tick of the clock...we are losing Jews..."[1]

— Rabbi Adin Steinsaltz

All over America, a spiritual re-awakening is unfolding. Dyan Canon throws "God parties"; Oprah features a segment called "Remembering Your Spirit"; the World Trade Towers fall and the nation prays.

The Jewish world is no different. The last few decades have seen an almost unprecedented return to Judaism, with thousands of secular Jews becoming observant. But while many secular Jews return to Judaism, thousands are casting off their religious upbringing for an alternative way of life. We are not too surprised when that occurs in secular, Reform, or Conservative Jewish families; but today, more and more *yeshiva*-educated children from classically observant homes are abandoning their tradition. This phenomenon, which in the observant world is referred to as "going off the derech" (going off the path), worries us. If it does not, it should.

I first noticed this phenomenon when I started dating my husband. As I introduced him to my friends, he would ask if they were observant, and almost every time, I found myself answering, "No, but he or she used to be." After a while, I realized that at least 75% of my friends had been raised in observant homes, but were no longer observant themselves. They were connected. They went to *shul* (synagogue) perhaps or they attended a Friday night dinner, but they were not living the *halachically* committed (committed according to Jewish law) lives of their childhoods. They were connected without commitment.

I couldn't understand it. My friends had the best Jewish educations money could buy. They came from a wide variety of backgrounds; many from warm, loving homes. They had all the tools necessary to continue observing Judaism whether they were raised in Modern Orthodox, 'black hat,' or Chassidic families, or whether their parents were *baalei teshuva* (returnees to observance). But they had all moved away, and at a time when so many are moving closer.

I myself had a similar experience. Although I was not raised in a technically observant home, I grew up in a traditional Sephardic one in which my parents had strong Jewish values and great respect for Judaism. They sent me to *yeshiva* day school, making many financial and personal sacrifices to do so, and they gave me a joyful exposure to Judaism. My education supported their positive regard for our tradition by teaching me our fascinating history, meaningful rituals, and reasons for our beliefs. In school, I questioned, worked hard, and I loved learning about Judaism so much so that by the time I graduated high school, I could think of only one direction for my future — learning in seminary in Israel. I went to *yeshiva* for a year, became *halachically* observant, and returned to continue my Jewish studies at Yeshiva University.

Five years later, I was in New York, going to *shul* almost every week and strongly believing in Orthodox Judaism, but no longer *halachical-*

ly observant. A typical Friday night involved five to ten of my friends getting together for a Shabbat meal, making *hamotzi* (the blessing for bread), eating, and then listening to music or watching TV.

Today I am observant again and always knew I would be. But that made my lack of observance all the more baffling. What had happened? Had my Yiddishkeit simply died? Had I become lazy? Was it the *yetzer hara* (evil inclination)? And had what happened to me also happened to my friends? Were we all experiencing something typical of young adults in a modern world or was it particular to each of us, as unique as each of us?

I started interviewing my friends to discover why they were no longer observant. Though we had spoken over the years about Judaism and our various struggles with it, the formal interview process was an eye-opener. While some had very intelligent responses and deep concerns, others seemed lost. One girl began her interview stating that she knew very clearly why she was no longer observant. First she told me it was her community; then it was her father; then negative educational experiences. Over the course of several hours, she gave so many different answers that by the end of the session she simply said, "I guess you could say I don't know why I'm not religious anymore. I guess you could say I'm confused."

Such is the case with many people. The answers that first come to mind are often superficial. Beneath them lie the deeper, more meaningful issues, which can take years of hard work and honesty to discover. As I conducted my interviews, I realized that many people were not in touch with those deeper reasons and that I would have to accept much of what I heard at face value. But even the superficial responses or confusing ones revealed something very important about why they had left observant life. They eventually revealed patterns and similarities which explained the issues properly.

The perspectives presented in this book result from over five years of research, including thousands of pages of in-depth, personal interviews with formerly observant Jews from across the religious and age spectrum, as well as interviews with prominent rabbis, educators, therapists, and program directors. In addition, I established a web site (www.offthederech.com) which anonymously surveyed hundreds of formerly observant Jews from across the religious spectrum. After all invalid and repeated responses were eliminated, there were 466 valid responses to the survey, although not all respondents answered all the questions. This unscientific study strongly supported the findings of the personal interviews, and its highlights are presented at the end of the book.

Through my research, I have learned that one of the great mistakes we make when we try to pinpoint the reason for people going off the derech is oversimplification. Everyone sees things through their own particular lens. Those who work with abused children point to abuse as the primary cause. Those who work with children with learning disabilities consider disabilities the principal factor. Drug counselors blame substance abuse. Rabbis, to varying degrees, believe the problem is contact with our open, hedonistic host culture, and educators dwell on negative peer group influences. Some simply finger-point; "It's not us, it's them."

They are all right. And they are all wrong. People do not leave religion for any *one* reason but for a host of them, for a series of complex factors that come together in a particular way over an extended period of time. The contributing factors vary according to personality and circumstance, and any attempt to answer the question through one particular lens will fall short.

Today, we have many pieces of the puzzle but no picture of the puzzle itself. We have answers to *parts* of the issue but no *overall understanding* of how the parts work together as a whole to affect our choices of faith and observance. I hope to create such an understanding, to delineate the complexities of the issue and create a framework for understanding why people stop being observant. In doing so, I will address when this phenomenon began, how big the problem is, and why the Jewish education we provide is not enough to secure Jewish identity for many of our youth. Where does free will come into the picture? Why do some eventually return while others never look back? And to what extent are we as families, schools and communities contributing to the exodus?

Answering these questions has proved far more difficult than I ever anticipated. Explaining why groups of people do *anything* is challenging. But this issue is particularly problematic. People feel strongly about it on all sides and there is much sensitivity and controversy surrounding it. Even defining observance, the first and seemingly most simple step, was complex.

What does it mean to be observant? This is not easy to answer. For clarity's sake, I use a classic definition of "observance" — the *halachic* observance of Shabbat and *kashrut*. The people I interviewed were raised with at least these two minimum requirements regardless of their placement on the spectrum of left, right or centrist Orthodoxy. They then crossed over to not keeping Shabbat and *kashrut*, no matter what else they did or did not do.

Although the group I surveyed includes what has come to be known as "kids at risk," this book focuses on the general population of Jews who have gone off the derech, including adults as well as those who have abandoned observance without exhibiting "at risk" behavior. The goal was to identify the underlying principles at work that would apply to *any* group of people or person who has gone off the derech.

As a result, the principles presented in this book should explain why anyone goes off the derech, regardless of their placement on the religious spectrum. In fact, they may well explain why people in general, even from Reform or Conservative families, move away from Judaism.

Having said that, it is important to note that the specific *application* or *expression* of these principles will vary from person to person or group to group. Each of us is a complex world with a myriad of unique needs. Therefore, while this book can present the principles which apply to us all, it cannot prescribe exactly *how* those principles express themselves in any particular person. Likewise, while this book strives to provide general solutions and guidelines for dealing with the issues, it cannot define *particular* solutions for *particular* cases.

In reading this book it is vital to remember what I quickly learned in conducting these interviews: that in order to understand why people stop observing Judaism, we have to see observant Jewish life through *their* eyes and hearts, not our own. In the most important sense, their perceptions *are* the reality that explains this phenomenon. Sometimes their perceptions correspond to reality; sometimes they do not. But their thoughts and feelings about Judaism and their decisions about observance were created by their *perceptions,* so that is the first place to look for answers.

It is also important to note that whatever the percentage we actually see leave observance, there are those whom we do not see leave — those who physically observe but whose hearts are empty, whose souls are thirsty, who go through the motions with little emotion or connection. They are the would-be dropouts, spiritual dropouts who are merely externally observant. And while these people maintain technical observance, odds are their children may not. So those who drop observance are the tip of the iceberg, and they indicate that, in many ways, throughout the observant Jewish world, we are losing our spiritual wealth. The chain of our tradition can only continue if observance is experienced as a privilege, and for too many, it has become a burden.

This presents a problem, not only for many who have gone off the derech, but also for Judaism itself and potentially the world at large. For our laws and rituals are the physical expressions of our spiritual values. They make Judaism a living, breathing part of us and losing them is often the first step inter-generationally to losing it all. That indeed is tragic for we Jews carry a unique and powerful voice "in the conversation of mankind,"[2] one that has revolutionized the world and inspired us to unimagined success in every generation. Perhaps most importantly, our voice keeps God alive in the world as the *midrash* (tradition) tells us: when the verse says in Isaiah (43:12) that "You are my witnesses says the Lord and I am God," it connects the two phrases to teach us that as long as we are here as witnesses, God exists in the world. If we are no longer here as witnesses, God is no longer the Lord.[3] So, as renowned educator Rabbi Adin Steinsaltz explains, "We not only maintain our own existence, but we also keep God in the world. And that is something that is worth doing."[4]

Some people minimize this issue. They claim that defection has always existed, that the numbers are minimal, or that whatever the numbers are, we should accept our "losses" as they come, concentrating on those who remain. Nothing could be further from a Jewish perspective in my opinion. Every person is a world, and every child who abandons observance, or becomes resentful of Judaism and Jewish people represents a tremendous loss to us.

So where do we go from here? As Chief Rabbi Jonathan Sacks says, "one of the advantages of being a four thousand year old people is that whatever happens, you have been there before."[5] We need only listen to those who are leaving to understand why. Rather than blame or fear them, it would help to approach each one like the gem that he or she is, to listen without judgment, and love them, with no agenda other than to understand. Once we have truly listened and their words have penetrated our hearts without judgment, anger or fear, we can effectively see what we can do to improve things.

After five years of doing little else but researching and thinking about this issue, I believe that there is no greater challenge facing the Jewish world today. Our Torah gives us the guidelines to meet it, and there is no need to move outside the structure of *halachah*, which has sustained us through the ages, to do so. But there is a need to re-think certain issues, to look with fresh eyes, and to dare to improve not only our communities, *shuls*, schools, and homes, and but also ourselves as individuals. We can make the religious Jewish community a model community for the world, and in many ways we have done so. With a little more effort and God's help, we can move even closer to inspiring our children and securing their commitment to observance.

I would be privileged if this book would be a small step on that journey. May *Hashem* give me the words and us the will to make it so.

CHAPTER 1

How Big is the Problem?

I n November of 1999, the *Jewish Observer*, a prominent Orthodox Jewish publication, did something it had never done before. It published an entire issue of its monthly magazine on one subject — kids at risk. They called it "Kids on the Fringe and Beyond." The magazine sold out. Parents, schools, and libraries asked for multiple copies for friends and relatives. The magazine needed a second reprinting just to satisfy demand and the response to that issue was so great, they did another unprecedented act: they printed an issue devoted entirely to readers' responses.

Both issues were fascinating. We heard from parents who stayed up all night worried about their children; from teachers witnessing surprising rebellion; from *gedolim* (highly respected rabbis) who offered words of comfort to a community struggling for answers.

The *Jewish Observer* was the first to confront this issue so publicly, to offer possible explanations as well as potential solutions. This broken silence elicited such overwhelming response that readers began to wonder just how endemic abandonment of observant life had become. It seemed like a plague, like tens of thousands of families were suffering from kids at risk.

For the observant this seems unthinkable. Our Jewish world has created strong, vibrant communities all over the world with schools and synagogues filled with prayer and learning. After thousands of years' persecution, we have managed not only to survive but to thrive, cherishing our rituals and passing them on. Today, our *yeshivas* are brimming with youth engaged with Jewish tradition, despite great challenges from a contradictory outside world.

On the other hand, there is alarm on behalf of parents, educators, kids at risk experts, and communal leaders. In referring to the issue of kids at risk, Rabbi Daniel Mechanic, Director of Project Chazon, who has taught Jewish Philosophy seminars to over 95,000 students in *yeshiva* day schools, says "the problem is one hundred times worse, both quantitatively and qualitatively" than anyone thinks it is. Yohanan Danziger, who studied at-risk youth in Brooklyn, asserts the problem is "at the level of a plague; it's out of control."[1] And Moshe Schapiro, who wrote "Ohr Samayach Addresses the Teen-Dropout Issue," says "the teenage dropout rate has reached epidemic proportions... and is widely regarded as one of the most pressing issues of our times."[2]

If our schools are brimming with students and our families are mostly successful in transmitting commitment to a Torah observant way of life: why the alarm? Where are all these dropouts everyone is talking about? Exactly how big is this problem?

My personal experience supports the theory that this problem is an "epidemic." Who, after all, were the multitudes of people requesting extra copies of the *Observer*? Who were they giving them to? To the same people I have met over the last four years at Shabbat tables all over the world. As soon as my fellow diners would hear the topic of this book, they would launch into an hour-long conversation which would inevitably end with a list of formerly observant Jews they knew personally. It never failed.

Many of us intuitively feel that the issue has reached epidemic proportions. But personal experience cannot accurately quantify the problem. For that, we need a more scientific examination of the facts and unfortunately, to date, no formal studies have been conducted on a national level. As a result, it is nearly impossible to ascertain exactly what percentage of observant Jews goes off the derech.

This is true, in part, because as experts point out, "It is extremely difficult to quantify a problem which still elicits silence and shame."[3] And this issue elicits great shame. Among the Orthodox Jewish community, there is almost nothing worse than children abandoning their parents' heritage. So when children come *close* to leaving the path, we remain silent. We fear communal ostracism. We fear secret conversations, condemnation, and criticism. We fear others saying what we ourselves may feel deep down inside — that we have been failures as Jews if our children go off the derech.

How then are we to proceed in understanding the extent of this problem? We can begin by examining related studies that shed light on the subject.

Indicator One: Kids at Risk

The first is kids at risk. "Kids at risk" usually refers to a population marked not only by abandonment of observance but also by engagement in socially delinquent activities such as vandalism, theft, substance abuse, promiscuity, and running away from home. In 1999, the Metropolitan New York Coordinating Council on Jewish Poverty commissioned Yohanan Danziger to conduct a study of at-risk youth in Brooklyn. The study surveyed observant parents as well as professionals working with at-risk youth including psychologists, social workers, teachers, principals, agency directors and others.

Interviewees were asked to estimate the prevalence of Orthodox at-risk youth in Brooklyn. Most speculated that about 1100 to 2200 Orthodox kids in Brooklyn are at-risk,[4] about 5 to 10 % of the Orthodox population. Hotlines and professionals who work "on the street" reported approximately 1500 cases of at-risk youth indicating a 6.6% level.[5] Most speculated that an additional 1500-2000 youth were "developing at risk behaviors...but had not, as of yet, become a full at-risk problem."[6] This would more than double the percentage, 13.3% to 15.5%.

These may not seem like high percentages. In fact, according to Rabbi Berel Wein, renowned educator and historian, "in an open society that accepts Jews the way Jews are accepted today in the United States, I would say between 8-10% [defection] would be expected."[7] According to Rabbi Wein, such an attrition rate still would be far less than it was 100 years ago, and is significantly less than in Reform and Conservative communities.

Yet if we use the Brooklyn study as a guide to shed light on how many people go off the derech, the percentages are much higher than might be expected. After all, this study only examined youth who were exhibiting the most *extreme* behavior. If between 6.6% — 15.5% of Orthodox Brooklyn teens are exhibiting or will exhibit at-risk behavior, what percentage are simply going off the derech *without* exhibiting socially unacceptable behavior? And what percentage is on the way out? Even the most conservative estimates based on this study would be much higher than the "expected" 8 or 10%.

Indicator Two: YU Education Study

This assertion is supported by a study conducted by Yeshiva University in 1994 which explored the effect of Jewish day school education on Jewish observance and behavior. Thousands of day school graduates were studied, the vast majority of whom had attended Orthodox day schools and came from observant families. Though the study did not specifically examine what percentage had remained observant over the years, Dr. Mareleyn Schneider who co-authored the study was kind enough to reexamine the data and provide me with the following information:

Of the approximately 2000 respondents surveyed who had two *halachically* observant parents and attended Orthodox day schools, 96.7% made Kiddush on Friday night; 89.2% made Kiddush Shabbat morning; 91.4% lit candles; 92.9% did not travel on Shabbat. In terms of *kashrut*, 87.7% observed strict *kashrut* at home. All these percentages fall within Rabbi Wein's expected figures for religious observance in an open society. What was somewhat surprising was the percentage of those who *did not* keep *kashrut outside* of the home. Of these 2000 respondents, 33.5% *did not* keep *kashrut* outside of the home. 25.5% kept it moderately or somewhat. 8% did not keep it at all.[8]

According to this data, if we use *halachic* Shabbat observance as our guide, approximately 3% to 11% have gone off the derech.[9] But if we use *kashrut* as our guide, the numbers are far higher, between 12% — 33%.

Indicator Three: Unobservant Jewish World

Finally, there is another way to think about the issue, one which may not provide clear numbers, but provides an alarming context for the problem, namely that today, about 90% of the Jewish world is not observant. Where did all these nonobservant Jews come from? Intergenerationally, they almost all came from observant homes.

Historically, for most of history that we can verify, the vast majority of Jews were *halachically* observant. According to Dr. David Berger, prior to the 1600's, those who publicly desecrated Shabbat were too small a number even to be counted.[10] But things began to change with the Enlightenment over the last couple of hundred years. More and more Jews moved away so that today, over 90% of the Jewish world is not *halachically* observant. To the best of our knowledge, this is a unique phenomenon in Jewish history — the first time that the vast majority of Jews are not observant.[11]

So today, for the most part, even the most disenfranchised Jew had a grandparent or great-grandparent who was observant. And that means that the process of *complete* assimilation often begins with the one observant Jew who goes off the derech. From there, his children move one more step away until finally, usually not more than three or four generations later, there is total assimilation. This process is reflected in an interpretation of the Four Sons of the Passover *Hagaddah*. One interpretation views these sons not as individual children but as generations. The first generation is wise, so to speak. He is committed to *halachic* Judaism; the second rebels and moves away. The third generation is "simple," confused between the parent who does not observe and the grandparents who do. The fourth generation is so far removed, it does not even know how to ask a question. And the fifth son, his generation is no longer at the Passover *seder* at all. He has totally assimilated.

If we think about the issue in these terms, we realize that whatever the percentage that have actually gone off the derech in any *particular* generation, over the last few centuries, the number has translated into a whopping 90% no longer observing. If the 90% of nonobservant Jews today came from observant ancestors, then the off the derech phenomenon has far more staggering consequences than we ever imagined. In fact, it is responsible for the new reality of Jewish life today in which most Jews are disenfranchised. This is an astounding reality, one which makes defection from *halachic* observance not only a cause for alarm among observant Jews, but for all Jews concerned with the continuity of Jewish identity and tradition.

The Trend

No matter how we quantify this phenomenon, there seems to be consensus on a couple of important issues. The first is that the numbers seem to be getting worse every year. Rabbi Daniel Mechanic recalls that, eight years ago, he received one call a month from parents of at-risk teens. Six years ago, it was one call a week. Three years ago, it was one a day, and by the time he began manning the hotline at Project

YES with Rabbi Yaakov Horowitz, over 700 cases were called in during a one year period.[12]

Rabbi Yaakov Shapiro, Director of Project Rejewvenation, who has spent over ten years working with kids at-risk in the tri-state area, has compiled research based on thousands of meetings with teens. He concludes that in 1998–2000, the numbers of kids at risk in the Orthodox Jewish world increased three times more than in any other two years in the past decade. He graphs the trend as follows:

% Increase Of Instances

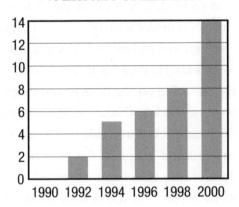

Furthermore, the age of rebellion seems to be decreasing. In 1990, he found that the average age of rebellion was 16 for boys and 15 for girls. By the year 2000, the age of rebellion had decreased to 14 and 15 for boys, and 13 or 14 for girls.[13]

Finally, most agree that no matter what the current percentage of observant Jews who go off the derech, it is only the tip of the iceberg. They are the ones who have left with their feet, whose lack of Jewish connection we see. But there are also those who have left with their hearts, whom we do not see. They continue to observe, but their observance is hollow, with no soul, no heart, no real belief at its core. There are still others who would stop observing if they could, but feel unable to do so due to familial or social expectations. These people are not externally or behaviorally off the derech, but we might say they are *internally* off the derech.

This group teaches us something vital about the quality of Jewish life and observance today, which may be a far better indicator of our success or failure than the *quantity* who remain observant.[14] And if we consider them part of this phenomenon, then the problems in our observant world are far more pervasive and dramatic than we might expect.

Those who are internally off the derech also teach us that the issues that cause complete defection affect us all to varying extents. Disconnection is merely a milder form of defection according to Rabbi Dovid Brezak, a well-known author and educator who counsels parents of off the derech kids. He explains that "when you put it in terms of what percentage are going off the derech, you destroy the true picture. The percentage of children that are going off only indicates the inner problem which exists even in children who are not going off."

So there is a spectrum of going off the derech, with three clearly defined groups: kids at risk, who are unobservant and socially delinquent; those who have gone off the derech *behaviorally* and those who have gone off the derech *internally*. While this book examines the second group, the principles at work are the same for all groups. Each group shares similar experiences to varying extents; each sheds light on how prevalent these issues are; and each indicates something about the quality of observant life today. And when we consider these groups in light of our new historical reality in which the majority of the Jewish world is no longer observant, we can begin to understand the dramatic nature of the off the derech phenomenon, and how it has already changed the character of our nation.

CHAPTER 2

Dispelling the Myths:
Assimilation, Then and Now

Before addressing the causes of defection from Judaism, it is worth considering whether or not this phenomenon is new. Has it always been this way? If so, is there any real cause for concern? And if not, how are things different today?

Rabbi Berel Wein answers these questions poignantly when he says that defection from Judaism is like "a recessive gene."[1] It has always existed but due to persecution from the outside world, has not always had the opportunity to express itself the way it does today.

From the very beginning of our story as a people, even before we received the Torah, Jews have been persecuted — first by the Egyptians, and then by nearly every other nation in the world. The nations of the world have chased us, started pogroms and set inquisitions against us, beaten us and treated us like slaves through one exodus after another, culminating in the horrors of the Holocaust. The 13th century in Europe alone saw the persecution of Jews from Spain, England, Italy, France, Austria, Germany, Hungary, and Poland. Middle Eastern Jews experienced sporadic violence from the inception of Islam in the seventh century until the re-establishment of the State of Israel when

600,000 Jews were forced to flee their homes in Arab lands. Through all this we feared, we hid, we practiced our beliefs quietly, and we taught our children to live humbly so that we might continue, at least, to live. That was enough and throughout much of our history that seemed to be asking a lot.

In such times of persecution, defection was difficult if not absurd. We did not really have the opportunity to assimilate; the hatred from the outside world established a natural barrier that kept us out. It also paradoxically strengthened us so that people did not *want* to assimilate. Persecution constantly reminded us of who we were, strengthening our religious identities and communal ties rather than weakening them. If nothing else, persecution revealed the cruelty of the outside world so that even if one hated Jews and Judaism, he would be loath to join a world as menacing as the one around him.

If for some reason a person did want to assimilate, the only hope of acceptance was through conversion, a move far too drastic for even the most dispirited Jew and one that often ended in persecution anyway. As a result, the 11th through the 18th centuries saw very little assimilation.[2]

The only exceptions to that rule were punctuated moments of freedom. During those moments when we experienced social acceptance and freedom, we have also experienced great upsurges in assimilation. For example, there was considerable assimilation in the time of the Second Temple, when Jews embraced Hellenism. Until the 19th century, such periods of assimilation were sporadic. But in the 19th century, everything changed. Freedom no longer existed as *moments* in time, but rather as a new *reality* that defined a revolutionary landscape of social, intellectual, and religious identity. And with it came unprecedented assimilation.

By the 19th century, an estimated 250,000 Jews in Europe had converted to Christianity. Between 1812 and 1848, 85 % of Berlin's Jews underwent conversion.[3] The rise of the Enlightenment, Emancipation and Reform movements — and the subsequent reigning ideologies of socialism, nationalism, and Zionism — all permeated the tone of Jewish life to the degree that when elections for Jewish Community Councils were held, secularists won every election.

Somewhere between 40% to 60% of Europe's Jews were in the process of assimilating. By 1929, about 30% of the Jewish community was intermarrying.[4] By 1930, over 70% of Poland's Jewish children were not attending Jewish schools.[5] Rabbi Ephraim Buchwald, founder and director of the National Jewish Outreach Program, explains that "because of the ferocious onslaught of secularism, some reports maintain that as many as 30% of the students of the venerated *yeshiva* of Volozhin — the Harvard of Jewish life — became Bundists, Bolsheviks and Mensheviks, some of them playing a prominent role in the atheist Communist revolution…"[6] And they were the best educated of society which explains why the rest assimilated en masse. At the time, Rabbi Buchwald explains,

> There were only about three to four thousand *yeshiva* students in all of Europe… Today, the *yeshiva* in Lakewood, New Jersey alone has 3000 students. But in all of Europe, there were only maybe 16 major *yeshivot* and only the best and most select young men attended. A good number of the *shtetel* Jews attended *cheder* (class), but that's like going to a poor quality elementary school, and on the basis of that education, you were expected to live your life as an informed and knowledgeable Jew.[7]

Only about 3% of Eastern European Jewish society consisted of scholars. The rest were ordinary Jews who were certainly not intellectually prepared to defend Judaism in the age of science, progress and equality.[8]

Europeans who immigrated to the United States often dropped observance in order to work and provide food for their families. And those who managed to remain observant often watched their children go off the derech, as one *baal teshuva* told me — his grandfather who came from Europe maintained his observance level, but all seven of his children "ate *treif* (non-kosher) in front of him and blew smoke rings on Shabbos."

The prevalence of this phenomenon is entirely new, for although there has always been defection from observance, prior to the Enlightenment, defections tended to occur over short periods of time with relatively small numbers in terms of the percentage of the entire Jewish world.

Recent decades have seen yet another change in the phenomenon, namely in the defectors themselves. No longer are those ranks filled with middle-aged immigrants, choosing painfully to work on Shabbat rather than let their families go hungry. Today we are faced with teenagers, who seemingly have everything they need in life, giving up on tradition.

In addition, the nature of defections in more recent history has changed. Our parents and grandparents may have lost the fight of holding onto tradition, but they *did* fight. As Rabbi Buchwald notes, "Our parents and grandparents fought with some sort of a mystical zeal to be here today. And what do we do — we give it away for less than a pot of lentils."[9] Put another way, Rabbi Yaakov Shapiro says that our "parents and grandparents would have gladly thrown themselves into a furnace rather than give up Yiddishkeit…If a kid is willing to throw it away because his parents got a divorce, he isn't living the same religion as his grandfather."[10]

Those who leave observance today seem not to be fighting for it. They drop observance sometimes without a second thought, sometimes with only a little guilt, and sometimes not with sadness, but with great feelings of resentment and bitterness toward Judaism and observant Jews.

The irony is that all this occurs at a time in history when in many ways it has never been easier to be a Jew. Freedom of worship has provided us with an unprecedented ability to develop our religiosity and communities, our *shuls* and schools. And we have succeeded in doing so. We have more Jewish books, more kosher restaurants, more students in *yeshiva* today than ever before. We are living in one of the most unique periods of Jewish history, one for which we have prayed for nearly four thousand years — to have "sovereignty in the land of Israel and freedom and equality in the Diaspora. We never had them both at the same time."[11] And now we leave in greater numbers than before, at younger ages, without a struggle? How can we understand this?

Myth #1 — Freedom as the Cause

One reason often given for the high rate of assimilation today is freedom. The freedom found in the modern world makes it easier to practice Judaism but it also makes it easier to leave it. Today, we can slip away into the outside world more easily than ever, and rather than be rejected for our Jewishness, we will be embraced and loved.

But it is important to realize that freedom is not the *cause* of defection; it is merely the *condition* that allows for it. Freedom itself is an inherently neutral condition. It does not determine the actual choice. When God gave Adam the freedom to choose, He did not *cause* Adam to eat from the tree. Rather He provided an opportunity for Adam to decide for himself. An open society can give us freedom, but it cannot force us to choose a particular side. It merely creates the context within which our Judaism lives and the challenges it must face. It opens the door and provides an alternative; whether or not we choose that alternative, however, is up to us.

The real obstacle to observance created by freedom today is that it levels the playing field. Freedom means that today our children can easily choose alternative lifestyles with far fewer negative consequences and under much less dramatic circumstances. Judaism is now just another contender for one's lifestyle as are other ways of life. As Rabbi

Dr. Norman Lamm, former President of Yeshiva University, puts it: "It's like sitting at a banquet and being free to take what you wish."[12] We compare Judaism to its alternatives and proceed accordingly.

In times of persecution, Judaism easily won when compared to the alternative. In fact, it needed only to be neutral to be chosen, for the alternative was perceived as "evil." If anything, persecution would drive you *toward* your Jewish community, for human nature is to avoid pain. Today, the opposite is true. The outside world is no longer painful or perceived as evil, but rather enjoyable, attractive and welcoming. So today, in order for observant Judaism to be chosen, it cannot merely be neutral. It must be better than the alternative.

And since observant Judaism requires discipline, work, and patience, it needs to be *much* better. It needs to be strong enough, meaningful enough, joyful enough to justify the "sacrifice." It can no longer exist passively, counting on persecution to drive us toward home; it must actively attract us and pull us there. The degree to which it succeeds at this task determines how likely the next generation will be to choose it.

So, freedom has raised the bar so to speak. But identifying freedom as the cause of defection begs the question. The real question is: why, when we are given freedom to choose, is Judaism not what we choose? Or to put it another way: why do we not perceive Judaism as the highest expression of freedom? We believe that freedom in and of itself is meaningless. In fact, Pesach celebrates our freedom but we count the *sefirah* in part to teach us that the freedom of Pesach is only of value when connected to *Shavuot* when we were given the purpose for our freedom. The *mitzvot* are meant to be the greatest facilitator of our freedom, creating far greater joys than can be found in freedom for its own sake, as expressed by King David, "I will walk in freedom for I have sought your law."[13] Yet today, we hear the opposite message. We hear that those who have left observance are "frei," free, implying that those who observe are trapped and bound.

Myth #2 — It's the Outside world

Perhaps one of the most often stated causes for those who go off the *derech* today is the outside world — its values, ideas, and shifting realities. This world assaults and challenges Jewish values at every turn in dramatic ways. The proliferation of the media, television, and the Internet has brought sex, violence, materialistic values, and foul language into our homes. Social realities have drastically changed as well. In the past forty years, "crime rates have risen 1000%...divorce rates have risen six times; the number of children born outside marriage has risen five times, the number of children living with a single parent has raised three times…"[14]

These stark realities are complemented by a secular value system which contradicts Judaism in both subtle and dramatic ways. Perhaps one of the greatest, most fundamental challenges has been the new mindset created by the Enlightenment. Ever since the Enlightenment, man no longer lives in a God-centered universe but a man-centered universe, in which science and reason rule and man is the measure of all things. Objective truth has been replaced by personal preference, and religion has become peripheral at best and irrelevant at worst.

Technology, too, has posed some unexpected challenges to Judaism. For example, technology has allowed us to travel far and wide, eroding communities and the family units within them. The world is now called a "global village," for it is getting smaller. But in reality, it is more like what Rabbi Yehuda Amital calls a "global metropolis."[15] The world is smaller, but it lacks the intimate atmosphere of a village in which we are known, cared for, and connected. In fact, we lack the support system once taken for granted in perpetuating an observant lifestyle.

Technology has also made everything fast and easy for us. From instant soups to instant messaging, we no longer have to wait for the most basic things in life. Dr. Marcel Perlman, a psychology professor at Stern College, once noted that the most aired advertisements on television are for pharmaceutical products, sending the message that there is no need to suffer for anything. Every pain or problem has a fast and easy remedy. To suffer even a headache is unnecessary.

To complicate matters, we are a more spoiled generation than previous ones. Leah Kohn, founder and director of the Jewish Renaissance Center for Women in Manhattan, recalls that when she was a child, getting a toy was an "event." In general, she and her siblings played with simple things—balls, ropes, dolls—and created make-believe scenarios for hours, using their imaginations to turn a shoebox into a personally decorated dollhouse. Today, when she wants to give something to her daughter, she says "I have a big problem. *Baruch Hashem* (Thank God) she has everything. Who doesn't have everything today? One more [thing]. Big deal! And if I want it to have meaning, I have to really come up with a creative idea so that she will appreciate the *idea,* not what she has…and she is not a spoiled child. But that's the reality today. We have everything."[16]

How does this challenge observance? Observing *mitzvot* should be enjoyable, but it requires investment. The more easeful our world has become, the less likely we are to work hard for things, and the less willing we become to maintain difficult practices. Observance requires work; it is not fast or easy. It inspires positive change slowly and with much effort, sometimes even with pain. If we are not willing to work hard or sometimes endure pain, we can easily lose the *mitzvot* or let them go. In addition, children today are far more sensitive to losing self-esteem. Since physical things are attained so easily, there is a "new psychological reality." We develop far less inner strength as we mature, making us more vulnerable to pain, criticism, and the challenges that await us in adulthood. As Mrs. Kohn explains, "Children respond to positive reinforcement in our time; rebuke or punishment must be used very carefully."[17]

It is obvious that these realities directly and indirectly assault Jewish values and create serious obstacles for becoming a "nation of priests." And today, these contradictory values not only *exist* in our world, they *infiltrate* it. We can delay exposure but we can no longer completely avoid it. We can limit it, but we must contend with it.

Having said all this, it is vital to realize that, in most cases, the challenges of the outside world do not *cause* most people to go off the derech. They may play a role, but they cannot adequately explain the phenomenon. Why is this so? Firstly, because our children are far more emotionally connected to us than they are to the outside world, so they have a vested interest in maintaining a connection with us — their parents, teachers, friends and mentors — than with anyone or anything on the outside. They are therefore more likely to perpetuate our values, assuming all goes right.

Beyond that, we are more influential than the outside world because long before our children know the outside world, they know us. We make the first impact and create the foundation for our children's lives. The outside world can play a role only *after* we have done so, at which point a child should have a well developed perception of life and Judaism. So like freedom, the outside world can create a context for Judaism and challenge, but it cannot determine how we meet those challenges. It cannot explain the nature of our Judaism, the character of our Jewish communities, or the choices of individual Jews.

Our world comes first; the outside world comes second. Thus, while the outside world is *a* contributing factor of the phenomenon, it is not *the* cause. It is where defection ends, not where it begins.

Myth #3 — It's the *Yetzer Hara* (Evil Inclination)

What about the *yetzer hara*? Is not the outside world incredibly alluring? As one formerly observant Jew who returned recently said, "Why do people go off the derech? Because it's fun!"

It seems to us that the outside world is constantly tempting our children and this is true to an extent. But to say that a Jew leaves observance because the outside world is just too irresistible is like saying that a man commits adultery because the other woman was just too beautiful. It is true; sometimes adultery occurs because a man or woman was tempted. But more often than not, it is because the marital relationship itself was flawed, opening the door for temptation. As they say, a wedge needs a crack. In the case of both marriage and Judaism, the crack occurs at home. Without it, the wedge — whether it be another woman or the outside world — would find no foothold to confront us.

So in most cases, temptation is a symptom, not a cause. In strong, happy, healthy relationships that are loving and committed, spouses do everything possible to protect the sanctity of their union and not get near even the *possibility* of adultery. And if, God forbid, a spouse does fall victim to the *yetzer hara*, he would struggle vehemently against it, not fall into a long-term extramarital relationship. He may lose a battle, but he usually wins the war.

And so it is with those who go off the derech. If the *yetzer hara* is at fault, at worst we might expect to see momentary infractions, but not an entire lifestyle of it. We might expect to see failure to keep certain *mitzvot*, but not wholesale abandonment of Torah life. In addition, we would expect to see a battle being waged which seems not to happen with most who go off the derech. In fact, they sometimes hardly seem to struggle at all, as if they *want* the behavior they choose.

The controversial movie "Trembling Before God" demonstrates an interesting point. The movie explores the struggle of Orthodox homosexuals. These people have a major *yetzer hara*, in what the *gemorah* tells us is one of the most difficult areas to overcome — sexual indiscretions. Losing this battle is called an "abomination" in God's eyes, and often results in dramatic rejection from the observant Jewish world. Did these people who had this major *yetzer hara* stop keeping Shabbat because of it? The answer is yes and no. Some had dropped observance; but others were still committed to it or struggling to hold on. Even as they lost the battle with their *yetzer hara* in a fundamental area, even when they were rejected by observant friends and parents, they struggled to hold on to whatever observance they could. They remained committed to keeping Shabbat and putting on *tefilin.* If the *yetzer hara* could not pull them off the derech even as it waged such great conflict within them, how does it manage to pull away our children?

Rabbi Dovid Brezak explains that, "The child will not start leaving religion because of the *yetzer hara.* He will have *nisyanot* (tests). He will be faced with challenges. But if he fails those challenges, it is not because of the *yetzer hara.* The *yetzer hara* provides challenges but how the child will react to those challenges has to do with a lot of other things....A person has *bechira* (choice). So it's not because of the *yetzer hara.* It's because he *chose* to go off."

The *yetzer hara* is a very good explanation for breaking individual *mitzvot* in particular moments in time. But, for the most part, it doesn't properly explain entire lifestyles or wholesale abandonment of Torah life. What makes more sense is that our children *want* to drop it all. As *Rashi* explains, the phrase in the *Shema,* "do not go after your heart and after your eyes,"[18] means that first the heart covets and then the eyes seek out. First we want to sin and then we find the means to do so. The question then becomes: Why do they "covet" what is outside rather than what they have been born into, especially since what they are been born into has a much greater influence?

Conclusion

The simple answer to this question is this: people leave observance primarily because when they compared Judaism to its alternative, Judaism paled in comparison. It just didn't seem worth it and in many cases, it seemed glaringly deficient.

Sadly, most formerly observant Jews today seem to have left, not because the outside world *pulled* them in, but rather because the observant one *pushed* them out. They experienced Judaism as a source of pain rather than joy. So they did what was natural: run in the other direction. Just as in times of persecution we run away from pain to find refuge in a safer place, these people ran away from the pain of the Jewish world to find refuge in the outside one. So they were not running *to* the outside world as much as they were running *away* from our own.

It is hard for us to admit this. It's easier to believe that it's them, not us, that we have little influence against the forces of the outside world, because if it's them, we feel less guilt and responsibility. But we must understand that this is a myth. It may absolve our guilt, but it robs us of the chance to improve our Judaism. It may temporarily appease us, but it also deludes us from realizing just how great a role we play in creating the experience of Judaism. As Rabbi Aaron Kotler said, if the Messiah tarries, it is not because of the sins of those who are ignorant or removed from Torah, but because of the sins of those who are committed to it.[19]

The acts of those who have a relationship with God carry more weight than those of the "outside world." We have more power than we think and this phenomenon is a call to *us* who are observant. As the Brisker Rav explained, when the ship carrying Yonah was engulfed by water, Yonah immediately perceived *himself* as the cause. "Though the ship was filled with idol worshippers and it would have been easy to point the finger at them, Yonah knew that God directs His messages primarily to those who acknowledge him."[20]

The phenomenon of those who have gone off the derech is a call to us to ask ourselves: Is our Judaism better than the alternative and if not, how can we make it so? If we face this question openly and realize that *we* are where the experience of Judaism begins and ends, we can make it better than the alternative, strong enough to withstand the challenges of modernity, and vital enough to inspire our children to observe. In that case, even if they falter, they will likely come home because we will have given them something worth returning to, a strengthened observance which can prevail through any persecution or freedom that comes our way.

I

The Heart of the Matter:
Emotions and Observance

CHAPTER 3

Religion and Its Practitioners

hen I first started researching this book, I was convinced that the most important factor in people's choosing to leave observance was their lack of belief in Judaism. After all, to be observant means to believe in many things: Divine Revelation, rabbinic authority, and our responsibility to follow the laws and customs arising out of both. These are great beliefs that are not easily proven or transmitted, but which are essential for committing to a properly observant life.

So the first thing I sought to ascertain was whether or not those who went off the derech believed in Judaism. During my interviews I expected to hear people tell me that they did not. I expected this in part because, like the experts I had interviewed, I saw things through my own particular lens. In my own experience, belief played a large role in religious commitment so I expected that to be true for others. Interestingly enough, it was not. In fact, 61% of those who responded to the web survey indicated that they believe that God gave the Torah; nonetheless, they had gone off the derech.

Belief was not frequently discussed in the interviews, and when it was, it was often not the real cause of defection. It was the tip of the iceberg. The more I listened, the more I realized that while intellectual issues play a legitimate role in people going off the derech, they are usually not the main cause. There are often other, deeper issues at work.

More often than not, what drives people from observance is not intellectual in nature, but emotional. How we *feel* about Judaism is far more important than what we *think* about it. Somehow the heart moves us more easily than the mind and, for better or worse, most people seek happiness before they seek truth. As one *baal teshuva* family who dropped observance after six years simply noted, "we realized we didn't *like* being Jewish and Orthodox [any more]."[1] That "like" or dislike, that simple feeling whether positive or negative, is enough to bring us closer or push us farther away.

Thus the most prevalent cause of people going off the derech is negative feelings about Yiddishkeit. Most people I have met who have gone off the derech have experienced Judaism negatively or painfully rather than joyfully and happily. As soon as they did not feel good about observance or they associated it with pain, the chances of their remaining observant significantly decreased.

To understand how negative feelings impact observance, we need first to understand one key fact: our feelings toward Judaism come primarily from the observant Jews we meet and the relationships we create with them. Observant Jews are the conduits for Judaism and it is through our relationships with them that our feelings and perceptions about Judaism are created. Relationships lay at the heart of every emotional issue. Negative relationships with the practitioners of Judaism tend to create negative feelings toward Judaism that compromise observance, while positive relationships create positive feelings toward it. Either way, relationships with observant Jews may well be the strongest factor in determining commitment to Judaism. Survey respondents supported this contention. When asked to identify *one* thing that caused them to move away from observance, 44% pointed to observant people.

My Story: The Importance of Relationships

I have experienced this most strikingly in my own life. Although my family was not classically Orthodox and I always had questions about Judaism, I loved it and knew that when I had a family of my own, I would be observant. In fact, ever since I was a small child I felt a significant connection to Judaism. I remember when I was only five or six years old, all I knew about being Jewish was that I was different from everyone else at my school. I didn't really understand how different. We were living in England at the time, far from a Jewish community, and my parents sent my sister and I to the local Catholic school. The school day started with morning prayers, and I remember clearly as the hundreds of students around me started to sing, I would stand in the middle of the crowd, different and proud about it. I would sing with them, but when the word *Jesus* was sung I would close my mouth defiantly and remain silent. They could make me sing, but they couldn't make me sing to Jesus; they would never make me utter his name. Even when I was too young to know what that really meant, being Jewish was something I took pride in, from my first day in Catholic school until I graduated from an Orthodox Jewish high school.

Perhaps because of that, throughout my years in the Orthodox Hebrew day school, which I attended from age eight, I was always one of the most vocal in class. I loved learning about Judaism and its laws. Every detail I learned fostered my respect and admiration for it.

While there were some holes in my belief, I listened in class with reverence and genuine respect. When I came home, my father would ask me about school and we would spend hours debating what I had learned. His not being observant was of great advantage to me growing up, because it allowed me to see things from a different perspective, to reevaluate what I had learned and go back to school with even more questions, which yielded even better answers. The more I learned, the more my reverence grew.

My classmates, on the other hand, seemed less impassioned. When we learned that taking an aspirin on Shabbat might be a problem, some of my friends left with an attitude of "that's nice, but I'll never do it," while I left curious and intrigued. Perhaps I had the luxury of respecting the *halachah* because it was theoretical for me. I could listen more dispassionately with nothing to lose, with a more objective ear. Whatever the reason, I came to one conclusion — that no matter what happened in terms of my becoming observant, I had to learn as much as I could in order to have my questions answered — especially the ones about God's giving the Torah and the rabbis applying it.

And so when I graduated high school, I wanted to go to Israel and explore Judaism even further. I had to find out — was it true or not? I knew that Judaism felt great. I knew it was something to admire. I just wasn't sure it was the Truth and unless I dedicated some time to figuring it out, I could not wholeheartedly commit to it. In short, I was looking to believe in order to follow my heart.

So the battle — a hard one — began. I had to convince my parents, who were bent on my staying home, to let me go to Israel. I was the first-born daughter of Sephardic parents and I was to stay put until I married. If I were to leave, surely it would not be to go to a seminary where I could be brainwashed. Although my parents had a lot of love for Judaism, they had had negative experiences with some observant Jewish people. Were my parents to entrust their child to such people and let them play with her mind? Religion had its positives but it could easily be distorted, and seminary was surely a place where that could happen.

But while my parents had strong views, they strove to recognize that I was my own person and needed to make my own decisions and mistakes. They knew that if I did not go to *yeshiva* in Israel, I might always resent it. My father was particularly sensitive to religious issues.

43

He remembered his own father, son of the Chief Rabbi of Tehran, who stopped speaking to him when my father refused to wake up at six in the morning to *daven* (pray). For three years my father suffered because he could not meet his father's religious standards before he finally left home. He was not about to impose his beliefs on me and possibly drive me away.

So I ended up in seminary in Israel. I was seventeen, and ready to have my questions answered with an open heart and mind. I spent my first Shabbat in Israel at the *Rosh Yeshiva's* home. He had met me and my parents in Los Angeles. I was not quite sure why he took an interest in me, but he did and I felt great about it. In fact, I felt great about everything there. The only difficulty I had was fitting in educationally. Having spent most of my education in *yeshiva* day school, I knew much more than those in the *yeshiva's* introductory courses. But that is where I could discuss my philosophical questions. The more advanced courses left little room for philosophical exploration. The school compromised and split my day between the introductory level courses and the most advanced ones.

It was perfect. The first few weeks at the school, I had the time of my life. I would wake in the morning for fascinating classes, learn in the afternoon with my roommate who had become my best friend, and spend the evenings going into town, which was a breath of fresh air for me. The social part of my life had been lacking in high school, and now here I was in Israel with thousands of other young Jews my age, hanging out and carrying on interesting conversations late into the evening. I connected with other intelligent, intellectual people who had deep questions about *Yiddishkeit* (Judaism) and this more informal learning bridged a gap for me. My friends quickly formed the kind of community I never had before, and there was nothing that was missing from my life. It was as perfect as I could have imagined.

Then, some weeks into the program I was told that I couldn't have it both ways, spending mornings in the introductory level and afternoons in the advanced level. I had to choose one program or the other, and there was a catch: If I chose the highest level, I had to commit to certain observances that I wasn't quite ready for, so that I would fit in with the other girls who were already committed. I would have to keep Shabbat and kosher. I would have to wear long skirts and dress more modestly, and I could no longer go into town to socialize. I didn't have to believe these things were God given, but I would have to observe them in order not to disrupt the program.

How could I decide? The hardest part of the decision was being forbidden to go into town because I really enjoyed my newfound social life. But I reasoned that I had not come to Israel to socialize; I had come to learn. And if I had to choose between the two — I would choose learning. And as far as the *mitzvot* that came with it — I would try them on and see how they felt. Maybe they would stick.

Having decided to switch to the highest level, it was not long before I wondered if I had done the right thing. My philosophical questions were not appreciated there. One day, when class ended, the head of the program took me aside and said kindly, "Listen, if you want to stay here, you can't ask questions like this." That surprised me, though it shouldn't have, and I tried to comply with his request. But for someone with many questions, who is philosophical by nature, who truly wanted to know and explore, being stifled in that way was a problem.

Still, I loved my learning. I had great relationships with my teachers. And I had made many friends. Stifled questions would not diminish my feelings toward *Yiddishkeit*. Unfortunately however, other experiences did.

I was struggling with the rule that I could no longer go into town. I don't know why it didn't occur to me that this would be so difficult to give up — but it didn't. After two weeks I broke down. My roommate and I figured we would spend a couple of hours in town and come back. On the way, we bumped into a male friend who lived nearby and was going to rent a couple of movies with his friends. We decided to join him. We all watched movies until six in the morning at which time the boy's father arose, made us coffee and sent us back to school. It was a Friday morning, so there was no need to wake up early for class and we walked back to school with a skip in our step. But as we approached the school, we heard our program director a few steps behind us. He saw us and angrily exclaimed, "What the hell are you girls doing up at this hour?"

We were caught. It was humiliating. We felt like criminals. The rav called us into his home and interrogated us separately about our activities. He wrote down every detail we told him and he promised not to call the boys' *yeshivas* and get them in trouble. I was demoted one level in my learning, and it felt like the program director would never look at us the same way again, all of which I expected the moment he caught us. What I did not expect was that this experience would be my first negative one with an observant Jew.

I am sure he was well meaning, but the rabbi went back on his word and called the boys' school. If I remember correctly, one of the boys was expelled as a result. And I, who had given him their names, felt betrayed. I had trusted him and I felt naïve for doing so. Punishing us was justified. But lying to us caused me to lose respect for him.

The Judaism I had been exposed to in my parents' house was warm and joyful. The observant teachers I had been exposed to in high school were dignified and supportive. I had always respected them and what they taught me. I never imagined that such a seemingly dignified man as my rav, such a representative of Torah, could lie. Perhaps I knew it intellectually, but in my heart I expected observant Jews to be above the rest.

I continued to enjoy my year at seminary. I continued to learn enthusiastically and I had a great time with my roommate who had become one of the best friends I had ever made. She was a second year student and it was my good fortune to room with her. The first day I arrived, she was putting her pants away. She had rebelled against her observant upbringing, but now after a year in Israel she was ready to return to observance. She strove to connect to God in everything she did. She *davened* with sincerity, learned with passion, and taught me through her behavior what it means to strive to grow. We spent hours discussing observance and Judaism, its reasons, its laws, its beauty and significance. And although we were not in the same place religiously and came from completely different backgrounds, we clicked in a way I had never clicked with anyone before.

But after the six in the morning incident, the program director didn't approve of our friendship. He made it known that as long as I roomed with her, he would not respect me. All he saw in her was a girl who was still smoking cigarettes and came home at six in the morning, and that was all he needed to know. Unbeknownst to him, my roommate was one of the most genuinely religious girls in the school and being around her was creating very positive feelings in me about observant life. I decided not to switch rooms and resigned myself to his disrespect, which was far easier to accept now than it had been before.

Over time, I asked my questions and slowly got them answered. I started to keep Shabbat — not because anyone forced me to, but because I wanted to. I kept kosher, and I *davened* with earnestness. I was touched by what I learned. But I continued to be disappointed by the authority figures I met. It culminated when I went to Netanya with a male friend again. Although the trip was platonic, I was almost expelled. The *Rosh Yeshiva* let me stay in the school, but things were never the same after that. Teachers who used to say good morning when I passed them in the hall now looked away. Until this point, whenever the *Rosh Yeshiva* asked a question in class and no one offered an answer, he would call on me and ask what I thought. Now, even when I raised my hand to answer, he ignored me. I remember sitting in class in the front row as he called on everyone else, with tears in my eyes. For half an hour I silently cried. I had ruined everything. I felt like a pariah. It seemed like as long as I was observant and did what they wanted, I was acceptable and could be respected. But now, I could no longer be tolerated, and it was unbearable.

As the year progressed, my relationships with the authority figures in the school deteriorated and so did my feelings about their kind of observant Judaism. I had come to *yeshiva* to learn. I had come with enthusiasm. And for the first time in my life, I felt terrible about observant Judaism and also about myself. I had graduated high school with a 3.9 GPA, all honors, and had been chosen twice for the Middot award at eighth and twelfth grade graduations — the first time in the school's history a nonobservant girl had won it. But here in seminary, I felt repulsive. A part of me, the part that was only seventeen, condemned myself. But another part condemned the "black hat" world. I began to associate its Judaism with the pain and rejection I felt. Black hat Judaism was painful and that colored everything.

So ironically, although I became technically observant, my feelings toward observant Jews changed. I still respected the Torah, but wanted little to do with the black hat world. And so, by the end of the year, the girl who had fought her parents to enter that world came home disdainful of it.

It all happened because of disillusionment and while my teachers were well intentioned and the reality of their feelings toward me possibly were not as negative as I thought, my perception was my reality. As is the case with others who have gone off the derech, the feelings are the reality that determine the outcome. And the feelings I experienced at the time were far too painful to combat. All I experienced was *yeshivishly* observant Jews hurting me. Whether or not they meant to, whether or not it was justified, was irrelevant to my experience as it often is for those who go off the derech.

Luckily, I had experienced a positive Judaism and relationships before I went to *yeshiva* so, intellectually, I knew that their behavior was less a reflection of Torah observance than it was of them. That enabled me to become observant even while I lost respect for the "system" and separated myself from it. But even the positive experiences of my youth, which perhaps enabled me to somewhat separate Torah from its practitioners, did not completely safeguard my observance. When I eventually lived on my own, I felt an aversion to becoming part of an observant community. After all, my first real foray into an observant world had been painful. So while I did not choose to venture into the "outside" world, I retreated into my own. I went to *shul* every week, but without becoming part of the observant community. I was observant in Manhattan but with little connection to an observant Jewish world, which made it difficult to remain committed.

So what should have the *rabbaim* (rabbis) in my *yeshiva* done? How should they have responded? In analyzing the verse "*tzedek tzedek tirdof*" — *justice, justice you shall pursue* — a commentator tells us that the word *justice* is repeated to teach us that it is not enough for the ends to be just; the means must be just as well.[2] The rabbis could have employed a variety of possible approaches — from not accepting students like me into the school to giving me more freedom to grow on my own. I can only say that whatever the approach, it should not have alienated or disillusioned me.

Why Practitioners Matter

Based on my experience and the hundreds of off the derech stories I have heard, I am convinced that when people say "you should not judge a religion by its practitioners" they are mistaken.

We say *Torah lo bashamiyim hi* — the Torah is not in heaven. It is here on earth, in our interpretations of it, in our commitment to it, in our love for it. We believe that Torah is not a theory to be studied, but a way of life to be lived. Judaism is ultimately about the way we live it. The Judaism that exists in books may be intellectually stimulating and essential to our observant lives. But what impacts us most dramatically in terms of our commitment to observance is the reality we create with it here on earth. And what impacts us most in terms of our feeling toward Judaism is the relationships and experiences we have with observant Jews. Negative relationships and their painful experiences push us away from both Torah and Jews.

This is true whether or not it should be. In an ideal world, perhaps we could successfully separate Torah from its practitioners, but in this world, it is extremely difficult to do so. It takes a lot of objectivity and self-awareness. People who are very analytical, emotionally mature, or who have experienced little pain in their observant Jewish lives might be able to do so. But many people may not be emotionally in touch with themselves, or may have been hurt so deeply, that the pain colors their perception of Judaism too strongly to get beyond. If the painful experiences are very negative, deep or pervasive, they may no longer be able to believe that it is only the practitioners and not the Torah they follow. And even if they succeed in separating the two in their minds, they may find it impossible to do so in their hearts.

Finally, even if somehow we could separate Torah from its practitioners, we cannot separate *ourselves* from the practitioners. We are required to engage with the practitioners of Torah. We must create relationships with them, learn, teach, pray, and raise families with them. We need each other in order to create our communities and to be properly observant; practitioners are an integral part of our observant lives and therefore of our experience of Torah. So when people say that we should separate the two — implying that the quality of the practitioners should be irrelevant to our observant lives — they fail to recognize just how much of Judaism and observant life is about the practitioners.

Even with my positive experiences as a foundation, it took years to get past the painful feelings of my year in *yeshiva*. Eventually I realized in my heart what I knew in my mind: that the negativity I experienced had more to do with those people's own personality weaknesses than with Judaism itself. Today I am more forgiving of those weaknesses, and I have more positive feelings toward the black hat world along with a respect for their commitment to Torah. But I never would have gained that understanding in my heart had I not been lucky enough to meet truly observant Jews who donned black hats, some of whom were among the most remarkable people I have ever met, who impacted my life in ways I could never have imagined. The positive relationships I developed with them and the warmth I felt from them counteracted the negative ones of my past. The new, positive relationships forced me to reevaluate my *yeshiva* experiences and taught me in my heart that black hat Judaism can be good.

In short, our commitment to Torah observance stems largely from our feelings toward it, and our feelings toward it stem largely from our relationships with Torah observant Jews. So, negative relationships with observant people will push people away while positive relationships can serve as one of the strongest deterrents for people going off the derech.

CHAPTER 4

Rejection

O f all emotionally negative experiences, rejection is arguably the worst. Throughout history, rejection has caused some of the most famous figures in history to go off the derech. Sometimes simple acts of rejection have had devastating consequences for generations.

Perhaps one of the most famous cases is that of Jesus (*Yeshu*). Why did he go off the derech? According to our tradition, Rabbi Yoshua ben Perahah found himself in an inn one night with Jesus. He complimented the beauty of the inn. Jesus, thinking that the rabbi referred to the innkeeper (the Hebrew word for both being *achsanai*), replied, "Her eyes are narrow." Rabbi Yoshua called Jesus a "villain" for looking at women that way and he excommunicated him. Jesus returned to ask forgiveness, but Rabbi Yoshua was reciting the Shema and although he only wanted Jesus to wait until he was finished praying, Rabbi Yoshua's hand signal looked dismissive. Jesus felt doubly rejected. When Rabbi Yoshua finally finished and asked him to return, it was too late. Jesus simply replied, "So I have understood from you that every one who sins and causes the multitude to sin has no chance to repent."[1] That dismissive hand wave may have ultimately prompted Christianity, which ironically focuses on unconditional love, forgiveness, and acceptance.

Similarly, the nation of Amalek, one of the Jewish people's greatest and most malevolent enemies, also sprung from an act of rejection. The Talmud tells us that Timna, the mother of the first Amalek, desired to join the Jewish people. She approached the Patriarchs Abraham, Isaac, and Jacob, but they did not accept her, so she left and eventually became the concubine to Eliphaz, the son of Esau. The Talmud tells us that Amalek arose to afflict Israel because "they should not have repulsed her."[2]

Even in our own patriarchal family, we have seen the disastrous results of rejection. The Ramban explains that Sara sinned in dealing harshly with Hagar, so God sympathized with Hagar and gave her a son who would bring suffering to the seed of Abraham. This, the Ramban contends, is why the Arab nations have shown so much hatred toward to the Jews.[3]

Rabbi Baruch haLevi Epstein, author of the Biblical commentary *Torah Temima*, notes that this phenomenon occurs in every generation. People whose opinions differ religiously only slightly are rejected. The rejection pushes them over the brink until they become disgusted with Torah and observant people and they forsake it altogether.[4] The results are devastating, not only for the rejected individual, but also for the Jewish people as a whole.

If the birth of Christianity and Amalek have been caused by the rejection of adults with presumably well established self-images, imagine how damaging rejection can feel when experienced in youth, when we are emotionally vulnerable, when acceptance and the development of self-esteem are paramount. Such was the case with countless people I interviewed for this book. I heard story after story of people who had been rejected in their youth by their parents and teachers because they failed to live up to religious expectations. In fact, 75% of those who responded to the web survey indicated that, at some point, they had felt rejected because they were not observant enough.

Chani

Chani Metzger is one such example. She was raised in a *yeshivish* family, went off the derech, and eventually returned to living a committed *halachic* life. Among other incidents, she recalls the following story as having pushed her away. When she was a Bais Yaacov High School student, she spent a night at a friend's home and watched a rated R movie. When her principal, who was also a teacher for one of her classes found out about it, Chani got in trouble. Punishment was warranted, but what happened next was devastating. The principal walked into Chani's class and yelled, "Peeeeyuuuu! Open the windows. Open the windows." She wailed with disgust as she waved her arms about her head to dissipate the stench. "It smells like bad *maasim* (deeds) in here. Chani Metzger — go to the back of the room!" Chani was mortified. Publicly humiliated, she moved her seat to the back of the class. Until today, years after the experience, she mocks the way her teacher treated her.

Jonathan

It is sometimes difficult to ascertain the real reasons people have left observance, but often when one reads between the lines, rejection seems to underlie the issues. Even those who have very intellectual reasons for not being observant, such as Jonathan, often have emotional feelings of rejection and alienation at the heart of their objection to Judaism.

When I began my interview with Jonathan, he told me that if he believed Judaism were true, he would have no problem following it. His issues, he told me, were intellectual.

> Philosophically, there is no room in my thinking for me
> to believe in God writing books. I just didn't buy that, and

once I didn't buy that, I didn't buy all the dogma that went along with it. So for a while, it made me reject the whole thing. Then eventually I started to see that there was a lot of wisdom in it, that it was a system that survived thousands of years...So I went back and learned Chassidut. I mean I go to *shul* pretty regularly even though I am not *halachically* consistent, but I do it because prayer is cathartic and because I have belief that there is a God and a force in the universe that you can tap into. ...but I think it's individual.

Jonathan is highly intellectual and introspective. Throughout the interview, he presented cogent philosophical and structural problems he had with Judaism, and for each of his problems, he had analytical explanations. But then another story began to unfold. From the time he was in fourth grade, he said, he was made to feel deviant.

If rabbis found out about boys and girls having contact, they would label you an "evil kid." I remember the *rebbe* (rabbi) calling me a wicked thing because he saw me talking to a girl in the parking lot...and you felt dirty about being that way ... You can't hang out with a girl, and if you do you're a modern bum. So I said OK, then I'm a modern bum.

He couldn't shrug off that label. It followed him and made it hard for him to get into certain schools, perpetuating further rejection. When he interviewed for the *yeshivas* his parents wanted him to attend, and he mentioned that he was interested in reading newspapers, he was told that "real *bachurim* (students) don't read the paper," and he was not accepted. In summer camp, Jonathan faced many of the same issues. Some teenagers were caught with a Playboy magazine and there was a scandal. In his words, they had a "McCarthy hearing. Think about it," he says, "you have teenage kids that are going around camp with Playboy — only in a fundamentalist world could you react this way. And to me that's a big failure. They are quick to label people and they are quick to throw you out. They'd rather get rid of you. It's like the rotten apple theory all the time."

Whether for his behavior or for interests, Jonathan experienced rejection in the observant Jewish world. Even his peers were not accepting. Kids in *yeshiva* used to call him "nigger" because he was Sephardic, and now he says, he feels a kinship with black people because of it, because he knows what it feels like to experience that.

David

Unlike Jonathan, David had difficulty pinpointing why he had left observance. He came from an observant home, had attended a black hat elementary school and modern orthodox high school. He explained his lack of observance at first by the fact that the rules never meant anything to him, that they were not logical. Then he went on to discuss his dislike for his rabbis. He explained that right away, starting from elementary school, he didn't like "anything to do with the religion" because of his rabbis.

> I just didn't like it all. I attributed everything bad with it. A lot of the rabbis were idiots that wouldn't have gotten by anywhere and they became teachers. They happened to be teachers that were rabbis. But they weren't bright. They weren't worldly. They never should have been teaching. That was a lot of my rabbis. Not all, but a lot.

David clearly has a problem with the practitioners of Torah who should have been his role models. In reality, his teachers might have been very bright, but David did not perceive them that way. And his feelings about Torah are based on those perceptions, regardless of what the reality might have been. Since his teachers represented Torah, and he did not perceive them as respectable, he began to lose respect for the Torah they represented as well. The two — Torah and his rabbis — seem interchangeable to him. He starts by saying he didn't like anything to do with the *religion,* but his examples have more to do with the people who practice it than with the religion itself.

But why did he disrespect his teachers and the rules they represented so vehemently? David continued the interview, telling me that in the mornings he would walk to school with a girl and some of the "religious people," from whom he now disassociates himself, told the principal and got him in trouble. He was made to feel like a reject over the incident and was reprimanded for it, until the principal learned the girl had been his cousin. David was left with the impression that his principal was "a fool."

His schoolmates were no better. "Other religious kids would attack me because I would talk to the girls in sixth grade. The older guys would call me names and hit me... *Shaygitz, shkutz....* (derogatory terms for a non-Jew)" To make matters worse, he was Sephardic, but the other students were all Ashkenazi — "white people" who were mostly from more religious homes. He remembers them calling him *shvartza* (derogatory term for Afro-American) in the same breath as he recalls being hit on the knuckles by his teacher when he was bad.

When David thinks about religion now, he can relate to Jewish spirituality but not to *halachah,* which he rejects as overly burdensome. When I asked him if he was ever explained the reasons for the rules, he said no, clarifying that sometimes rules were explained, but more often the teachers didn't know the reasons for doing things. What my question reminded him of, and what he thought was more representative of his education, was a tape of *gehenom* (hell) he heard in second grade. "Basically, they shut off the lights and there was music in the background and people were screaming things like 'oy vey, I am hanging from my tongue. If only I wouldn't have spoken loshon hara!'"

David admits that he was not an easy child. He remembers lighting smoke bombs in school, but he also recalls that he would only get in trouble for *halachic* infractions.

> I went to a high school which was more modern and that was even worse in a way because at that point, a bunch of us started smoking pot, drinking, and not keeping Shabbas — experimenting. And we would get screamed at by a rabbi for not wearing *tzitzis*. They weren't even realistic about what was going on. I remember out of everything that I did at that school, the one time I got suspended is when I talked during *minchah* (afternoon prayer) when I was a chazzan. I did things that were a hundred times worse, but the rabbis punished you for the *tzitzis* thing or because your *yarmulke* was too small or because you went out with girls. They were really focusing on the wrong things... If you broke something religious, it made much more of a negative impact than if you lit smoke bombs in school.

He got the message that observant people didn't really care about fundamental things like *derech eretz* (Jewish ethical behavior). They only cared about *halachah*, and this caused him to lose even more respect.

His negative memories continued for the three-hour interview. He played ball in Brooklyn with other local Jews. They were "very religious, but liberal" and for the ten or fifteen years that he played softball there, a local father and daughter who were not Jewish joined them. Then —

> A Chassid comes to play one game and leaves because a girl is playing. He tells the others that you are not allowed to play softball with girls. Now, probably according to the rules, you might not be. But there was no *negiah*

(prohibited contact), no attraction. She was almost 35 and the father was 65. It was probably a big *chilul Hashem* (profaning God's name), but the community caved in and kicked out the father and daughter. It made me feel really disgusted.

Over time, the community moved religiously to the right and there was increased infighting and disrespect between the various Orthodox groups. He remembers the Satmer and Lubavich fighting because one group wouldn't drink the other group's milk. He remembers the Chassidim not liking the *mechitzah* (physical separation between men and women) and "sneaking in" to raise it. "The *mechitzah* had been that way for 40 years," David explained, "but no one put it back down again because they were afraid of being perceived as less religious."

After a long series of such experiences, David went to *yeshiva* in Israel. His second day there, a rav saw him missing class and said, "You are not learning? Why don't you just leave?" Later in the year, when he wanted to visit his uncle for Shabbat, the school encouraged him not to go because the uncle was not religious. The uncle was having an operation, so David went; but he was made to feel an outcast for it. Later in the year, David went to visit Rabbi Sheinberg, a greatly respected rabbi throughout the world. A neighborhood kid asked David whom he had gone to visit, and when David said Rav Sheinberg, the child said, 'oh, my father says he's a *shaygitz*.'

What is particularly interesting about listening to David's stories is that there is such a wide variety of experiences that were problematic for him — his school, its rules, *tzitzis*, name calling, his community, *mechitzahs*. David's mind flowed from one thing to another. But underneath them all was a feeling of rejection.

The "stupid" rules and the teachers who enforced them, all caused him to feel rejected. He felt rejected for walking to school with his cousin and rejected when he was called a *shvartza* and beaten up by his classmates. He heard about rejection when he listened to the *ge-henom* tape which told him at the tender age of six or seven that God would reject him if he didn't keep the *mitzvot*. Every single story he related involved rejection, even the experiences that had nothing to do with him — the old man and his daughter who were rejected from the softball game; the *mechitzah* being taken down which represented a rejection of the community's standards; the community "caving in" because they were afraid they would be rejected; the different Chassidic sects not drinking each other's milk; his *yeshiva's* rejection of his uncle in a time of need because he wasn't religious; and finally, even Rav Sheinberg, a holy man, shunned by a young child who was taught to reject before he could even think for himself.

All these are examples of rejection, and every one contributed to a growing sense of anger and disrespect for observant Jews. David was so scarred by them that even when a *frum* (observant) Jew treats him badly *outside* of anything to do with Judaism, he feels anger. "Again I am dealing with another religious person who is treating me badly." What does it all add up to? Now he says, "I like the religion. I hate the people, and I just left it at that."

These experiences would not have been as damaging had they not been so prominent and pervasive throughout every stage of his educational and personal development. Each incident in isolation might have made a limited impact on him. But together, they were devastating because they created a pattern, one in which he began to associate Torah, rabbis, and observant Jews with rejection and pain.

In addition, what David learned over time was that being a good Jew meant rejecting others, judging others and even calling them names. He says that "at my work, I'm the biggest Jew. The girl who is next to my office works on Yom Kippur and she is dating a non-Jew. And I keep calling her *shiksa* and *shkutz*. 'Oh look at the *shiksa*,' and I'm friendly with her and its funny." David and his co-worker might be able to laugh at his name calling, but it is interesting to note that this is the example he uses to prove that he's "the biggest Jew." He seems to have learned that the bigger the Jew you are, the more you alienate and taunt others.

The Impact on Observance

Unfortunately, these stories are not unique. I have heard countless such stories of rejection, labeling, and harsh judgment for everything from seemingly small issues to larger ones. But why is rejection such a big deal? And what does it have to do with being observant?

Rejection is destructive because one of our most basic needs is to be accepted and loved for who we are. Rejecting a child because he is not properly observant makes him feel valued for what he *does,* not for who he *is.* It undermines his self-worth and sends the message that he is good, lovable, and worthy only in so far as he perpetuates our beliefs and Judaism.[5] He is merely a means to an end.

This is antithetical to Judaism, which strives to teach that we are valuable in and of ourselves.[6] Many of our *mitzvot* such as the laws of *tzniut* (modesty) and *taharat mishpachah* (family purity), for example, aim in part to de-objectify women and men in relationships.[7] They teach us to value and respect each other not for the pleasure, happiness or pride we give each other or the number of *mitzvot* we keep, but rather for our unique souls.

Home is ground zero for teaching this basic lesson. It is perhaps the *only* place in the world where you are not valued for what you *do,* but for who you *are.* Young children and teenagers need to feel this message of unconditional love and acceptance above all else if they are to feel self-worth.

As soon as we make acceptance contingent upon observance, we deny them that. We remove the safety net of our love and teach children that they are not valuable for who they are but rather for the extent to which they comply with our expectations. In doing so, we fail to acknowledge the image of God in them and make their ultimate haven of safety — their home — unsafe.[8]

We may wonder: if one's self-image depends so much upon acceptance, why not simply *be* observant to gain it? After all, as Rabbi Yaacov Shapiro points out, "For the teen, Judaism is the most convenient path to take, not the least."[9] Why not simply follow the rules and avoid rejection?

The answer is that the child will naturally strive to do so. If he succeeds, he will not feel rejected and can easily feel good about himself and Judaism. But if he fails, he may feel negative about both. And even the most perfect child is destined to fail in his observance sometimes, in some ways, the same way a child who is learning to walk is destined to fall. After all, adolescents are *practicing* to be adults; they have not yet arrived. And most adolescents are faced with so many physiological, social and emotional changes that just surviving in good health is a challenge.

For the observant teen, these challenges are compounded by a daunting set of religious responsibilities, as well. For the observant child or teen, potential failure lurks around every corner. The question then becomes: how do those whose love and acceptance he needs *react* to that failure? The stronger they react, the more they reject him, the worse he feels. The worse he feels, the less likely he is to try, for the price of failing becomes too high to pay.

Eventually, not only will he likely feel negative about himself and his parents or teachers, he may also feel bad about Judaism. After all, the source of his pain, the rejection — whether in the form of labeling, admonishing, criticizing, shaming or embarrassing — resulted from his inability to be properly observant. His need to avoid pain can lead him to run in the opposite direction from its source, in this case observant Judaism and potentially the parents, teachers and community that rejected him as well.

This process occurs because the need to avoid pain is greater than the need to be observant. Emotional needs tend to precede spiritual ones. If we are to satisfy our spiritual needs and live an observant life in the long run, we must first meet our emotional ones. When those are not met, Torah either becomes irrelevant or it becomes an obstacle to happiness. As a result, it becomes difficult to experience its beauty or see its Truth, and it may even become necessary to discard it to achieve emotional health.

The psychologist Abraham Maslow explains this process with a hierarchy of needs. According to Maslow, "human beings are motivated by unsatisfied needs, and certain lower needs need to be satisfied before higher needs can be satisfied."[10]

Maslow categorizes these needs in the following order :

SELF-ACTUALIZATION
The need to reach our personal potential, achieve fulfillment and growth.

ESTEEM
The need to feel respectable, valuable, competent, and approved of; thwarted when we experience disrespect that results in a feeling of inferiority, weakness, helplessness, worthlessness

LOVE
The need for affiliation, acceptance, and belongingness; thwarted by rejection, loneliness, alienation, lack of affection

SAFETY
The need for comfort, security, freedom from fear; thwarted when psychological needs are unmet such as in dysfunctional homes or with abuse

PHYSIOLOGICAL NEEDS
The need for food, water, oxygen etc.; thwarted by hunger, persecution

We all need safety, love, self-esteem and self-actualization. These are all aspects of our fundamental psychological needs. But, according to Maslow, they are not equally important. They are prioritized in a specific hierarchy. For example, the physiological needs of food, air, and water are the most fundamental. If we are deprived of all our needs, these physiological needs will be most dominant. All our being will focus on satisfying hunger and all other needs will become secondary. Maslow explains that

> It is quite true that man lives by bread alone — when there is no bread. But what happens to man's desires when there is plenty of bread and when his belly is chronically filled? At once other (and 'higher') needs emerge and these, rather than physiological hungers, dominate the organism. And when these in turn are satisfied, again new (and still 'higher') needs emerge and so on. This is what we mean by saying that the basic human needs are organized into a hierarchy of relative prepotency.[11]

When our needs are thwarted in a particular area, we stagnate in our growth focusing on fulfilling the unfulfilled need. The more fundamental the unfulfilled need, the more likely we are to abandon higher needs in order to meet the more fundamental one. So for example, if our physiological needs are not met, we cannot move on to feeling safe and secure. We are likely to abandon safety and security in order to fulfill our physiological needs. If our need for safety is not met, we cannot afford to worry about love and self esteem. And without love and self-esteem, we cannot afford the luxury of fulfilling our potential. This does not mean that these needs must be completely satisfied in order for us to move on; nor does it mean that, once they are fulfilled, they are never a concern. Needs must be met throughout life, and each acquires a level of primary importance at different stages in life. But it does mean that if we are to actualize ourselves, we must basically have our fundamental needs met.

This poses a challenge for observing Judaism because ultimately religion and observance are a matter of self-actualization, addressing the highest need on the hierarchy. Observance may also serve to fulfill our more fundamental needs for love or acceptance. But we can achieve these things without religion and observance. What we may have a more difficult time achieving without observance is our need to become the best we can — personally and spiritually.

All this means that in order to maintain observance and fulfill our potential, we must first feel safe and secure, loved and accepted. Observant children and teenagers who are rejected experience a lack of love and their self-esteem is compromised. They therefore stagnate at the level of love and esteem, making observance a luxury they cannot afford. They then become willing, unconsciously, to discard observance in order to fulfill their more fundamental needs.

So unfulfilled emotional needs sabotage observance and create an obstacle to it. And when those needs are sabotaged *because of observance*, they become a more direct obstacle to observance, rendering observance something that must be eradicated. Thus a child or adult who has been rejected by observant people has a significantly increased chance of going off the derech. And one who has been rejected by observant people *over issues of observance* will be even more likely to do so, for then Yiddishkeit *itself* has become a source of pain. In most of these cases, only when he fulfills the fundamental emotional needs that have been sabotaged will there be hope for his Yiddishkeit to flourish.

CHAPTER 5

Imposing Religion: Free Choice and Conditional Love

Like rejection, imposing observance is one of the surest ways to inspire our youth to reject Judaism. Interestingly, many who feel they were rejected during their religious upbringing also feel that observance was forced upon them. For example, while David was experiencing rejection in school, he was being pushed to be observant at home, which mirrored and amplified his negative experiences. His mother would tell him to wear a *kippah* (skullcap), insist that he go to *shul* on Shabbat, and demand that he wear a black hat. In his words, "she tried to shove religion down my throat." While his mother was surely well intentioned, her actions created even more negative associations for David, pushing him farther and farther away from observance. 66% of those who responded to the web survey indicated that they had similar experiences, feeling that observance was imposed upon them.

There is a fine line between forcing and teaching, pushing and leading. That line shifts as a child grows, and it will vary from child to child. It is therefore sometimes hard to know where *chinuch* (education) ends and coercion begins. Properly answering this question depends upon a child's perception and individual needs rather than upon the reality of the situation or the parents' intentions. The most well intentioned parents who strive to educate can push a child away from observance if they do not recognize a child's needs or his reactions to their expectations.

How can we know when *chinuch* ends and coercion begins? If a child starts to become resentful, developing a negative attitude about observance or lying about it, he is probably feeling coerced which is counterproductive to his future observance. If, on the other hand, he is developing a positive, respectful attitude, the parents are engaging in *chinuch,* which serves their child well. Again, the reality of a parent's actions or intentions will have far less to do with a child's future observance than the child's feelings about them.

While imposing observance is always problematic, it is particularly troublesome in adolescence. Young children expect to be told what to do; they need this kind of guidance in order to learn. But as children become adolescents, they require greater independence and telling them what to do or forcing them to comply becomes more and more counterproductive. As Rabbi Shapiro explains,

> Children obey. Teens *choose* to obey.... The greatest mistake parents of teenagers make is trying to manage their teens instead of relating to them. The parents treat the teen like an employee, insisting he carry out the decisions of the management. They don't realize that they have been transferred out of Management and now find themselves in Sales.[1]

During adolescence we need room to grow, to explore our selves and the world around us. When Judaism is imposed on us, it destroys our ability to do so. It compromises not only our fundamental emotional needs, but our religious ones as well.

Imposing Observance is Ineffective

Imposing observance undermines Judaism in various ways. First, it creates negative rather than positive motivators for Judaism. It creates an environment in which kids observe *mitzvot* merely to avoid getting in trouble. In these situations, the adolescent may go through the motions but does not experience the positive Judaism he needs to maintain commitment in the long run. He may comply but fail to develop an independent relationship with God and Torah. He may act the part but do so for the wrong reasons — to avoid rejection and pain. He may observe out of fear rather than love. Sometimes, he will not observe at all and lie about it.

Dena is a perfect example. She remembers the following conversation that occurred every Sunday morning in her home. She would come downstairs and her father would ask, "Dena, did you *daven?*" She would say "No, not yet." And her father would say "Go *daven.*" So she would go back into her room for a half an hour where she would read whatever book came to hand, and come back downstairs to declare, "I *davened.*"

Dena was motivated not by a love for connection with God through prayer, which is positive, but rather by a fear of parental rejection. As a result, in the long run, Dena dropped *halachic* observance. She explains that she did so because she "didn't like being told what to do." She liked to do things on her own, and observance was never something she did on her own. It was something she did for her father. Observance was her father's way; therefore dropping it was hers. "I think, for a long time," she says, "I would do things because my father told me to. But he's not God. And maybe I should do things because *I* believe in doing them for God-fearing purposes." She believes that many children observe out of routine because that's what their parents want, and she did not want to be one of those people. "I wanted to do it because *I* wanted to do it," she says. Dropping observance was her way to develop her own relationship with God — a religious need, while at the same time becoming independent of her father — an emotional need.

Sabotages Fundamental Emotional Needs

In addition to creating negative associations with observance, imposing religion can undermine the fulfillment of all our basic emotional needs. Abraham Maslow explains that there are certain prerequisites to fulfilling our needs. These include the "freedom to speak, freedom to do what one wishes ...freedom to express one's self, freedom to seek and investigate information..." He explains that "danger to these is reacted to almost as if it were a direct danger to the basic needs themselves," for they are almost ends in themselves. Without providing these conditions, we deprive our children of the basic requirements for fulfilling their emotional needs.[2]

Sabotages the Fundamental Need for Love

In addition, imposing religion directly sabotages one emotional need in particular, the need to be loved. Dena's story indicates that imposing religion can create a feeling of conditional love. Of those who responded to the survey, 51% felt that their parents' love was conditional or somewhat conditional on their observance.

If Maslow was right in identifying love as one of our most basic needs, then feeling conditionally loved, especially as a result of religion, undermines emotional and therefore religious development. The parent-child relationship may be the only one in the world defined by unconditional love. The more unconditionally children experience that love from their parents, the better their self-esteem and ultimately the more loving their relationship with God, the ultimate parent. When children are denied this basic need at the hands of observant parents, Judaism suffers. If they are denied it as a *direct* result of Judaism, they are almost sure to resent religion and drop observance altogether.

Dena felt that her father loved her conditionally because of his religious demands. Even though he didn't come out and say it, she felt that if she would not comply, he would love her less, and not consider her a good person. This being too high a price to pay, she continued to lie to him about her lack of observance until her late twenties. As she puts it, "I didn't tell him [about it] until I was pretty much on my own because I was afraid that he would say 'if you're not going to do it, then you're not my daughter and I'm not supporting you.'"

Her father never explicitly said that to her, but his expectations told her that every day. Last year, he went so far as to express it verbally. He told her that she didn't turn out "how he had hoped," but nonetheless he was proud of her. What Dena heard was conditional love, a backward compliment. "He could have just said I'm proud of you," she laments. Instead, he qualified it by referring to her unobservant lifestyle, which once again resulted in Dena's feeling conditionally loved. This reinforced her negative association with observance.

One could argue that despite her father's anger or disapproval, she still had free will. And technically this might be true. But pitting a child's observance, in Dena's case her *davening*, against her parent's love is like putting a gun to a child's head. Parental love and acceptance is too essential to lose and invariably children in this situation will comply in order to gain a parent's love. They simply cannot afford to lose it. So although the child might technically have free choice, for all practical purposes, he has little if any at all.

Perhaps because her father's behavior tied her value as a person to observance, Dena now makes a point of distinguishing between the two and says that a person's worth or Jewishness has nothing to do with observance. "I can be a good person and a spiritual person and just not be observant," she explains. The distinction allows her to heal her childhood wound by valuing, loving and accepting herself in a way that her father may not have done. Since she felt deprived of love and respect because of Yiddishkeit, she needs to emphasize that she can be loveable and acceptable without it.

In addition, because, for all practical purposes, she was deprived of free choice, freedom has become of paramount importance to her. In discussing her religious beliefs, she emphasizes the importance of freedom and choice, explaining that she would never tell anyone what to do in terms of religion. She believes, "To each his own. If you are going to light candles and then watch TV and that's what you want to do, then that's fine." This philosophy extends to educating children as well. She hates to hear her sister Devorah tell her children to make a *bracha* (blessing). Instead, Dena believes that Devorah should make a *bracha,* wait for her kids to ask about it, explain it to them, and let them decide what to do. In Dena's opinion, they should never be told to make a *bracha.*

Dena's reaction is human nature; we tend to overemphasize the importance of things we are missing. Dennis Prager humorously alluded to the phenomenon in his book *Happiness is a Serious Problem.* He explains that he and his friend, Joseph Telushkin, would often try to identify the most important trait in a woman, and found their definition constantly changing. After a particular date, Dennis called Joseph to announce that he had finally identified the most important trait in a woman. But Joseph interrupted him, saying that he already knew the answer. How could he have known the answer when he didn't even know the woman? "It doesn't matter," Joseph replied. "You're about to announce the most important trait in a woman is whatever trait tonight's date didn't have."[3]

Whatever we are deprived of in childhood often assumes critical importance in adulthood. Thus kids who are rejected tend to feel that acceptance is most important. Kids who have been abused tend to feel that safety is most important. And kids who have been deprived of choice feel that freedom is most important. In their adult lives, they either compensate or overcompensate for the areas they lack. Dena's deprivation of free choice heightened her sensitivity so that anything that even *smacks* of imposing religion is off limits.

71

Interestingly, Dena's heightened sensitivity may result in her doing the same thing her parents did but in the opposite direction. When walking the fine line between *chinuch* and coercion, they tended toward coercion. Dena may tend toward too much freedom in an attempt to overcompensate. They focused too much on observance; she may focus on it too little. This tendency to overcompensate for what we were denied in our youth means that children often repeat parents' mistakes in different ways. The exact expression of the mistake varies from one generation to the next, but the issue remains the same.

Sabotages Healthy Religious Development

So, imposing observance sabotages a fundamental emotional need to be loved unconditionally. But imposing observance also undermines the fundamental religious need to acquire and develop our own Jewish identity. Professor Shraga Fisherman, who interviewed hundreds of formerly modern Orthodox kids for his book *Noar Kippot Zerukot*, Youth of the Discarded Kippas, explains why this is true. He believes that as children we have an immature faith, which is marked by a shallow, weak observance, disconnected from the essence of who we are; we practice religion because we are told to, because our parents do, because that is all we know. We do not have life experience or well-developed intellectual faculties. But when we reach adolescence, things change. We start to develop our critical thinking. We become more aware of the world around us, and eventually start to question things in order to develop our own worldview and identity. This is the beginning of establishing a mature, strong and lasting faith.

We bridge the gap between childhood and adulthood — between immature and mature faith — by going through a period of conflict. One can understand this conflict if we think about it in physical terms. How could we go from being a child to an adult without the physical awkwardness of adolescence, without growing pains? Those pains are an essential part of the transition, necessary if we are to grow into healthy adults.

The same is true in the spiritual sense. If my faith is to mature from a reactive to a proactive one, from 'my father told me so,' to something deeper and more meaningful, I must explore it and make it my own. As Rabbi Avraham Kook explains, *tzadik beemunato yichiye* (a righteous person lives by *his* faith)[4] means that a *tzadik* lives by the faith he acquires for himself, the one he works for, not the one given to him or imposed on him.

According to Professor Fisherman, struggling adolescents sometimes conduct themselves contrarily. They deviate from the norms of observance as part of the process of searching for identity. They vacillate between behaviors that comply with and deviate from observance.[5] This vacillation is necessary for solidifying their beliefs and acquiring their own Judaism.

Whether adolescents stagnate in an immature faith or develop a mature faith depends, in part, on the degree of coercion and freedom to choose. If they are coerced, they are likely to stagnate in an immature faith that is less personal, less strong, less meaningful and less enduring. If, on the other hand, they are given latitude to explore and to fail, they will be more likely to acquire their own Judaism and emerge with a stronger, more passionate conviction.[6]

Understandably, it is difficult to let adolescents mature this way and try to find their own Torah when there is a chance they may not find it at all. It is risky and frightening for parents, both religiously and emotionally. But it seems that God Himself took that risk with Adam, the first child, even when He knew that sin was inevitable. God created Adam and immediately gave him free choice, knowing full well that not one page later Adam would stumble and choose sin. But God determined that it was better to allow Adam to fall, better to have him betray His will with free choice, than not to have that choice at all.

God wants us to walk in his ways, but he doesn't force us to. He leads, but does not push. He gives us free will and then does what

He can to preserve it by delaying punishment. Removing immediate consequences from our sins helps to ensure that we do not develop a "lightning strikes" mentality that might deprive us of real choice.[7] It helps us develop a positive relationship with Him, to serve Him from love rather than fear. This teaches us how critical choice is. Without it, Judaism and life itself become meaningless.[8] We are told that this is the very thing that makes us unique as human beings[9] and makes us able to serve God's ultimate purpose in a way angels never can.[10]

Children cannot live *our* Torah; it must be their own if it is to endure. The mature faith, the lasting one is personalized, acquired through a struggle that makes observance alive and meaningful. In fact, the greater the struggles, the stronger the commitment can become. We see this with *baalei teshuva*. They often have more passionate commitments to observance than those born into it. How did they become this way? By asking, exploring, making mistakes, struggling to balance their old lives with their new ones and finally finding their own unique place in Judaism. The struggle helps them to acquire Judaism, strengthen it and make it their own which ultimately makes it more personal and valuable for them.

The story of Jacob wrestling with the angel teaches us the value of such struggle. Jacob is called *Israel* only after he struggles with God. Only after the struggle does he acquire his identity, his destiny, and realize his potential. The birth of our individual identities mirrors the birth of our nation. Our Jewish identities are born when we begin to struggle with God. Perhaps that is one reason why *bar* and *bat mitzvah*, which marks our attaining spiritual responsibility, occurs at preadolescence, precisely when we begin to develop our critical faculties and independent personalities.

Gaining the ability to struggle with God in pre-adolescence, we finally gain the responsibility to bond with Him and follow His ways. And like Jacob, whose body was marked forever by this struggle with the angel, our souls are marked forever by the struggle of adoles-

74

cence. In turn, our Jewish identity is forever defined by the results of that struggle, as our nation is forever defined by the name *Israel*, meaning *He who struggles with God.* Whether individually or nationally, that struggle is essential for developing an inspiring and enduring Judaism.

Rabbi Dr. Natan Lopez Cardozo, renowned educator and Dean of the David Cardozo Academy for Judaism, alludes to this in explaining Moses' error in hitting the rock. Why, Rabbi Cardozo asks, was it so great a sin for Moses to hit the rock rather than speak to it? Why did it warrant losing the privilege of entering the land of Israel, especially when the miracle of the rock springing water was just as great if it had been spoken to or hit?

His answer is that Moses was punished because hitting the rock signified coercion; speaking to it, as God intended, would have signified persuasion, an act that allowed room for the rock to choose for itself, so to speak. At that time in our history, the Jewish people were at a crossroads, on the brink of entering the land and becoming an independent nation; they were emerging from their childhood in the desert where they had been utterly dependent on God, forced by the barrenness[11] of the desert to comply with His will and coerced at *Har Sinai* (Mt. Sinai) into accepting the Torah, into adulthood. To mature into a strong, independent nation, they would now have to choose Torah for themselves, through persuasion rather than coercion. The miracle of the rock was meant to demonstrate this reality to them and all their future leaders. Maturation requires the persuasion of speech, not the might of dictatorship.

Conclusion

Free choice is the most precious gift we have, one that makes not only Judaism but also life itself meaningful. Taking it away from an adolescent child is akin not only to taking away his Torah, but even his life. As the Maharal says, "Life means autonomy, not being dependent on anyone else. The absence of [autonomy] is death."[12] Therefore "an assault on a person's ability to make independent choices is an assault on his life."[13] If God, the ultimate parent, would not do such a thing, how can a human parent?

Unfortunately, sometimes parents impose observance as a way of fulfilling their own needs rather than their child's. Sometimes they feel insecure about their own Judaism, they lack confidence in Torah or in their children's ability to see the truth and act accordingly. Sometimes they see deviation as a threat to their authority, a poor reflection on their parenting skills or a mark of shame in front of the community. Each of these feelings can compel parents to buckle down and impose observance on children. But doing so can cause children to lie or to develop a negative attitude about observance; it can cause them to observe out of fear rather than love or to feel that parents love them conditionally; and it can deprive them of the growing opportunities they need to develop a mature, personal and inspiring faith. In that case, it may be far better to take the chance and give them freedom, as God did with Adam, than to impose observance. That way at least there is the possibility of creating a positive, personal relationship with Torah and *mitzvot*; the other way there is far less hope. If we work to foster security in our own Judaism, to improve our schools, and to have faith in the beauty and truth of the Torah and our children's ability to recognize it, we will help ensure that the reward will justify the risk.

CHAPTER 6

Shalom Bayit and General Happiness

While our relationship with Judaism and how it makes us feel is very important, how we feel in *general* may be more fundamental. It is the foundation upon which all else rests. When young people feel unhappy in life they are likely to feel unhappy in their observance. As Leah Kohn says, "You cannot be a happy Jew if you are not a happy person." And if you are not a happy Jew, there is good chance you won't be a truly observant Jew or remain one in the long run.

But why is feeling good so vital to maintaining observance? On the surface, these seem like two distinct areas in life. We all know observant people who are unhappy and remain observant. Feelings about their job, family, friends or spouse do not cause them to stop keeping Shabbat and *kashrut*. So how does general unhappiness contribute to the off the derech phenomenon?

Clearly, when we are unhappy, our interpersonal relationships suffer. We do not have as much patience for others, and cannot give as much, for our energy is sapped by unhappiness. At such times we may tend to speak more *lashon hara* (negative speech about someone), do less *chessed* (acts of kindness), and react to situations with anger and frustration. As one prominent educator explains, "The happier we are with ourselves, the more tolerant we are of others and their faults."

Unhappy Jewish children tend to have compromised relationships with the practitioners of Judaism and, by extension, with Judaism itself. And because of their unhappiness, they tend to be less forgiving of any negative role models they encounter, and have a harder time maintaining a positive feeling about Judaism. In the least, their unhappiness tends to affect the quality of their internal experience with observance and diminish their joy for it.

The Role of the Family

There are even more direct, dramatic ways in which general unhappiness causes people to go off the derech. In order to understand how this occurs, we need first to consider where these feelings generally originate. Where do our emotional worlds begin and develop? The answer lies in our families.

We experience family before we experience anything else on earth. Our familial relationships, particularly with our parents, are the most fundamental and influential in our lives.[1] It is through those relationships that we first experience feelings and establish our primary emotional experiences. So family relationships are the foundation of our emotional lives and create the lens through which we experience the world, including God.

We can think of our emotional lives, the story of our family, as a fabric woven from two different threads — our parents' relationship with each other, and our parents' relationship with us. When either one suffers, observance suffers.

Parents and Children

Yaacov told me that he was observant in his youth, but, after his parents divorced, things changed. They were struggling financially and his mother stopped caring as much about observance. His father, who had never been particularly kind to him or his mother, did nothing to help out. They struggled to hold onto a semblance of normalcy, but observance became particularly challenging. When his father left, there was nobody in the house to make *kiddush* and no structure for him to come home to. "There was no family," he sadly recalls.

Over the years, Yaacov's observance deteriorated. In the *yeshiva*, he would maintain whatever observance he had to, but outside of the *yeshiva* he would sneak into pornography theaters and do a little shoplifting. Instead of learning, he played video games all day. He was looking for something, he says.

> I was looking for something — for identity, for love ... I felt that I had tried everything to be happy. I had tried working. I put on a suit every day, and walked into an office building. That didn't make me happy. Pot didn't make me happy. Losing myself in girls didn't make me happy. I was a punk rocker for a while; that didn't make me happy. Eventually I had gotten as far as I could in pop-culture and I still wasn't happy... What else was I going to do? Then one night, I met a girl. I was at a party in Harlem, tripping on acid, and she was a stripper and I was talking about how I wanted to go cross-country on a motorcycle. And she said 'Me, too.' And the next thing I know, I was traveling cross-country on a motorcycle with a stripper named Crisco. A boy from Brooklyn! It doesn't get any better than that. This was it; this was the pinnacle. I had gotten as far away from my roots as I possibly could. But on the trip, I sat there thinking about what would make me happy, what was real. And I discovered that if someone said 'live a good life and you will be happy,' I was in trouble because I had no idea what a good life

79

meant....I came to the conclusion out of total desperation that I couldn't ask anybody how to be happy because everybody's got their own sketch of reality, including philosophers and psychologists. So who is going to tell me with absolute certainty how I should live my life — except for some being who is transcendent.

Yaacov decided to look for an answer in the revealed religions and, recognizing Judaism as the source of Western religions, he decided he would give it another chance. He would practice being observant again for a three-year trial period, at the end of which he would evaluate whether or not he was happy. What enabled Yaacov to take that leap, change his lifestyle and give Judaism a second chance?

Because I dealt with my father. I wanted to be [observant], but I didn't like my father. So if I didn't like my father and he was [observant], I wasn't going to be observant either. I was repelled by Judaism because of him. And I realized one day that if you're really pissed off at your father, the best revenge is to become nothing because then look at what you've done to his son. You are saying 'I don't want to be anything because of you' and that's a really tough blow.

Yaacov's turning point came when he met a rabbi who made an impression. Yaacov told the rabbi his family's story and called his father a *baal mussar* (a moralist). The rabbi stopped him saying, "If that's how your father acted, he wasn't a *baal mussar*." Yaacov was taken aback. He recalls that "with that one sentence, the rabbi separated religion from my father and that was tremendous."

After the conversation, Yaacov began learning in the rabbi's *yeshiva*, went to Israel, stopped using marijuana and became observant again. It took years of struggle for him to come to terms with how he felt about his father, but when he did, the obstacle to his religiosity was removed. Today Yaacov is a rabbi who works with kids at risk.

The Parent-Child Relationship and Observance

Yaacov's story demonstrates a number of ways in which unhappiness that stems from the parent-child relationship can compromise observance. First, when a religious parent — like any parent — does not appear to his child as a decent human being, he fails to earn his child's respect and ceases to function as a role model. When the child no longer respects or likes his parent, he no longer wants to emulate him. Yaacov disliked his father, so he didn't want to be like him. Since his father was observant, he couldn't be.

If the child experiences enough pain at the hands of the parent, things can deteriorate to the point where the child actually wants to hurt the parent as punishment or revenge, and there is no better way to hurt an observant parent than by not being observant. This will likely be the case even if the child's pain has nothing to do with Yiddishkeit, as was the case with Yaacov. His father's apparent rejection of him and his mother had nothing to do with Judaism, but Yaacov's rebellion did.

Also, the worse the pain, the more dramatic the rebellion, so that sometimes it is not only observance that suffers, but the child's life in general. For example, Yaacov did much more than simply drop observance. He shoplifted, did drugs, and engaged in sexually inappropriate behavior. To really hurt his father, Yaacov had to do more than merely drop observance; he had to "become nothing."

Finally, Yaacov's story demonstrates how a negative relationship with a parent can be experienced as a negative relationship with God. When our relationship with our parents suffers, our relationship with God suffers as well because our parents are the model for our relationship with God.

Since we cannot know God directly, we know him indirectly through our parents. Like God, they created us and they feed us, clothe us, love us, and teach us. They are the most God-like figures in our lives, and so the kind of relationship we have with them tends to define our view of God. If our parents or parental figures are predominantly loving, we tend to view God as loving and nurturing. If, on the other hand, they are mostly harsh and rejecting, we tend to consider God that way as well. If they are merely absent, we may fail to have a model against which to understand God and our relationship with Him. In such cases, the best hope for creating a healthy relationship with God and Judaism is healing the parent-child relationship. As Dr. Meir Wikler, distinguished therapist in the observant world, explains, often when people work through the relationships with their parents and "unravel their emotional difficulties," a miraculous transformation occurs, enabling them to have a better relationship with *Hashem* (God).

Dr. Wikler believes so strongly in the influence of the relationship between parent and child on observance that he says he had never seen, met, or heard of someone who grew up in an Orthodox home who became non-Orthodox and had warm, close intimate, relationships with their parents."[2]

So when our relationship with our parents suffers, our Judaism will often suffer as well. Rabbi Shlomo Riskin, the Chief Rabbi of Efrat, summed it up when he said, "If I am at peace with my parents on earth, I'll be at peace with my parent in heaven."[3]

The Parent-Parent Relationship

Not only can a child's poor relationship with a parent compromise observance, but so can his witnessing a bad relationship *between* his parents. For example, Chani Metzger spent the first 15 years of her life living in a home filled with conflict. When her parents finally divorced, her observance began to deteriorate along with everything else.

At the time of her parents' divorce, she was at the height of her popularity as class president. But, when she became the only girl in her Bais Yaacov class with divorced parents, she started to act out. Chani started to dress a little differently, tying her shirt in a knot. Although she made sure to wear another shirt underneath, so her skin would not be exposed, she was considered to be dressing immodestly and was rejected — not only by her teachers but also by her friends. She remembers a friend writing her a note that she still has today. "I understand what you are going through and I have always loved you even when you were different." But, she continued, the knot in her shirt indicated that Chani wished to go in a different direction, which would have a negative influence on her, and so she needed to disassociate from Chani. "She loved me anyway," she said, "but she could never talk to me again."

That one rejection might have been bearable, but the rejection continued and intensified. Chani remembers one day wearing a skirt with a slit. Bais Yaacov required that a slit or button-down skirt had to be machine sewn, closed with a double seam. Lacking a sewing machine, Chani closed the seam with two rows of tiny safety pins. When she wore the skirt to school, she was humiliated.

> The teacher bent down, picked up my purple snap down skirt, and saw that there were two rows of safety pins as opposed to two rows of stitching. She ripped it open and brought me into her office. I was wearing a slip, thank God. So I went into her office in my slip and waited for my mother to come to pick me up...I sat there in that slip for three hours. It was terrible.

Chani was "dying to break out" of her world. Her home was a source of pain and now so was her school. She felt confined and unhappy. She wanted her parents to notice and help, but they didn't. She longed for something different where she could feel joy. She would ride her bike at three in the morning, alone into the night to feel free. And she would write scenarios in her diary in which she was trapped on an island, waiting for a guy to arrive and rescue her.

One day, as she was sitting down to eat a bagel, she got up to wash and all of a sudden asked herself: "Why are you making a blessing? You are being dishonest if you make a blessing. You don't really believe in this anymore. You don't want it. You are looking for a way out." So she didn't wash her hands and she didn't make a blessing, and thus began her formal break with observance.

Chani remembers trying to reach out before she made the break. Her father was a *Rosh Yeshiva* (the rabbinic head of a *yeshiva*) who had brought many people closer to Judaism. And she would ask him questions about Judaism; but he would dismiss them, not taking her seriously or realizing she was reaching out. She says that she was open to his answers and might even have been turned on to observance if he would have only smiled and given her the same courtesy he gave his students. But he didn't, so she stopped trying.

Miserable at home and unable to fit in at school, Chani eventually left Bais Yaacov for a more modern school away from home. The girls at her new school were allowed to have boyfriends and behave more freely, which gave Chani permission to see herself as acceptable.

> ...it made me feel like I can still be good and have a boyfriend. Bais Yaacov girls can't be good and do this other stuff. Once they get involved in *any* deviant behavior, even if it's not that terrible, they lose all their self-respect. And I was able to maintain some of that because I saw other *frum* people respecting themselves even if they watched movies and had boyfriends.

During that time, Chani met a guy named Eli with whom she fell deeply in love. But her parents found out about it and intervened. Eli got kicked out of school and the two spent a number of months apart. Finally they were going to reunite, but Chani's mother threatened Eli and he stayed away. Chani was dejected. Alone and away at camp, she ended up running away into the arms of an older man she had met. She spent only one week with him, but it scarred her for years to come. During that week, he physically abused her and eventually sexually abused her as well. She never told her parents or anyone else about it. She carried the pain inside when she returned home, but she was no longer the same. She was now wearing skirts that were shorter — just below her knees — which embarrassed her father terribly, especially given his position within the community. Things exploded when one day he read Chani's diary, which was full of stories about her and Eli. Her father became enraged, condemning her and calling her a prostitute. She fled to her mother's house and refused to return to school.

Eventually, Chani developed close relationships with a rabbi and teacher who took an interest in her and persuaded her to return to school. It was hard, but she returned to Bais Yaacov. Unfortunately, she carried the pain of her sexually abusive experience with her; it was a deep scar that needed to heal. Chani began writing about her experience in the form of a novel. She created a fictional character that experienced what she did as a means of releasing the pain inside. In her words, it was "the dirtiest novel you ever read. It was disgusting," presenting the graphic details of her experience starkly and honestly. Soon after she started the novel, her mother found it and history repeated itself. Shocked, her mother showed the novel to the rabbi and teacher who had befriended her.

The teacher, whom Chani loved and respected, berated her, "I am sitting here helping you and being there for you and I feel fooled. I feel disgusted. I can't believe it. All this disgusting stuff is in your head! I don't know what we're doing with you. I don't know why we're trying to help you. You're schizophrenic." The rabbi responded that he no longer knew her, and there was nothing more he could do for her.

Chani felt rejected and betrayed and she internalized their condemnation of her.

After that incident, she dropped out of her senior year of high school just three months shy of graduation, and things spiraled out of control. She started wearing pants, completely went off the derech, and began to engage in a lifestyle of sex and drugs, all of which she had success-fully avoided until that point.

Many years later, she dealt with her emotional issues, including the divorce of her parents and the traumatic experiences of her adoles-cence, which enabled her to return to her *halachically* observant way of life. Today the girl who was rejected by her parents, role models, teachers and friends for not being observant enough is happily married to her teenage sweetheart Eli, raising their numerous children as obser-vant Jews, and working in *kiruv* (bringing people closer to Judaism).

The Importance of *Shalom Bayit* (Family Harmony)

The Steipler Rabbi has said that "success with our children is 50% *sha-lom bayit* and 50% prayer."[4] That is because *shalom bayit* is the context within which we experience everything else. When that suffers, so does every other part of our lives. As Yaacov Horowitz explains, a lack of *shalom bayit* —

> …creates unhappy distracted children who are unable to concentrate in school. They develop an intense distrust of authority figures and harbor a simmering rage at an adult world that cannot seem to get its act together and provide them with a peaceful environment in which to grow up.[5]

This may be why Rabbi Moshe Prager, who specializes in work-ing with kids who have gone off the derech at Neve Tzion *yeshiva* and throughout Israel, notes that 40% of the formerly observant boys he works with come from broken homes.[6] And it may be why in the Talmud, our sages identify lack of *shalom bayit* as a cause of rebellious behavior. When the Torah discusses a man who marries an *Aishet Yifat To'ar* (woman who was captured in war), our sages say "If he marries her, he will end up hating her and have a rebellious child with her."

First he will come to hate his wife, and then *because* of his hatred for her, a rebellious child will result from their union.[7]

Conflict Undermines Need for Safety

Chani's spiral away from Judaism illustrates exactly how *shalom bayit* issues can ultimately push one off the derech.

A lack of *shalom bayit* undermines the need for emotional safety, Maslow's second emotional requirement. This need is even more fundamental than the need to feel loved and accepted. Parental conflict destroys a child's ability to fulfill this need, as it did for Chani. Chani's home was filled with negative feelings of pain, anger and unhappiness. But even worse, it was unpredictable, an environment which might be angry one minute and loving the next.

A child cannot feel safe and secure when he doesn't know from day to day or hour to hour what kind of emotional world he is walking in to. In such cases, the basic need for safety remains unfulfilled, which compromises a child's ability to achieve any others on the hierarchy, including love, self-esteem, self-actualization and the Torah that goes with it.

Confusing Unhappiness with Judaism

A child in these troubling circumstances may also begin to create a subconscious association between Judaism and pain since the pain emanates from a religious world. As a result, he may confuse the source of the pain, thinking that Yiddishkeit is the problem rather than the familial relationships.

When Chani rode her bike alone at three in the morning, it was not observance that she was running away from; it was the conflict at home. But when Judaism is so much a part of the home it becomes hard, on a subconscious level, to separate the two. They are too closely associated. And so it is interesting to note Chani's first break with observance — the blessing on the bagel. She said that, as she was about to make the blessing, she realized that she "didn't want it"; she was "looking for a way out." But was she looking for a way out of making *brachot* (blessings)? Not at all. She was looking for a way out of her pain, her predicament, her environment. Since her environment was so inherently defined by observance, breaking free of one seemed like breaking free of another. Since she didn't want her world, she figured she also didn't want the observance that came with it.

It is easy and almost natural for a child to confuse the pain emanating from the home as pain emanating from *the way of life* at home. When that happens, Yiddishkeit is perceived as the source of pain, and is often discarded. Thus the general emotional problem becomes a Yiddishkeit problem.

Family Problems Become Religious Problems

Chani's story also demonstrates how *shalom bayit* issues can snowball into religious issues. Chani's problems started at home. But, as is often the case, problems that begin at home do not end there. It all stemmed from her parents getting divorced. At that point, she was not unhappy with Judaism; she merely felt unhappy in general, with life itself. But her general emotional issues became religious issues.

Chani expressed her familial pain at school by changing her dress and deviating from the norm. These are natural responses for teenagers who are suffering. At this point in the story, Chani's relationship with Yiddishkeit and her other role models were still positive. There was still a chance that her general unhappiness might not have colored her experience of Judaism. But her acting out was met with rejection, which compounded the problem. Now the practitioners of Yiddishkeit *themselves* had become a source of pain. Now another series of needs, the need for love and acceptance, were also undermined. So she started to associate Judaism and observant Jews with the negative feelings of unhappiness and lack of self-worth. These feelings were reinforced more painfully when she was rejected and alienated by her mother, father, close teacher and rav. The dramatic condemnation from her primary role models not only shattered her self-esteem, but also created even stronger negative associations with observant people.

Unfortunately, it didn't occur to anyone that her acting out in school resulted from pain and so they didn't help her. And it didn't occur to her parents or mentors that Chani's novel might have been a way of dealing with her pain. Ironically, it might well have been *because of* her earlier positive relationship with these mentors that she started to write it: When Chani's mentors gave her love and approval, they gave her emotional safety — the very thing she had always lacked and needed in order to achieve emotional health. Thus it might have been precisely *because* she was healthier that she started to write the novel. She did not intend to hurt, embarrass or betray anyone, but her father, mother, teacher and rabbi all took her novel *personally*. Instead of wondering why she was writing the novel, they condemned her for it. Instead of talking to her about it, they rejected her. Instead of giving her the unconditional love she needed, they further exacerbated her pain and unhappiness.

Chani's parents and teachers may have been well intentioned. They were probably reacting the only way they knew how. But even with the best intentions, their response was destructive. By condemning Chani instead of talking to her, by pushing her away instead of pulling her closer, by making her feel inadequate instead of worthy, they denied Chani the safety and love she desperately needed. They ensured that the pain of her home would not only create general unhappiness but also create negative associations with Judaism and its practitioners, diminishing her ability and desire to be observant.

Judaism Should Make You Happy

It may complicate matters even more if children are taught to believe that simply being observant makes one happy. A child who is taught to expect that committing to Judaism brings happiness may question

Judaism's effectiveness and truth when he sees pain in his family or experiences it personally in his adult life. In such cases, the unhappiness will damage his perception of Judaism and cause him to lose faith in it or in the teachers who taught him.

That is why it is vital to separate the two for children, to teach them that Judaism *alone* will not necessarily make us happy. It can bring us meaning and fulfillment more powerfully than anything else. It can provide wonderful insight and depth to our life. But it cannot replace the fundamental things in life that we should have gained from our parents or teachers. It cannot create happiness where there is none. It must rest upon an emotional foundation, which is most effective when built in our youth. This is perhaps another way to understand the term — *derech eretz kadmah leTorah* (common decency precedes Torah).

Shalom Bayit Doesn't Mean Absolute Agreement

It is important to note that *shalom bayit* does not mean that parents should agree on everything. In fact some degree of disagreement is healthy and beneficial for the emotional development of a child. Dr. Wikler explains that if "children get the impression that spouses in a marriage must always agree on everything, they get a distorted impression."[8] They think that a healthy marriage means complete agreement with no conflict. As a result, when they grow up, they may be unable to tolerate any dissension, certainly not from their spouses and potentially not from others either. Even normal, healthy disagreements may make them feel insecure, unhappy, and unsuccessful.

Parental disagreement can be positive. It can send the message that being different or having differences of opinion is a normal part of a healthy marriage. In fact, as Debbie Greenblatt, former director of Project YES, an organization that helps kids at risk, notes, "The best marriages in fact are the ones where the people are different"[9] for that creates the greatest potential for growth, assuming the two sides respect each other, move toward each other, and learn from one another or, in the words of a friend, "celebrate" each other's differences.

So when do differences and conflicts become problematic? Dr. Naftali Reich, a psychologist who has spent years counseling couples explains that "within reasonable parameters, it is not the *differences* that are the problem; it is *how they are communicated.*" If parents communicate respectfully and listen attentively to each other, they will not undermine the child's needs or make him feel insecure, but rather teach him how to love, how to listen, how to tolerate differences in others, and how to negotiate those differences.

It is when those disagreements become abusive, angry, intolerant, disrespectful, or frequent that the child suffers. In such cases, safety and happiness are eradicated. In addition, Dr. Wikler believes that, "…the children get the impression that they cannot please both parents which could lead the children to reject parental authority." So children need to see a relatively united front while also seeing some difference occasionally so that they can learn how conflicts are negotiated.[10]

This principle may hold true for differences in Judaism as well. Over the years my father became more observant than my mother, which could have created great conflict in our home. But, though they differed in their actions as well as in some of their beliefs, they were always respectful of each other. When they disagreed, they did so respectfully, both in their words and their actions. When my father wanted to keep Shabbat *halachically,* my mother learned the *halachot* (Jewish laws) of cooking on Shabbat. She bought a *blech* (hot plate) and learned how to use it. Likewise my father never required her to change her personal habits and become *halachically* observant herself. He respected her religious choices and gave her the freedom to do as she believed.

Surely not every marriage could have successfully bridged these kinds of differences. My parents were lucky in that these changes came after many years of marriage, after they had already established a strong foundation to tackle change and accommodate difference.

In addition, they had always shared certain religious values; for example, Shabbat was always a special day for my mother. She would start shopping and cooking early, always made special food, set a beautiful Shabbat table, and refrained from some of her hobbies, like sewing, in order to maintain the sanctity of the day. So though my parents did not share the same *behavior*, they did share certain *values*. And because the relationship that lay at the heart of the differences was strong and respectful, the differences enhanced the relationship rather than weakened it.

Conclusion

When discussing observant life and the possibility of children going off the derech, the first place to look is in the home. Everything begins there, including Judaism. It is where our feelings are created, where our concept of God is developed, where the foundation for our general happiness and relationships with others is laid. When life at home suffers, so does everything else. A lack of *shalom bayit* can push children off the derech. It can do so as it did for Yaacov, by creating disrespect for primary role models of Judaism; by undermining belief in God's care; or by creating a desire to rebel and hurt the parent, which is most effectively accomplished by dropping observance. Or it can do so as it did for Chani, by undermining the feeling of safety and therefore the ability to self-actualize through Torah; by making Yiddishkeit mistakenly seem as the source of pain; or by triggering other painful experiences with the practitioners of Torah.

No matter how, the conflicts that undermine *shalom bayit* and general happiness ultimately undermine observance. Therefore, the best way to strengthen the possibility of future observance is to strengthen the family — the parents' relationship with their children, and perhaps more importantly, with each other.

CHAPTER 7

Who are the Parents

A t the heart of all familial relationships that influence a child's observance are the individual parents. Their unique emotional make-up, personalities, and value systems all affect a child's observance in numerous ways. They affect observance directly in that they determine the nature of the familial relationships, the general atmosphere of the home, and the child's general happiness. But they also affect observance more indirectly in that parents' emotions, personalities, and value systems create the parents' own relationship with Judaism, which determines the effectiveness of their role modeling.[1]

No doubt parents have the most difficult jobs in the world and, consequently, no matter how dedicated, caring, loving, and sacrificing, they are destined to make mistakes. After all, parents were also once children, raised by imperfect parents. But unlike children, parents are confronted with tremendous responsibilities — financial and otherwise — and the stresses that come with those responsibilities. Under such circumstances, simply raising emotionally and physically healthy children is a significant accomplishment, let alone raising God-fearing children who have strong ties to Torah and the Jewish people.

So it is almost inevitable that observant parents in particular will fall short in some regard. Nonetheless, it is helpful to try to identify potential problems in order to preempt or mitigate their affect on a child.

Emotional Issues

Parents' emotional and character-based strengths and weaknesses help determine the nature of the familial relationships, the atmosphere in the home, and the parents' own relationship with Judaism. Generally speaking, if parents are unhappy, the relationships with their spouses and children will suffer. Unhappy parents tend to be less loving, less patient, or less tolerant of their children's mistakes, creating distance and pain. In turn, the parents' own observance[2] and ability to model Torah may suffer. Their *mitzvot bain adam lechavairo* or *bain adam lemakom* (commandments between man and man or man and God) may suffer or they may lose their joy for observance.

Their emotional issues or character flaws can ultimately affect the way they transmit Judaism. For example, parents who lack self-esteem need outside approval so they often impose observance on their children in an effort to gain it. Parents who are self-centered might value their children only in so far as they provide *nachas* (joy). Or, as Rabbi Shlomo Wolbe, a leading Torah authority, points out, parents who are jealous by nature may look at someone else's child who excels in a certain area and impose those expectations on their own child. As a general rule, the less the "self" is developed, the more problematic the familial relationships and transmission of Torah. The more the self is developed, the more room there is for others and the better the transmission of Torah.

Personality

Parental personality also plays an important role in familial relationships. For example, perfectionist parents may demand too much of their children whereas free-spirited parents may deprive their children of necessary structure. In regards to observance, personality may determine our tendency toward certain *mitzvot* and how much joy we exude in their practice. For example, parents who are naturally giving may gravitate toward deeds of kindness and goodwill between people, whereas parents who are more intellectual in nature may tend toward the *halachic* study of Torah. Sometimes personality affects what we value as well. For example, a creative person might consider the *mitzvot* that foster and express creativity, like building a *succah* for example, of paramount importance whereas one who is less creative by nature, might value the more technical aspects of observance. These tendencies are natural and even positive. But they can hurt children's observance if they are confused with "truth" or if they are imposed on children with different character structures and needs.

Values

As with emotional make-up and personality, values largely define the nature of our Torah as well as our relationships. It is important to realize that children internalize values whether or not parents express them verbally. They learn from actions as well as words so that parents are constantly sending subtle messages whether or not they realize it. Such was the case for Elisha Ben Abuyah, one of the more famous people who went off the derech in Talmudic times.

Elisha was a very learned man, dedicated to God and Judaism. But in his adult years he went off the derech, and our sages discuss the possible causes. In one place, they claim that Elisha was turned off from Judaism because he witnessed the disgrace of a holy Jewish man. Alternatively we are told that he went off the derech because of his father, Abuyah. Abuyah had put Elisha on the path of learning when he witnessed Torah scholars learning and was impressed by the honor they received. Since his motive was glory rather than truth or a desire to serve God, the foundation of Elisha's commitment was weak and impure. Both explanations hint at potential causes of people going off the derech. But which was the real cause — Elisha's disillusionment or Abuyah's ulterior motives? Rabbi Yaakov Shapiro explains that both were true.

> Yes, Elisha was "turned off" by witnessing the unspeakable disgrace of someone who deserved only honor. But where did Elisha acquire this weakness in his personality? Surely someone of Elisha's stature should know that God's ways are beyond understanding, and that the atrocities of this world are not a contradiction to the truth of the Torah.
>
> But, with a father like Abuyah, that's what can be expected. To Abuyah, dedication to Torah depended upon the glory it bestowed. He never [explicitly] taught this to Elisha, but Elisha acquired his father's imperfection just the same. For someone whose commitment is due to the spectacular glory it brings, seeing the horrifying disgrace of a righteous sage can be devastating.
>
> Elisha went off the path because he was raised by a man with an inadequate attitude toward Torah learning. Deep down he acquired that attitude himself, and [it] positioned him for failure...because parents' actions leave an impression on children stronger than words can tell.[3]

Parents teach primarily through their own value system and the behavior they model. So, if parents want their children to respect Torah, the best way to do so is by respecting it themselves.[4] They must make it a priority in their actions and not just their words.

While personal weaknesses and mistakes are inevitable, parents can mitigate them in order to safeguard their children's emotional health and commitment to Judaism. One way is for parents to know their characters, strengths, weaknesses, and value systems. The better we know ourselves, the better we can anticipate problems and potentially avoid them, and the better we can know others, especially our children, which is vital for maximizing their relationship with God.

We can also forgive ourselves for our weaknesses. Forgiveness not only relieves pressure and guilt, but also enables us to be more forgiving of others. In addition, parents can be open and honest about some of their issues when children are old enough to understand. Honesty, simply admitting errors, has a way of diminishing their negative consequences and improving our relationships.

Perhaps most importantly, parents can value growth and dedicate themselves to self-improvement. In that case, no matter who they are today, they will be better tomorrow. Dedication to growth is so important that Rabbi Wolbe, says that "a person who does not work on improving his character cannot be a proper parent or teacher."[5] In fact, this may be the only thing we can truly control. We cannot change our past, the legacy whether good or bad that our parents left us; we cannot eliminate the external stressors that infiltrate our daily lives; what we can do is determine how we react to them, strive to minimize their negative effects on us and those around us, and meet the world and our own personal issues with a positive, growth-oriented attitude. When we commit ourselves to growth, we help ensure that personal weaknesses do not forever define the nature of our relationships or observant lives. We become better parents and role models. And, if nothing else, we help teach our children to grow and strive to overcome whatever emotional or religious obstacles we might inadvertently put in their path.

CHAPTER 8

Abuse and Safety

O f all emotionally devastating experiences for children, abuse may be the worst. Whether sexual, physical, or verbal, abuse eradicates a child's feeling of safety in the world. Verbal abuse eradicates emotional safety; while physical or sexual abuse will go one step further and eradicate physical safety as well. Abuse also betrays trust, humiliates and painfully rejects, undermining self-esteem, a child's feeling of love, and the ability to establish trusting relationships.

With these most fundamental needs compromised, a child who has experienced any kind of abuse at the hands of his parents is almost sure to go off the derech. He will find it difficult to reach his emotional and spiritual potential, and will likely associate Torah and its practitioners with pain and degradation.

While abuse may not seem to be a prevalent problem, 51% of those who responded to the web survey indicated that they had been physically or verbally abused by someone observant.

The extremely destructive nature of abuse can be seen in the kind of rebellion it produces. Dr. Jerry Lob, Chicago-area psychologist who has extensive experience working with kids at risk, explains that rebellion in families where there was abuse is the worst kind of all. In such cases, "the kids want not only to hurt their parents, but to embarrass them, for example by walking around in public in the community with tongue rings, smoking a joint." Dr. Lob says that he has "never seen a case of a child wanting to humiliate his parents publicly where there wasn't abuse. We pay for our crimes with our kids,"[1] he explains.

While abuse is most destructive when experienced at home, like all other negative experiences, it can be problematic when experienced at school as well. Parents are not the sole contributors to a child's emotional development nor are they its sole guardians. Once a child enters school, teachers and school administrators begin to spend more time with a child than parents do, and they quickly become secondary authority figures, role models, and representatives of Torah for a child. This gives teachers significant influence over a child's development and also significant responsibility for it.

Shlomo, a Chassid from Brooklyn, is an excellent example. In the course of my interviews, he was one of the most interesting and conflicted people I met. He walked in wearing traditional *Chassidishe* garb — a long black coat, white shirt, and *tzitzit* hanging out from beneath his jacket. He wore his black hat high on his head and his *payas* (sidelocks) hung down to his chin. He was only about twenty-four, and what I noticed about him first were his eyes — young, innocent, and kind — which he averted from mine until long into the interview.

Shlomo is no longer observant. He is married with a child and he lives a lie; on Shabbat he tells his wife that he is going to learn, but he walks out of the community, gets in a car and drives to Manhattan where he smokes and hangs out. On Yom Kippur, he walks outside of the community, eats in a coffee shop, and returns to *shul* because he loves the *nigunim* (melodies). He lives in the *Chassidishe* world unable and unwilling to leave it.

Hearing Shlomo describe his life was astounding. It was nearly impossible to reconcile his outer religious appearance with his inner experience. But about an hour into the conversation, things became clearer. Shlomo looked at me with his kind eyes, dressed in his pious clothes and said that "If there is a God, He is a bastard." I could see the pain and anger on his face as he continued in his broken English:

> There is no God. It looks like there is a God in this world? Do you see judgment in this world? I want to ask you, if there's a God in this world, He's not someone that is a *rasha merusha* (truly evil)? Look how many people dying; look how many children. Look what's going on in this world. How many people have pain and pain and pain? No one is happy in this world. You can't find happiness in this world.

Shlomo sees pain everywhere he looks. He sees pain in the religious world and pain in the secular world. He even sees pain as the cause for the Torah itself. He explains that "…everyone has pain in this world so Orthodox people decided we have to think of something that will make easier life for people. And they make up something."

Needless to say, Shlomo keeps these ideas to himself. He says that if the community knew that he was not observant, they would pressure his wife to divorce him. As it stands, "they don't have enough proof" so he still lives with his wife, who knows something of his "questions" but not the full extent of his disbelief and disconnection.

Shlomo would leave the community and Judaism totally if not for two things. First, he does not believe there is a better alternative. Shlomo says,

> My father told me 'You can go wherever you want. Take your *payas* off and go. Where do you think is going to be better for you? You think you're going to go make a new community? New friends? New life? You think your

100

life is going to be easier for you?' He told me if you find
a place where life is going to be better for you, call me. I
will come also.

For Shlomo, the outside world seems just as miserable as the observant one, so he may as well be miserable at home. He says, "When I will know that someplace [else], it will be better for me, then I will do it. But the world is not that good. Wherever you're going, there is pain...so why should I?"

The second reason Shlomo remains is that he loves and respects his family and doesn't want to hurt them. "I'm doing it only for respect — because I love my wife; I love my kid; I love my family. Why should I destroy everything?" If not for the great respect and love of his parents, Shlomo says he might well have divorced his wife and left the Chassidic world already. But Shlomo's parents are supportive and kind, and he respects them both too much to hurt them. He recalls that when he first heard about sex, he was close enough to his father to ask him about it, and always felt his father respected him despite their differences of opinion. Shlomo remembers that one night he came home at three in the morning while his father was talking to a guest.

> I heard the other guy say, "He's coming home now?" My
> father says "yeah." "You're not asking from who he's coming?" And my father told him, "If he's coming now from a
> *blatt gemorah* (page of *gemorah*), sitting and learning, so
> he will tell me. If he's not telling me from who he's coming, he probably don't want to tell me. So if I will ask him,
> he will not answer or he will tell me some lie. So I have
> two problems. One, he will not answer so I will not know.
> The second, I make him to lie. I can't do it."

Shlomo's father respected him and Shlomo respects his father, so much so that until today he awakens at four in the morning to hear his father's *shiur* (class).

If his impression of Judaism had been gained solely from his family, perhaps Shlomo would not be living his contradictory life. But, unfortunately, his *yeshiva* experiences played a part as well, and they were so negative that they compromised not only his observance, but also his emotional well-being.

Shlomo's issues began with not being able to ask important questions at school. He says he certainly never had the "guts" to ask questions about God because that was taboo, and when he asked about other things, he got into trouble. Shlomo was a gifted child, a couple of years ahead in his studies and when he once asked a lot of questions, his teacher accused him of wanting to waste time. Rejected and hurt, Shlomo stopped asking questions altogether, but that angered his teacher even further. Now he was viewed as *chutzpadik* (insolent) and the teacher eventually kicked him out of class.

He had problems with his classmates as well. Shlomo was the youngest in his class and also the smartest, and when he started passing tests that everyone else was failing, his older classmates began beating him up. Eventually they threw his bags out of the dormitory and rejected him completely. Nothing ever happened to the boys who attacked him, and Shlomo continued to suffer their abuse. He could not understand why his trying so hard to be good was met with so much pain. Eventually his *davening* started to suffer, and he was teased even more that because of that — "You're not *davening* so long anymore? What happened to you?" Shlomo became dejected. He started to fade into the background. He decided it didn't pay to excel in his learning. From then on, he would be a "regular *bachur* (student)."

His connection to the Torah world continued to weaken during his adolescence. He started to go out with people who were not observant in the Chassidishe way, and he started to go to movies. Eventually his daily observance waned too.

At age seventeen, he no longer wanted to put on *tefilin* (phylacteries). But it had been so much a part of his life, he couldn't merely let it go. He had to struggle with himself to stop. He would tell himself he wasn't going to put on *tefilin* that day, and then as the day progressed, he would feel worse and worse until he couldn't take it anymore, and at the last possible moment before the sun was about to set, he would give in and put them on. This went on for days until he managed to finally let go. He calls the day he first skipped *tefilin* an "ugly day."

Although Shlomo does not believe or practice properly, he wishes desperately he could. He said he prays for God to make him a believer because he was happier when he believed. At least then, he felt protected; he could believe that if he suffered today, at least he could have pleasure in *olam haba* (the next world). He says the only happy people he knows have been religious. But he simply doesn't believe it's true, so he can't bring himself to believe or to practice.

Since his home life was so positive, Shlomo's deep connection to observance and his strong desire to believe could only be severed by something dramatic. His teacher's rejection and his peers' abuse, though devastating, were probably not enough in and of themselves. What underlay all these experiences was something that happened many years before, when he was only six or seven years old. His religious teacher molested him. At a tender young age, when he should have been nurtured, he was betrayed and disgraced by a representative of God and Torah. He felt unsafe and powerless, confused and alone. He could no longer trust the trusted, including God. How, after all, could he trust or love a God who had allowed such cruelty toward him? He didn't provide more detail than to say that the sexual abuse occurred around the same time that he first started to question God, the truth of the Torah, and the goodness of the world. Life no longer seemed kind; God no longer seemed just; happiness no longer seemed possible.

Shlomo explained his pain at the end of the interview by saying that "people may think that taking away life is only with a knife, only with a gun. Sometimes, you're taking away the life from someone, because you're making them feel miserable, like it's not a person, like when he's young. Then you can kill him forever. So it's also a kill."

Shlomo's story indicates clearly that there is a powerful interplay between family and school environments. Shlomo's primary relationships with practitioners of Torah — his parents — fulfilled his basic emotional needs creating positive feelings toward Yiddishkeit. With these positive feelings and relationships as a foundation, he was strongly drawn toward Judaism. He associated it with happiness and developed a deep connection with it.

However, his school environment completely undermined the successes of his positive family life, repelling him from God and observant life. Since his positive experiences occurred in his primary relationships, they could go far to counteract the pain experienced in his secondary relationships at school. But they could not compensate completely for it. So with deeply positive experiences on one hand and deeply negative ones on the other, Shlomo exists in limbo, dressing piously but speaking heretically, loving *nigunim* but eating on Yom Kippur. He is drawn and repelled from Yiddishkeit at the same time, unable to reconcile his heart with his mind, unable to live as he believes, unable to believe as he truly desires.

Shlomo is not alone in this regard. Dr. Lob says he has worked with numerous boys and girls, like Shlomo, who had positive home lives but such horrible experiences at school that it was enough to drive them away from Judaism.[2]

*　　*　　*

Abuse need not be pervasive or dramatic to destroy emotional and religious health. One interviewee, Moshe, told me that his anger toward Judaism started in first grade when, as punishment, his teacher would put Moshe under the desk and kick him to the rhythm of his words. With every second word, the teacher would kick him three times, like the chorus of a song. Moshe eventually left the school, but the rabbi who kicked him continued teaching there for the next 36 years. Today, when Moshe talks about Orthodoxy, he uses words like "disease" and "mental illness" to describe it. He associates it with "*karet, cherem, chilul Hashem, apiokeres, goy*" — all words of rejection, intolerance and negativity.

In Avraham's case, the physical punishment was not as dramatic, but it was pervasive. It occurred throughout his education, and eventually led to his dropping out of school at age seventeen. He says he was "tired of rabbis smacking" him around. He was tired of his parents not doing anything about it. So one day, when a teacher struck his brother so hard he needed stitches, Avraham dropped out of school.

In addition to ruining emotional health and positive feelings toward Torah, these kinds of incidents destroy the teacher-student relationship which is essential for learning. Without a positive relationship with a rebbe, children will have a hard time learning Torah. They may gain ideas, but Torah learning is about more than imparting ideas. It is about imparting *a way of life*, a value system, which can only be successfully learned from someone whom we admire and respect. Where there is abuse, there is a lack of respect and relationship which means there is probably no real learning. A teacher's words will not penetrate a student's soul. This may be why the Chazon Ish felt that the "necessary prerequisite to influence one's students is a genuine love of people."[3]

Sometimes behavior can compromise learning and future observance in seemingly harmless ways. For example, Yonatan's teacher teased him for having long hair. He would call him "Yoni Shaygitz." Surely the teacher viewed it as harmless teasing, but the kids in Yonatan's class jumped on the bandwagon and took it to the next level. They began to beat him up for it. The teacher's seemingly harmless teasing had created an atmosphere that condoned hurtful behavior. When Yonatan came to class disheveled one day from a beating, he reached out for help — telling the teacher that "The kids beat me up because you call me Yoni Shaygitz." Instead of seeing the error of his ways, or even simply trying to console him, the rabbi replied, "Well, are you going to cut your hair?"

Yonatan's teacher was oblivious to his own role in the bullying, oblivious to the damage it was doing, and oblivious to Yonatan's cry for help. As soon as he failed to help Yonatan and recognize his suffering, he became an accomplice to it. Thus, although the actual abuse came from his peers as opposed to role models, it was enough to turn him off to Yiddishkeit. It created pain and anger not only regarding the abuse and those who abused him, but also toward the teacher and environment that enabled it. The teacher was not a direct cause of his pain, but an indirect cause of it and that was enough for Yonatan to reject not only the teacher but everything he stood for.

The word *rabbi* means teacher. But when Rabbi Chaim of Brisk was asked to define the role of a rabbi, he did not emphasize the intellectual, educational function of a rav, but rather the interpersonal, emotional one. He responded that the role of a rabbi was "to redress the grievance of those who are abandoned and alone, to protect the dignity of the poor, and to save the oppressed from the hands of his oppressor"[4]; certainly, not to become the oppressors themselves.

Children need the protection of the adults around them if they are to grow into emotionally and religiously healthy people. They need authority figures to create safe, secure, caring environments. That is why, when the Chazon Ish chose a candidate for *mashgiach* (supervisor) in a *yeshiva*, he selected a man "'with a good heart'" rather than a great scholar. He explained that a man with a good heart "'will make every effort to help the boys through their pain'" which was perceived as most important.[5] In fact, a teacher's care for his students is supposed to be as great as his care for his own children, as the Talmud tells us: the verse "You should teach the Torah to your children," means to your students who are always referred to as one's own children.[6]

It goes without saying that such statements assume teachers will never physically or verbally abuse their students. But it means that beyond that, they should actually play a proactive role in protecting them. Since teachers create a child's second home, they can play a unique role in doing so. When other children are the source of abuse, teachers must step in to "save the oppressed from hands of his oppressor." And when abuse occurs at home, they must strive to do the same. In fact, they are uniquely equipped to do so because they have the most exposure to the child and therefore the greatest ability to identify potential signs of abuse. In addition, teachers are the child's secondary authority figures whom a child hopefully trusts, likes, and respects.

In the case of parental abuse, therefore, teachers may be the only one who can help. Unfortunately many teachers have not been taught how to identify signs of abuse so they cannot do so. In that case, the abused child is left to deal with his torment alone — neglected by his role models, destined to suffer his pain both at home and the school. He is then likely to reject not only the abuser, but also the environment that allowed it and everything that environment stands for.

Short of preventing abuse altogether, we can at least strive to create positive relationships with children, which can go a long way to mitigating pain and preserving a degree of emotional health. As a side benefit, those relationships may also help preserve some connection to Yiddishkeit as Shlomo's story indicated well. The deep bonds created through relationships can be harder to discard than observance itself, and, for better or worse, can keep one connected to the observant world long after belief has died.

— CHAPTER 9 —
The Little Things

Rejection, imposing observance, and *shalom bayit* issues all play significant roles in children's attitudes toward observance. They compromise what Maslow identifies as a person's second, third and fourth needs for emotional safety, love, self-esteem, and self-actualization and therefore his perception of observance.

But it is not dramatic experiences alone that create a child's emotional world. Feelings about life and Judaism also result from a myriad of seemingly insignificant daily experiences, which combine to create patterns that define a child's life and shape his perspectives. These little things can be far more significant than the dramatic experiences for they tend to occur far more frequently. They may bruise our souls only slightly, but when they recur before the small bruise has had a chance to heal properly, they can become very painful wounds. Each minor negative experience can be like a blow to a fresh bruise, becoming more and more painful.

In this way, seemingly insignificant negative experiences can damage a soul, and its connection to Torah, slowly, quietly and dramatically. They are most harmful when experienced at home, but can also be damaging when experienced at school. If, God forbid, they are experienced in both places, the result can be truly traumatic, leaving no safe haven, no happy place for the child to develop emotionally and feel secure.

Physical and Emotional Safety

The most significant little things are those that compromise the need for physical and emotional safety. As discussed, abuse may be the most devastating, but other less extreme versions of physical retribution, such as hitting, can also compromise a child's feeling of safety. Rabbi Shlomo Wolbe explains,

> …when the child reaches his teenage years, parents begin to complain. "I don't understand what's with my child. He never talks with me. He never shares anything with me. I have no idea what's going on with him." When the parents experiencing this rejection approach me for advice, I often ask "tell me, did you strike the child when he was two or three? The parent usually responds "of course, but only for the sake of the child's education." Then I must offer the painful explanation. Now you are paying for the blows you gave him back then: the blows and harsh treatment seethe in the child's subconscious, often without even the child's awareness. The events remained concealed within the child's soul until adolescence reveals the deep wounds.[1]

Rabbi Wolbe explains that "Punishment expresses a parent's desire to control. A person feels that if he can punish he has control."[2] Such an approach, Rabbi Wolbe explains, "is totally perverse and unworthy" of educators and parents.[3]

There is much debate over whether it is proper to hit a child as a form of discipline. Some argue that today's generation is less likely to accept this form of discipline and more likely to rebel as a result. All Torah authorities, however, seem to agree that hitting must *never* be done out of anger, and must never be done severely or frequently.[4]

Verbal abuse also eradicates feelings of safety as does its lesser expressions of harsh language. The man who said that "sticks and stones may break my bones but words will never hurt me" was speaking only of our physical selves. Harsh words and criticisms bruise our souls and break our spirits. Like serious physical wounds, they can leave our souls significantly diminished. That may be why Rabbi Wolbe considers "harsh words" worse than a light spanking.

Harsh words spoken in anger or criticism compromise a child's feeling of safety.[5] When parents relate to children in cold, withdrawn ways, they are punishing the child.[6] While sporadic occurrences of such behavior may not have lasting effects, frequent or unpredictable harshness can become problematic. The more frequently and unpredictably such behavior occurs, the less a child feels safe — because in order to feel safe, people, especially children, need a consistent environment in which they can reasonably predict consequences. Without this, we never know where we stand. We become unstable, insecure and uncertain.

Behaviors like hypocrisy, dishonesty, broken promises, and *lashon hara* can all have the same kind of effect — making a child feel insecure and unsafe — which leads to a lack of trust in parents and eventually to a lack of trust in God.

So how can parents foster emotional safety and stability? First and foremost, by creating a happy, healthy relationship between each other, which translates into a happy, healthy atmosphere in the home in which there is no abuse of any kind. Next comes a healthy, loving relationship with the child, one without frequent, unpredictable, or intense anger or harshness.

Finally, all this must be achieved within the context of clear, consistent rules, discipline and structure. Without these elements, children feel unprotected. Of course, rules and discipline must be verbalized and enforced in loving ways that are kind and gentle, but they must be enforced.[7] A lack of rules can not only compromise fundamental emotional needs but also observance itself, for part of serving God is subjugation to His will, knowing that there are rules, that there should be rules, and sacrificing for them.[8] Structure, rules and discipline in the home create the model for one's relationship with God and observance.[9]

So when observant parents give their children love and nurturing within the context of discipline, structure and rules, they achieve two things at once: they create the emotional safety for becoming a healthy person as well as the discipline necessary for becoming a healthy Jew.

Love

Once children feel physically and emotionally safe, they must feel loved. The punishment, criticism, anger, abuse and harsh punishment that compromise safety can also compromise a child's feeling loved. These behaviors melt messages of love toward our children, the way hot water melts ice.[10] Though sometimes necessary in doses, these behaviors can become problematic depending on their frequency, intensity, and delivery.

This is particularly problematic for observant children who need to feel loved unconditionally not only for their emotional health, but for their religious health as well. Observant children need to learn that God, the ultimate parent, will love them no matter what. This feeling is essential for creating a positive relationship with God and also for growing as a Jew. For only if God loves me unconditionally, which I learn from my parents loving me that way, can I hope to repent and grow even when I fail miserably.

Feeling loved is more than merely belonging; it is the ability to hope, to continue striving, to believe in oneself and grow, to keep one's connection with God despite failure. It is about more than creating emotional health; it is about creating spiritual health as well.

How then can parents foster a loving feeling? Through three principal things: affection, attention and time.

Of these three, affection may be the most obvious. When we think of love, we think of hugs and kisses, smiles and kind words. We think of warm positive feelings and emotional embraces. Affection comes both physically and emotionally and the more it exists, the more a child feels loved. At the heart of affection is simple happiness as author Sarah Radcliff explains, "parents who are happy and content with themselves emit positive and loving vibrations."[11]

Affection however cannot in and of itself make a child feel loved. Children also need attention. Rabbi Moshe Speiser, who runs a hotline for religious teens and their parents in Jerusalem, recounts a story of a son who had become rebellious. The rabbi advised the father to pay him some personal attention. The father took his son out for a meal and his son later remarked, "What took him so long? It took me becoming irreligious to get my father to start listening to me."[12]

We can understand how important attention is by considering its absence, neglect. Psychologists have tested the effects of neglect on children with fascinating results. One study examined children in orphanages in Romania, where babies were lined up in cribs and fed at a particular hour. They were not held or cuddled and were given little or no affection. Surprisingly, these babies soon stopped crying; they were silent even when they were hungry, wet, or in pain. Unless it was changing time or feeding time, their cries were ignored. They therefore learned that their tears would accomplish nothing so they stopped crying altogether. Even in less extreme cases, children who have been neglected often develop speech problems in part because they learned through neglect that speaking was of little use.

One of the most important ways of providing attention is by actively listening. Rabbi Speiser explains that in training hotline helpers "the crucial factor is simply learning to listen."[13] Listening actively means not talking, not offering opinions immediately, and moving from hearing information to thinking about it, processing it and then, after consideration, responding to it accordingly.

This kind of listening has many benefits. Most importantly, it conveys a feeling of interest, love and concern. But it also enables a parent to know a child, and helps the child feel loved and accepted. As Rabbi Yaakov Shapiro explains, a child who is not truly known can feel like "a stranger in his own home,"[14] suspecting deep down that if his parents really knew him, they might not love him as much.

Active listening also opens the door to conversations about Judaism and problems that may compromise observance. Conversation can enable parents to understand a child's personality and particular challenges, help anticipate and prevent problems, or simply create a more positive relationship.

In some cases, communication might enable parents to answer questions for a child as was the case with Yochanan. When he had issues with Judaism, he was always able to discuss them with his father. At 16, he told his father that he was not interested in being religious anymore. He felt close enough to his father, safe and loved enough to be honest with him about his doubt. Thus his father was able to speak to him, and what might have become a terrible rift between father and son brought them closer, and brought Yochanan closer to Judaism as well.[15]

Of course, the listening in Yochanan's home began many years before there was a problem. In general, the more attention and listening there has been in the past, the more a parent can be assured that a child will approach him with problems in the future. The more conversation there has been in good times about mundane issues, the greater the chance there will be conversation in bad times about problems.

Finally, feeling loved requires time, both quality and quantity. In today's world children get less and less of the time they once seemed entitled to. Parents today work longer hours and tend to be less accessible to their children, often leaving them to be raised by themselves, their housekeepers, or nannies. Alan Sirote, Director of the Jewish Board of Family and Children's Services clinic in Brooklyn, cites financial stress, the need for longer work hours, and dual incomes as the most prevalent factors leading to abuse and neglect in Orthodox families.

Orthodox families tend to be bigger than most and their education far more expensive. In *kollel* (*yeshiva* for post Talmudic studies) families in particular, a father's Torah studies often shifts the responsibility of child-rearing and income-earning to the mother. In some cases, as one former *kollel* student explained, fathers learn while mothers are pressured, even by other women in the community, to seek jobs to support their spouses. As a result, children lose both quality and quantity time with both parents.

Children need the time and attention of *both* parents. Each parent helps the child feel safe and cared for in unique ways. When one is absent, it becomes all the more important for the other to try to compensate. When children are deprived of this time and attention because of Yiddishkeit — for example, the father's learning — the problem can deepen and Yiddishkeit can become associated with pain and negativity.

This can be avoided by spending quality and quantity time with children. Sometimes, a parent's simple presence can help a child feel protected and loved in a way that no one else can. Rabbi Riskin relates the story of a cab driver he met in Manhattan who had worked very hard to support his family of three children. Now they were grown — one had become a doctor, one a teacher, one a nurse; each had succeeded beyond his parents' expectations and each had a good relationship with his father. Rabbi Riskin had to ask: how did you accomplish this? The cab driver responded that he made sure to always

114

be home to have dinner with his family. At the table, each person was asked to share something about his or her day and everyone listened to each other. That simple act, which surely required sacrifice, made a huge impact on the children.

While many parents today simply cannot be home for dinner, it is essential to strive for time with children. Quality time can compensate for a lack of quantity of time; but it cannot replace it. Both are essential for a child's feeling safe, secure and loved. Without it, a child may start provoking the parent into giving him attention, often by misbehaving inside or outside of Judaism. When he does so and the parent responds by clamping down in "a rigid, authoritarian way," Dr. Wikler explains, "...he may complete the process of the child severing himself from Yiddishkeit."[16]

Providing children with affection, attention, and time is a vital way to make them feel loved. However, it is important to note that these things should be offered as unconditionally as possible. It is relatively easy to provide these expressions of love when a child behaves according to a parent's desires. It is far more difficult when a child misbehaves or defies parental expectations. In these instances, it may be natural to withdraw affection or spend less time with a child. Doing so however can undermine the feeling of unconditional love children need from parents. In general, the less conditional these expressions of love are on a child's behavior, the more loved and cherished a child will feel.

Self Esteem

In order for children to become healthy adults and Jews, they also need healthy self-esteem. This means feeling strong, worthy and capable. These feelings are ultimately based upon our selves — our accomplishments, characters, and ideals — but in our youth, they are based on the perception of others.

Children and teenagers are vulnerable because they are only beginning to develop their identities and self-esteem. So when role models, authority figures and nurturers see them positively, children tend to develop a positive self-perception. When, however, role models view them negatively, children feel unworthy and inferior.

What then threatens self-esteem? Sarah Radcliff writes, "Any statement implying that a person is neither lovable nor likeable, neither competent nor normal, constitutes a threat to his positive self regard."[17] This threat is not limited to our words alone, but also includes our behavior, which helps to communicate whether we feel our children are normal, competent, and lovable.

Shloime Mandel, a *Rosh Yeshiva*, tells the story of a boy he met in a neighborhood meeting of teenagers who had experimented with drugs. One of the adults running the meeting asked the boys what they were doing for the summer and, as one of the boys was about to answer, the adult interjected, "Pot?" One of the boys later remarked that "I know I'm a piece of garbage, but did they have to advertise it in public? Maybe if he would have told me that I am a '*tyere Yiddishe kindt*'...I would think differently about myself. My problem is that I think of myself exactly as he said it."[18]

The most threatening behavior to self-esteem may be rejection. But less dramatic actions such as criticism can severely undermine self-esteem as well, especially if frequent or harsh. Criticism sends the message that a child is not accepted or loved unconditionally in which case he begins to feel unworthy of acceptance and love.[19]

A particularly harmful form of criticism is labeling, which stigmatizes and belittles by ignoring a person's unique personality. It assumes, from the identification of one or two characteristics, that the child shares other, intolerable attitudes with these "types" of people. It brands him unworthy without considering the totality of the person and removes the permission he needs to see himself as respectable.

Needless to say, public criticism or labeling exacerbates a feeling of unworthiness, for the recipient is now also demeaned in the eyes of others. When criticism occurs in front of others, it makes us self-conscious before those who witnessed the criticism. It can then follow us everywhere we go, making it difficult to develop a positive self-perception. This is why Torah scholars such as Rabbi Shimon Schwab have asserted that one must never reprimand his children in front of others, not even in front of siblings.[20]

Basy Shaked, Founder and Principal of Tzofiah, a high school in Israel for American girls at risk, relates a telling story. A father once called her about his daughter who had not only dropped observance but had also started engaging in dangerous, antisocial behavior:

> "You have to help us," he said. "My daughter is so defiant. She won't listen to anybody. She's an unhappy person.... she needs serious, serious help... We gave her Prozac; she didn't even take it..." He repeated over and over again how she has problems and after a few minutes he said, "I mean she is just sitting here, looking at me."
>
> Mrs. Shaked was shocked. "You mean you are saying this in front of her?"
>
> "Yes," he admitted.
>
> "I can't imagine she feels very good about this," Mrs. Shaked responded.
>
> "I don't care what she feels. This is the truth and she should know it."

This parent wrongly prioritized the truth at the expense of his daughter's feelings and his relationship with her. No doubt he had done so throughout her life. Now he was doing so publicly and harshly which only humiliated her even further and closed the door to potential help. Needless to say, when Mrs. Shaked called back to speak to the daughter, the daughter refused to speak to her.[21]

By humiliating her publicly, the father sent his daughter an important message: that her feelings, her desires, and her needs, in fact her whole self, were unimportant to him. And if she was unimportant to *him*, the one who created her and was supposed to protect and love her unconditionally, then how could she be important to anyone else, including herself or even God? And if she is not important, then why would her actions be? If she is worthless, then her actions are meaningless.

Ironically the criticism, labeling, and public embarrassment that end in no expectations at all, often originate in high expectations or unrealistic ones. When parents or teachers expect too much, a child will find it hard to succeed. The parents may then criticize the child's failure and ultimately abandon all expectations of him, which further diminishes self-esteem. Although a child's failure to meet expectations may say more about the expectations than it does about himself, children generally don't blame the expectations. Instead, they tend to think of themselves as inadequate.[22] This perception is reinforced if the failure to meet expectations is met with criticism or labeling.

That is not to say that we should not have expectations of our children. When set appropriately in accordance with the child's age, personality and ability, expectations can provide healthy goals which promote growth and self-esteem. But this only occurs if the expectations are realistic. When they are not, they doom the child to failure. The question then becomes: how does the parent deal with that failure? If he recognizes that the expectation was unrealistic, and becomes encouraging and supportive of his child, the parent can temper the feeling of failure. Unfortunately, parents' expectations sometimes result from their own unfulfilled desires or other weakness of personality, which leads them to react to the failure harshly and inappropriately, instead of honestly identifying the expectations as the problem.

To work, expectations must be age, personality, and ability appropriate. As Rabbi Wolbe explains, "A child loathes and often shirks an inappropriately sophisticated request, and forcing him to attempt tasks that are beyond his ability could seriously damage his long-term spiritual development. ...Parents must ...constantly adjust their expectations to the child's changing ability. If parents demand too much…they sabotage the educational process."[23] So for example, it is counterproductive to force young children to sit at a Shabbat table for hours when they need to run around and play, or to push them to pray at too early an age (seven or so).[24] Such attempts will often backfire.

In addition to appropriately adjusting expectations, it may be wise to exchange specific expectations for a general one: that a child do his best. Using this criterion can help a child to define success not in terms of objective criteria, which may be unrealistic, but rather according to personal effort. With such a perspective, rather than competing with others or with unrealistic expectations, he will compete only with himself. He will be encouraged to examine his own abilities and strive to grow and improve.

In addition, since the expectation is a general one, it can apply to every area of life — personal or professional, academic or religious, and the nature of the expectations will shift as he grows into a more capable, developed person. In addition, if the child fails to achieve the objective goal, but succeeds in doing his personal best, he can maintain self-esteem, which will empower rather than diminish him.

Doing one's best is a standard that is general enough to be adapted to any situation, but specific enough to be meaningful. Such a standard can relieve unnecessary pressure and can help define realistic, achievable goals. The "doing one's best" standard does not impose external expectations, but rather leaves room for and encourages a person to evaluate himself, which in and of itself empowers, for it assumes that a person can and will do so honestly. It respects our children's abilities, honesty, and desire to grow which may foster the greatest self-esteem.

Conclusion

When a child is deprived of safety, love or self-esteem, whether through dramatic experiences or more innocuous ones, his emotional and religious development suffers. "His main energy is channeled into self defense. He cannot move forward because he is too busy preserving his self-esteem and fighting for his self-respect."[25] The more extremely this occurs, the more a child may have to distance himself from the source of the problem in order to heal his wounds and develop a healthy self-image. As we have already noted, this can mean not only moving away from the parents or teachers who are the source of that criticism, but also the Judaism they represent.

On the other hand, when a child is tended to, laughed with, sacrificed for, respected and loved, encouraged and supported, hugged and kissed by his adult role models, he not only feels safe, secure, loved, and confident, but also achieves self-actualization through Torah observance. This works in part because meeting a child's emotional needs removes stumbling blocks to observance and facilitates health. But it also works because it enables parents to gain their children's respect and inspire their emulation. The great sage *Seforno* explains, "A parent can lead his children even when they disagree because the children perceive him as someone who loves them and would labor with all his energy for their good."[26] Gaining a child's respect also makes parents better disciplinarians, as Rabbi Noach Orlowek explains, "the best disciplinarians are the ones most beloved by those they rebuke.... effective discipline depends on the relationship between the person disciplining and the person being disciplined."[27]

CHAPTER 10

Understanding and Dealing with Rebellion

As we have seen in previous chapters, the seeds of rebellion are sown when Judaism is associated with rejection, conditional love, harsh discipline and other destructive behaviors. In such cases, Judaism is experienced as painful rather than joyful and ceases to fulfill our basic needs for safety, love, esteem, and self-actualization. Rebellion then ensues in a variety of ways and for a number of reasons.

A primary reason for rebellion is the natural tendency toward self-preservation. We naturally retract from the things that cause us pain in order to protect ourselves, the way one retracts his hand from a fire. When we think Judaism is the cause of our pain, the natural response is to move away from it in order to avoid that pain. If it is the family or school that causes the pain, a child may move away not only from Judaism, but also from the people who embody it.

According to Dr. Lob, sometimes retracting from the source of pain is not only a natural response, but also a way of achieving emotional health. If a child's parents or school failed to fulfill his fundamental needs for safety, love and esteem, a child may strive to do so for

himself. It can be very difficult to do so in the environment that compromised those needs in the first place. Successfully healing emotional
wounds therefore may require breaking away from painful environments that created them in order to gain the space and objectivity to
develop a healthy self-esteem and identity.

Sometimes, observance is lost in the process. Not because a child
is angrily rebelling, but rather because he is busy concentrating on
fulfilling his more fundamental emotional needs. If Maslow's theory
is correct, a child who has been deprived of fundamental needs cannot concentrate on self-actualization through observance. He must first
fulfill more basic needs as a foundation for observant life. Pulling away
from an observant environment may be the first step, a healthy retreat
rather than a problematic rebellion. If the retreat enables him to fulfill
his needs, it may open the door for a healthy return to observance
later.

Finally, rebellion may be a form of revenge, a way of punishing the
Torah observant parents or teachers. One way of dealing with people
that hurt you is to hurt them back. When Judaism or observant people
hurt a child, especially if the pain is deep, a child may want to retaliate.
How can he best do so? By going off the derech. This enables him to
strike the parent with the very thing the parent values most, and with
the very thing that hurt the child most. In going off the derech, he can
kill two birds with one stone; he can punish the parents and move
away from the source of the pain.

Not All Conflict is Rebellion

It is important to realize, however, that not all conflict is rebellion.
Adolescents naturally express differences, deviate from the norm, and
vacillate in their observance, developing their own faith and unique
identities as part of the maturation process.

As Dr. Meir Wikler explains, "Some conflict is natural and healthy.
If there is never any conflict with the parents… then there is probably

something wrong. But if there is too much it can be destructive and harmful, and when it goes beyond the normal healthy range, it leads to an abandonment of Judaism."[1]

So how are we to identify normal, healthy conflicts? According to Dr. Wikler, healthy conflict occurs when "kids are able to express differences with parents..." This kind of rebellion will not necessarily lead to abandonment of observance. Much will depend upon how it is dealt with. Rebellion that is dealt with appropriately can end un-dramatically and serve as a means to developing a healthy, religious identity. On the other hand, rebellion that is dealt with inappropriately can compromise not only observance but also the healthy development of the child.

Preventing Rebellion

Of course, the best way to deal with rebellion is to prevent it in the first place. The most effective way of achieving that is to address a child's fundamental needs of safety, love, self-esteem, and self-actualization, through healthy relationships with the practitioners of Torah and with Torah itself. When this is accomplished, Torah is experienced as a source of pleasure, and since we naturally move toward the things that give us pleasure, healthy relationships with observant people and Torah are most likely to motivate a child toward observance. His basic needs will be fulfilled and the door will be open to achieving self-actualization through observance. This does not mean they will never veer away from *halachic* observance, but rather that any lapses will most likely be temporary. With a generally positive attitude to observance, a child will eventually move closer to observance; with a generally negative attitude, he will tend to move away even if he observes in the moment.

Thus, the overall attitude may be more important than the behavior itself. While observant behavior with a negative attitude may compromise observance, un-observant behavior with a positive attitude toward observance may ultimately foster it.

So addressing fundamental emotional needs is the best way to prevent rebellion. It can help sustain a positive relationship with Torah and its practitioners, which will help establish a positive overall attitude to observance and foster long-term commitment.

Dealing with Rebellion: Prioritizing Values

Part of creating a positive attitude and preventing rebellion is prioritizing values and picking battles. This is also the most important element in dealing with rebellion once it begins as Dr. Wikler explains, a healthy parent-child dynamic involves "a balance in which sometimes the parents give in and back down and sometimes they enforce limits."[2] This enables a child to express healthy difference, which may be all he needs to grow into observance in a healthy, joyful way.

Picking battles effectively can only be achieved if there are issues for the parent to "back down" on, some issues that are less important than others. This requires clear priorities. In Dr. Wikler's words:

> Parenting a rebellious adolescent is a war that will only be won by surrendering some battles...they have to decide priorities and create red lines, and for the long-term goal of painting a positive relationship with adolescents, look away from some things. Those parents who are able to bite the bullet, become more flexible, and give in are able to go through their child's adolescence unscathed. But those parents who fight every battle are the ones who drive the adolescent further and further away from themselves and from Yiddishkeit.[3]

Dr. Wikler explains that, when it comes to raising adolescents, what you see is not what you get. Just because a child behaves one way today, does not mean he will continue that behavior for the rest of his life. Some parents clamp down because they are afraid of a slippery slope — that not wearing a black hat today will lead to not keeping Shabbat tomorrow. So they fight every battle to ensure they don't lose any territory. But Dr. Wikler says that parents — like wise generals — need to know that in order to win the war, you have to surrender some battles.

This is always true, but it is most important when rebellion has already begun. In that case, insisting on compliance to observance can lay the groundwork for even greater conflict. As Dr. Wikler explains, great rebellions often start from small ones. For example, he relates the story of a fourteen-year-old boy he once counseled who did not want to wear a black hat. The issue became so intense in the family that he and his father came to blows over it. Dr. Wikler believes that, if this kind of conflict continues, the child "will eventually leave [observance] altogether." As soon as the parent blows up the hat into a major issue, the rebellion will escalate. The issues will no longer stop at wearing the hat but will likely progress to issues of not keeping Shabbat and *kashrut*, and could even lead to more deviant behavior like vandalism, drug use, and promiscuous sex.

Why so? Because the rebel has now met with rejection. The more the parents enforce Yiddishkeit, the more the child feels conditionally loved and potentially rejected. His self worth will suffer and he will begin to feel pain in his connection to Yiddishkeit. If those feelings ensue, his fundamental emotional needs will be undermined — a much bigger problem than if his Yiddishkeit alone were compromised.

Dr. Wikler explains that "In one family this becomes Hiroshima or Nagasaki. In another family, it will be a blip on the radar screen." What makes the difference is not the rebellion itself, but rather "how the independent striving and initial incidence of rebellion are handled that will determine the outcome."[4] If "parents can prioritize and keep their eye on the big picture — that it is more important that the kid is shomer Shabbat than wear a black hat — if they look away, he can end up shomer Shabbat and maybe even wear a black hat as well."

But if the parents require compliance with all *halachot* and all *minhagim* (customs) equally, there may be no room for the child to deviate or express himself. Everything is likely to suffer as a result. A parent's need to have it all can mean he ends up with nothing. If, on the other hand, a parent can surrender some battles, the rebellion can be defused, the relationship with the parents and with Torah can be better preserved, and the child may end up doing everything the parent wanted anyway.

Prioritizing Within Judaism

So prioritizing successfully begins with prioritizing within Judaism, picking our battles when it comes to observance itself. But how should parents prioritize within Judaism?

This question is difficult to answer. Our religious priorities are personal, the parent-child dynamic sensitive, and the needs of each particular child varied and complex. Properly responding to rebellion depends largely on who the parents are and who the child is. But, as a general rule, the Torah itself may provide some guidelines.

For example, the Torah tells us that *derech eretz* is fundamental to the functioning of society. Without it, there can be little else, especially not spiritual development and growth, which needs a strong foundation to stand upon. We learn this in part from the Tower of Babel and God's bringing a flood upon the world. Rabbi Samson Raphael Hirsh explains that although the society was rife with idolatry, it was destroyed because of stealing; a *mitzvah* between man and man, for when man neglects such fundamental *mitzvot*, the world can no longer be redeemed.[5]

This makes a good argument for prioritizing *mitzvot bain adam lechavairo* before *mitzvot bain adam lemakom*, especially when dealing with rebellious children. Rebellious children in particular need a strong foundation in basic human decency if they are to develop spiritually. And since these societal norms are ubiquitous, they are easier to request. Everyone can intuitively appreciate their value and that makes it easier for children to comply with them. So for example, a rebellious child can and should maintain respect for his parents in his tone and behavior even if he deviates from their religious expectations. Such expectations are usually easier to enforce and more productive to a child's spiritual development.

Whatever our actual priorities, the key to prioritizing successfully is flexibility — the ability to change our expectations from year to year, from child to child, from circumstance to circumstance. Flexibility creates room for our children to grow, a lesson that can be learned from the physical world. People who exercise know that to achieve physical health, you must work on flexibility. Why? Flexibility creates room for our muscles to grow and therefore become stronger and healthier. Spiritual flexibility creates room for our souls to grow. Parents who are flexible in their expectations help create the necessary room for their children to grow spiritually stronger and healthier.

Prioritizing between Yiddishkeit and Emotional Needs

So prioritizing within Yiddishkeit can go a long way in preventing and dealing with rebellion. But it may not be enough.

Prioritizing effectively and picking battles becomes more and more complicated as children grow. As adolescents, their behavior can increasingly conflict with observance and their emotional needs can conflict with observant life. When they do, parents may also need to prioritize not only *within* Yiddishkeit but also between Yiddishkeit and their child's emotional needs. Sometimes, it will be easy to address both and create balance; but sometimes, one will have to be chosen over the other. In those cases, prioritizing Yiddishkeit at the expense of emotional needs can be devastating to observance. This may be one of the greatest mistakes parents make in dealing with rebellious adolescents. Although seemingly reasonable to put Torah observance above else, when it comes to children's fundamental emotional needs, prioritizing

127

Yiddishkeit can undermine it.

When parents make Yiddishkeit of paramount importance, above their child's emotional needs, they tend to impose observance on him. They tend to clamp down more than necessary and have a hard time picking battles. Rather than provide space for their child, such parents are more likely to deny him the necessary room to grow. This not only stifles the child's emotional development, but also his religious development.

A child may begin to feel rejected because of Yiddishkeit; he may feel his parents' love is conditional on observance. He may begin to feel unsafe and start to associate Yiddishkeit with pain, resenting it for taking away his parents' love and acceptance. He may begin to perceive it as an obstacle to achieving the most fundamental needs in life, and feel that he must discard observance to achieve health and happiness. Alternatively, the child may become angry at his parents for depriving him of basic needs and may rebel in order to hurt them.

In many cases, when observance is prioritized above all else, the child begins to feel that his parents care more about Yiddishkeit than about him. Dennis Prager, who grew up in an Orthodox home but no longer identifies with Orthodoxy, feels that this is one of the significant causes for movement away from traditional Judaism. He calls it "making *halachah* more important than the human." Mr. Prager explains that this can occur when, for example, a parent tells an adult child, "I'd rather you not come for Shabbat dinner than have you drive to us for Shabbat."[6]

Inviting a nonobservant person to your home for Shabbat when you know he would drive to get there is a delicate *halachic* issue that can be viewed from a number of perspectives.[7] But putting aside the *halachic* permissibility of this situation for the moment, the point here is that when these kinds of statements are made to a child, especially one who has rebelled or might rebel, it can send the message that observance is more important to the parent than the relationship with the child. In such cases, whether the parent is objectively right or wrong, the child may begin to resent Judaism. Dr. Wikler explains why:

> If it gets to the point where the child gets the feeling that you care more about the *mitzvot* than you care about the child, then there is going to be a terrible rift. I know children who have gone off from solidly *frum* homes, who as adults have told the parents, "You know what used to upset me more than anything else was when I was growing up? You cared more about whether or not I conformed to your religion than you did about me as a person." And when a child gets that impression, rightly or wrongly, then the child feels uncared for, unloved, unappreciated. Then the religion becomes almost like a rival."[8]

Specific instances of prioritizing observance may not create a feeling of resentment in a child if those instances exist as *exceptions* within the context of a generally loving environment that prioritizes the child's needs. However, when Yiddishkeit is always of paramount importance, a pattern is created in which the child feels that his parent truly does care more about Judaism than about him. Ultimately, not only will his relationship with his parents suffer, but so will his relationship with Yiddishkeit.

Children who are commonly referred to as "kids at risk" are the best example of this. Kids at risk are those whose rebellion is the most intense. They not only drop observance, but also engage in delinquent behavior — stealing, doing drugs, engaging in promiscuous sex. If their pain resulted merely from negative experiences within Yiddishkeit, they would likely have simply dropped Yiddishkeit. This alone would suffice to remove the pain and create happiness. But their extreme rebellion indicates that there is more going on. It is not only observance which has become a problem for them, but also their unfulfilled emotional needs. Since those needs — to feel loved, accepted, worthy — are so fundamental, their deprivation results in the most dramatic rebellions. If these needs were sabotaged *because of* Yiddishkeit, it becomes all the more logical and perhaps necessary to abandon Yiddishkeit as well.

So kids at risk teach us most dramatically that, when we prioritize Yiddishkeit above a child's emotional needs, we can end up losing both his Torah observance and his healthy emotional development. Needless to say, doing so once rebellion has already begun can be even more problematic, rapidly fueling the fire.

Interestingly, when we do the opposite, namely place a child's emotional needs above his Torah observance, we seem to gain both his emotional health and his Torah observance. Consider this common experience: people who were never given a Torah life, but whose emotional needs were met, generally become healthy contributing members of society. Some even become observant, and when they do, their observance is quite meaningful and fulfilling. How can this be?

It happens because addressing emotional needs creates emotional health, which is a positive foundation for observance to rest upon. When emotional needs are met, children feel loved and accepted by their parents. They tend to have healthy self-esteem because they know they are always most important to their parents and worthy of their love. This creates the ability to be a healthy and contributing member of society. But it also creates a positive foundation for observance. For the nonobservant, it does so by giving them the tools and desire to self-actualize properly which some will choose to do through Judaism. For those raised in observant homes, it creates the desire to emulate parents, and in the least ensures that Judaism is not a source of pain.

All this may be one way to understand the phrase — *derech eretz kadmah letorah*. Those who strive for *derech eretz* first — those who prioritize the fundamentals — seem to gain both Torah and *derech eretz*. Those who prioritize Torah seem more likely to lose both.

So preventing rebellion and reacting to it effectively requires somewhat counterintuitive thinking. It requires that, rather than prioritizing Yiddishkeit at the expense of children's emotional needs and making it of paramount importance, we make our children's emotional development paramount. Ironically, de-prioritizing Judaism in the short run may be the only way to secure it in the long run. Doing so can help ensure that Judaism is not experienced as an obstacle to achieving emotional health and can provide children with room to create a personal relationship with God and Torah. It can also help the parent-child relationship, making children more likely to emulate their parents; and diminish the possibility that Judaism will be used as a weapon against the parents. Thus, the child wins, Yiddishkeit wins, and the parent-child relationship wins.

It may seem that placing Torah observance second compromises truth. But it is interesting to note that truth does not always take precedence in living a Torah life. For example, the Talmud notes situations for which we are allowed to equivocate the truth. One is *shalom*.[9] When truth conflicts with *shalom*, peace takes precedence. This makes sense because without *shalom*, especially within the home, truth itself and Torah observance can be compromised.

So when it comes to *shalom* with our children, especially if those children's Yiddishkeit or health is threatened, there may be room to de-prioritize truth (ie: what is objectively right, Torah observance), at least temporarily. Obviously, these are delicate and complex issues which are best determined by a family rav who knows *halachah* as well as the child and his family. But with all there is to gain — emotionally and religiously — it is surely worth an inquiry.

Having said that, it is vital to realize that accommodating our children by de-prioritizing truth does not mean compromising truth *altogether* or making Yiddishkeit unimportant. Placing a child's emotional needs first does not mean neglecting Yiddishkeit. Nor does it mean allowing children to do whatever they want. Rather it means deciding what battles are most important in the context of a given situation.

131

It also does not mean that serving God is not of paramount importance. In a vacuum, nothing takes precedence over it. But practically speaking, when it comes to our children's observance, there are times that the *halachah* itself would dictate doing the unexpected in order to help a child, in the same way that if someone were being kidnapped, the *halachah* could allow us even to be *mechalel* Shabbat to save him. In the case of a child who is struggling with observance, de-prioritizing his requirements in the short run may be the only way to secure his observance in the long run. It may in fact be prioritizing service of God because it means doing exactly what the *halachah* would require in such a situation.

The Importance of Acceptance

In addition to establishing priorities within Yiddishkeit and recognizing our children's emotional needs as paramount, it would help to practice a degree of acceptance when dealing with rebellious children.

If rejection is one of the strongest deterrents to observance, acceptance and the love that comes with it can be among its most powerful motivators. Rabbi Riskin shared an extraordinary story that illustrates the advantages of accepting a child who becomes rebellious. A friend's son gave Rabbi Riskin's friend "a real run for his money." He was a wonderful boy, intelligent and loving. But in his teens he was having a hard time and became very rebellious. He had dropped out of school and let his hair grow.

The father was an outreach rabbi who had brought many people closer to Judaism but he was unsuccessful with his own son. The man worried about the impact it would have on his other children and told his wife, "We have to kick him out of the house." His wife said, "No. He's testing you: who is more important — the community or your son? He's rebelling, but he's doing it in the house. Don't push him away." Rabbi Riskin recounts:

That night the distraught father was coming home from a lecture, and on the radio there was an interview. The person being interviewed was a professor with a name that woke him up. The professor's father had been a *dayan* (Jewish judge) who had written a commentary on the *Toseftah* that was quite well known in religiously educated circles. Then the interviewer asked the professor... 'Why did you not Hebraisize your name? You have such an obviously Polish Russian name. Why didn't you do it?'

The professor said 'I would never do that.' His whole voice changed. 'I had a father who was considered a great rabbi. And we always fought about Shabbas, Yom Kippur even. And he kicked me out of the house. He died. I don't know if the soul lives after life. But if his soul is still alive, he would love to know that I changed my name. But I want him to know, wherever he is, that he has a son with his name who eats on Yom Kippur.'

Rabbi Riskin's friend started to cry. He came home and woke up his wife and said, "I never want our son to say that about me. You are right." He then went to see a psychiatrist who told him, "Listen, I know you and I know your wife. Trust your son."

The father did so. He relaxed his expectations and things started to improve. Some time later, the reason for the rebellion became clearer. The son left a note on his father's pillow that read:

> Dear father,
>
> We are both blind. You don't always see how much I have done for you and I don't always see how much you taught me. But you think that I took the Tablets and I just threw them to the ground. That's not what happened. They were too heavy and they simply dropped from my hands.

Today, the boy is observant and, ironically, the man blames himself for the rebellion saying he was not spending as much time with his son as he should have. He says, "When I look back I realize that every time I looked at him, I felt guilt and that was very hard." But at the time of the rebellion, the man was astounded. If not for the love of a wise wife who refused to reject her son, who knows what might have happened. What is clear is that the rebellion certainly said less about the child's future than the father thought it did. This is often the case. Often rebellion says less about who the child will be in the long run, than who he is in that moment. In this case, the man's acceptance of his son helped ensure that the temporary did not become permanent.

Acceptance, therefore, especially parental acceptance, can be a powerful tool against permanent disengagement. As Rabbi Riskin explains, the Torah uses three analogies to describe our relationship with God: the relationship of master-slave, parent-child, and lover-beloved. One may see these as representing a progression: the most primitive relationship is that of master-slave, where there is total submission and service through fear; the next is parent-child, in which fear is tempered by love; and finally the lover and beloved, a relationship in which there is only love. Rabbi Riskin asserts that of these relationships the parent-child is actually the strongest, for, while a master can sell his slave and a lover can leave his beloved, a parent can never abandon his child. That love and acceptance make the parental bond more precious and powerful than anything else.

So maintaining that bond can significantly help preserve Yiddishkeit especially when offered in times of rebellion. In such times a child can learn that, even in the face of deviant behavior, his parent still loves and accepts him. This can motivate the child to respect his parents even more and reap the benefits of emotional safety.

Love and acceptance also create the kind of environment necessary to heal the wounds that caused the rebellion in the first place and provide a warm home worth returning to when the rebellion ends. In speaking of his friend's son, Rabbi Riskin says, "I don't know where that boy's anger came from or where it went. But my fundamental theory is that, if the parental home is good, they'll come back to it."

Acceptance Fosters Honesty and Averts Loneliness

Acceptance and understanding can also foster communication and honesty and avert loneliness.

When a child feels accepted, he is more likely to express his problems in life and with Judaism. This can help parents and teachers deal with rebellion and address the child's needs. When, however, a child fears rejection he may stifle his problems, feelings, or doubts about Judaism. As a result, he will have little chance to address those issues with his parents or teachers, and he may begin to feel more lonely and isolated, distant and secretive. He may fear that, if he reveals his true self, he will be shunned, lonely and rejected. Ultimately, the child may associate 'being himself' in an observant world with the pain of loneliness, fear, dishonesty, and rejection. He may then either rebel or observe *halachah* on the outside while he retreats and disconnects on the inside. Such was the case with one man I interviewed, Avi. He was in his mid forties and said that he had struggled with Judaism his whole life. He loved learning, but had many questions which needed to be addressed.

> I was in this *yeshiva*. I was feeling very disturbed about my conflicts and I felt very alone because I couldn't speak to anyone. And there were a couple of guys that I had befriended. I was around nineteen or twenty and I thought I could speak to them; I just felt I had to speak to somebody. But I was afraid that if they knew what I really thought, they would reject me. So I used to joke with them — "If one day I will have nothing and I'll come to your door begging for a crust of bread, you'd slam the door in my face."

And they used to say I was nuts…And then one day I told them why I said that, and they said "It's true. We will slam the door in your face. If you go away from religion, that's it. Judaism is everything." And they didn't want to hear that I had any questions. They said that Judaism demands blind faith. No questions. *Naaseh venishma* (we will do and we will listen).[10] And they confirmed my suspicion.

Avi was not rebelling, but his doubts were perceived as rebellious. So he kept his doubts to himself. As a result, he could not seek God properly. Because he sensed potential rejection, he never addressed his issues and he lived in silence, feeling more and more isolated and lonely as time went by. How long could he remain observant under such circumstances? He struggled to do so for a long time, but eventually he stopped practicing and found a place among other formerly observant Jews where he could speak his mind without feeling fear or rejection. Now among others who went off the derech, he no longer feels alone and alienated. Unfortunately, neither does he feel at peace with his Judaism.

Relationships teach us, inspire us, draw us near, motivate us, and connect us to each other and to God. If we do not have healthy, meaningful relationships with our parents, we cannot have them with God. If we have superficial relationships with them because we are fearful of being rejected and judged, then we may well have a superficial relationship with God. If we fear that if they knew the truth about who we are others would condemn us, we may believe that God will condemn us also. We may feel shame and react as Adam and Chava did when they felt shame — by hiding from God instead of seeking Him.

In this sense, rejecting a rebellious teen may even be an issue of *lifne iver lo titian michshol* — not to place a stumbling block before a blind man — because rejection can cause people to hide and lie and deny themselves the dialogue and relationships needed to heal pain and address religious issues. Acceptance, on the other hand, can combat loneliness and alienation by creating an open atmosphere. This may reveal things which are unpleasant to see or hear. It may challenge our sense of accomplishment as parents or teachers. But it may also help the child and enable us to address emotional and religious issues more effectively. Where the child goes from there is his own doing but, in the least, we will have fulfilled his needs and given him the tools to succeed emotionally and spiritually.

The Limits of Acceptance

Of course, the difficulty is in knowing where to draw the line between rejection and acceptance. The balance may shift and elude us. Limits and rules are necessary, but how do we define them? A number of experts provide some surprising responses.

Rabbi Dr. Norman Lamm suggests that parents should pull back and accept the child as he is when they see that their efforts have become counterproductive and the child is pulling away or becoming unhappy.[11] If his overall attitude to Judaism and relationship with his parents starts to deteriorate, it is time for acceptance, which can temper the negative feelings.

Dr. Wikler says that he has seen kids "who were pretty far off…it was hard for their parents to accept the idea that they have to accept the child as a person and look away from *mechalel* Shabbat (profaning the Shabbat) and other things; the parents who were able to accept this advice came back to thank me."[12]

Mrs. Leah Kohn went so far as to say that, in terms of observance, parents should never reject a child — perhaps not even if they intermarry — because, as long as the relationship exists, there is always hope for a return. Of course, the parents should make it clear that intermarriage is unacceptable. But they should leave the door open for the child by not rejecting him. She knows of people who intermarried, whose non-Jewish spouses brought them back to Judaism. By maintaining positive connections to the observant world, return is possible. Had the relationship been severed, there would have been little hope.

Many parents feel that the line should be drawn when it comes to other children who might be affected by rebellion. They feel the proper response is to remove the rebellious child from his home environment so he won't negatively influence his brothers and sisters. While addressing this issue is tricky, Rabbi Moshe Prager of Yeshiva Neve Tzion, who has spent years working with kids who have gone off the derech, asserts that kicking rebellious children out of the home is counterproductive. He has found that often the other children relate to the rejected child and come to resent the parents for taking him away. Once they relate more to the rebellious sibling than to their parents, the children are more likely to emulate their sibling rather than their parents and more likely to go off the derech. There may be exceptions to his general rule if rebellious behavior becomes dangerous to younger siblings or if the younger siblings emulate the older one.

But in most situations, even when things seem intolerable, Rabbi Prager suggests making space for the rebellious child within the home, an area where he can seclude himself while remaining a part of the family. If some general rules of respect are then established — requiring basic *derech eretz* and not necessarily *halachah* — many rebellious children will try to comply. This may be especially important when rebellion goes too far. The worse the rebellion, the more important it is to keep a child safe, and he is usually safer in his home. Kicking him out of the home destroys the one safe haven he might have. And when his feeling of safety, one of the most fundamental emotional needs, is eradicated, his feeling of love, self worth and potential observance become compromised as well.

Maintaining Love and Respect

Adopting an accepting attitude when children challenge and defy the very truth and values we hold most dear can be exceptionally difficult, if not impossible. But parents can at least temper their disapproval or rejection with love and respect which can help alleviate the sting of rejection. A good example of this was published in the *Jewish Observer*.

> My principal entered my circle of friends, pulled me into the center and danced with me. I was so shocked. "Was this the same principal who had just criticized me?!" But upon further thought, I felt the message loud and clear. It was her responsibility as my principal and fellow Jew to reprimand me. But the way it was done with such love…Somehow, after that dance with my principal, the sting of her rebuke was not as strong. She was telling me: "Sometimes, kid, in life we make mistakes, but we still love you. You're still a great person.[13]

Those who work successfully with kids at risk in the Jewish world seem to share one unusual characteristic — respect for the rebellious child. Because one tends to gravitate to where he feels special, wanted, and valuable, a positive perception of the child opens the door to relationship and often keeps him connected. As one off the derech teen said of his mentor, Rabbi Shapiro, "I expected him to be hostile, like all other religious people were towards me. But he wasn't. He embraced me, he took me into his group and he cared about me…. Rabbi Shapiro was a real friend. That does not mean he approved of what I was doing. He was my friend despite his disapproval. And he always treated me like a *mensch*."[14]

Rabbi Shapiro explains that the usual pitch made to a child who wants to leave Orthodoxy is, "Don't go; what you're giving up is too valuable to lose," which is ineffective. "When Jethro wanted to leave for Midian, Moses' plea to him was just the opposite: 'Please don't go — for *you* are too valuable for us to lose….A child will feel attracted to those who say 'we need you' far more than to those who say 'you need us.'"[15] The focus is not on Judaism but on the child and, with respect, a child moves closer.

Rabbi Moshe Prager goes one step further. He says that it is vital to treat these children like *tzadikim* (righteous people). We must remember, he says, that when kids have been rejected, abused, neglected, and dealt with harshly, it is a miracle if they are still interested in Judaism at all. If they have any connection to the Jewish community, they should be regarded as *tzadikim*.[16]

How can we maintain a respectful attitude or take it to Rabbi Prager's level of admiration?

First, we can remember we don't fully know what rebellious teens are experiencing and therefore we need to give them the benefit of doubt. If we knew their internal struggles, they might appear to be far more successful in their observance or general behavior than we originally thought.

Second, we can remember that accepting a rebellious teen is not the same as accepting his behavior. We can separate the rebel from the rebellion. This will make it easier to show him love, support, and warmth, even though we disapprove of his behavior.

This may be hard to implement and may seem contradictory to a Judaism which asserts that our actions play a significant role in defining who we are. But it is important to remember that we are not *only* what we do. We are also what we feel, what we desire, where we have been, and where we are going. Rebellious actions and *halachic* infractions may be *one* part of a rebellious child, but they are not the *only* part. And even though actions define a person, they take time to do so. External behavior *ultimately* affects the internal soul; but it begins as a mere *reflection* of internal reality. It takes time for behavior to *affect* the soul and define the person. So rebellious behavior may say less about the person than we think, and separating the behavior from the person himself can go a long way to foster a positive relationship.

Likewise, it can help to separate our selves from the rebellious behavior. Often parents react more strongly than is desirable because they take the child's rebellion personally. They see the child as a reflection of themselves and their parenting skills, which leads to a feeling of failure and guilt. Failure and guilt taint their reactions to the child and lead to rejection.

But as a child matures into a teenager he starts to become his own person, spiritually responsible for himself. He learns to take responsibility in part by separating himself from his parents. That is the point at which parents, too, would do well to separate themselves somewhat, providing room for the child to act independently and viewing his actions as independent of themselves. Doing so can help a parent create the distance necessary to react appropriately. As Judy Young, educator and founder of the Machon Academy for Girls in New York, explains, "It's not my responsibility what they're going to do at the end. That's between them and God."[17]

Striving Not to Judge

Finally, perhaps the most effective way we can maintain love and respect is to remember that we cannot judge where anyone else truly is in life. We see only a part, a piece of who they are, a brief moment in time. But to judge, we would need to see the whole picture the way God does. We would need to know not only what the Torah expects, but also what a particular person's capabilities are. It would seem that knowing the Torah's expectations of us would be enough of a basis to judge. After all, it is the ultimate guide of our behavior, the objective standard we should all strive to achieve. But even God, in his infinite wisdom, does not judge us solely by that objective standard. He includes in His evaluation our subjective capabilities — our particular personalities, needs, abilities, and life experiences.[18] It is the interaction between our selves and the *chiyuv* (requirement) that determines where we stand in God's eyes.

Thus we could say that the Torah is an *objective* standard that is *subjectively* applied according to who we are. Leah Kohn explains:

141

In objective terms, he is not where he is supposed to be. But in subjective terms, he might be where he is able to be and we cannot judge. In objective terms, we say every Jew should keep the Torah. But was this person doing what he could, even though he didn't do anything at all? Only *Hashem* can judge. If he does the things that he can do, then *Hashem's* attitude is that he is where he is supposed to be. In ultimate terms? He is not yet where he is supposed to be…but he could be righteous in the eyes of *Hashem.*

Our observance is not judged in a vacuum, but rather within the context of our potential and life experiences. That potential is a mystery to those around us. Where exactly people are meant to be at any particular time is also a mystery. And while we can say that in a perfect world, Jews in *general* should be observant, we cannot say whether or not God expects a *particular* Jew to be observant at a *particular* moment.

In fact, there seems to be no timeline for movement toward observance, as Mrs. Kohn explains:

Is it possible to embrace Judaism now fully? Maybe not. It could be a very long process…It might be that a person will die not *frum,* but over the years had some inner problem nobody knew about. Or [maybe] at least he tried to fight [his problems]…These are things only God knows. So we cannot say when this person dies not religious that he is a failure. We don't know what is going on inside. His choice might not even be about keeping Shabbat. It might be about whether he can even accept God as a reality in his life or not, on whatever level. Sometimes moving from one stage to another can take a lifetime. For example, a person who went through the Holocaust and lost his

142

faith and trust in *Hashem*. It might take years until the pain will subside such that he will be able to even start thinking about the issue. Whereas if a person who has had a good environment and education and normal life circumstances, and doesn't keep one *mitzvah*, God might not be pleased.[19]

Somehow, with the extreme example of a man who suffered through the Holocaust, we can intuitively understand that God may have different expectations of us as individuals. After all, is it really hard to understand why a Holocaust survivor would question God, lose faith, or stop observing altogether? Especially when we understand that it can take a lifetime to resolve certain issues, we find it hard to condemn those, like Holocaust survivors, who leave observance or lose faith due to great suffering.

But a child from an observant family who goes off the derech is no different in principle. We cannot know his pain, his potential, or his ability to cope. We cannot know exactly what God expects of him. We tend to consider *halachic* observance as the baseline for those who are born into observant families. Since they are given Shabbat and *kashrut* and Torah education, we feel their job is to move beyond these. It seems hard to imagine that God may require less of them than these basics. But our *bechira* levels — our points of choice — our challenges and abilities and therefore God's expectations of us can change depending upon our personalities and life experiences.

For those who have suffered particularly painful experiences in observant life, minimum *halachic* adherence may no longer be the baseline as far as God is concerned. Their challenge may no longer be in keeping Shabbat and *kashrut*, the *halachic* observance they were born into, but rather something more basic, such as maintaining belief in God or simply keeping a positive attitude toward observance.

It is interesting to note that, in a sense, it may be easier for a person from an unobservant family to become observant than it is for a child from an observant family to return. For a *baal teshuva* starts from a neutral point and may even be pushed *toward* Judaism if he has had negative experiences in the outside world. But the formerly observant child, in order to return, may have to overcome negative feelings to reach the neutral point that the *baal teshuva* usually starts with. His challenges, therefore, can be far greater.

The child who has gone off the derech might need many years or even a lifetime to overcome his challenges, no matter how basic they may seem. In that case, we may be wrong to expect a child who goes off the derech to be *frum* on our timeline or even perhaps in this particular lifetime. If we consider the idea of reincarnation, which many Torah sages throughout time have acknowledged as possible, we might gain some insight. If we are, in fact, given multiple lives, it may be to give us time to move through the stages of spiritual development until we reach our potentials. The journey of doing so is long and deep. It takes time, lifetimes maybe, for even the most committed among us to achieve their spiritual best. So perhaps in this life, we are meant to achieve only a certain level with the rest of our spiritual growth coming in later lives. In that case, our spiritual mission in any particular life may be far less encompassing that the total observance we expect of children.

What we see in any particular life is a brief moment in a soul's long journey throughout time, a small part of its total experience. Where it has been and where it is headed, what is expected and what has been achieved exists in unknown dimensions. If we can remember this idea and hold onto it, we might be able to see a little of the *tzadik* that Rabbi Prager sees when he looks at kids who have gone off the derech. We might be able to maintain the positive, respectful and loving attitude necessary to fulfill their needs and move their level of *bechira* (choice) one step closer to God.

CHAPTER 11

Neutrality and Beyond

T he previous chapters focused on issues that compromise observance, namely negative feelings that form negative associations with observance and lead to its abandonment. But these issues do not explain why children from happy, healthy homes, who have *not* suffered emotionally in their Yiddishkeit or relationships, go off the derech. If negative emotions are primarily to blame for people leaving Orthodoxy, and these children's emotions are not negative, why do they move away?

Julie, now in her late twenties, illustrates this phenomenon well. Julie enjoyed a happy home life. She attended Orthodox day schools and suffered no significant negative experiences at home, at school, or within her community. She maintained observance throughout her college years but started to move away from it when she was about twenty-one and on her own. She explains:

> Religion didn't really add anything to my life. It didn't take anything away either....I just never really felt positive about it. My friends were all religious just because we

grew up that way. I don't hold any resentment or grudge against Judaism or religious people. I think I just stopped one day. I think I hadn't felt anything for years and years, probably ever. I don't think I've ever felt anything for it. When I broke Shabbat, I had no regret. Nothing! I didn't think twice about it. I just don't feel it and I can't do something I don't feel.

Years later, Julie remains unobservant and doesn't know if she ever will be, though she remains connected to God. She tries to have God in her life, or at least in mind, in whatever ways she can. She says that, whenever she makes a toast on a drink, in her head she is always toasting God. And surprisingly, though she does little else, she reads the *parsha* (weekly Torah portion) every week. She is happy about maintaining that kind of connection. And, even if she never returns to observance, she likes the way she grew up and wants to send her kids to *yeshiva* so that they "have the option."

Julie never suffered because of Yiddishkeit, therefore she has managed to remain connected to it. She values and appreciates it, and wants to give her children the option to choose it. But she can only connect to it at a distance; she cannot fully engage in it because, although she never experienced it as particularly negative, she never experienced it as particularly positive either. Observance was not particularly joyful, pleasurable, or meaningful; it was merely neutral. She never really felt anything for it. And, as she puts it, she can't do something she doesn't feel.

Where there is neutrality, there is no connection and certainly no passion. Judaism fails to touch our hearts. It remains a superficial, external way of life without affecting our internal reality, our souls, and our relationship to God. Neutral feelings fail to inspire. They make it easy to discard Judaism in adulthood, when one is confronted with more pleasurable options. Unlike Shlomo, for example, who struggled for days to stop wearing *tefilin*, Julie broke Shabbat easily with no regret as soon as she lived on her own. The reason is simple. Since she had never bonded with Judaism, such that it became a part of her identity and soul, she never lost a part of herself when she dropped it. It remained merely an external behavior which was easily replaced with something else.

Neutral feelings or indifference toward Judaism is a major reason that kids from relatively happy, well-adjusted homes end up leaving Yiddishkeit. The modern Orthodox community is an apt example of this trend. Unlike more Yeshivish or Chassidic communities, they tend to live in less restrictive homes, and their families' definition of proper observance tends to be broader, providing more freedom to deviate from societal norms with fewer consequences.

Why do these children drop observance? Because like Julie, although they did not develop negative feelings about observance, they also failed to establish positive ones. Sometimes this occurs because parents are inconsistent in their observance or are not as strongly committed to it as their *yeshivish* counterparts may be. Sometimes they are strongly committed, but they fail to exude joy and enthusiasm for Torah. Whatever the reason, for these children, observance remains an external behavior rather than a deeply embedded way of life that touches the soul.

In a sense, it would not be inaccurate to say these kids dropped observance because they never really had it in the first place. What they had was behavior without feeling, action without connection. Judaism never became a part of who they are, so it is easy to discard without guilt or sense of loss. Under these circumstances — when children later live on their own and walk the delicate line between the Jewish world and the outside one — they can end up either consciously choosing the outside world or unconsciously slipping into it. For when their neutral Judaism is compared to a pleasurable, joyful alternative, Judaism pales in comparison. A neutral feeling about Judaism means the outside world need only be slightly positive to be more attractive than the Jewish one.

Feeling joy, pleasure and fun

The Torah tells us *soor merah veasai tov — veer away from the bad and do good.* In doing so, it teaches us not only how to behave but also the way to inspire our children. The first step is to avoid the negative feelings mentioned in previous chapters. But that merely brings us to a place of neutrality, which is insufficient for proper observance. Then we must move beyond neutrality to joy, to fill the absence of pain with pleasure and love. Only then can Judaism inspire and motivate a person to battle the outside world. Judaism cannot merely be good; it must *feel* good as well. It cannot merely be better than the alternative; it must *feel* better than the alternative.

This message is clearly repeated in a number of places. One of the most obvious is the Shema, the prayer which sits within every mezuzah on every doorpost of a Jewish home. It tells us about educating our children, and begins with the word love — you shall love *Hashem* your God with all your heart. It tells us to let the words that He commands be upon our heart. In the second paragraph, the phrase "if you keep My commandments that I command you today," is followed by "to love *Hashem* your God and serve him with all your heart" as if all God commanded us was to love Him. And, when the Shema warns us not to sin, it describes the process as our "hearts" being led astray. This all seems to indicate that, if we are to follow in His ways, it is of primary importance to gird our hearts with love.

A particularly striking example of the Torah's emphasis on love is in *Devarim* (Deuteronomy), where Moses recounts the curses that will befall the Jewish people if they don't live up to their covenant. He starts by saying that if you do not "keep and perform all His commandments and all his decrees...then all these curses will come upon you..."[1] But then when fifty three verses later the Torah finishes the list of curses, it

148

does not say if we fail to "keep" His commandments, which is how the verses begin, but rather if we fail to serve God "with gladness and with goodness of heart out of an abundance of everything."[2]

The Torah is clearly indicating that keeping *mitzvot* is not enough. If you do not observe them with joy, they will not endure; they will not become a part of your soul and curses will befall you. Thus, in a sense these verses begin by telling us to abide by the letter of the Law, but they end by telling us to connect to the *mitzvot* emotionally, as if to say the letter cannot survive without the emotional connection to it.

Particularly interesting is one of the curses buried within the fifty-three verses. God tells us that one of the repercussions of joyless observance is that *your sons and daughters will be given to another people and your eyes will see and pine for them all day long, but your hand will be powerless.*[3] We immediately think of Assyria, Babylonia, and the destruction of Jerusalem. But in these cases, our sons and daughters were *taken* from us; they were not *given* away.

According to the Rambam, these verses refer to our own exile. And in our exile, the one in which we live in an open society, our children are not taken away from us; rather, we *give* them away by virtue of not serving God with joy. It is as if the Torah is saying that we ourselves play the central role in our children's dispersion. Without joy, the nations of the world will not *have* to take our children; in failing to feel the requisite love for Judaism that keeps them strongly connected, we will have *given* them away.

So it is not enough to ensure that Judaism is not a source of pain; it must also create feelings of love and joy. Joy is so vital to proper observance that the Talmud tells us one of the ways we can identify the *mashiach* (messiah) is through his capacity and willingness to sing. Without the joy of song in his heart, a man cannot serve as the ultimate leader.

The Talmud goes on to explain that, in the absence of such joy, evil ensues as was the case with King Chizkiyahu, one of the most righteous leaders of the Jewish people who was supposed to be the *mashiach*. Chizkiyahu failed to merit that position and was also unable to educate his son, Menashe, in the fear of heaven. Menashe became a wicked king because, commentators explain, his father did not know how to sing and therefore could not inspire him. Without joy, Chizkiyahu not only failed to reach his own potential, but failed to transmit Judaism to his son as well.[4]

Chizkiyahu's story teaches that the most effective way for children to feel joy in observance is for the parents to feel it themselves. Love, like many other feelings, is contagious as Rabbi Moshe Ibn Ezra says, "What comes from the heart goes to the heart."[5] When parents feel love and joy for Judaism, those feelings will usually transmit and penetrate the hearts of their children too. In fact, the 16th century commentator Rabbi Moses Alsheich explains that the verses in the Shema — "you shall love the Lord your God with all your heart and with all your soul" — and the following one, "and you shall teach these things to your children" are connected in order to teach us that we can only pass on to our children what we ourselves love.[6] Parents, therefore, are not only role models for behavior, but also conduits for feelings and attitudes toward observance.

Parental love for Judaism can be so powerful that, even in the absence of observance, it can motivate children toward Judaism. Children from unobservant homes whose parents love Judaism inherit that love and often become observant despite their parents' *halachic* infractions.

Chief Rabbi Jonathan Sacks explains that his parents were not technically observant, but all four of their children became observant, and progressively more so, because his parents loved Judaism. His father, the president of the *shul*, would spend his evenings going from home to home in search of *mezuzahs* and, when he found one, would knock on the door and invite the family to come to *shul*. Likewise, his mother ran the ladies' guild and was dedicated to the Jewish community. Rabbi Sacks explains that, because they loved Judaism so much, their overwhelming sense of love penetrated their children's souls.

Such stories seem to indicate that feelings toward Judaism make a greater impact and are far more important in fostering observance than *halachic* behavior. Positive feelings often bring children closer, even when there is little observance; whereas negative or neutral feelings often push children away, even with complete *halachic* observance.

So parents are well served to observe Judaism with loving feelings that will help transmit a sincerity, joy and love that endure in their children's hearts. Their positive attitude will likely prevail even over *halachic* infractions and motivate further observance in their children. Observance without such joy can provide a weakened legacy, one in which children inherit a Judaism that feels burdensome and leads them off the derech.

So how can we help children find joy and pleasure in observance? Techniques for doing so will vary from age to age and personality to personality. But, for example, a Shabbat table can be filled with songs, laughter and fascinating stories. Torah learning can be reinforced with the use of games, humor, and prizes.

Judy Young was even more creative in inspiring her children. Every week she would bake something into her *challah*, a clue related to the Torah reading of the week. Her kids would then become active, enthusiastic participants in the meal by figuring out how the secret clue was connected to the *parsha*. That small but thoughtful effort turned the act of eating *challah* on Shabbat into an exciting game, one that connected the food to spirituality, fun, and enjoyment all in one.

Just as important as creating a joyful observance at home is teaching about it in the classroom. *Mitzvot* should be seen in a positive light and the Torah as a means for pursuing spiritual and physical pleasures in the best possible way. Basy Shaked explains that it is vital to see the Torah as "a structure which gives us the perfect formula for happiness." She explains to her students that, "Life without restriction, is chaotic and unsafe. Life with structure, on the other hand, helps us constantly remember that every action has meaning." In this way, the Torah itself and all the *mitzvot* within it become means to pursue both pleasure and spirituality. This perspective provides a positive context for *mitzvot* and helps children experience them not as restrictive or difficult, but rather as a means to joy and pleasure.

In conjunction with this, it may be helpful to focus on the positive *mitzvot,* rather than the negative ones, which can be learned from the story of creation. In the story of creation, it seems that God's first command to man is a negative one — not to eat from the Tree of Knowledge. But the commentator, Meshech Chochma, explains that this is not the first *mitzvah* at all. The first commandment was not restrictive or negative, but rather positive. First God tells Adam *to eat* from all the other trees, and then tells him not to eat from one particular tree. The Torah starts with the positive before it introduces a restrictive negative. Rabbi Cardozo explains that this makes it easier for man to deal with prohibitions. "Once religious life starts on a positive note, and God's first commandment to man is to enjoy His creation... [Man's] attitude towards restrictions is ...penetrated by optimism... [but] if one does not teach oneself first to enjoy God's world, one will end up in transgression"[7] for without pleasure, we cannot abide pain or restriction.

The Torah then goes one step further than creating a positive context for *mitzvot.* It actually makes the pursuit of pleasure a *mitzvah* in itself. According to the Meshech Chochma, this is the first *mitzvah*, as he explains, the expression used in the creation story is not "You are permitted to eat" — which would make eating of the trees in the garden a neutral and dispensable experience, but rather "You shall eat" making it a commandment to do so. Thus the Torah's first real commandment to us is to eat from the trees of God's garden, to enjoy that which we can, and take pleasure in the world around us. This is not only good and important; it is a requirement of being Jewish. As it is written in the Jerusalem Talmud, if you come to an orchard, and there is a new fruit or vegetable that you haven't tasted, and it doesn't belong to anyone, you are going to have to account for why you didn't taste it because each new experience brings you back to the source, which is God.[8]

Educators agree that this kind of joyful approach to life and to Torah education is vital for keeping children connected. Leah Kohn explains that "this is the real way to fight outside temptations. The most important thing is to show the beauty of Torah, to teach with love."[9] Rabbi Cardozo puts it differently, that to "turn the tide" of assimilation, we need first to "show our people that Judaism is foremost the art of enjoying God's world."[10]

Conclusion

Although the primary reason people go off the derech is negative feelings toward Judaism, neutrality or the absence of feeling can be equally harmful. In order for observance to stick, it must move beyond neutrality to joy, pleasure, and meaning. It must move beyond something we *do* to become something we *are*, something that lives within and stirs our hearts. The most effective way for parents and other mentors to impart these feelings to others is to love Judaism themselves and exude joy in their own observance. Such feelings are contagious and more deeply motivating than anything else. They enable us to experience Torah as a privilege worthy of effort and even of sacrifice. As Rabbi Mordechai Eliyahu, former Chief Rabbi of Israel, says: With such love of God, it is impossible to feel observance as a burden[11], which is probably why the Torah emphasizes love in as many places as it does.

One of the best ways therefore to protect our children's observance is to gird it with love and joy and remember that, while actions speak louder than words, they do not speak louder than feelings. Our feelings, whether they be of joy or pain or neutrality, are contagious and they play an important role in defining our children's attitudes.

CHAPTER 12

Conclusion and the Role of God

S o far we have seen that the primary causes for discontinuing observance do not lie within the external reality of the outside world or the internal desires of the *yetzer hara*, but rather within the Jewish community itself. Personal experiences with observant Judaism and its people most significantly influence our future commitment to observance because they create our emotional attitude toward Judaism. And since emotions affect our decisions and perspectives so greatly, negative experiences with Judaism or its practitioners can significantly undermine potential observance.

The most problematic kind of experience occurs when demands of observance or its representatives ignore or sabotage our fundamental emotional needs, for example by eradicating or diminishing the feeling of love or self-esteem. When these fundamental emotional needs remain unfulfilled — whether as a result of a few traumatic experiences or a series of less traumatic, but more constant ones — Judaism is eventually experienced as painful, as an obstacle to happiness. Once Judaism is associated with pain, a child may drop observance, either as a natural way of escaping pain, as a means to achieving emotional

154

health, or as a way of punishing the observant people who caused the pain. The greater the pain, the greater the likelihood and extent of rebellion, sometimes not only against Judaism, but also the family, schools and communities that perpetuated it.

So, in order to understand why a person is no longer observant, we first need to ask whether he experienced pain in his Jewish life. We need to ask: Did Judaism or its practitioners sabotage or fulfill the person's fundamental emotional needs? Did he experience pain through verbal, physical, or sexual abuse? Did he experience constant anger, over-punishment, hypocrisy or dishonesty, all of which induce pain by eradicating emotional safety? Did he experience the pain of rejection, or a lack of acceptance, attention, affection, time, or listening, all of which undermine the primary need to feel loved? Did he feel unworthy, incapable, or inferior through rejection, criticism, labeling, or public embarrassment?

Finally, if there was no pain in these areas, we need to ask whether there was joy. The absence of pain is not enough to motivate observance; it merely creates a neutral environment, which can also cause one to go off the derech.

After ascertaining the *nature* of the negative feelings toward Judaism or its representatives, we need to ascertain their *source*. Our emotional worlds are primarily created through relationships with our family, school, and community who largely influence our emotional development and relationship with Judaism. But not all relationships are equal. Just as some painful *experiences* are more fundamental than others, some *relationships* are more fundamental than others as well. Pain experienced in primary relationships compromises observance more than pain experienced in peripheral ones. For example, the most destructive pain occurs within the parent-child relationship. Our relationship with parents is the most fundamental, with the deepest emotional ties, and therefore pain within it most dramatically affects our lives and observance. Relationships with teachers and other role models, on the other hand, are less fundamental and more peripheral to observance while still playing a significant role.

The more fundamental the relationship, the greater the influence it garners upon our emotional development and relationship with Judaism. Thus, in order to properly understand why someone has gone off the derech, we need to ascertain not only the nature of the pain, but also its source, examining both primary and secondary relationships. First we need to ask: What is the nature of the child's relationship with his parents? This includes his parents' relationship with each other, and their individual emotional makeup, which combine to determine the general emotional atmosphere at home. Next we must examine relationships with teachers, other primary role models, and, finally, other more external relationships.

Whether examining the nature of pain, or the source of it, the same principle applies: the more fundamental the emotional need or relationship that sabotages it, the more dramatic the pain and the greater the challenge to observance. If we illustrated the issues and players in order of importance, it would look something like this:

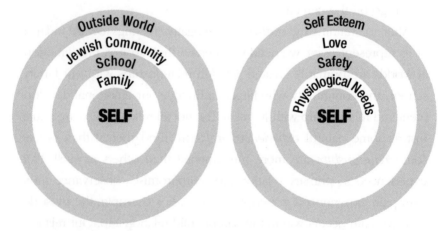

All of these relationships and needs play a significant role in the process of going off the derech. But they vary in power. Those elements which are closer to the core, the 'self,' exert the greatest influence both emotionally and religiously; those farther away exert the least. Once we understand the hierarchy of influence, it is important to realize that neither the players nor the issues work in a vacuum; they work in conjunction with each other to influence observance.

The more pain there is in a greater number of areas from a greater number of sources, relative to the proximity to the core self, the greater the risk of going off the derech. Alternatively, the more joy there is in each of these areas and within each of these relationships, the greater the chance of remaining observant. So for example the most painful experiences and deterrents for observance would be when familial relationships compromise physiological or safety needs. These two elements are closest to the core self and therefore garner the greatest influence. So when they come together — the most fundamental player and the most fundamental issue — they are likely to have the greatest negative impact on observance.

Given the complex interplay between the players and issues, one of the strongest ways to assure observance is for families, schools and communities to work together to address a child's fundamental emotional needs: directly, through positive experiences with Yiddishkeit, and indirectly, through positive relationships with *frum* people.

What About God

Interestingly enough, throughout these discussions, one player has been conspicuously absent: God. While it is outside the scope of this book to properly examine God's role in faith, it is important to realize that He, too, may play in people going off the derech.

It is possible to consider God responsible for everything that happens to us. Whether or not we suffer at the hands of observant people or the world at large, God can be deemed the cause of *all* our experiences, the source of all pleasure and pain, as the Talmud says, "Everything is in the hands of heaven, except for the fear of heaven."[1] According to this perspective, while we control our moral choices and our observance of *mitzvot*, God controls everything else. We have free will, but He determines the context and circumstances within which free will exists. Therefore, He may be ultimately responsible for what happens to us. Thus, though a person may suffer at the hands of observant people, he could ultimately blame God for allowing that suffering to occur in the first place.

This may be the ultimate challenge to observance for, while we expect human beings to have flaws, which makes it somewhat easier to forgive them, we expect God to behave perfectly. We expect Him to exude the ultimate in loving kindness toward us. So when we suffer at the hands of God, though we know intellectually that we cannot understand His ways, we sometimes find it harder to forgive Him.

In some circumstances, however, God is perceived to play an even more direct role in suffering. These circumstances tend to involve our most fundamental need — not yet discussed — namely the physiological need to be fed, to breathe, to sleep, which precede even our need for safety. These needs are the most basic, and we tend to perceive God as the ultimate provider of them. Whether we are rich or poor, healthy or sick, persecuted or free, these circumstances are often attributed to God more directly than others which are somewhat filtered through other people.

Since these needs are the most basic and since God is perceived as their direct cause, the suffering in these areas creates some of the most challenging obstacles to belief and observance. As one formerly observant Jew put it, "Allowing children to die of horrible diseases and allowing the Nazis to butcher our people, being oblivious to the suffering that permeates our world, brings me to one of two conclusions: either this personal God is sadistic or he just doesn't care. Either way, He serves no useful purpose in our lives."

The Holocaust is perhaps the most dramatic obstacle to belief. Although perpetrated by man, the Holocaust is often attributed to God. It involved suffering of the most fundamental and dramatic kind. The horrific extent of the suffering made for unprecedented challenges to faith. The Holocaust eradicated well being along with basic physiological needs and, since God was perceived as the direct source or passive participant of that deprivation, the Holocaust has generated some of the greatest anger toward God. That challenge to observance is so great that even those who did not personally suffer at its hands find themselves troubled by the question: Where was God during the Holocaust?

If Maslow's hierarchy is correct, we can understand why. To suffer a lack of love because of Judaism is one thing; to starve and be persecuted because of it is another. The physical need is most fundamental and therefore its deprivation leads to greater anger, pain and rebellion. When God is perceived as the source, the rebellion is likely to focus more directly on Him and His religious requirements.

So suffering, whether nationally or personally through disease, poverty, and misfortune, can foster serious anger and mistrust toward God. Our relationship with God and our commitment to observance can then falter. As with many things in life, however, the outcome has less to do with the challenge than how we meet it.

For this reason, Leah Kohn asserts that it is vital, especially in the classroom, to address the issue of why good people suffer. Developing the emotional and religious strength to combat deep and fundamental pain is a challenge for any Jew. But it is particularly difficult for children who lack emotional and religious maturity. As a result, Mrs. Kohn explains that the issue should be dealt with from kindergarten on, in every stage of life. From stage to stage, she says, one must deepen children's understanding of the issue or eventually they might come to question Judaism altogether.

On the surface, this may seem like an esoteric philosophical issue, one which we can never truly answer well. But in truth it is a very real, practical, and important issue. It is not theoretical at all for our suffering and how we meet it is largely influenced by the strength of our belief.

To gird belief with intellectual understanding can help temper pain, guide our feelings, keep them in check, stop them from translating into anger and rebellion, and thereby reconcile pain with belief and observance.

Another intellectual safeguard can be to instill a feeling of justice in children. As Debbie Greenblatt points out, studies have shown that children who believe in an underlying justice in the world tend to be more resilient than children who lack that view.[2] Believing in justice, or that there is a reason for everything, provides a meaningful context for suffering that can help alleviate its sting.

The most effective safeguard of all, however, is to foster positive feelings and relationships that can combat and mitigate painful experiences for, while the intellect can be an effective tool in tempering emotions, other emotions can be far more powerful. Therefore the most important way to protect children's observance is to ensure that observant people themselves do not become a source of pain, but rather a source of joy from which the strength to meet all of life's challenges flow.

II

Mind Over Matter:
Truth, Meaning, and the Intellect

CHAPTER 13

The Role of the Intellect

A lthough the majority of people go off the derech because of negative emotional experiences with Judaism and its practitioners, these issues do not fully explain the phenomenon. Many people have been raised in happy, healthy homes, experienced Judaism positively and still abandon observance. Why? If emotions are the greatest motivators, why do those with *positive* feelings drop Yiddishkeit?

The answer lies in the intellect, one's belief in the truth and meaning of Torah. The heart and its feelings may be the strongest motivator for observance, but they do not act alone. The intellect plays a secondary role for all of us, to greater and lesser extents. It is the supporting cast to emotional experiences, secondary but essential for ultimate observance. Usually when a person has positive feelings toward observance, but drops it anyway, lack of belief is the culprit.

Many people have a hard time believing that people really go off the derech because of intellectual issues. Even some experts contend that *hashkafa* — intellectual or philosophical understanding of observance — plays no part in the phenomenon, that it can be explained by emotional experiences alone. One expert made this point dramatically in relating the story of a Bais Yaacov girl who wanted to go off the derech. He said that, after a brief conversation with her, he was sure her problems were not *hashkafic,* but rather emotional. How did he know? The tip off, he said, was that she was willing to throw away her mommy and daddy, her school, her *bubbe* and *zaide* (grandmother and grandfather), *shidduchim* (matches for marriage) and friends all for the sake of discarding observance. "Because of *hashkafa?*" he remarked. "Bologna!"

He makes a good point. Teenagers generally have a lot to lose when they go off the derech. In addition, their intellectual capacities are only beginning to mature so, for them in particular, emotional issues usually come into play. But this is less likely to be the case with adults who go off the derech, and sometimes even for teenagers the intellect can play a role.

Attributing intellectual issues to emotional problems over-simplifies the issue because people's religious decisions and relationships with Torah are complex. Some people from difficult backgrounds manage somehow to maintain observance, while others with very healthy upbringings may drop it. Thus, emotions are complemented by other factors, the most significant being intellectual issues, issues of belief.

If we doubt this, we should consider the phenomenon of *baalei teshuva.* Why do these people *become* observant? Our answer is simple: they have found the truth. But they too often throw away their mommy and daddy, friends and lifestyles. Would we dismiss their intellectual motivations? No. In fact doing so would disrespect their choice. When it comes to *becoming* observant, we readily accept the idea that people turn their lives upside down for intellectual reasons. But, if the intellect plays a role for those who *become* observant, it must also play a role for those who *discard* observance. The intellect either plays a role in religious choices or it does not. And if it can motivate a person to turn his life upside down *for* Torah, it can surely also motivate one *away* from it.

The Danger of Confusing the Intellect with Emotions

Failing to acknowledge the importance of the intellect in observance not only oversimplifies the issue, it can also be dangerous especially for those who sincerely struggle with intellectual issues. Avi's story is a case in point. As a young man, Avi dreamed of becoming a Torah scholar and had the exceptional intellect to accomplish his dream. But he harbored doubts about whether the Torah was true. These doubts persisted and plagued him for much of his life. In his youth, he stifled his questions. At that point, they were not central to his observance anyway and Avi's love of learning compensated for his doubts to a great extent. As he explains, he was constantly "seduced by the Talmud" so that his questions disappeared into whispers of learning.

But occasionally he would experience a crisis of faith. His love of learning was insufficient to establish belief and, being a truth seeker, he needed to believe in order to remain observant. His religious crises intensified as he matured so that, in his mid-twenties, he found himself studying in *yeshiva* but plagued by doubt.

Feeling afraid to ask his questions in his *yeshiva*, Avi left for Israel hoping to find answers. He rented a little apartment in Israel and started speaking to rabbis. But it didn't go as well as he had hoped. Though some rabbis did offer good answers, others shunned him. One rav, well known for his brilliance and ability to answer philosophical questions, was particularly hurtful. Avi approached him with the question: How do we know the Torah is true? At first, the rabbi seemed very respectful and open, praising the importance and validity of the question. But after a while Avi explains,

> I found myself in the situation where he was doing this whole thing that they love to do — "what kind of childhood did you have?" as if I only have these questions because I have emotional problems. I have always had a problem with that attitude because I don't find these ques-

tions so difficult to think of; I don't find them so unreasonable that they should be attributed to some psychological problem. I think that is the main way they fend off questions. It always comes down to some personal problem. You are a *baal taayveh* (pleasure seeker) or your question comes from the fact that you don't want to be *frum*; you don't want to be bound by the Torah. Or there's something personal — this happened when you were a kid so you're angry at God. That's the way they explain it.

My experience in that world is that... if they are less gentle, they just curse a kid out and make him feel guilty for having these doubts. And, if they are gentler, they speak about his psychological problems...That type of thing makes me angry. It's somewhat Stalinesque — Stalin sending off all the dissident intellectuals to an insane asylum [as though] if you don't see the revolutionary truth, you must be insane... If you have any doubts about the party line, there must be something wrong with you.

Avi was a genuine truth seeker. He was philosophical in nature, respectful of Torah, and desirous of living a religious life. But he was taken for a pleasure seeker, an emotionally unhealthy person who was looking for a way out of responsibility. This false assumption meant that the rav failed to take his questions at face value and answer them seriously. In doing so, he dismissed and belittled Avi and his sincere quest; he minimized Avi's commitment to Torah and intellectual honesty. Now what was once a purely intellectual issue for Avi became an emotional one as well. The rabbi added the negative feelings of rejection and anger to Avi's doubt, obstacles which would be far more difficult to combat than intellectual questions alone. In addition, the rav's failure to acknowledge the sincerity of Avi's quest denied Avi the real, valid answers he needed in order to remain observant.

In the end, Avi went off the derech — not immediately, but years later. He struggled for many more years to find the answers he needed; but he never did. And finally, since he could not make his beliefs comport with his behavior, he changed his behavior to comport with his beliefs by dropping observance. It was the only way he could resolve his religious crises and find some peace.

Dismissing the Intellect Can Cause Pain and Ignorance

Avi's story demonstrates that dismissing a sincere intellectual quest as emotionally motivated is dangerous. Doing so misjudges, undermines, and rejects, creating negative feelings where there should be closeness and enlightenment. It also fosters ignorance, which can indirectly cause negative feelings. Where there is ignorance, there is lack of meaning and connection to Yiddishkeit, which makes it impossible to fulfill one's unique potential through observance. The intellectual issue then becomes an emotional/spiritual one, triggering a movement away from Judaism.

Even when intellectual issues are emotionally motivated, the emotional catalyst does not invalidate the question. A question may be valid and may require a thoughtful response even if it stems from a negative emotional experience. And the questioner may be just as sincere if motivated by negative experiences as if he were motivated by the intellect alone.

Addressing it Can Help Emotional Issues

In fact, sometimes the only way to properly address the emotional issues beneath the intellectual ones is to address the intellectual ones. Basy Shaked explains that if there are truly emotional issues at the heart of the question, answering the question may remove the intellectual smokescreen and reveal the emotional reality. If the questions have been answered and the questioner still cannot or will not commit to it, he may be prompted to examine why. If he is honest with

166

himself, he may be able for the first time to realize that the intellectual questions were not the real problem but rather his emotions and experiences that were the obstacles. In that sense, providing answers can strip the questions of their mask and assist in addressing the real cause of the problem.

In any event, since we can never know the true motivation of a question, giving benefit of doubt may be the only appropriate approach to take. That way, whether the questions are emotionally based or not, whether they are sincere or not, we respect the questioner, create a positive relationship with him, foster positive feelings toward Torah, and provide the intellectual answers which can help establish belief. Anyway, as Avi points out, many questions, even fundamental ones, are not that revolutionary. Especially when the Jewish world calls upon the truth of Torah to validate itself, it should expect children to ask the first and most obvious question — How do we know the Torah is true? — without attributing it to emotional problems.

The Role of the Intellect

So what role does the intellect play and why? It varies from person to person. For most of us, it plays a secondary role to emotions. But for others who are in the minority, for example "truth seekers" or those who are intellectually oriented — it may play a more primary role. These people may need more comprehensive answers than the rest of us. And a lack of intellectual belief can cause them, more than others, to move away from observance. But, for all of us, the intellect plays a role and that role increases as we mature and our capacities develop.

Why and How it Plays a Role

Whatever its degree of influence, the intellect is essential for securing observance, and it can weaken observance to the point that people go off the derech as a result.

This is true for a number of reasons. First, feelings alone are a poor foundation for long-term commitment to observant life. They are less secure, predictable, and objective than beliefs. A feeling can change from year to year, from day to day, or hour to hour. But intellectual understanding, a strong belief in Torah, tends to be less volatile and subjective and therefore establishes a stronger foundation for observance.

People who feel good about Judaism but lack true, abiding belief can easily find their commitment to observance weakened in the face of pain or conflict. The greater the pain and the less developed their belief, the more likely they will drop observance if their positive feelings falter. The intellect, therefore, serves as an anchor that girds our Judaism through the storms of emotional change and challenges to faith.

In addition, the older we get, the greater the role intellect plays and needs to play in observant life. In our teens, intellectual capacities begin to develop and they must be used if observance is to mature and become secure. Our reasons for remaining observant must evolve from purely emotional reasons to a combination of emotional and intellectual ones. Those who fail to develop an intellectual understanding of Judaism will experience a Judaism that speaks only to part of their being rather than their entire being. Theirs is a weaker connection than those whose observance rests on feelings *and* understanding.

Finally, as we mature into adulthood, not only do we mature intellectually, but we mature emotionally as well. When our basic emotional needs for safety, love and self-esteem become satisfied, they no longer motivate our behavior as strongly as before. For example, we are less likely to act in order to gain approval, love or acceptance. We then often begin to act more in accordance with our intellect.

We become free to address our intellectual needs and establish other reasons for our observance. Rather than be motivated by a desire to be loved and accepted by parents and community for example, we become more able to serve God from true belief in Torah. In fact, we must begin to address our intellectual needs if we are to achieve ultimate health and happiness. Why so?

Because ultimate health and happiness requires something greater than addressing our emotional needs through safety, love, and self-esteem. It requires one thing more, what Maslow defines as self-actualization. Self-actualization involves becoming the best of who we are, reaching our potential, and perhaps contributing to the world in a meaningful way. While addressing fundamental emotional needs may lay the foundation for doing so, it cannot create ultimate fulfillment. Emotional fulfillment may satisfy the heart, but it cannot satisfy the soul. It cannot create meaning, pride and fulfillment. It cannot enable us to utilize our complete selves to achieve meaningful goals. That kind of ultimate health and happiness requires attention to our intellectual and even spiritual needs. It may even require living a meaningful life and striving for truth as Rabbi Nachum Braverman explains in his article entitled "Falling In Love with Judaism":

> The experience of meaning is a greater pleasure than love. When we feel our lives have a goal and purpose, it gives a sense of deep-rootedness…we long for the ecstasy of committing ourselves in the service of some great mission. We may even risk death, so nourishing is the experience which gives our life ultimate purpose.[1]

A person who does drugs all day may experience pleasure, but he can never know the ultimate joy of living a meaningful life. One who knows ultimate joy must emotionally mature and move beyond the needs of the heart to meet the needs of his mind and soul, in order to reach his ultimate potential.

What is true in terms of reaching one's general personal potential is also true of reaching religious potential. Ultimate growth and fulfillment in Judaism requires moving beyond positive feelings toward Judaism to creating an intellectual foundation of belief. Intellectual examination of Judaism's core tenets makes Judaism meaningful, relevant, and true in a way feelings alone cannot. Through our intellects, we can begin to experience Judaism as something more than a positive feeling. We can begin to experience it as meaningful. In that case, it can come to be experienced as an essential part of achieving health and happiness. It can become a source for fulfilling our potential, fostering a sense of pride and ultimate pleasure, that of a higher kind.

When this occurs, reaching our personal potential can be experienced as one and the same with reaching our religious potential. For only by achieving ultimate meaning — the kind that comes from observance — and striving for ultimate truth, which observance is all about, can we reach ultimate health and happiness.

Without intellectual understanding, we are likely to fail to appreciate observance on its own terms, fail to perceive it as a means to living a meaningful life, and fail to experience it as the ultimate means of reaching our potential. Since reaching our potential is at the pinnacle of our needs, we will strive to do so one way or the other. And if Judaism is not perceived as the best way to reach our potentials and achieve meaning, we are likely to search for an alternative, perhaps moving one step closer to going off the derech.

The intellect, therefore, is an essential partner to positive emotional feelings. It strengthens us in times of trouble when our positive feelings may falter. It addresses our higher capacities as they develop, and serves as the ultimate tool for establishing Judaism as the best means to self-actualization. As such, the intellect seals the success of positive emotional experiences in a powerful way.

The Heart-Mind Connection

A great sage once said that the distance between the heart and the mind is greater than the distance between the heavens and the earth.[2] One of the main purposes of Judaism is to bridge that distance, to bring the heart and the mind together so they can work in harmony to fulfill the purpose of the soul. The more they work together, the more one experiences the wholeness of spirit for which he was created, and the stronger his observance will be. The more the heart and mind conflict, the more the soul is disturbed and the less likely one is to find ultimate fulfillment. The internal conflict will make it harder to stand up to external challenges, which confront one from the outside world.

If one is to remain observant through each stage of life, no matter what his environment, the heart and mind must work together. Especially today, one's Judaism must stand on at least two legs: the first is that of the heart, how he feels about Judaism, and the second is that of the mind, what he thinks regarding its truth.

When the heart and mind work together in a particular direction — either toward Judaism or away from it — the future of observance is most clear. A Jew whose observance stands on both legs is most likely to remain observant, while the one whose observance stands on neither is most likely to go off the derech. But most of us experience something in the middle, some combination of these elements, which makes the outcome less clear and more complex. When we experience some combination of the heart-mind connection, observance is possible but not inevitable; it can go either way depending on circumstances and personality.

For example, one who loves Judaism but doesn't believe in it experiences an observant life that stands on the strongest leg, in terms of motivation for observance, but lacks the support of the other. So, if his feelings are challenged or his intellectual belief is weakened, he may lack the intellectual ammunition he needs to stay the course, and may drop observance. On the other hand, if that person is not intellectual in nature or his feelings are never challenged, he may not need strong intellectual understanding. He may not need to question or if he does question, he may not be troubled by unanswered questions. His positive feelings may bridge the intellectual gaps for him. His form of Judaism may not be the strongest but it may be enough to maintain his observance.

Those who believe in Judaism but don't feel particularly good about it can also go either way. Their observance stands on the weaker of the two legs, but it may endure nonetheless. Their intellect can establish the truth of Judaism and create a meaningful connection to it. This may ultimately create positive feelings, for the mind can affect the heart just as the heart affects the mind. In these ways, especially for truth seekers or the intellectually oriented, the intellect can compensate for negative feelings and may, over time, replace them with positive feelings that foster observance. On the other hand, if the negative emotions are too powerful or the intellectual connection too weak to compensate for them, the person will likely drop observance.

The relationship between heart and mind is complex. They not only interact with each other in a state of tension too complex to predict; they also interact with our personalities, our unique needs and tendencies making it nearly impossible to isolate the roles of each or predict their outcomes in a particular person's religiosity. Only one thing is certain: that no matter what the personality or life experience, the heart and mind, the emotions and intellect work together to greater or lesser extents to either motivate observance or hinder it.

So after understanding the role of emotions, we must examine the role of the mind — how it causes people to go off the derech and how it can be utilized to strengthen observance. We need to examine the intellectual relationships with Torah — whether or not those who go off the derech believe the Torah is true and meaningful, and whether or not we succeed in presenting it as such. In doing so, we need to consider not only what is taught, but how it is taught, and by whom, which will help explain the second category of reasons that cause people to go off the derech.

CHAPTER 14

Truth

"The more true something is, the less likely people are to believe it."

— Rabbi Adin Steinsaltz[1]

Jacob Neuser has said that "When we know *why* we want to survive — what difference it makes for us to continue as a distinctive group — we shall have no problem finding out *how*."[2] Educators today lament the fact that observant children who have spent their entire lives in *yeshiva* often do not have a reason for being observant. They do not know why they are Jewish and they lack intellectual fundamentals necessary for maintaining observance in our increasingly challenging world.

Educators say that, when they ask Bais Yaacov girls why they are observant, they often hear "God told us so." But, all too often, when they ask *why* God told us so, the girls have no answer. Leah Kohn explains that she has asked many Bais Yaacov girls why we are here, and they respond as expected "to serve God." But when she asks, "Does He need your service? No. So why are we here?" the conversation ends. They have no answer.[3]

Rabbi Daniel Mechanic, Director of Project Chazon who has spoken to thousands of *yeshiva* and Bais Yaacov students, explains that, when he asks them why they are observant, over 98% respond "because that's the way I was raised." To date, he has spoken to over 95,000 observant teens and he confidently asserts that "We are producing generations of kids who went to *yeshiva* for at least twelve years, yet, in many cases, remain totally unprepared and unable to explain to themselves and others why they are Torah observant."[4]

That means that for most of these children, observance is nothing more than a cultural experience. They fail to believe in Judaism's truth and fail to experience it as meaningful. Lacking answers to fundamental questions, their faith never matures and strengthens the way it should, and the Judaism they live and pass on to their children wanes. It becomes emptier and emptier until it is lost altogether. Even children who are still technically observant suffer in this respect. Without a strong, meaningful understanding of Judaism, without a deep personal appreciation of it, they may soon have no compelling reason to stay.

Generations ago, Judaism might have endured under such weak intellectual foundations. But in today's challenging world, in which Judaism strides against the tide and competes in a free market of ideas, a shallow intellectual understanding and belief in Torah will likely not suffice. The heart needs more support than ever. Without understanding, there can be no comprehensive connection; without connection, there can be no meaning; without meaning, there can be no ultimate joy, and without ultimate joy there may well be no motivator powerful enough to endure the lifetime of challenges to observance.

The Importance of Truth

So how can we create a strong belief in Judaism? First and foremost, by establishing the truth of Judaism, by answering the question: Why be Jewish?

Perhaps the most powerful answer to this question is that Judaism is true. Truth can lead to meaning and purpose. When Judaism is considered true, it is perceived as the best and *only* way to live, one that fosters fulfillment, enables the reaching of potential, and inspires pride.

Rabbi Shaya Cohen, founder and director of Priority One, an organization that helps kids at risk, says "People are only really happy when they feel that what they are doing is real and true." A woman who rejoices in a beautiful diamond engagement ring will instantly lose her joy if she discovers the ring is cubic zirconium. It may shine as beautifully but, if not real, it lacks inherent value and diminishes her happiness.[5]

Believing that Judaism is true also provides intellectual ammunition to overcome obstacles to faith and make sacrifices we might not otherwise. So it empowers us to remain committed when we might otherwise falter.

The observant world has always asserted truth is a primary reason for being observant. The *aseret hadibrot* — the Ten Commandments — begin with belief in God, all-powerful and all-knowing, who defines Jewish law for eternity and thus establishes objective truth as the foundation for everything that follows.

Of course people maintain observance for a variety of reasons. For some, the connection is cultural, for others, social, and for yet others, emotional. All these can inspire and sustain a certain degree of observance. But to commit oneself to the *totality* of Jewish Law, to observe even when a commandment does not seem to make sense, even in the privacy of one's own home, even when extremely difficult, that requires a belief that Judaism is based on Divine truth.

Many people who go off the derech for intellectual reasons do so because they fail to believe that Judaism represents objective truth. And they often feel justified in doing so because we tend to emphasize objective truth as the main reason for being observant. To prevent that, we must secure a strong intellectual belief by attempting to establish the truth of Judaism.

How can we do so? By addressing three fundamental components of belief: the existence of God, His giving of the Torah, and the authority of rabbinic leaders to apply the Torah for each generation. These fundamental tenets of belief establish Judaism's truth by addressing the Divine source and development of Judaism.

Is there a God?

Most people raised in observant homes, including those who go off the derech, tend to believe that God exists. In fact, Debbie Greenblatt, former director of Project YES, notes that she has yet to meet someone who has left observance who does not believe in God.[6] We tend to believe in God not as a result of personal intellectual exploration that leads to the active choice to believe but rather as a result of upbringing. Our parents believed, they told us we should believe, and therefore we do, without giving it the kind of thought and exploration that makes it our own. Thus belief in God begins in childhood and pervades the lives of observant people. But it is almost as though we take Him for granted, as if He must exist because He has always existed for us. When God is such a given reality, questioning Him can become akin to questioning our own existence.

Since belief exists so strongly in our observant worlds, it may seem superfluous to teach about belief in God. But doing so can be important, first because there are degrees of belief, and intellectual exploration can strengthen and improve the degree of belief. Second, belief can weaken over time. A child who begins with a strong belief in God may find himself doubting later in life, for example, if he suffers greatly. A stronger intellectual foundation can help him meet that challenge successfully.

Finally, we are commanded to believe in God, which implies the obligation to study His existence. Why would God command us to study about His existence? Because doing so can help us move beyond *passively* receiving the belief to *actively* gaining it for ourselves, and this would strengthen and personalize the belief in a way being raised with it alone could not.

So how can we strengthen belief in God? By discussing with students and children, on a level they can understand, the reasons for believing in God: why it makes sense, if it makes sense, what the alternatives are, what some of the arguments are for God's existence and against it.

This is not easy to do. In fact, it can be quite tricky for, while we can make good arguments for the rationality of God's existence, we cannot *prove* it. Not acknowledging this limitation can create problems as evidenced by Rena, a girl who went off the derech in her late teens and then returned to observance years later. In high school, her teacher announced that he was going to "prove" God's existence — which got her very excited. Although she believed in God, she was looking forward to learning "proofs." But as the classes progressed, her enthusiasm turned to disappointment. She was able to poke holes in his assertions. His "proofs" were fascinating; but they weren't proofs, they were just interesting arguments.

While Rena didn't lose her belief in God, she did lose belief in her teacher and the system, and began to feel that *frum* Jews would try anything to make others believe — even pretend to know what they don't.

Philosophers have been trying to prove God's existence for thousands of years. All have failed and for very good reasons. Rational arguments are limited, and trying to prove God — who exists beyond our world — with the tools of our world is futile. We cannot use the experiences and tools of *this* limited world to comprehend His, especially since He is intangible, ethereal, and eternal. Merely comprehending Him is impossible, let alone trying to prove He exists. Perhaps that is why we are told the Torah begins with the letter *beit* (second letter of Hebrew alphabet), which is closed on one side and open on another. That is meant to teach us that we can examine everything from creation on. The things in our created world are open to us, but that which existed before our time and outside of our world is beyond our reach.

Our reason, language, and intellect can take us a long way, but not all the way. They can solidify belief, but they cannot unequivocally establish it. That is why we can be commanded to believe in God. Commandment implies choice — that we can choose to follow what is commanded or not. If it were possible to intellectually "prove" God's existence, there would be no real choice. Having been intellectually shown the truth, we would *have to* believe. The mere fact that God *commands* us to believe means there must be the ability to choose otherwise, which means there must be the legitimate possibility of doubt. After all is said and done, we must take a leap if we are to believe in God

Unfortunately, we often do not acknowledge this. When we do speak of God, we often act as though His existence can be proven, as if it must be obvious. Sometimes we strive so vehemently to establish belief in God that we denigrate those who don't believe. A teacher once told a class that it was ridiculous to be an atheist. "Ask the *apikores* (heretic) 'Did you ever read Aristotle? Plato? *Moree Nevouchim?* No?' Then tell him you are not an atheist. You are an *am haaretz* (ignoramus)"

His statement was very dramatic. But it was also based on false premises and could be misleading to a young observant Jew. A student hearing this may think that, to believe, all he has to do to is read these books. He might read them and still not believe, which might give him permission to abandon the search or go off the derech. Or he may try to use his teacher's arguments on an educated atheist only to be surprised when they are knocked down. The student might end up feeling ignorant and foolish; he may create a *chilul Hashem* (desecration of God's name), and even begin to doubt his own education and belief.

At best, students who hear denigrating, simplistic messages may fail to appreciate the complexity of belief in God, the limitations of our intellect, the beauty of belief, and the importance of being able to take a leap in the service of God.

This does not mean we should shy away from such conversations. Instead, we should acknowledge the difficulties in doing so and move ahead anyway. Educators such as Rabbi David Gottlieb, who presents the issue of God's existence to *baalei teshuva,* can show us how. He does not shy away from discussing the matter simply because he cannot prove it. Rather he asserts at the outset that, in its pure form, certainty is almost always elusive. We do not generally base our decisions on certainty but rather on *probability*. There is always an element of doubt when it comes to our life choices and beliefs, but we pick a side anyway — we take a leap. The question is how big a leap and whether or not we are willing to take it.

The intellect will not make the leap for us or make it disappear. It can only lessen the gap, making it easier to leap if we choose to. We must use the intellect to understand the issue, but we cannot expect it to prove God's existence or choose to believe.

The Experiential Side of Belief

Of course, classroom discussions must work alongside a familial and social framework that acknowledges and lives with God, which discusses Him whenever possible, as the *Shema* says — *when you are sitting in your home and when you are on your way, when you lie down and when you get up.*

This experience of God in our everyday lives can be far more influential for establishing belief than intellectual arguments. Educators like Daniel Mechanic assert that we do not talk about God in a real, relevant way nearly often enough. How many parents or teachers speak regularly about the Divine intervention, point out possible examples of *midah keneged midah*[7] or point out God's splendor in a flower or tree.

The Kotzker Rebbe was once asked "Where is God?" and he profoundly answered, "Anywhere you allow Him to be." If we want our children to believe in God, genuinely and deeply, then we must show them God everywhere He can be found — in the beauty of a flower, the power of a storm, in the rising and the setting of the sun. We must see Him and seek Him everywhere, not only in the Torah, but in every area of life.

Did God Give the Torah?

Belief in God creates the necessary foundation for believing in the truth of the Torah. But it is not enough. In order to live a fully committed observant Jewish life, it is important if not essential to believe that God gave the Torah. This solidifies our commitment to the commandments in a way few other beliefs can.

Educators say that, when you ask most children why they keep the Torah, they give the same resounding response: Because God told us to. But when you ask them how they know this, you get another resounding response: silence. This would not be such a problem if they had other reasons to be observant — if they believed that Judaism fostered happiness and fulfillment, provided meaning, inspiration etc... But many do not. We hinge our children's entire commitment upon the Torah's Divinity and then inadequately equip them to believe in it.

Sometimes that's because we lack the answers ourselves, having not received them from our own parents and teachers. Sometimes we simply don't take the *time* to answer them. And sometimes we consider these vital questions heretical. Whatever the reason, ignoring such issues weakens observance and threatens it. The best indication of this is found in *baalei teshuva*. They are among the most passionate in the Jewish world about Judaism. They often exhibit a stronger, more abiding faith than those who are born into religious families. And where does their education begin? What is the foundation of their belief? These very issues, which are first addressed when they enter *baal teshuva yeshivas*.

Yeshiva high schools all over the country are starting to recognize the benefits of addressing these issues by means of seminars such as Project Chazon. These seminars complement day school education in important ways. They strengthen belief and demonstrate that answers do exist if people search for them. And they can legitimize the quest for truth and make children realize that it is normal, productive and healthy to ask questions as a means of developing faith and commitment to Torah.

On the other hand, these seminars cannot cover enough ground in a short period of time. If we teach a crash course and leave no time to properly explore the issues, the students may fail to truly understand and internalize the answers. They can become confused or feel uncomfortable asking sensitive questions from a seminar lecturer whom they have never seen and will never see again. Successful examination of these issues requires more time, the kind that comes from making them an integral part of the educational curriculum.

Some will argue that issues of belief should not be addressed in class because they can confuse or create doubt in other students. Nonetheless, there are vital reasons for doing so.

Most significantly, the student who might become most confused may be the one who needs answers the most. Perhaps it is *his* faith in particular we should strive to strengthen. If we fail to do so today, he may abandon observance tomorrow when his faith is challenged and there is no one to answer his questions. What, after all, does the Passover *Hagaddah* tell us to do with the child who does not know how to ask a question? It tells us to ask it for him, not to assume that he knows, or thank God that he has no questions, or console ourselves with the belief that he is secure in his faith. Rather we are to ask and answer for him in order to strengthen his belief and help him serve God with strong conviction, for the right reasons. Failing to do so can deny him his rightful heritage and perpetuate dangerous ignorance. So, answering questions of belief, when the teacher actually has answers, may be the safest thing to do.

Rabbinic Authority

The final element of believing that the Torah is true is belief in rabbinic authority, namely that the spiritual leaders of our age, and every age that preceded ours, hold the authority to establish binding law on the individual and communal levels. If children believe in God and that He gave the Torah, but they fail to believe in rabbinic authority, they will not fully believe in the truth of observant Torah life as it is lived today.

Unfortunately this issue too is often ignored, sometimes because we lack the answers, sometimes because we think our students already believe in rabbinic authority, and sometimes because we consider the students' questions heretical. What we forget is that even observant students have doubts about rabbinic authority and even those who don't could use a strengthened belief.

So although these issues are complex and sometimes touchy, we must try to address them. Most importantly, we must try to establish rabbinic authority in real life as well as in the classroom. Parents cannot expect students to respect their *rabbaim* (teachers) if the parents don't. And it is important to realize that our respect for *rabbanim* (rabbinic communal leaders) of yesteryear stems from our experience with *rabbaim* today. Since we cannot know the leaders of hundreds of years ago, we extrapolate about them from those we see today. Our children look at their own rabbis as representative of those who preceded them. If they see truth and righteousness, belief in rabbinic authority will likely strengthen. But if, God forbid, they see the opposite, their belief in the system will likely erode. They may lose faith in the rabbis of today and by extension those of previous generations. If our children's real life experience contradicts our intellectual arguments, belief and observance may ebb away.

So, everyday rabbis, the ones who teach our children, who run our *shuls*, who are the principals and program directors in our communities, hold an awesome responsibility. They not only represent

Judaism and God, but rabbinic authority itself. Improper behavior such as hypocrisy or acts of *chilul Hashem*, which might go unnoticed in an average Jew, can have devastating effects when practiced by a rav. Our *rabbaim* and *rabbanim* are meant to be the best of us, and need to act accordingly to help establish belief in Judaism.

In the alternative, we might consider a radical change to the system. Perhaps we might consider returning to the traditional *semichah* (rabbinical ordination) process in which the title of "Rav" was bestowed only upon the best and brightest, an elite few who carried the title with integrity and brought it honor. To become a rav, one had to exhibit not only exemplary knowledge, but also exemplary *middot*. It was not enough to *know* Torah; they had to *be* Torah, to radiate its values. These prerequisites of the title preserved the integrity of Jewish leadership and its system of law.

For others, there could be alternative titles. Perhaps they could earn a Jewish equivalent of a BA, Master's, or PhD — something that acknowledges their learning without pronouncing them exemplary in behavior. This would respect their knowledge while preserving the sanctity of the title and with it the people's respect for rabbinic authority.

Practicing What We Preach

If we succeed in intellectually establishing that there is a God, that He gave the Torah, and that rabbinic leaders have the authority to make *halachah*, we will have succeeded in establishing an important foundation for observance. We will have also created an open, affirming atmosphere in which students can develop their belief effectively.

In doing so it is vital to remember that real life experience plays an important role. Our everyday actions either establish the truth of Torah or diminish it. We cannot claim that truth is of paramount importance if it fails to be so in our teaching methods and in our lives. Intellectual and practical dishonesty can greatly undermine Torah, us, and our arguments for the Torah's truth.

Michael, who went off the derech as an adult, experienced intellectual dishonesty when observant people would engage in what he calls "selective reporting" as they tried to prove that Judaism was true. He says they would "sometimes look for various scientific discoveries to prove certain age-old truisms in the Talmudic system and, at the same time, disregard scientific studies that disprove them." As Michael puts it, "They don't necessarily even believe in the tools they are using to prove the Torah. They just figure, 'Hey. It's useful. Let's use it.' And when someone discovers that it's not useful, they dump it....It is not the evidence that drives the system; the system drives the evidence."

This caused Michael to lose respect for the system and for observant people. And it created a sense of hypocrisy. People claimed that he should make important sacrifices in his life for the sake of the truth, but it seemed they didn't really care about truth at all.

Likewise, those who work in *kiruv*, sometimes find it particularly difficult to admit troubling realities in the observant world to those who might become observant; they fear it may turn them away. Sometimes they may begin to distort the truth. But, even in the best situations, unrealistic depictions of observant life create problems. They can eventually create distrust and sometimes disrespect of observant people.

Such has been the case with numerous *baalei teshuva* who were painted a rosy picture of observant life and were disillusioned years later. Some have gone off the derech as a result. Others, already having wives and children, live in a terrible crisis of faith, with bitterness toward those who they feel deceived them. Part of their attraction was built on falsehood and thus it can easily deteriorate.

The Torah seems to tell us that, even in pursuit of the most noble of causes, we must not distort truth. *Tzedek tzedek tirdof— righteousness, righteousness you shall pursue*. Why, asks Rabbi Bunam of P'shis'cha, is the word *righteousness* repeated twice? In order, he answers, to teach us that not only must the end be righteous but also the means. We must pursue righteousness *righteously*. Unrighteous means to achiev-

ing a righteous end undermines the Torah. And distorting truth to inspire commitment to truth can be even more absurd. It undermines the
very Torah we are trying to perpetuate, like stealing a *lulav* to make
a *bracha*.

So truth must be acquired truthfully. If we want to argue effectively
for the truth of Torah, we must not only speak *of* truth, we must speak
with it — in the classroom, in our actions, and all our pursuits. We must
be honest about ourselves and honest about Judaism. Hiding the truth
undermines truth, which is one of the strongest arguments for Torah
observance, and it likewise undermines people's respect of observant
Jews, which is one of the strongest glues to the observant world.

True confidence in our Judaism means recognizing that no problem
or negative reality in the Jewish world can jeopardize Judaism's truth,
that has lasted thousands of years, survived persecution, and succeeds
until this day in inspiring its people to unprecedented and disproportionate achievements when compared to the rest of the world. Judaism
stands, thrives, and depends on truth. The Jewish people, therefore,
must teach truth, must speak truth and live truth if they are to establish
a strong belief in its cause.

CHAPTER 15

Meaning: A Universal Vision

Of all intellectual issues that cause people to stop observing Judaism, lack of meaning is probably the most significant for it is through meaning that we find fulfillment and pride, joy, and purpose. It is meaning that makes Judaism an integral and uplifting part of our identities and daily lives.

Many who drop observance do not experience Judaism as meaningful. They fail to experience observance as relevant to their lives; they fail to see how it improves their lives and connects them to what is good. They often know what Judaism says, but not why. As Rabbi Ahron Kaufman says in the *Jewish Observer*, they do not understand their Judaism.

> If they do not understand, they cannot appreciate. If they do not appreciate, they cannot be enthusiastically involved, and it is not meaningful to them. If it is not meaningful, they are on their way to dropping out. Dropping out is not our main enemy; superficiality and ignorance are.[1]

Truth is Not Enough

Establishing the truth of Judaism can help to make it meaningful. But it is not enough to secure observance. Truth and meaning are two different things. It is true that the ocean is blue. But what does that mean to me? Nothing unless it is relevant to my life in some way. What gives truth meaning is relevance, the ability to affect our lives, for better or worse. What gives truth meaning is a purpose, context, and greater reason that inspires, uplifts, and motivates us to act.

So, believing that the Torah is true is only the first rung on the intellectual ladder of observance. Judaism must then become relevant in a significant, positive way. It must improve life and provide it with a greater vision and purpose; it must enable self-actualization and connect us to the world as well as to God.

What Makes Judaism Meaningful

There are two different and equally important ways of experiencing meaning in Judaism. The first is by understanding its micro-elements, its details and *halachot*. The other is by understanding the bigger picture, the greater whole to which the details connect, the context for the *mitzvot*, and the inspirational vision they realize. A meaningful context connects the details to a whole which is greater than itself. It brings them to life and imbues each one with greater significance. It not only makes Judaism meaningful, but makes our lives meaningful as well. It inspires us, lifts us, and makes Judaism the vital, breathing part of the soul it needs to be in order to thrive in today's contradictory world.

Achieving this holistic Judaism requires both these elements, macro and micro. Our children often lack inspiration because, while we teach them the details of living an observant life, we often fail to transmit the bigger picture. Today we tend to focus on the microelements of Torah, the *mitzvot* and how to practice them. But we almost entirely neglect to transmit the purpose, the vision and context for the *mitzvot* we teach. We focus on how and what to observe, but not why. So our children know exactly what to do when a drop of milk falls into a pot of chicken soup, but they do not know what that means, why it is relevant, how it transforms them and connects to something greater. In short, they fail to experience its meaning. As Rabbi Sacks explains, we are losing the plot.

> If Judaism is only the six hours between milchig and fleishig…where is there room for the soul? *Min hamaitza karati ya — from the depths I call to you —* I feel claustrophobic and I'm calling for the *Ribono Shel Olam* (Master of the Universe) to give me a breadth of vision to lift my spirits, to give me something that is ethically challenging and spiritually demanding and intellectually coherent so that I do not have to believe in Alice in Wonderland's famous phrase, 'six impossible things before breakfast.'[2]

There is a story of the Jewish people, one in which we each play a vital part, and which no one else can play. It is our duty to teach our children this story, to give them not only the lines, but also the plot, the purpose, and direction. We have been at the center stage of history, playing a pivotal role in the advancement of the world. We have propelled humanity forward in seminal areas of life. It is our duty to show our children their role in the process.

Judaism sets forth a utopian vision of peace and righteousness that has captured the imagination of half the world. It serves as the foundation for two other major world religions. Yet it uniquely remains truly universal, speaking to all but recognizing differences, by specifying unique and individual *mitzvot* for Jew and non-Jew alike. Such a vision is greater than us, greater than the commandments, greater than the Jewish people, and it makes even the most seemingly mundane holy and important.

This is our children's rightful heritage and if we fail to give it to them, they will be more likely to abandon observance. Instead, we must give them a greater vision, tell them who they are, where we came from, what our history is, what we have been chosen to do and why, and how to fulfill that vision. We must tell them how doing so will enhance not only our own lives but also the lives of those around us, Jew and non-Jew alike. We need to get back to the big picture and connect each individual *mitzvah* to the fabric of our lives and the story of humanity.

Establishing the truth of the mission is an important first step. But without building upon that foundation to create a meaningful purpose, vision, and context, people will continue to go off the derech.

So how can we create a meaningful Judaism? By explaining *who* we are, *why* we are here, and *how* we best achieve our goals.

Who We Are

On the individual level, everybody needs to know who they are: their unique strengths and weakness, likes and dislikes, their past as well as their potential future. Taking pride in ourselves begins with knowing our selves. And knowing ourselves begins with knowing our past: our parents and grandparents, their histories, personalities and value systems, the decisions they made which shaped our lives. Discovering this past is essential for self-actualization and achieving personal and religious meaning.

The same is true on the national level. Jewish pride and the achievement of Jewish goals require understanding who we are as a people. Where did we come from and why? How did we develop as a nation into the dramatically diverse people we see today? What are our strengths and weaknesses and how do they affect our current reality and future prospects?

Thus we must understand not only our modern history, but also our ancient roots, where we were born and how. Perhaps that is why God begins the Torah not with what we must *do*, but with who we *are* — the story of our ancestors from Adam to Abraham which provides a meaningful context for our lives and mission.

Why Are We Here?

Once we understand the fundamentals of who we are, we must identify why we are here, not only as individuals, but also as a nation. In short, what is the meaning and purpose of life and what role if any does Judaism play in that?

The Jewish answer to this is straightforward, important, and rarely discussed, in a word, actualization — reaching our potential and doing so on three levels — personally, nationally, and universally. We are here to become the best of who we are as people and as Jews and, in doing so, help the world to reach its potential. On the individual level, we are meant to grow spiritually, to improve our characters, learning, and deeds, to strive for Godliness, to move beyond who we are today to become something better tomorrow.

This goal is challenging, important, and meaningful. But it can provide meaning only to our own particular lives. It is hardly grand and inspirational. It becomes grand and inspirational when connected to something greater, like the entire world.

The Jewish nation is also delegated with the unique responsibility of serving as a light for the world at large, of striving not only for a *tikun* (fixing) in ourselves, but also for *tikun olam* (fixing or improving the world). We are supposed to spiritually revolutionize the world by inspiring it to achieve spiritual fulfillment. We are meant to model the ways of justice and righteousness, to go against the natural grain that seeks materialism, self-interest, and personal preference and strive instead for spirituality and objective truth. We are supposed to achieve a moral peak that inspires the world to emulate God and spiritually actualize.

This is a national goal, because changing the world on a global level cannot be accomplished by individuals alone. A goal so lofty requires a nation of people who join together so that they can model not only how individuals should behave, but also how nations as a whole should behave. In doing so, their individual power and influence becomes unlimited. They become empowered to achieve God's vision on a much larger scale and accomplish on a global level what they could not alone.

This vision connects our individual existence to that of a nation, and connects the existence of that nation to the world at large so that there is tightly woven fabric of existence, a holistic vision of life which makes Judaism more effective, meaningful, and inspiring than it would be otherwise.

The Universal and Particular

To achieve our universal mission, we must not only know who we are as Jews but also who we are *vis-à-vis* the world. We must recognize *both* our similarities and differences with other nations. Understanding both perspectives is essential for achieving the Jewish mission as the Torah itself seems to teach us in its structure.

For how does the Torah begin? Not with the birth of the Jewish people but with the birth of the world. It begins with the creation of one man, in order to teach us that we all come from the same place and share a common core that unites us. This is the very first lesson we are taught. In teaching us how to live as Jews, God begins by teaching us to recognize our common humanity with all people, perhaps because only with this recognition will we be sufficiently moved to improve the world and lead it properly.

Recognizing commonality fosters respect, caring and the ability to relate to our fellow men. Without this, we would not care enough to help the world and be properly motivated to do so. And without this, we would fail to assist, teach, and lead with humility and respect, for we might fail to recognize the *tzelem elokim* (image of God) in us all. Rabbi Abraham Isaac Kook explains how essential this is:

> It is impossible to reach the exalted state of reciting 'Praise the Lord, call upon His Name, declare His works among

the nations' without an inner love which fills the depths of the heart and the spirit to seek the betterment of all of the nations, to improve their material status, and to further their happiness....the noblest love for one's own nation, in its broadest practical and spiritual reaches, appears only in a person who is rich in love for humanity and for every individual man. And the narrow viewpoint which causes one to see everything which is foreign to a particular nation, even what is outside the Jewish people, as ugly and defiling, this is one of the awful darknesses which bring general destruction to every edifice of spiritual goodness, whose light every sensitive spirit longs to see.[3]

But appreciating the universal is not enough for the Jew. He must then appreciate his unique identity and utilize it if he is to contribute to the world. To deny that uniqueness or chosenness is to deny the very essence of who we are. And no man can be happy for long or live a meaningful life if he denies his essence. That which makes us unique is as vital as that which makes us similar and to deny either is to cripple our ability to live a meaningful life and achieve our goals as a people.

That may be why *Bereishit* (Genesis) serves only as the *beginning* of our story. It continues with the establishment of the Jewish people, how and why we came to be who we are. It is as if to teach us that once we know what we have in common we must understand how we are unique. Our foundation is the same as everyone else, but we are also different, chosen for a unique task and endowed with unique attributes and potentialities to achieve it.

Understanding our similarities is essential for connecting and leading with humility and respect; understanding our differences is vital for maintaining, developing, and utilizing our unique abilities. One without the other is insufficient.

So to empower our children to live meaningful Jewish lives, we must straddle two seemingly divergent conceptions of religion and identity. On the one hand, the universal — this asserts our commonality and connection with the rest of the world — and on the other hand, the particular and exclusive — our separate roles and unique identities.

Unfortunately, we find it difficult to maintain both at the same time and often emphasize one at the expense of the other. Today it seems the observant world focuses on the exclusive elements of Judaism at the expense of the universal ones, while nonobservant Jews focus on the universal at the expense of the exclusive. Either perspective diminishes Judaism's mission and vision.

When the observant Jew focuses on the exclusive elements of Judaism at the *expense* of the universal, he undermines the desire and ability to respect and influence the world at large. Then, stripped of its ultimate vision, Judaism loses an important part of its meaning; it becomes hollow and more easily discarded, especially in an open society that values universal ideals.

On the other hand, when the nonobservant Jew focuses on the universal and neglects particularity, he loses the means to achieving that universal vision. He loses the unique Jewish identity through which he is meant to improve the world. With the birth of the Enlightenment, many Jews sacrificed the exclusive elements of being a chosen people in favor of a universal vision that denies or minimizes differences. As Rabbi Shlomo Carlebach once noted, "I ask students what they are. If someone gets up and says, 'I'm a Catholic,' I know he's a Catholic. If someone says, 'I'm a Protestant,' I know he's a Protestant. If someone gets up and says, 'I'm just a human being,' I know he's a Jew."

Rabbi Kook explains that at the heart of the Jewish soul lies the longing for universality which expresses itself in Jews turning to communism, art, psychology, humanitarianism, and philosophy.[4] But perhaps because the nonobservant world has focused so much on the universal at the expense of the particular, observant Jews have done the opposite, reasoning that if unbridled universalism has threatened observance, stressing exclusivity will maintain it.

But both the universal and particular are necessary for serving as a light unto the nations, and providing the tools that make Judaism ultimately meaningful. Neglecting either foundation weakens Judaism; but neglecting to provide the universal vision can create particular problems in terms of people going off the derech. It can lead people to believe that if they want to achieve more universal goals, they will have to step outside of the observant world to do so. As Susannah Heschel points out in the study "What Do American Jews Believe":

> Chosenness strikes me as a very modern formulation; it is barely an issue in classical Jewish texts. When I was growing up, being Jewish was always associated with generosity and devotion to others, and a *mitzvah* meant doing something for another human, or for God. My father used to say that a *mitzvah* is a prayer in the form of a deed. I also learned from him that religious life and social justice were intertwined. The great concerns of the prophets and the rabbis were not the minutiae of *halachah*, or the refinement of personal piety, but the treatment of widows and orphans, cheating in the marketplace, and atrocities committed during war.[5]

Chosenness, of course, is not a modern formulation at all. Nor is it at odds with personal piety or the treatment of widows and orphans. The two can and should work together. But, when they are considered contradictory, chosenness often loses. Universal ideals tend to resonate so strongly that when faced with the need to choose, many would rather compromise their unique and chosen identity for it.

An observant Jew need not choose. He can and should have both if he is to live a fulfilled life that achieves personal, national, and universal actualization. One need not come at the expense of the other.

Understanding the universal vision makes Judaism more meaningful. Understanding our commonality with others fosters humility and inspires *tikun olam*. And understanding our particular heritage enables us to make a unique contribution through our particular heritage. Denying either perspective on the other hand, compromises these things.

Establishing a meaningful Judaism requires the understanding that our essence can be the same while our task is different. The goal can be universal, while the means are particular. If children understand these things, they will know who they are and why they are here. They will be better equipped to reach their personal potentials and help the Jewish people and outside world to do the same. And in the process they will likely find greater meaning both in their Judaism and in their lives. The only thing they will need to know then is how to accomplish these goals.

CHAPTER 16

Mitzvot: The Means to Actualization

hen children know their mission, they can appreciate Judaism and experience it more meaningfully. But then they must understand: How do we achieve our mission? The Torah answers this question with the *mitzvot*, our game plan for actualizing ourselves and the world at large. Truly appreciating the *mitzvot* and their role in creating a meaningful life begins with a general understanding of the system as a whole and ends with appreciation of the individual *mitzvot*.

Why Follow a System?

To fully appreciate *halachic* Judaism, we first need to understand the value of having a system to begin with. Why prescribe such a well-defined route for achieving our goals? How does subjugating yourself to *any* system bring righteousness to the world?

There can be many beautiful explanations for doing so. One poignant one was expressed by Rabbi Pesach Wolicki, *Rosh Yeshiva* of Yesodei HaTorah. He explains that through the *mitzvot* we achieve liberation of the soul. How does being bound to something achieve freedom? Rabbi Wolicki quotes a Bengali poet, Rabindranith Tagore, to explain:

> I hold in my hand a violin string.
> It is free to bend and move in any direction,
> But it is not free to sing.
> I bind the string to my violin.
> It is no longer free to move and bend in any direction,
> But now, for the very first time, it is free to sing.[1]

Why Follow This System?

Like violin strings, binding ourselves to Torah may limit our movement, but it allows our souls to sing. Such a positive perspective can create new appreciation for structure and commitment.

Now we can begin to understand why *this particular system* is best for us. Why these particular *mitzvot*? We can begin to explore each *mitzvah* on its own merits, in order to understand how each one works and why. Why does God care about ripping toilet paper on Shabbat or a drop of milk that falls into a pot of chicken soup?

The answers to these questions can help us to appreciate Torah better, to see it as a recipe book for life such that we not only know what the ingredients are, but also why each was selected: how it flavors the food, what happens to the meal if there is more or less of one ingredient or another, and how they all work together to create ultimate nourishment for the soul.

Self-Actualization as a Reason

The most powerful reasons for *mitzvot* are the ones that show their relevance and demonstrate their benefit for us because these kinds of reasons make *mitzvot* potentially more meaningful than any other. Of all potential reasons (or benefits), perhaps the most significant is that they help us to actualize ourselves, our nation and the world at large.

Mitzvot enable us to achieve our mission as individuals and as a nation, to become *Kiddushei Hashem* (those who sanctify God's name), to serve as a light unto the nations and ultimately to achieve *tikun olam*.

When *mitzvot* are explained this way — as the means to achieving self, national, and global actualization — they acquire the greatest significance possible. Actualization is at the pinnacle of our needs, so if *mitzvot* can achieve it on all levels, they become the means to achieving the ultimate happiness and fulfillment in life, something everyone wants. In addition, they not only become meaningful and relevant in and of themselves, but also become connected to something greater, first to ourselves, then to our nation, then to the world at large. This broader perspective provides an understanding for *mitzvot* that transforms each individual deed and greatly magnifies its significance.[2]

The best place to start in creating this perspective is by demonstrating the *mitzvot* as the best means to actualize your self: your body, your mind, and your soul.

This is particularly important in the modern age. Prior to the Enlightenment, in theory at least, God was the center of man's universe. Life revolved around religion and God was the measure of all things good. With the rise of the Enlightenment, however, man became the measure of what is right and good. This fundamental shift in mentality has affected the Jewish world as much as the world at large, the result being that today it is more difficult for people to accept God's word as the measure of what is good.

Today, to experience something as good or right and therefore meaningful, it must be good in one's own eyes. Moreover, for something to be good, it must now also be good *for* me, the individual. This is why the great sage Maimonides wrote, "you must make [a person] know that you are telling him [to change his ways] for no reason other than his benefit."[3] That which successfully advocates my needs and wants, is good.

This is the age in which we live, one where man is not only the primary *arbiter* of the truth, but must also be the primary *beneficiary*. As Aron Kaufman notes: "Among the numerous unmotivated and even motivated teens with a broad range of problems whom I've met, one common denominator is this lack of understanding of basic Judaism… They frequently ask, 'What do I gain in this world from Judaism? How do I benefit from being *frum?*"[4] The more effectively we can answer these questions, the stronger the identity and commitment to observance.

Torah can only survive when it is experienced as a privilege; it wanes when experienced as a burden.

The more we see *mitzvot* as helpful to us, the more likely we will experience them as a privilege, to value and perpetuate them. Understanding how particular *mitzvot* affect us, how they transform the soul, advance happiness, and promote self-actualization can actually motivate observance and commitment where there otherwise would be none. For example, I remember learning about *brachas* throughout my *yeshiva* day school education. I knew all the details about what to say and when to say it. But I never made blessings on the things I ate. Then one day, the teacher discussed the reasons for making blessings. Of course the underlying reason was that God told us to. But that is not what he focused on. What he discussed was happiness. Happiness, he said, is an essential thing in life. How do we achieve it? The key is to appreciate every little thing we have. The more we appreciate the more room we make for happiness. He explained that each time we make a blessing, we become aware of what we have to appreciate, and food is the perfect place to start. It is the basis of all life, something so mundane that we often take it for granted. On a subconscious level then, we experience appreciation and make room for happiness in our lives. From then on, I started to make blessings.

That reason inspired me to commit to making *brachot* for it made the *mitzvah* relevant, important, and valuable for my life. It transformed it from a routine deed into a spiritual act and created a greater appreciation for *mitzvot* in general.

The more *mitzvot* we can explain this way, the more relevant and meaningful they become, and the less likely our children are to drop them. Why so? First, because it is human nature to value what benefits us personally. So if Judaism makes our daily lives meaningful by helping us to self-actualize, it becomes directly positive and relevant to us. Second, self-actualization is at the pinnacle of our needs and creates ultimate happiness in life. So if we see the *mitzvot* as a means to achieving that, we are likely to consider Judaism as ultimately meaningful. We are more likely to perceive it as an integral part of our happiness, which will help us value it and commit to it. Finally, while we can and should try to change the world directly, we do so primarily and most effectively by changing ourselves. The daily acts which improve our own souls and lives indirectly affect the world in mysterious but important ways. When we change ourselves, we create ripple effects of *tikun olam* that eventually change the entire world. So when we establish that Judaism best advocates self-actualization, we indirectly argue that it best achieves universal-actualization as well.

National Actualization as a Reason

The next layer in making *mitzvot* ultimately meaningful for our children is to establish them as a means to national-actualization, the best way for the Jewish people to reach their national potential.

When we show our children a universal vision, we create a meaningful context for Judaism. When we explain how the *mitzvot* advocate that vision, we connect the details to the greater whole. And when we explain *mitzvot* in terms of self-actualization, we connect the individual to the details and to the greater vision. The national component is the last piece of the puzzle. It is the bridge that connects the individual to the entire world. This is vital in part because, although it is my goal to change the world, I as an individual cannot do so alone. I can only change the world *in me* and that in turn changes one little part of the world. As an individual, I can achieve *Kiddush Hashem* but not *tikkun olam* on the level that God intended. To achieve that, I need to bind with other Jews. As part of a group, I can better maximize my positive influence on the world.

There are many *mitzvot* that enable this national-actualization and emphasize the national component of Judaism. But two in particular bear mentioning: *yishuv Eretz Yisrael,* settling the Land of Israel and *ahavat Yisrael,* loving our fellow Jew.

When considered alone, these *mitzvot* are like any other. But when considered in the context of our universal and national goals, they take on greater significance because we can only properly serve as a light to the nations when we unite in a homeland.

When we consider *Bereishit,* we see that God gave the Jewish people His goal and His vision. But He did not stop there. Then, he gave them a home. The tie that binds us is not only our belief system but also the home in which we observe it. This is because without a land, a people can only do so much. They can serve as *Kiddushei Hashem* on the individual level, but not on the national level. To magnify the impact of Judaism, we need to move beyond individual role-modeling to national role-modeling. We need to have our own home in order to establish a model society with all its relevant institutions — judicial, military, political and social. This enables us to serve as a model nation, showing the world the Jewish way to implement justice, feed the poor, and educate children.

Of course, having a land is not enough to achieve our national goals. A house is not always a home. To make the land a place really worth emulating, it must become a home. It must have *shalom bayit.* Only with unity and love for each other can we truly achieve *shalom bayit* and serve as a model society worthy of emulation. This may explain why hatred toward our fellow Jews was enough of a reason to disperse us from the land of Israel in the time of the Second Temple. If we failed to love each other, we could not serve as a light for the nations. Our mission would become impossible to achieve and our home would be rendered useless, for even within it, we could not achieve our purpose.

But these two *mitzvot,* living in the land of Israel and loving our fellow Jew, though central to our mission as a nation, seem neglected in our educational system. How many of our teachers and parents strive to inspire a true love for *Eretz Yisrael* and for *all* Jews regardless of background or religious affiliation?

Regardless of perspectives on Israeli politics or the religious commitments of individual Jews, we can all agree on the importance of our national vision and the *mitzvot* which foster them. But the land of Israel and even the idea of *mashiach,* which are fundamental to Judaism, are hardly discussed today outside of Chabad or religious Zionist circles.

Rabbi Wein suggests one possible reason for this:

> Mashiach got a bad rap in the last few hundred years. We had a lot of false messiahs. The utopia never arrived so it's not factored into our lives. Mashiach will come tomorrow — good, fine. We always say in America — people say — gee I hope he doesn't come before the Super Bowl. It's not really factored into our lives.

In addition, our national vision is very obscure. There is no clearly defined path for achieving it or solving our national problems, which makes Judaism irrelevant today on the national level.

Rabbi Wein identifies this as one of the main causes of defection from Judaism today:

> To a great extent, I think one of the greatest problems that Orthodoxy faces is that it doesn't promise anything. It should. On an individual basis perhaps it does; but [not] on a national basis. I mean let's say everybody would vote for the Orthodox parties tomorrow. What would be its

platform? What are we going to do? We have no idea.

The Torah [has ideas], but someone has to articulate them. What's our attitude toward labor unions? What's our attitude toward the poorer section of society? Toward the Arabs? Toward anything? So now the attitude is: do Torah and *mitzvot*. But doing Torah and *mitzvot* is not a foreign policy and it's not a domestic policy either. We don't promise anything to anyone....We don't say that we are going to fix the world; we don't say those things even though it is part of our heritage, even though that's part of Torah. We don't express it. It could be the reason we don't is that we have been under attack for so long; we have been a minority within a minority so we can't afford grandiose dreams. But I think that if we don't express grandiose dreams, we doom ourselves to remain the minority within the minority.[5]

Failure to project a national vision makes Judaism less meaningful and relevant than it can and should be and ignores its most potentially inspiring aspects, those that take it beyond individual importance to a national importance. Without this element, children may be prompted to abandon observance and historically have done so precisely for this reason.

Consider that in Eastern Europe, 70% of the Jewish children in Poland did not attend Jewish schools. Why? Rabbi Wein explains that the reigning ideas of the time were socialism, nationalism, and labor Zionism, all of which promised a utopia and offered potential solutions to problems. Orthodoxy, on the other hand, never promised anything except more of the same. So there comes a point where it is certainly more appealing to listen to someone who says he's going to bring the utopia than to someone who says — "listen, we just have to tough it out for the next hundred years."

Conclusion

Presenting *mitzvot* as the means to personal, national, and universal actualization establishes them as an inspiring and meaningful part of our lives, the means to achieving ultimate health and happiness on the individual and global levels.

When we succeed in portraying *mitzvot* as a means to achieving these goals, as a vibrant way of life that touches every part of us in deep and meaningful ways, our children will more likely appreciate the importance of their role in the world as part of the Jewish people. They will feel connected to *mitzvot* and to each other, and they will feel like an important part of the world at large, responsible for and vital within it.

Take that away from them and what do they have? Judaism in a vacuum; deeds without meaning, actions without a goal, pieces with no greater picture, a Judaism less worthy of committing to.

CHAPTER 17

Reasons and Relevance

stablishing the *mitzvot* as a means to personal, national and universal actualization is a vital way of infusing them with meaning. But we can do so only if we are willing to provide reasons for the *mitzvot* — both the system in general and for individual *mitzvot*. Unfortunately, we seem to have a strong aversion to providing reasons or benefits for *mitzvot*. As Dennis Prager notes, when he was a young student, "despite all the encouragement of questioning at *yeshiva*, one seminal area of Judaism seemed to be off limits to questions: reasons for the laws. Not only were reasons not given, but we were largely taught that looking for reasons bordered on the sacrilegious."[1]

The Role of Reason: God is Not Enough

We seem to believe that the only worthy reason for keeping *mitzvot* is that God commanded us to and if we provide a reason at all, that is the one we give. But, especially in today's modern world, this is an inadequate answer. As one Bais Yaacov girl said:

I don't feel like we're really explained anything. All questions are answered along the lines of "this is what *Hashem* told us, or what *Hashem* wants us to do," and that's it. We should not ask questions and should basically accept everything because of that reason. But between you and me, it's a hard thing to do. Sometimes I really feel ignorant about my Yiddishkeit even after going all my life through a Bais Yaacov system school. When someone asked me once "Why am I Jewish" my first thought was "what do you mean? My parents are Jewish."[2]

Why is this so problematic? Because after the Enlightenment, not only did man become the center of the universe, his reason became supreme. It became the sole arbiter of right and wrong. Reason became considered "the most significant and positive capacity of the human" enabling one to break free from "primitive, dogmatic, and superstitious beliefs." According to Enlightenment doctrine, "beliefs of any sort should be accepted only on the basis of reason, and not on traditional or priestly authority."[3]

Whether or not we like it, these ideas have created a new reality which must be acknowledged if Judaism is to compete in the modern world. Judaism can no longer solely rely on God, for God is no longer naturally at the center of our world. And it means that Judaism must now appeal to reason for reason is now the ultimate tool for ascertaining truth. Our children are not likely to simply accept *mitzvot* if they lack compelling reasons. God's giving the Torah can be a good reason. But it can only go so far in today's world. It can be a great *first* answer, but it cannot be the last answer.

This is true for many reasons, the first of which is that "God Told Us So" establishes truth but not necessarily meaning. Truth does not necessarily make Torah meaningful. Providing reasons is essential for accomplishing that. Reasons turn a simple deed into a spiritual endeavor. They make *mitzvot* meaningful, relevant and capable of sustaining observance today. Reasons ensure that Judaism is experienced as a privilege and considered the best of all alternatives.

In addition, offering God as the reason for observance pins our entire commitment upon one idea which is both difficult to prove and changeable throughout life. This can be dangerous to observance as demonstrated by Shai's story. Shai became famous through a *Wall Street Journal* article written in 1991 when he started an organization called "*H'agudah Lechozrim Leshala.*" It was an 'underground railroad' established to help people who wanted to leave religious life.[4]

Shai grew up in a sheltered *Chassidish* world but eventually went off the derech. Having suffered great pain in his Chassidish world, he began to question God and began engaging in delinquent behaviors such as stealing money from *tzedakah* (charity) boxes at *shul*. How could he have gone so far from his upbringing? Shai explains that, "Once God no longer existed, there were no more rules. I had already broken the Sabbath, so why shouldn't I steal."

No doubt, Shai was taught to keep *mitzvot* because "God told us so." This worked very well as long as he believed in God and cared about His will. But when God disappeared, all the commandments went with Him, even the ones involving common decency.

Perhaps had Shai understood the *mitzvot* in a broader context, as a means to developing the soul, improving society, connecting with his heritage, he might have been more inclined to keep them. In that case, even if God disappeared for him, other reasons might have remained to maintain some commitment or observance.

For example, had Shai seen commandments as a means to becoming a good person, he might have maintained some *mitzvot* no matter how angry he became with the observant world, or how much he doubted God. Despite his negative feelings, he at least would have been left with the basic fundamental desire to be good, which seems common to all people. And understanding *mitzvot* as a means to that end might have helped him maintain at least the *mitzvot* he felt were good for him. Or he might have at least maintained appreciation for the *mitzvot* which might have prompted a future return. But with God as the only reason, there was nothing left when God disappeared. There was nothing to take Shai beyond his moments of doubt.

God's existence is difficult to prove and what we feel about him today can change tomorrow. Life's circumstances can weaken our belief. And when our commitment to Judaism rests *solely* upon God, it is more likely to falter in those circumstances.

But if we have a broader base for belief, we are more likely to remain committed. Broader connections can more easily prompt a future return.

"God Told Us So" Fosters Obedience Not Understanding

In addition, teaching children to observe because God told them to limits their ability to understand and appreciate Torah. It fosters obedience, not understanding. They may then observe the *mitzvot*, but without appreciating the principles behind them; or they may comply now, but may not remain committed in the long run.

When a parent tells a child to do something "because I told you so," the child will comply. But he will not necessarily understand. When he grows up, he may observe out of rote or may stop observing altogether because he was negatively motivated by fear rather than by love and respect. In addition, he may fail to internalize the value of *mitzvot*. Rather than touch his soul, they are more likely to remain external behaviors that fail to inspire.

But when we explain why, a child can understand the principle behind the behavior. This will make him more likely to continue the behavior on his own and also more likely to understand the principle behind it and extrapolate it to other situations. For example if, without providing a reason, you tell a child not to hit, he may refrain from hitting but may engage in other hurtful behaviors. But if you explain the importance of sensitivity and care for others, he will be more likely to refrain from other similar situations because he understands the principle behind "not hitting."

This does not mean we should never say "because I told you so," or "because God told you so." These are important teaching mechanisms for establishing authority. But teaching Torah must go beyond that. It must transform the soul — and this requires teaching *principles* — explaining and instructing so that a child can develop a Jewish *consciousness,* not simply a Jewish behavior, so that he can appreciate, respect and value the *mitzvot* and learn how to apply their lessons in every area of life. "God told us so" can establish authority and inspire commitment, but cannot develop proper appreciation and respect.

Reasons Create Trust in God

Providing reasons has the added benefit of fostering trust in and love for God. When we learn, understand, and appreciate the value behind the command, we also come to value the Commander, to trust in Him and see that what He requests or demands is not for His sake, but our own. We can see this clearly in the parent-child relationship.

Imagine if every time a child was told to do something, and the child asked why, he did not receive a reason. The child, seeing his parent as a dictator, would likely become frustrated and never come to appreciate the parent's wisdom and concern for his well-being. He may never establish proper trust in his parent. True, sometimes the child simply cannot understand, or the parent needs to establish authority. But those times must be the *exception*, not the rule. The same is true of God. How do we come to know God's love? By seeing that what He tells us is for our good.

So when we deprive our children of reasons for commandments, we not only deprive them of the meaning of Torah, but also of the understanding that God loves them, that He wants for their best, that the Torah is the manual for living the best kind of life. With this kind of trust in God, we can have greater faith in the things we do not understand. The love and trust we develop in the 80 or 90% of commandments that we *do* understand can carry us through the 10 or 20% that we don't. But if the whole Torah is a mystery to us, commitment is far more difficult.

This doesn't mean that we provide reasons for all the *mitzvot,* all of the time. It means we must try. Rabbi Shaya Cohen of Priority One explains that the Rambam strove to provide explanations for the *mitzvot,* but he was at a loss in the Book of Leviticus when it came to the commandment not to "bring yeast or honey on the altar." Nonetheless, he said he would try to provide an explanation so the commandments wouldn't appear like a closed book; because if they would appear that way, children might reject it in their youth and forsake it forever. The Rambam was successful in providing reasons for 612 of the *mitzvot.* But he was afraid that if he missed one it would sabotage the rest, because reasons can be powerful tools for establishing trust.

Dr. David Pelkowitz gives the example of ten people standing on line for a Xerox machine. If one guy breaks in with no excuse, everyone gets angry. If another cuts in, saying his wife is giving birth, no one cares that he cut in. And if yet a third cuts in and mumbles something that no one hears, but they believe he had some reason, they are satisfied even if they are not sure what the reason is.[5]

The Importance of Relevance

Finally, providing reasons makes the *mitzvot* relevant, and this is the most important element for making them meaningful.

In a recent article entitled "Religious Graduates Becoming More Secular," Matti Degan, a former Director of Israel's national religious school system, explains that lack of relevance is a significant cause of disenfranchisement from Judaism. As he says, teachers simply "don't make the Talmud relevant to the students."[6] Educators such as Rabbi Cardozo agree:

A lot of information is given, but it is often irrelevant to the lives of the people they are trying to inform. You can teach *Chumash* (the Pentateuch) but they may wonder, what does this have to do with me? Why do I need to know this? The children walk away uninspired. There is no connection between what they learn and who they are. ...You have to teach *chumash* in a way that shows how this story says something about his or her life — how it can guide them, warn them, inspire them.... the question of Jewish education should be what it has to do with the child's life.[7]

So showing reasons for individual commandments is not enough. Those reasons must also be made relevant to each person. How does keeping the Sabbath make me a better person? How do keeping kosher and making blessings improve my life? What does it mean to me, rather than my ancestors or my parents, and how does it connect to my life.

Such relevance can be established by making the values of Judaism explicit. Rabbi Norman Lamm explains that "We have too much emphasis on text and too little emphasis on the values that emerge from them... We concentrate on the texts and we don't leave very much time to the values that emerge from them...The result is that the kid emerges with a bunch of amorphous, almost chaotic ideas about Judaism, and he has no grounding in the educational realities which an observant Jew needs. We must strike a balance between text and values."[8]

I remember a unique class in which, instead of teaching *Chumash* with the commentaries as any typical teacher would do, our teacher, Judy Young, gave us charts. These charts included five sections. For every word of the Torah and every commentator we read, we had to fill in the chart with the following information: What is the word we are analyzing? Which commentator is attempting to provide an answer?

What is his problem or issue with the word or phrase? What is his solution? And then the clincher — the thing that brought the Torah to life and made it relevant — how do we apply that solution to our everyday life? What unique message or lesson can we learn from the commentator's solution? She called this the "application." Every student had to come up with her own application for every single word or phrase.

It was a very difficult thing to do. When you are learning about the most obscure details of the tabernacle, you wonder how this could ever teach a greater principle about life. But my teacher forced us to think creatively, to think out of the box, to find a way to make even the most obscure words in the Torah relevant. Though sometimes this was difficult, it was rarely impossible, and it prompted us to see how every aspect of the Torah applied to ourselves.

This ensured that we walked away not with information, but with lessons for life. It ensured that we learned not only the details, but the greater values they connect with.

This simple technique made a great impact on my life. I came to see the Torah not only as a guidebook — what to do and what not to do — but as a teaching, a perspective and value system made for me, to help me become the best person I could possibly be.

Torah can be either a past-oriented, isolated expression of God in history or it can be vital and alive, touching a student with every word, teaching something important about his life. The best educational approaches take the Torah from the past into the future, making it more than a book of "do"s and "don't"s and transforming it into a relevant, meaningful, and inspiring way of life.

Conclusion

Providing reasons can help transform commitment to passion. They can strengthen the truth of the system in general and make each *mitzvah* more relevant, meaningful, and inspiring than they would be otherwise. They can take Torah beyond truth to meaning, connect it to a greater vision, and infuse every *mitzvah* with a purpose that moves us to commit.

It is worth reiterating that reasons need not come at the *expense* of faith and tradition. Reasons or benefits for particular *mitzvot* can work in conjunction with God to solidify belief. The point is that God should not be the only reason, for this ignores a host of elements that make observance most meaningful and awe-inspiring. When combined with belief in the Divine origin of Torah, reasons create a dual foundation for belief which is stronger than either one alone and which can motivate us to commit with enthusiasm.

CHAPTER 18

What Compromises Universal and National Meaning

Those who have gone off the derech for intellectual reasons either do not believe in the Torah's truth or fail to experience it as a meaningful way of life. The school plays the primary role in establishing these essential elements for commitment. Of course parents play a role as well. A child's education begins at home, but it doesn't end there. Parents are primarily responsible for it, but they entrust teachers to carry out the task.

Outside of the family, the school is the first world our children encounter. They spend more time there than they do at home and it is the only place solely dedicated to developing an intellectual connection to Yiddishkeit. So while the parents develop the first layer of connection to Torah — the emotional foundation — the school and its teachers create the next layer — the intellectual understanding, the knowledge, the meaning and the answers to life's most fundamental questions.

As such, the school plays a significant role in fostering or undermining observance. A study conducted by the Guttman Institute examining the National Jewish Population Survey concluded that "enrollment in day school is more important for Jewish involvement than being raised in an Orthodox home."[1] Another famous study called "Will Your Grandchildren be Jewish" found that the "strongest counter-assimilation effect is exerted by Orthodox day schools."[2] A Yeshiva University study also indicates how significant Jewish education is. In families with two *halachically* observant parents, a child's likelihood of maintaining observance rises significantly with the number of years of Jewish education.[3]

What We Teach

One of the most important elements in effective Jewish education is teaching the right subjects. And one of the greatest problems in our system today is that we do not focus nearly enough on *hashkafa,* the philosophical underpinnings of Judaism.

If students are to establish a strong belief in Judaism, they need to understand the universal and national visions of Judaism and the meaning and relevance of *mitzvot.* But these philosophical concepts require time, energy, and concentration, which we do not provide. We relegate *hashkafic* discussions to brief moments in time, assuming that our discussions about everything else will indirectly address it. Often they don't and, even when they do, they may be insufficient for establishing solid belief.

Hashkafah

Interestingly, *baal teshuva yeshivas,* which successfully inspire their students to believe, do the exact opposite. They dedicate a lot of time to *hashkafa* and they address it before anything else. Rather than begin with *halachah,* history, or holidays, they begin with ideas, reasons, a vision; everything else comes later. This lays a strong, broad foundation for belief, something substantial for the *halachic* details to rest upon. It creates an educational model that looks something like this:

Our children's educational model, on the other hand, is the exact opposite:

This foundation rests on a point — a detail, a *mitzvah*. It lacks a broad base needed to create context for the details and provide a firm foundation. Therefore it cannot meet intellectual challenges as effectively; a strong wind can easily tip it over. In addition, since the foundation rests upon details, *halachot,* observance rather than ideas and beliefs, when ritual is discarded for whatever reason, the whole structure crumbles. In the *baal teshuva* model, which has a philosophical foundation, even if the ritual is lost, there is belief to rely upon, which connects and may ultimately lead to renewed observance.[4]

Observant children today are far more like *baalei teshuva* than we think. They may not choose whether or not to become observant, but they do choose on some level whether or not to remain observant. Rabbi Mendel Weinbach of Ohr Somayach explains, "Both the religious dropout and the *baal teshuvah* must cross the same gate — the *hashkafa* barrier; one contemplates whether to get *out* through that gate while the other deliberates whether to go *in* through that gate."[5]

Providing our children with the educational model of *baal teshuva yeshivot* can help establish the same strong, passionate belief that *baalei teshuva* so admirably exhibit. This can be done throughout the educational process, addressing philosophical issues on a level children, and certainly teenagers, can comprehend. Seminars such as Project Chazon have already begun to address these issues; but they are insufficient responses to so fundamental a challenge. As external solutions, they can only go so far. Real change, the kind that lasts, demands that our current system change the status of *hashkafa* from a marginal to an integral part of education.

Talmud vs. Everything Else

Just as we focus on *halachah* at the expense of *hashkafa*, we focus on g*emorah* at the expense of other fundamentals. We teach Talmud disproportionately to everything else and we begin to do so at too young an age. This compromises our ability to establish a firm foundation in the basics of Judaism.

Educators echo this refrain in many ways. Rabbi Avi Rothenberg, an educator who specializes in *frum* kids-at-risk, recounted a story about a fourteen-year-old boy he met who came from a *yeshivish* family. The boy wore a black hat and had attended prestigious *yeshiva* day schools. But in the course of the conversation, Rabbi Rothenberg mentioned Yitro's name and the boy responded, "Who is Yitro?" This student could clearly answer questions about the minutia of *halachah*, but he was ignorant of basic Jewish history.

A few years ago, on Shabbat *Parshat Yitro,* I was trying to remember the Ten Commandments — pretty basic for someone who spent over 12 years in *yeshiva* day school. I could only come up with nine and felt ashamed. Later that day, we attended a lunch at the home of a local Rabbi whose son, in his late teens, was home for Shabbat with two of his friends. The three of them attended a world renowned (black hat) *yeshiva*. Surely they would know the Ten Commandments, especially after having read them in *shul* that morning. Between the three of them, they also came up with nine.

On a personal level, I didn't feel so bad anymore. But as a Jew, I felt even worse. Here we were — different kinds of Jews, with different kinds of educations, all observant, all serious about learning, all incapable of recounting details of the most fundamental experience the Jewish people ever had — the Revelation at Sinai.

It seems that, while there are more *yeshivas* today than ever before, there is also less knowledge of the basics. The worst part is that it seems not to bother us too much. After all, we know so much about so many aspects of Judaism, these basics feel insignificant. But they are not. They are the most significant of all. Look at how God Himself educates us. He took one moment in history to speak to man on the national level, and what did He choose to say? The Ten Commandments, the foundations of moral living, from which it has been argued all other *mitzvot* stem. And long before giving us any particular *halachot*, God started with creation, the history of the world and our people. Only after this knowledge do we receive our *halachic* obligations. If God is the ultimate parent, He is surely the ultimate educator. Why not emulate His approach in our educational curriculum?

Women's education tends to emulate this pattern. It is broad enough to incorporate *Chumash, Navi* (Prophets), holidays, women's issues, and sometimes *hashkafa*. But men's education is Talmudically centered, far too narrow to address fundamentals. Knowing who we are and what we are here for — the very things that provide an inspiring connection to the Torah — are to be found in the very things our young men are missing today in their education. This is not to say that there is something wrong with emphasizing Talmud study, which has carried Judaism through the ages. Rather, when we do so without a proper foundation in the fundamentals or at the expense of them, we lose a precious and essential tool for keeping our children connected to Torah.

Addressing fundamental subjects can also help students who are not Talmudically inclined. Excelling at Talmud study takes a certain kind of mind that not all children possess. These children may lose interest in learning, develop feelings of failure, low self-esteem, and may eventually turn away from observance as a result. A broader curriculum could provide other opportunities for these boys to shine, develop healthy self-esteem and love for learning, which ultimately is likely to create positive associations with Torah observance and draw them closer.

Unfortunately, as Eliyahu Bergstein explains in the *Jewish Observer*, unhealthy competition fueled by parental anxiety often prompts schools to focus more and more on Talmud and to do so at younger ages.[6] Rabbi Shapiro notes that over fifty years ago, the previous Bostoner Rebbe suggested creating a school with a broader curriculum to better accommodate students who found *gemorah* learning too intense. He was told by Reb Mendelovitz, "You are right; but what parents will send their kids there?"

As long as parents consider Talmud study more prestigious than other areas of Torah, as long as they compete — explicitly or implicitly — with other parents in terms of their children's *gemorah* learning, children may lack the very things they need to be inspired, remain observant, and create a strong foundation of belief in Torah.

Our schools serve our families. They are created by us and are therefore a reflection of ourselves and our values. They will not change until we, as parents, change.

The Past vs. the Future

As discussed in previous chapters, an important part of making Judaism meaningful is a vision for the future. The past is an essential foundation of our lives, what Rabbi Wein calls our "rearview mirror." But

219

the future holds our hope, inspires our souls, fulfills our potential, and provides Judaism with much of its value and relevance. Teaching Judaism without reference to the future is like writing a business plan without reference to future earning potential. No one would invest in such a business, and likewise, such a religion is missing great potential value. But today, at least in the classroom, we focus on the past at the expense of the future.

To complicate matters, when we do speak of the past, we tend to idealize it. Rabbi Ephraim Buchwald, who has inspired thousands of unaffiliated Jews through his National Jewish Outreach Program, explains that we tend to do this today more than ever, thus creating credibility problems for Judaism:

> ...the greatness of the Bible is that it freely exposes us to the shortcomings of the ancients, and demonstrates how great they became despite these issues! Jews do not subscribe to papal infallibility. It is not part of our tradition. Moses made mistakes. David made mistakes. Abraham made mistakes. They all made mistakes. Ours is suddenly the first generation when religious educators declare that such discussion is off limits.

Even the recent past is idealized. Rabbi Buchwald explains that "We look back upon pre-Holocaust Europe as if it was the most pure and pristine era in Jewish life. It wasn't. It was a generation that was on the verge of self destruction." But some "highly regarded publishers whitewash the prewar European reality. Pictures are airbrushed. They avoid showing photos of rabbis who weren't wearing hats," when in fact, "they all wore yarmulkes. They never show photos of *rebbetzins* (rabbis' wives) who didn't wear their hair covered," when in Lithuania, many women didn't cover their hair. Such truth is distorted in a variety of ways and Rabbi Buchwald believes this plays a role in people going off the derech.[7]

Why? Because in order to learn from the past and connect to it, we must be able to relate to it. If our forefathers or the rabbis in Lithuania were perfect, they become irrelevant because we will never be perfect. Their perfection makes them too different from us to learn from. When, however, we see their shortcomings, we feel more connected to them and are more willing to learn from them.

In addition, we often learn from others' mistakes more than their accomplishments. Through the imperfections of our leaders, we learn that greatness does not mean perfection, that mistakes do not demonize or absolve us from striving for holiness. It is precisely the imperfections that connect us to the people of the past and allow them to serve as role models for us. An ideal approach would balance a realistic examination of the past with a vibrant picture of the future.[8]

Ritual vs. Ethics

The final issue that can compromise meaning is our focusing on ritualistic *mitzvot* rather than ethical ones.

Mitzvot between man and man, the ethical ones, are essential for achieving a national vision, creating *kiddush Hashem,* and inspiring others to emulate Judaism. Our ability to wash our hands correctly or make the right *brachas* on food does not nearly accomplish these things as much as conducting business honestly, behaving with humility or honoring parents. These interpersonal actions inspire admiration in others. They create the kind of nation that can serve as a light. When compared to ritualistic *mitzvot,* they seem to be more effective for sanctifying God's name and creating a strongly bonded Jewish nation that can achieve Judaism's mission.

In addition, the ethical *mitzvot* seem to create more awe and respect for Torah and its wisdom than ritual *mitzvot* do. That may be why the sages explained that loving God means learning his Torah and then behaving socially in a way that makes God beloved. How do we make God beloved? The Talmud answers: with behaviors such as

221

speaking respectfully to others and doing business honestly.[9]

The ethical *mitzvot* also connect us to other Jews more directly than most ritual *mitzvot* do. And finally these *mitzvot* are the training ground for our relationship with God.[10] So when we fulfill these ethical *mitzvot*, we establish the foundation for doing so in all other *mitzvot* as well. This may be why the *Mishnah* tells us that a sin *bain adam lemakom* is a sin against God, but a sin against our fellow man is a sin both against man and against God.[11]

Although these *mitzvot* inspire, foster self-actualization, national-actualization and ultimately universal-actualization more than ritual *mitzvot*, we tend to focus on rituals almost at the expense of ethical *mitzvot*.

Children spend hours learning the details of hand-washing, but they have no idea what exactly *chessed* means or how to prioritize *tzedakah* funds. This is exacerbated outside the classroom as well where we often focus on ritual *mitzvot* almost to the exclusion of others, and where our expectations of children focus more on ritual *mitzvot*. After all, ritual infractions often spark more anger and rejection toward our children than interpersonal infractions.

In addition, what is our criterion for being an observant person? The criterion seems to be almost wholly observance of ritual *mitzvot* — *mitzvot bain adam lemakom* as opposed to *mitzvot bain adam lechaviaro*. As Rabbi Joseph Telushkin, the well known Jewish educator explains:

> Among many Jews, Orthodox and non-Orthodox as well, the word 'religious' has acquired an exclusively ritualistic connotation. If two Jews are speaking about a third and the question is raised as to whether or not the person is religious, the answer will be based exclusively on the person's level of ritual observance: 'He keeps Shabbat and *kashrut*, he is religious. He doesn't keep them, he is

not.' Ethics are treated almost like an extra-curricular activity — nice, but not that important in defining a person's religiosity.[12]

It would be wiser to shift our focus and at least make more room for ethical *mitzvot* that are *bain adam lechavairo*. This is true for many reasons. First, everyone can relate to the importance of *mitzvot* like kindness and charity. Everyone wants the goodness they foster and no one needs to be convinced of their value. So they are an easy avenue for drawing people close to Torah and creating respect for Torah.

They are also an easier avenue for making Torah relevant to today's Jew because as long as man exists, interpersonal relationships will be important. That is why though you hear people argue that rituals such as Sabbath, Passover, and prayer belong to the world of the past, you rarely if ever hear people say that ethics are no longer relevant.

So, if the Torah does a good job of addressing ethics and improving interpersonal relationships through them, it will always be perceived as relevant and important and people will more likely pursue it. As Rabbi Riskin says, "It will always be relevant if it creates more secure families, better kinds of people....Religion has to be identified with morality if people are going to respect religion.... "[13]

In addition, people who are not ritualistically oriented will benefit from a focus on ethics. There are those among us who simply do not relate to ritual observance as well as others. The rituals are laborious and uninspiring for these people, not because they have the wrong values but simply because they have unique personalities. Addressing these other *mitzvot* can provide an outlet for less ritualistically oriented people to take pride and feel connected in ways they may not otherwise.

The most important reason to focus more on ethical *mitzvot* may be to help kids who have gone off the derech. When a child goes off the derech a number of things happen. Religiously, he no longer sees himself as observant and often begins to feel different, disconnected and apart from his observant neighbors and their values. Emotionally, on some level, he might feel like a failure for not living up to their expectations. His self-esteem may then suffer and he may spiral into deviant behavior or complete disconnection from his world. Emphasizing ethical Jewish values and *mitzvot* can be a safety net for such a child.

If he has learned to value interpersonal *mitzvot* as uniquely Jewish, if he believes that keeping them properly also makes him *frum*, he might feel more connected to Judaism, his family and community. That feeling of connection alone can temper some of the other problems associated with going off the derech and help him to eventually return. In addition, he can take pride in keeping these *mitzvot*, and feel good about himself as a person and as a Jew — because at least he can live up to some of God's expectations of him.

If focusing on interpersonal *mitzvot* has so many benefits, why do we focus on ritual as much as we do? Perhaps because the rest of the world focuses on being a good person, we focus on being good Jews. Perhaps we do so because *mitzvot* between man and God and their rituals distinguish us from other nations and from nonobservant Jews. After all, everyone believes in being a good person, but we alone believe in keeping the laws of Shabbat.

The problem is that this is not entirely true. It is not only Shabbat and *kashrut* that make us unique, but rather the whole of Torah. It is true that other peoples and religions believe in giving charity, honoring parents, and not speaking ill of others. But how many define these matters as sensitively and specifically as we do? How many translate those values into real life in such moving and sensitive ways? One cannot help but be awed by the Torah's foresight, detail, and revolutionary definitions of proper interpersonal behavior.

So it is not Shabbat alone that makes us unique, but every *mitzvah*. There is a Jewish way to be a friend, a child, a teacher, and a doctor. There is a Jewish way to give charity and express kindness. To ignore these *mitzvot* is to deny the unique and powerful meaning of half the Torah. And that half may be the more inspirational one that can best promote pride, create *kiddush Hashem,* and foster personal and national actualization.

If we want to create more inspiring connections to Judaism, it would help to teach our children Judaism's vision of ethical obligations. This would help them respect our tradition, find meaning and relevance in it, and gain the tools to achieve our national goals through *kiddush Hashem.* For those who have gone off the derech, focusing on ethical *mitzvot* can help maintain connection and self esteem. Of course, this requires not only teaching these principles, but also living them and including them in our definition of a good Jew, which can make a strong impact in creating the holistic approach to a meaningful Torah that our children need.

CHAPTER 19

What Compromises Personal Meaning

As the previous chapter indicates, emphasizing certain subjects in Jewish education at the expense of others can compromise the very information that makes Judaism most meaningful. The principle that applied in the previous chapter in terms of finding universal and national meaning in Judaism, applies to finding personal meaning as well. There are certain approaches in education today which compromise our ability to find personal meaning through *mitzvot.*

Love vs. Fear

One of those approaches is our focusing on fear rather than love. Numerous people I interviewed said that they felt that if they broke Shabbat, lightening would strike — not literally of course, but there is a sense of fear surrounding observance that creates that feeling.

Sometimes they get that feeling explicitly, as did David when in second grade he heard the tape of screams from *gehenom*: "'Oy vey. I am hanging from my tongue. If only I wouldn't have spoken loshon hara." Sometimes that message comes less explicitly, like when parents or teachers react dramatically to *halachic* infractions. Such was the case with Dena whose father forced her to *daven*. He behaved in a way that led her to believe she would experience devastating consequences for breaking *halachah*.

The "lightening strikes" mentality indicates a fear-based observance rather than a love-based one, and fostering a fear-based relationship with God, whether in the classroom or in life, can hinder commitment to observance.

Joseph was raised in Israel and educated in the national religious school system. He says his doubts about Judaism began at age fifteen when he started to realize that "one does or doesn't do all sorts of things, not from religious conviction, but from fear." The more he realized this, the less inclined he was to keep the *mitzvot*. He says that he was "somewhat afraid because of the threats and punishments I hear about all the time; but to my relief nothing happened, the sky didn't fall." Joseph ended up taking off his *kippah* and going off the derech. Fear was just not enough to keep him connected.

Fear works well when we are young but loses its power when we mature. For many, especially in this generation, it will not work in the first place. And children whose observance is based on fear will likely lose their observance when their fear disappears.

In general, fear is negative rather than positive and therefore less effective than love as a motivator for observance. So if it works well to motivate observance, it does so in a supporting role to love, which is the positive, more mature motivator for observance. As our Sages say: "The reward of one who fears God extends to one thousand generations; while the reward of one who loves God extends to thousands of generations."[1] The Rambam goes one step further stating that we come to fear God by loving Him first, by contemplating His wondrous creations and thereby standing in awe of Him.[2] This creates a positive relationship to God, in which we serve Him as a lover to a beloved rather than a slave to a master. The alternative relationship is more of slave to master, one which the Torah itself seems to deem a necessary evil not to be perpetuated indefinitely.

Negative vs. Positive

Connected to this is our focusing on the negatives within Judaism at the expense of the positives. There are many no's in Judaism — *mitzvot lo taaseh* — prohibitions we must refrain from in order to be holy. But the more we focus on those, the more negatively we frame observance and Judaism. The more we focus on positives, on the other hand, the more pleasantly we tend to see Judaism and its overall mission. We currently spend a lot of time discussing prohibitions and not enough time focusing on things that are permissible and inherently positive.

How then can we focus more on positive elements in Torah? First, by preempting the negative *mitzvot* with positive ones, just as God does by telling Adam to eat from all the trees before telling him not to eat from one. This creates a positive association and foundation for all of Torah, including its restrictions. Second, we can balance and temper restrictions with pleasurable activities so that children are not deprived of joy and pleasure because of Torah. Last, we can strive to paint even the negative elements with positivism. One way of doing so is to make the values that underlie the *mitzvot* explicit. The *expression* of a Jewish value may be difficult or restrictive, but its *purpose* is always positive and beneficial. For example, being required to make *brachas* can seem cumbersome. But when we focus on the underlying purpose — creating appreciation and happiness in life — the potentially cumbersome becomes more freeing. Teaching *mitzvot* in this light can make the seemingly negative, positive and can turn prohibitions into opportunities.

Happiness and Pleasure vs. Duty

Connected to this is a focus on duty and obligation rather than pleasure and happiness. Perhaps because secular society overly focuses on happiness, we focus on duty. But while society at large goes too far in valuing happiness, we have gone too far in almost ignoring it completely.

The truth is Judaism mandates that, when happiness conflicts with moral duty, duty takes precedence. But they do not always conflict. Often the two work together. Judaism rarely advocates duty at the *expense* of pleasure and happiness. In fact, one might say it advocates the *mitzvot* as means to pleasure and happiness. It is just that in most cases, rather than foster physical pleasure, Judaism strives for spiritual pleasure and happiness. It seeks long-term happiness that is experienced on a deep and lasting level which sometimes requires sacrificing momentary happiness. But the fact remains, Judaism values happiness and the *mitzvot* are the means to achieving it in the ultimate way.

But often we do not send this message. We tend to ignore the importance of happiness and the *mitzvot's* ability to foster it; and the value of striving for it in our daily lives. We tend to ignore the value of experiences that foster pleasure such as dancing, listening to music, and eating gourmet food. Instead of defining how and when these experiences can provide positive pleasure and growth for the soul, we seem to minimize or ignore them altogether — both in our classrooms and in our daily lives. Duty often comes at the *exclusion* of the pleasure and happiness it is meant to achieve.

This squeezes the joy out of living a Torah life. It ignores one of the important strengths of Judaism. This can prompt our children to feel that somehow the secular world offers them something that Judaism does not — the chance to be happy and feel proud about valuing happiness. If the secular world is the only one talking about happiness and pleasure, it can seem that it alone has the answers for achieving it.

Rather than perpetuate that illusion, Judaism should make its case for happiness. Since people value happiness, this may be one of the more important ways of drawing people, especially our children, toward observance.

The Physical and Beautiful

The same goes for the physical and beautiful. We seem to ignore the fact that body and soul work together and each play important roles in serving *Hashem*. The Baal Shem Tov explained this relationship by comparing the soul to a king who hears beautiful music as he walks down the street. The king wants to dance but can't for he lacks a partner. Soon a man approaches, but he doesn't want to dance. So the king gives him a few drinks to intoxicate him to dance. And after a while, the two begin dancing.[3]

Our souls are like the king, who wants to dance but needs a partner. The body is the partner of our soul, and it must be satisfied if it is to join us in dance. Sometimes we can feed the soul only through the body; sometimes what seems to speak to the body really speaks to the soul. Physical experiences that seem superficial may in fact be deeply spiritual. Nature, beauty, art, and music are filtered through the body, but they speak to our souls. They seem to be physical experiences, but they move the spirit. That may be why Rabbi Shlomo Wolbe asserts that an appreciation for beauty, as in nature, is essential in a religious child's development. He explains that:

> We must show our children the world's beauty... It would be sad if a child grew up lacking the emotional development to respond with real awe to *Hashem's* handiwork. When we contemplate the creation's wonder, we see and absorb *emunah* (belief); and we all need well-developed *emunah*.[4]

What Rabbi Wolbe applies to nature, Rabbi Cardozo applies to art and music. He explains that beauty and art belong "to a world beyond words."

> Real art does not record the visible but rather it reveals the invisible...natural beauty and art are conducive to religious awakening...It is a means of giving form to our

inner feelings and consequently to be in touch with the mystery of our inner lives. It is our duty to stand in awe and this is provided for in all that is beautiful. ...To look at a Rembrandt and to have its beauty flowing through one's veins is not only a delight, but above all, a religious experience that God in His kindness granted His creatures. To deny oneself this opportunity is turning his back on the Creator. To refuse to listen to a refined piece of music is to close oneself off from life itself.[5]

These principles apply to all majestic creations, whether the handiwork of God or man. They should be valued because they are a means to achieving the Godliness we seek in a way that other *mitzvot* may not. Perhaps this is why the Talmud tells us that "A beautiful wife, a beautiful dwelling place, and beautiful furnishings broaden the mind of man" and why the Temple service was full of music and song.[6] It is also why Samson Raphael Hirsch went to Switzerland in his old age. When asked why, he responded that when God would ask him "'Samson Raphael! Did you see My mountains in Switzerland?'" he wanted to have an answer.

Information vs. Inspiration

Knowledge without inspiration is like a marriage without love. All the pieces may be there, but the tie that binds the two is missing. Today we have a lot of knowledge and not enough inspiration. This is unfortunate because while information is easily forgotten, inspiration lives on and brings us closer to Judaism.

When children gain information without inspiration, the seeds of learning are sown without nourishment. But when they are inspired, with or without information, they gain positive feelings which in turn often motivate them to continue seeking knowledge on their own, long after they leave school. So the learning experience that is pleasurable and inspirational will foster future growth and learning even if it comes at the temporary expense of learning itself. This may be why William Butler Yeats declared that "education is not the filling of a pail, but the lighting of a fire."

Educators can light a fire by choosing inspiring topics, using colorful materials, and incorporating activities and games into the learning process. The most effective element may be a teacher's passion for a subject — for passion is contagious. There are many ways to inspire our children. The point is to find one that can make Torah learning "the lighting of a fire" that can turn an ancient tradition into a living fountain of enthusiasm, longing, personal meaning, and satisfaction.[7]

— CHAPTER 20 —

The Role of Questions

What we teach is essential to establishing a strong belief in Judaism. But it must be complemented by a student's ability to ask questions. This should not be too problematic, for Judaism has always been marked by a tradition of questioning and debate. It seems almost a part of our national character.

Our great Biblical leaders throughout Jewish history have been those who dared to question, seek the truth, and challenge the status quo — sometimes even God himself. Our great Talmudic leaders have done the same, using argument and questioning to decipher and apply Torah. In fact, "The entire Rabbinic literature is nothing less than an anthology of what the Sages called 'argument for the sake of heaven.'"[1] Debate developed the Torah, brought it to life and allowed it to remain relevant for all time.

In Torah study, challenging and examining issues from opposing sides is essential. It strengthens our understanding, broadens our insight, and solidifies our belief. The giants of Jewish tradition always understood this, which is why Rabbi Hayyim Volozhiner taught us that "to differ with a revered teacher is a *milchemet mitzvah* (a holy war) in which we give no quarter to an intellectual opponent because of station or prestige."[2]

Understanding an alternative viewpoint is so important that, the Talmud says, Jewish law sides with the Academy of Hillel rather than the Academy of Shamai precisely because "they were much more accommodating and accepting of insults and, whenever they were asked a question, they first presented the opposing view."[3]

The Danger of Stifling Questions

Despite the history and importance of debate, we seem to have a hard time with questions today. Sometimes we do not accept them at all. At other times, we accept them only if they are "within the system," as long as they don't challenge the fundamentals of Torah.

Students repeatedly express frustration and sometimes bitterness about this reality, and some go off the derech because of it. In fact, 51% of those who responded to the web survey indicated they felt they could not ask questions in class, and 64% felt that when they did, their questions were not answered satisfactorily.

An organization in Israel, which helps *charedi* (Ultra-Orthodox) people who want to leave the fold, includes stories on their web site of those who have left observance. When introducing the stories, they say:

> The interviewees differ widely in their personality and in the way they reached the decision to leave. But they share a common overwhelming motivation: the desire to stop living a lie. They all testify to the loneliness and isolation they suffered when they began to question the Orthodox life. There was no one with whom they could share their struggle because no one is allowed to doubt the validity of Orthodox beliefs and social structure; such doubts are considered grave crimes. Punishment can be severe.

Stifling questions is a common phenomenon and it easily causes a fear and loneliness that can be hard to bear. It can cause people to go off the derech and, beyond that, can create great bitterness toward Torah and *frum* people. As one formerly *yeshivish* Jew told me, "Orthodoxy says, 'this is the truth and if you are different then you're an idiot, or wrong, or blind.'" Fear kept him "in the closet" for years. He felt he would be ostracized if he raised questions, a feeling which trapped him and made him feel he was "contemplating evil."

Why is stifling questions so devastating? How can it cause people to go off the derech and to become so bitter? Dr. Meir Wikler explains that when a child asks an intellectual question and is stifled or condemned for it, the potentially intellectual experience turns into a negative emotional one for "The child reached out and was rejected."[4] He also experiences a lack of safety, which can easily make him feel isolated and alone, confused and dejected. These emotional consequences can easily cause him to go off the derech.

Truth seekers, questioners and intellectually oriented people especially need a safe environment to express themselves. They, more than others, tend to need room to explore, search, and give voice to their doubt. If given a safe environment in which to do so, they may remain interested and engaged even if they never find answers to their questions. But if silenced by fear of rejection, they can suffer greatly. They may well develop negative feelings about Judaism and learning that cause them to go off the derech. The same is true of those with low self-esteem and those who are curious by nature.

The stifling of questions can also hinder one's relationship with his teacher and association with learning. Consider the following story that was recounted by Rabbi Avraham Goldhar, an educator who has developed a new method for memorizing the Torah. In one classroom he visited, a young boy raised his hand and asked a question and his teacher, who was standing on the side of the class, interrupted before Rabbi Goldhar could respond. "Why do you ask such a stupid question!" he shouted. "It would have been better if you had kept your mouth shut and we wouldn't know how stupid you are!"

Can we imagine how humiliated, ashamed and belittled this child must have felt to hear his role model attack him that way? Can he possibly feel good about Torah learning or develop respect for his rebbe? Worst of all, can he feel confident as a person, and how many more such instances will it take until he loses all self-esteem?

Often teachers do not attack the student himself, but they attack the question so strongly that the child himself feels attacked. One girl on the *Frumteen* website says that when she asked her teacher how Rashi knows the answer, her teacher "got red in the face and started screaming" telling her that she goes to Bais Yaacov and shouldn't ask questions like that. The teacher went so far as to say that if she persisted in asking such questions, she would "go to *gehenom* (hell)." The girl wrote on the website that she didn't want to go to *gehenom*; she just wanted to understand. She ended her comments with the question, "Am I really a bad person for asking questions?"

Luckily, experiences are not usually that extreme. They are usually more along the lines of the following story: A high school boy said that a phrase in the Torah "made no sense," and his teacher yelled at him, "It makes no sense? Who are *you* to say the Torah makes no sense! You mean you don't understand it!" The student's question was meant sincerely. But when he was berated for asking it, he lost the ability to respect his teacher and therefore learn from him.

So, negative reactions to questions compromise the student, his relationship with the teacher, and eventually his learning and observance as well. Once a child's question is rejected, he loses the safe and accepting environment he requires to fulfill his emotional needs. This in turn affects his relationship with his rebbe, his learning in general, observant people, and sometimes Yiddishkeit itself.

To compound these issues, the inability to ask questions also creates intellectual problems. Questions are a vital means of gaining information. Without them, a child may be unable to build a sufficient foundation for belief. The more fundamental the question is — revolving around God or His giving the Torah — the more important it becomes to address. Of course, these are the very questions we have the most trouble accepting. But our inability to do so can leave a gaping hole in a child's belief. Even smaller questions, if there are enough of them, can compromise belief, for eventually they can add up to one big question mark. And as one formerly observant Jew put it, "I cannot worship a question mark."

The Advantages of Encouraging Questions

Rather than stifle questions, we should do everything to encourage them. There are numerous benefits to doing so such as fostering safety, acceptance and self-esteem, which creates positive associations with Torah, teachers, and learning.

In addition, asking and answering questions makes learning active and interesting. In fact, the question-answer method has been proven the most effective way to learn. That may be why the question-answer method pervades the Talmud as well as other texts like the Pesach Haggadah. Question-asking makes the difference between the excited voices in a room full of *bachrim* (students) studying Talmud and the stale, stoic environment of a lecture hall where students formally, quietly and passively receive information. One is alive and stimulating, while the other is uninspiring.

Create a Personal Connection

Questioning also makes learning more personal. It allows us to bring ourselves into our learning, to extend ourselves to the Torah. It creates the moments in which we acquire the Torah, where the God of our fathers becomes our own, and the Torah transforms from something that is meaningful in general to something that is meaningful to me.

We all hear the same things in a classroom, but we are intrigued or disturbed by different things in different ways. When we question, we respond to our learning through the filter and expression of our unique personalities. In essence, when we question, we are saying: I connect with this in some way, but something is missing. Help me fill the hole; close the circuit and make this information a part of who I am. This is the moment when Torah can become most personal to us, most relevant, and most likely to become an integral part of who we are.

Questions Cause Teachers to Learn

Questions also help the teacher to learn. They are opportunities for the teacher to grow as well the student. A wise teacher knows he can learn most from his students, even the seemingly heretical ones. Rabbi Meir continued to learn with his teacher Elisha Ben Abuya, even after Elisha had became a heretic. When his colleagues chided him for doing so, Rabbi Meir replied, "I take the fruit and cast away the rind."[5] We may need to look behind the sometimes defiant attitudes of our students to find the "fruit."

Demonstrates the Strength of Torah and the Value of Truth

When we respond to questions appropriately, not only do we strengthen positive qualities of the student and ourselves, but also of Torah. Allowing questions to be asked demonstrates the strength of Torah. When something is strong, stable, and well founded, it can withstand challenge. When it is weak and unstable, it will cower and hide. So when Judaism welcomes questions and criticism, it demonstrates strength. This is essential for making Judaism's case and fostering pride in Torah.

Every time we stifle questions, we inadvertently send the message that we, too, believe Judaism cannot withstand intellectual scrutiny, that we are afraid questions may reveal an ugly truth — that Judaism has no answers and that it is not true after all. This is why the Maharal of Prague says that:

...It is proper, out of love of reason and knowledge, that you not reject anything that opposes you own ideas, especially so if [your adversary] does not intend merely to provoke you, but rather to declare his beliefs. And even if such [beliefs] are opposed to your own faith and religion, do not say, "Speak not, close your mouth.' ... on the contrary, you should, at such times, say: 'Speak up as much as you want, say whatever you wish and do not say later that had you been able to speak, you would have replied further.' For one who presses his opponent to hold his peace and refrain from speaking, demonstrates the weakness of his own religious faith... curbing the words of an opponent in religious matters is naught but the curbing and enfeebling of religion [itself]...Thus it is wrong simply to reject an opponent's ideas; instead, draw him close to you and delve into his words....[6]

We should not be afraid that questions or our lack of answers will undermine Torah.

Judaism has answered many questions. It has survived generations of challenges, verbal and otherwise; it has outlasted many belief systems and it still thrives today. Surely it can withstand the questions of our six year olds, sixteen year olds or sixty year olds. And even if it fails to answer them sometimes, it will survive. There are some questions that cannot be answered, that should not be answered. Some things are meant to be mysterious. There are other questions which cannot be answered quickly, which require years of struggle and life experience before the answer is understood. There are yet others which have only personal answers, not generic ones. These require each of us to make a journey throughout our own lives to find our own answers.

If we understand this, we need not find questions or a lack of answers as threatening. We begin to see them not as weakening Torah, but rather as revealing the Torah's true nature — that of a deep, complex, and sometimes mysterious entity that beautifully mirrors the nature of life and the mysterious God who created it.

Why We Stifle Questions: We Consider Them Heretical

It is worth asking: if questions are so important, why do we inhibit or reject them? One reason is that we consider them heretical, especially when they are fundamental in nature. Alternatively, it may seem that our children should have a *naaseh venishma* attitude — *we will do and we will listen* said the Jewish people at Mt. Sinai, meaning that they would observe first and listen to the reasoning later. But our children do not live in an ideal world of faith. They have not seen God like the Jews in the desert nor do they live in a God-centered world. They experience, on their own level, great challenges to faith. In their world, faith needs reason. God cannot be accepted on blind faith[7] but rather upon a faith that challenges, that questions and that answers.

We Consider Them Challenges, Not Questions

Sometimes we dismiss questions because the questioner himself seems disingenuous or defiant; or we take them as a personal affront. This can cause us to respond with anger, disdain or even mild dismissal, which may easily result in a feeling of rejection in the child. In such cases, it would be wise to give the benefit of doubt, to remember that our perceptions may be wrong and that, even if we are correct, it is important to take the question itself seriously and respond to it respectfully for a number of reasons.

First, doing so fosters an open and accepting environment which benefits *all* students. It creates a feeling of safety so that students feel they can be honest and open with their doubts and concerns. In addition, other students may share the question but simply not have voiced it. Or they may have the question in the future in which case answering the defiant student's question today can help other students tomorrow.

Finally, if the student really is defiant or embittered about Torah, answering his question appropriately becomes all the more important. It is precisely the defiant student who needs to be embraced by his teacher's response, who needs to feel warmth and acceptance. He, of all students, needs to be treated well, taken seriously, and respected for his mind and his search.

The defiant students — though the hardest and perhaps most frustrating for teachers — may present the biggest opportunity. That may be why when asked how a *yeshiva* should treat a troublemaker, the Chazon Ish responded that the student is not to be blamed and the school should make every attempt to put up with him and draw him near. The process of doing so might take months or even years. But if a teacher can stay the course and respect the child, he will earn the child's respect and make a significant impact on his education and personal development.

We Are Insecure in Ourselves

Some teachers stifle questions because they are insecure in their knowledge, afraid that they are ignorant or will be perceived that way.

But we are all ignorant of some things, and admitting that to students with the words "I don't know" can have numerous positive ramifications. These words can help a student feel proud; he was able to stump the teacher, which creates an affirming emotional experience. They also demonstrate the teacher's honesty and humility. This inspires awe and confidence, as well as trust, which helps foster relationship. These educational benefits of humility may be why Moshe Rabbeinu — our Teacher — was of all things humble.[8]

Admitting ignorance also teaches that there is no need to feel shame. Ignorance can be the beginning of great knowledge if followed by a search for an answer. Especially when a teacher follows up his "I don't know" with "I'll find out and get back to you" he teaches vital lessons about growth and education.

First, he demonstrates with his actions that he believes there is an answer out there which establishes confidence in Torah; second, he demonstrates that he cares enough about learning and the student to seek an answer on his own time and get back to the student with it. Third, he shows the student that learning is a process, one that continues throughout life. It never ends — not even for teachers who are experts in their field. He role models for the student in a way which words alone cannot do. And what a powerful moment it is when the teacher comes back in a few days with an answer. The teacher has cared enough to invest time for the education of that one particular student.

So, rather than feel insecure about our inability to answer questions, we should embrace those moments as rare teaching opportunities, as unprecedented opportunities to affect a child, to role model for him, and to develop our own education as well.

Afraid it will Compromise Other Students

Finally, we sometimes stifle questions because we fear confusing other students or because we simply don't have time. In these situations, we could at least address questions outside the classroom so that the student gets his answer without sacrificing the needs of the class.

Conclusion

When we think of this issue as merely stifling questions, it is hard to understand how it can cause people to go off the derech. But when we understand the emotional, intellectual and spiritual ramifications of denying questions, it becomes clear. That may be why it has been said that it is not for the lack of answers that our children go off the derech, but for the absence of questions. Respecting and fostering them, therefore, plays an important role in helping kids stay on the derech.

CHAPTER 21

What Compromises Learning: Teachers, Students, and Parents

The things we teach and the attitude with which we teach them are the most important elements of successful education. But content alone cannot create belief or secure observance. The educational process is not only about what we teach, but who does the teaching, who the learning, and what kind of support there is for the educational process. The quality of the teachers, the nature of students, and the attitude of parents can all either serve to support or compromise what is taught in school.

Teachers

As discussed previously, teachers play the greatest role in education and the establishment of belief in Yiddishkeit. According to a *BusinessWeek* article entitled "How to Fix America's Schools," few factors "affect students' performances more than the quality of their teachers. A Tennessee study in 1996…found that fifth-graders who had three years of effective teaching improved their math scores by 83%, vs. a 29% gain for students with ineffective teachers."[1] What makes teachers effective? The requirements in Jewish education are somewhat more stringent than general education.

What They Know

First, Jewish teachers need to be highly educated in Chumash, Tanach, *Halachah* and *Hashkafa*. We take this for granted but teachers themselves are often ignorant of the basics. Nowadays, the need for teachers to know may extend to a secular education as well. As more and more *yeshiva* kids are exposed to the outside world, they increasingly see teachers who are ignorant of the outside world as "primitive" — as one interviewee put it — which undermines respect and relationship.

In addition, teachers should be taught to recognize and address different learning styles. As Dr. Lazerson explains in his article in *Jewish Action* magazine,

> The general *yeshiva* system has been far too inflexible. We have built institutions that cater to a certain kind of student: the child who wants to learn and who doesn't mind sitting in one place for most of the day...Many of our children simply do not fit this mold. Some require more individualization. They need work sheets and homework sheets suited to them. Others need a different approach entirely. The visual learner will be lost in a Talmud class taught orally. In such a case, the rebbe will need to draw diagrams on the board and make sure the student isn't drowning in a sea of words. Disregarding the Torah-honored principle of *"chanoch lanaar al pi darko"* (teach a child according to his way), we have changed the passage to read *"al pi darkeinu,"* according to our ways! This slight grammatical difference has created a demanding stifling system where individual learning styles are largely ignored.[2]

Finally, according to Nefesh, the International Network of Orthodox Mental Health Professionals, teachers must learn to identify the signs of child abuse, learning disabilities, eating disorders, depression, drug problems, AD(H)D, and symptoms of molestation.[3] Teachers often have more exposure to students than anyone else, so if they fail to identify these problems, it can mean that a child struggles with them indefinitely. This can compromise his emotional health and intellectual development and may lead him off the derech as well. But success in identifying these can turn a potential problem into an asset, especially in the case of those with learning disabilities who are often blessed with other exceptional talents that compensate.[4] If we can identify these and work with them, the potential liability can become an asset.[5]

Who They Are

Who teachers are is just as important as what they know. Teachers with poorly developed characters compromise the learning process as well as Torah in general. Their students may get knowledge but not values. This is uniquely problematic in Torah education, for Torah is about imparting a way of life, a value system, and this can only be gained from someone whom a student admires, respects, and wants to emulate.

As Rabbi Yaakov Shapiro puts it, "A student who despises his rebbe — or is despised by him — is much more likely to drop out than a student who cannot make the grades."[6] It is of the utmost importance therefore that teachers be sensitive, kind, respectful, honest, and exemplary of Torah values.

Relationship with the Students

Good *middot* must then translate into a loving and respectful attitude toward students. Rabbi Nosson Einfeld of Bnei Brak, faculty member of Kollel Chazon Ish and student of Rav Chaim Kanievsky, says "…every *mechanech* (religious teacher) must love and care for his *talmidim* (students) as though they were his own children. If he is unable to do this, his *talmidim* suffer, with some going so far as dropping out of *yeshiva* completely. Everything else is handling the symptoms, not curing the cause."[7]

Part of developing a loving relationship involves knowing who students are and being able to relate to them. One interviewee remarked that his *yeshivish* teacher was so out of touch with his Modern Orthodox students, that he would condemn them repeatedly for playing basketball on Shabbat. This made the students feel distant from him, as if their teacher had no right to try and influence their behavior.

The Haggadah and its four sons show us the importance of relating to a student. The four sons each have questions. But before telling us what those questions are or how to answer them, the Haggadah tells us who is doing the asking. You must know whom you are teaching in order to teach effectively and earn the right to influence them. This is where *mashgiachim* whose sole purpose is to get to know a child can be so effective. As Rabbi Shaya Cohen notes, in developing caring relationships and relating to students, they supplement education and make it more effective.[8]

How They Observe

Exemplary Torah observance is also essential. The more attractively teachers observe Torah, the more effectively they inspire our children. It is hard to define what makes observance attractive but we know it when we see it. It starts with an admirable character and extends to things like a love and passion for Torah, a positive attitude toward *mitzvot,* and even dressing presentably or fashionably. All of these make *halachic* observance attractive.

Since they are teachers, the most important part of observance may be their attitude toward learning. Rabbi Moshe Ibn Ezra tells us that "what comes from the heart goes to the heart," so the best way of ensuring that our children love learning is to have teachers who love it themselves. If teachers are excited and passionate about Torah learning, they will infect students with that spirit and children will likely continue learning long after their *yeshiva* education has passed.

Where They Teach

Just as important as what we teach, how we teach, and who is doing the teaching is the environment in which that teaching occurs, both physically and emotionally. The physical environment can do a lot to help or hinder learning. Factors such as cleanliness, overcrowding, adequate heating, or air-conditioning can all affect the educational process. They can either make learning easier or harder, creating positive associations with Torah or negative ones.

The emotional environment is important as well. For example, students' spying on each other in order to help educators enforce rules can be detrimental to the learning environment, as Rabbi Shapiro explains, a "spy vs. spy environment in a school generates animosity, and distrusted students often live up to the negative image their role models have of them. A positive, friendly atmosphere is crucial for healthy development."[9] Anything that compromises that — whether it be invading privacy, not respecting students' feelings or intelligence, passively allowing teasing to occur or directly instigating it — can create an unsafe, unpleasant environment that undermines learning and therefore observance.

Students: Learning Disabilities and Emotional Issues

Learning disabilities too — Attention Deficit Disorder, Oppositional Defiant Disorder, Depression, Dyslexia, and Language Disorders — can play a role in complicating the educational process.

Nefesh has estimated that 6 to 10% of the school-aged population in the United States is learning disabled.[10] ADD affects 7 to 10% of the Jewish community nationwide.[11] Although these disabilities are considered physical in nature, they can create emotional obstacles for learning.

Children with learning disabilities are emotionally vulnerable, perhaps more so than the average student. It is harder for them to learn in conventional ways and therefore harder to achieve the success that parents and educators are looking for, which can create negative feelings or associations. If a disability is identified or if a child learns to naturally compensate for his limitation, it may not present much of a problem. But if not, it can create great problems. A child may become frustrated by struggling with things that come naturally to other students. He may fail to meet expectations, which can lead to low self-esteem. If out of ignorance or frustration his parents or teachers berate or criticize his failure, his negative feelings will magnify and intensify. These experiences can ultimately compromise his love for learning as well as for Yiddishkeit. This may be why experts have long noted that there is a disproportionate number of learning disabled children among those who drop observance.

Like learning disabilities, emotional issues ranging from mild unhappiness to larger issues of divorce and abuse can affect the student and learning process in general. They can result in passivity, disinterest, active disengagement; or a negative, disrespectful attitude to teachers, other students or the subjects being studied.

The Parents and Their Interaction with the School

Finally, it is worth noting that parents too play an important role in supporting or hindering their child's education. In the first place, they themselves must foster education and help their children find the school that best addresses their particular needs. They must also establish a working relationship with the teachers and administration.

In part, that means that as much as possible, the school and home must present a unified front when it comes to matters of Jewish *hashkafa*. When either side compromises the authority of the other, the child's relationship to Torah is undermined. That does not mean that the philosophies must be identical or that there can be no disagreement on fundamental issues. But any disagreements must occur respectfully, with each side supporting the other as much as possible. Sometimes a simple conversation can prevent tremendous conflict.

Parents must strive to abide by school rules both inside and outside the classroom. In return, schools should be afforded respect for the great responsibility they bear in educating children. Making their job more difficult is unfair and counterproductive. If parents are primary authority figures, the school and its rebbes are secondary ones. And to undermine or ignore the school's rules is to undermine the child's respect for his rebbes and the Torah they teach.

In part, this means choosing the right school in the first place. Dr. Lob explains that oftentimes a student's problems result from being placed in a wrong school. One environment may make him feel like a terrible person whereas another environment might bolster his self-esteem.[12] If the child or his parents are simply unable to comply or meet expectations, it might be right to find another school. Unfortunately, sometimes due to societal expectations, parents find it shameful to do so. Alternatively, they may be unaware of their child's needs, have limited financial resources, or may lack available options. But if they keep their children in the wrong school or they undermine school rules, a pattern of conflict can occur that compromises the educational process, the child's self-esteem, and ultimately observance itself.

When all is said and done, as Dr. David Pelcovitz explains in the *Jewish Observer,* kids do best when "expectations at home and in school are clearly spelled out and consequences are immediate, consistent and calmly implemented."[13] Calm implementation must go hand in hand with as consistent an environment as possible and one in which schools, teachers, and parents work together to achieve educational goals.

Committees, conferences, and events can help schools and parents develop positive relationships through which they can develop goals and understand methods for educating the child. In doing so, schools and parents must respect the boundaries of their respective authority. If the two conflict, a good case can be made for the school backing down.

The authority of the home is more vital to the child's development and observance than the authority of the school. That may be why when the Chazon Ish was asked how a school should deal with a child in the class whose parents are *mechallelei* Shabbat (those who profane Shabbat), he replied that "one must never disgrace parents in the eyes of their children."[14]

Some Educational Solutions

Teachers, students, and parents can all compromise the learning process in their own ways. Though not all problems can be solved, there are ways to help ensure that these problems do not compromise the educational process too much.

Parents can choose schools more carefully, with greater regard to their children's particular needs, and they can do a better job of cooperating with the schools they do choose. Parents and teachers need to form partnerships, more effective relationships that create more effective education.

Schools can hire more effective teachers, as defined above, and train them more adequately to identify learning problems and deal with them appropriately. When students' needs cannot be addressed within the conventional school system, new schools like Hevruta in Israel should be created to address their needs. Hevruta offers an entirely different curriculum than most *yeshivot*. At Hevruta, sports, music or hiking can become majors rather than merely extracurricular activities, whereas English, Math, and History are after-school activities. This approach is ideally suited to the non-academic student that allows him to thrive at school. As Rabbi Yoram Shamir, the *yeshiva's* principal, contends "In the regular school system…all people tried to do was to strengthen our students' weak points. …this didn't help them. So let's forget the weak points and works on their strengths…the more our students succeed, the more they begin to believe in themselves and the greater the chances are that they will want to deal with those things they failed at in the past."[15] And the greater the chances they will love their learning and associate Yiddishkeit with positive feelings.

Torah giants such as Rabbi Eliezer Shach have long advocated creating such schools in addition to vocational schools, but, to date, few have been established. Until they are, we might try incorporating more creative courses into existing curricula, or providing them after school.

All of this must go hand in hand with higher salaries to attract the best of the observant world to its most important profession and to properly compensate those who are already making great sacrifices to educate our youth. *Business Week* conducted research on how to best improve American schools and cited raising teachers' salaries as the *number one* method for improving the quality of schools and education.[16]

At the very least, we could offer teachers more honor and respect, the prestige they deserve. At the least, we can say "thank you" for their efforts and teach our children to respect and appreciate their work. Until we find a way to compensate them better, we can make a difference in our attitude alone.

CHAPTER 22

Conclusion

Although emotional factors are the primary reasons people stop observing Yiddishkeit, belief and its corresponding intellectual issues play a part as well. For some, that role will be primary; for others it will be secondary. But it is more than likely that if someone has *not* gone off the derech because of emotional reasons, he has done so because of intellectual ones — either because he did not believe in the Torah's truth or in its providing a meaningful way of life.

Our school system plays the most significant role in establishing or hindering these beliefs, just as the home plays the most significant role in the emotional area. In fact, 72% of those surveyed indicated that their educational experiences, particularly with teachers, contributed to their move away from observance.

Establishing a strong intellectual belief in Judaism requires a number of components. It starts by providing our children with a universal vision that creates a meaningful context for Judaism. Then, by explaining how the *mitzvot* advocate that vision, we connect the details to the greater whole. And by explaining the reasons for the *mitzvot* and applying them to the individual, we connect the individual to the details and the greater vision. Thus the universal, national, and individual goals become united into a cohesive entity that inspires and makes Judaism a most meaningful way of life.

Currently what and how we teach compromises this process: We focus on:

1) Everything else at the expense of *hashkafa*
2) Truth at the expense of meaning
3) *Mitzvot* at the expense of a universal and national vision
4) Particularism at the expense of similarities with others
5) *Gemorah* at the expense of basics
6) The past at the expense of the future
7) Ritual at the expense of ethics
8) Fear at the expense of love
9) Negatives at the expense of positives
10) Duty at the expense of pleasure and happiness
11) Information at the expense of inspiration
12) Blind faith at the expense of reason (we stifle questions).

In many cases, these choices seem to be reactions to the modern world and its challenges to Judaism. Perhaps since the modern world values reason at the expense of belief, we focus on belief at the expense of reason. Perhaps since the world focuses on universal elements at the expense of unique differences, we focus on our differences to keep us apart. Since the modern world speaks only of "being a good person," we speak of being a good Jew. Since the modern world emphasizes love and denigrates the desirability of fear, we speak primarily of fear and ignore the positive influence of love. Since the world values happiness, pleasure, and physicality above all else, we put these things at the bottom of our list.

By emphasizing values opposite to those of the world around us, we try to protect Judaism and to eradicate seemingly anti-Jewish values from our education. Unfortunately, this is ineffective for creating the inspiring Judaism we need.

Eradicating these things within our own world does not eradicate them outside of it. Rather, it causes us to lose some of the most precious, unique, and inspiring parts of our own tradition. After all, where did the modern world get many of its current values? From Judaism. Of course the world at large has distorted them, focusing on one end at the expense of the other. But by distorting values in the other direction we do not bring things into balance, but rather deprive our children of the beauty of their heritage.

For the beauty of Judaism cannot be seen by what it *excludes* but by what it *includes*. Judaism is great, in part, because of its ability to balance seemingly contradicting values, to give each its place; to ensure that happiness and truth work together; that our past history serves our future vision; that our particular uniqueness as a nation serves our commonality with all other men. In part, our religion is great precisely because it does not make the kinds of choices the secular world does. It is broad enough to make room for many seemingly oppositional values, and in doing so, creates a healthier approach to life.

Rather than fight the world outside, perhaps we should work with it. Rather than teach children in our schools that happiness is not particularly important, we should teach them that it is very important, and that Judaism is the best way to achieve it. Rather than prioritize rituals, we should teach that ethics are fundamental but ritual makes them complete. Giving these things — universalism, love, pleasure, happiness, the future — their place again in Judaism can show our children that Judaism promotes many of the same things as the outside world, but in a way that achieves ultimate truth and meaning. It will bring back some of the beauty of our tradition, and make it easier to teach and inspire.

No doubt these are revolutionary changes. And it is easier to seek slow and gradual evolution rather than radical change. But there are moments in history that demand revolution, as when Sarah Schneirer created Orthodox schools for women. Her revolutionary but visionary efforts might have saved Judaism in the modern era.

We are living in such a time. As Leah Kohn says, "in the same way that when she saw a need for a change and initiated it, we are now in a place where we need a change in the way we teach."[1] We can wait and see what happens and eventually, over time, things are bound to evolve in the right direction. But it would be far better to take an active approach, organize our efforts as Sarah Schneirer did, and implement these changes now — to teach *hashkafa*, focus on the basics, allow room for questions, and emphasize our vision for the future.

III

Implementation:
The Final Step

— CHAPTER 23 —

Implementing Observance: The Role of Character

D aniel grew up in the Tri-state area in a Modern Orthodox home. His father was a doctor who *davened* with a *minyan* (quorum of ten males) every day and learned on a regular basis, and his mother was a homemaker who dressed *tsniustically* (modestly), though she did not cover her hair. Unlike most children in his community, Daniel attended right wing *yeshivot*. His *rabbaim* and classmates were more *halachically* observant than Daniel's community and home. They all wore black hats, took Torah very seriously, and none of them had televisions at home.

Interestingly, while this discrepancy could have created problems for Daniel, it did not. Daniel explains that before attending the *yeshiva*, he did not really understand the black hat world and may even have looked down on it a little. But after attending, everything changed. He respected the school, its *rabbaim* and students, and his respect grew and developed over time. He began to feel that the "right wing" school presented a true picture of observant life, one he wanted to emulate. His affiliation with the school was so positive, in fact, that over the years both he and his family became more *halachically* observant.

In terms of both areas we have discussed — emotional and intellectual — Daniel was blessed. He had positive experiences with Judaism and received an excellent Torah education. He felt good about observance and believed Torah to be true. He had good relationships with his parents and also with his teachers. But soon after going to Israel for his post-high school year in *yeshiva*, he went off the derech. He was learning all the time, and loving his *gemorah shiurim* (classes), but he was no longer keeping Shabbat.

According to everything we have said so far, we must ask: Why? Why would someone like Daniel, who had positive foundations in both emotional and intellectual connections, drop observance?

He explains that it happened gradually and resulted from peer pressure. He made non observant friends outside of his *yeshiva* who became his main social group. They did not actively try to pull him away from observance, but their lack of commitment affected him. He wanted to fit in with them and he began altering his behavior to do so. First, he hung out in places he normally wouldn't have. After a while, he started going to bars on Shabbat, although he would not break *halachah*. Soon he stopped wearing his *kippah*; it was just too incongruous given the things he was doing. Eventually he ended up breaking Shabbat altogether. It was too difficult not to.

Once the spirit of the law was gone, the letter soon followed. Neither his positive feelings about observance nor his strong belief in it were enough to keep him committed.

Why did Daniel go off the derech? Initially, because he wanted to fit in with an un-observant crowd. But soon, as he puts it, the reason changed. "It was just more fun not to" keep Shabbat, he says. Today, many years later, he explains that he has been disconnected for so long, it just feels too hard to get back on the path.

Daniel is very unusual in that his belief in Torah and desire for observance are still fairly strong. He has not done what many people in his situation might — rationalize his behavior or dismiss Torah. Rather he lives in cognitive dissonance, not keeping Shabbat but believing wholeheartedly that he should.

Daniel's story teaches a number of important lessons. First, it dramatizes the Talmud's statement that *averah goreret averah* — sin leads to sin. Daniel's innocently going out on Shabbat led to breaking it, which led to not wearing a *kippah,* which ultimately took him so far away, he now feels it is too hard to come back. Most importantly, his story dramatically indicates that believing in and feeling good about observant Judaism are not enough to keep one on the derech.

Positive feelings and belief will not translate into action if we do not have the tools to implement them. We can believe that something is right. We can know it and want it, but still be unable to achieve it. Think of the smokers of the world who know they are harming themselves but are unable to stop. Their hearts feel and minds know, but their actions do not comport. Why? Because there is a missing link that jeopardizes the smokers' ability to bridge the distance between their thought and action.

What is the missing link? The ability to implement. That is what bridges the distance between the heart and the mind, connects them and allows them to translate their feelings and beliefs into action. It is the third and final leg of observance. Without it, observance is impossible.

So we could say that observance stands on three things: feeling, belief, and the ability to implement them. So far we have discussed the first two elements — love of Yiddishkeit, which involves our feelings, and belief in it, which involves our intellect. The third component — the ability to implement — is the last vital piece. It stabilizes the other two legs and secures observance.

The Tools of Implementing Judaism

So what are the tools of implementation? There are two parts to this answer — one internal, one external. The first is the ability *within* the individual to translate his beliefs into action — this involves his *char-*

acter and personal strength. The second is the *supportive environment* necessary to do so.

These two elements — personal character and environment — are the primary tools of implementation. They either serve as obstacles to implementing observance or facilitators for it. They may not be as fundamental to observance as the positive feelings of childhood or the philosophical inquiry of young adulthood, but without a strong character and proper environment observance is impossible.

Of the two components — internal character and external environment — character is probably most important. Daniel's story illustrates this. His external environment challenged his observance and prompted his departure. But it seems that his character played the most important role.

It was not the group that *pulled* him in as much as it was his *desire* to join them. His *internal* desire for fun and acceptance meant that he wanted to be a part of them, even if it came at the expense of his *kippah*. His character was the primary culprit. His parents did not wrong him. His school did not fail to educate him. Even his environment is not ultimately to blame. It is he, himself, who failed to implement his beliefs into action. While the environment presented challenges to his observance and may have tempted him with opportunities to sin, it could not force him to choose.

Whatever our environment, ultimately our internal character chooses and fights the battles. It is within ourselves that battles are fought and won, or lost.

This idea is at odds with our modern thinking. Our generation tends to blame society for its failures, as Dennis Prager explains, "A generation has been raised to believe that its greatest problems emanate from hostile and oppressive outside forces such as racism, sexism, and economic inequality."[1] When society is not to blame, genetics is the culprit for which, of course, none of us can be blamed. Rarely do we hear that the culprit is the self. Judaism, on the other hand, supports the idea that the primary battle for most things, including observance, begins and ends within ourselves.

When the Talmud asks: *What leads to sin?* It answers: *Kinah, cavod,* and *taavah* — jealousy, honor, and desire. All three of these are internal factors, things which result from weaknesses in character. The Talmud does not blame environment, but rather ourselves and, upon closer examination, we can see its reasoning in action. Think again about Daniel's story. Why did he sin? *Kinah* — he may have been *jealous* of the fun his friends were having; he didn't want to miss out. *Cavod* — he may have sought *honor,* the respect of others, which required him to fit in with their behavior. *Taavah* — he *desired* to have fun on Shabbat rather than stay at his *yeshiva* engaging in activities that were not as alluring.

A person with a weak or immature character or one whose character is still developing, such as a teenager, is more prone to sin than a person with a strong, developed one. He is more likely to act in variance with his beliefs and true values or abandon them altogether. That may be why Rabbi Mordechai Eliyahu feels that people primarily go off the derech because of laziness. In fact, he believes that even more subtle character traits can cause abandonment of Torah, for example when people learn for the wrong reasons. When people learn for admiration or pride or to please their parents, their learning fails to penetrate. Their impure intentions prevent proper connection to their learning, which jeopardizes observance.[2]

Character Development

We might say that religious decisions are made when character meets environment. And it is best to strengthen both the self *and* the environment if we are to facilitate observance. But character development is a good place to start — for whether the environment challenges our observance momentarily or altogether, it can be fought with a strong, well-developed character. Of course if we do not feel good about

Torah or do not believe in it, we will not have the desire to fight — in which case having the ability to do so is irrelevant. But assuming we have the desire, a developed character can make the difference in winning the battle. The *baalei mussar* understood this well, which is why books like *Mesilat Yesharim* that focus on character development are cornerstones of the *yeshiva* world.

Self-Knowledge and Esteem

The first component of effective character development is self-knowledge — of our limitations and strengths. Knowing our limitations helps us anticipate problems. It can help us avoid temptation and build barriers against it, and can also help us identify the areas we need to work on so that we can overcome temptation when it does arise.

But knowing our strengths is equally important. Without this, we can lose hope and the resolve we need to grow. If we don't acknowledge our strengths, we can forget how much we have to contribute and character development may seem futile.

Dennis Prager alluded to this in a lecture called "Obstacles to goodness." In it, he defined the obstacles to goodness as self-absorption, laziness, weakness, lack of empathy and, finally, thinking that what you do doesn't matter.[3] All are character-related issues but the last is of particular interest: Thinking that our actions are not significant can lead us to sin. This may have played somewhat of a role in Daniel's move away from observance.

In his interview, Daniel said that he would not break Shabbat in front of his children, even if he were not really keeping Shabbat when he has children. Why not? He explains that as a married man without children, he is not really hurting anyone but himself by not being observant, although he might be hurting the Jewish people in some grander, esoteric scheme he cannot relate to. But breaking Shabbat in front of his kids is different. It would directly and significantly hurt them by setting a bad example. So he would rather hide his nonobservant behavior in order to model the right behavior.

In Daniel's explanation, one sentence stands out — *by not keeping Shabbat, he's not hurting anyone but himself.* His one act isn't that significant in the grand scheme of things. And if his actions are not so important, what difference does it make if he is observant or not?

Where does that feeling come from? Possibly from the belief that he, himself, is not that important. Once you cease to value your behavior, it makes no difference if you are observant or not. And if not being observant hurts only yourself and you do not matter, then even if you believe it is hurtful not to be observant, you will have no incentive to change. Perhaps this is why, though the Torah tells us to remember we are nothing more than a speck of dust, we are also told to balance that awareness with the belief that the entire world was created just for us.[4]

But it seems we sometimes forget the importance of self-esteem and pride in character development. For example, in trying to demonstrate that there are no valid counterarguments to the truth of Torah, a teacher once said, "Everyone's bluffing. Don't buy it. They think they have thought of something that Rav Moshe Feinstein never thought of? Huh!"

This well-intentioned message has an undermining subtext: that no one, including the children in the classroom, can think of something Reb Moshe didn't think of.

Now, perhaps the chances of any child in this classroom doing so are slim. But it is possible and we should be encouraging our children to try.

Torah is a wellspring of knowledge rediscovered in every generation, including our own, and people think of new things every day. It is true we say that there is nothing new under the sun. But anyone who appreciates great poetry knows that life's oldest truths and greatest wisdoms are constantly expressed in new and unique ways that can touch us like never before. Surely our children are capable of such thought. And they may be capable of much more. One might in fact be the next

Reb Moshe and unless we believe that, we may miss the opportunity to help him achieve that.

If Reb Moshe Feinstein would have looked at the Rambam and thought that he could never think of something the Rambam never thought of, he never would have become Reb Moshe. That is why in relating the principles of *chinuch* (education) taught by the Chazon Ish, Rabbi Zvi Yabrov emphasizes that we should not withhold from our children the possibility of becoming a *gadol* (great leader). "We have to ensure that every child has the opportunity to be that 'one out of a thousand', however improbable it seems. Hence a *yeshiva* must never devalue any student, for it is impossible to know which young *bachur* will one day be the *gadol hador* (great leader of his generation)."[5]

If sending affirming messages helps create the next *gadol hador*, it also helps our children reach their particular potential, and enables them to develop character, without which observance is weakened.

Discipline

Once we know ourselves and develop a level of esteem, we must develop discipline — for without discipline, observance is impossible.

We can say many positive things about observant Judaism, but we cannot say it is easy. That does not mean we need experience it as a *burden*. On the contrary, some of the most difficult things in life can be the most rewarding — for example becoming a doctor. Doing so is certainly not easy, but neither is it a burden. Something one wants, commits to, understands and values, even when extremely difficult, is not experienced as a burden but a privilege.

Experiencing Judaism as joyful and meaningful can help to transform it from a burden to a privilege; but it won't make it easy. Observance will always require discipline. Even for the most committed Jew, there will be difficult moments or areas of observance. When those moments arise, man's character is tested and revealed. Meeting them successfully requires strength, the ability to say "no," to put aside momentary desire for a greater cause. This is particularly difficult for teenagers, which is why they also need a supportive environment to maintain observance. But even with a supportive environment, if there is not enough discipline, there can be no long-term observance.

Hard work

The ability to work hard, sacrifice and persevere goes hand in hand with discipline. Since character development and growth in Torah observance are life-long endeavors, they require the ability to work hard and persevere despite great challenges. As Rabbi Sacks has said, "Religion is like being married to the Divine Presence. It is about the long stretches of loyalty between the moments of high passion."[6] In Judaism, as in marriage, things will not always be easy or exciting. Moments of boredom or difficulty will require hard work to overcome. The greater the discipline and willingness to work hard, the less difficult commitment will be — the more it can be sustained between moments of "high passion."

The *Yetzer Hara* and Its Role

So developing a strong character is vital for staying on the derech. But doing so presumes that we accept one important idea, namely that whatever our external challenges, ultimately we fight the battle within ourselves, against the *yetzer hara*.

The concept of the *yetzer hara* is somewhat esoteric and therefore difficult to discuss. It is usually defined as "the evil inclination," a desire within us to sin, a longing to rebel against what God wants and sometimes even what we ourselves want and know to be right. Especially today, belief in the existence of the *yetzer hara* cannot be taken for granted, as noted in an anecdote told by Dennis Prager:

> One night when my older son was in third grade, I asked him what he had learned that day in school. 'That I have a

yetzer hara,' he responded. I was delighted for both psychological and moral reasons...the moral reason ...was that he would know...that life is a constant battle with his *yetzer hara,* i.e. with himself. This traditional Jewish belief is at total variance with the intellectual mindset of our time, which holds that the most important battle for us to wage is with our environment, with our society....The awareness that the battle is within oneself is a defining characteristic of the truly religious person...[7]

The *yetzer hara* certainly plays a role in challenging us and our observance of *mitzvot.* Having said that, it is important to realize that, in most cases, giving in to the *yetzer hara* does not lead to living a nonobservant life. In fact, of all those interviewed for this book, only Daniel seemed to fall into this category. *In the majority of cases,* the *yetzer hara* or lack of discipline does not take one *completely* off the derech. Rather it leads to *moments* of sin, which exist within the greater context of a committed life.

It seems that for the most part, the *yetzer hara* can only take one off the derech when the connection to Judaism is weak to begin with, the same way that "the other woman" generally causes an extramarital affair only when the spousal relationship was weak to begin with. The *yetzer hara* has little hope of taking one off the derech when there is a strong foundation of love for and belief in Judaism.

Why so? Because when we love Judaism and believe in it, we want it in our lives and will do everything we can to protect it. Even if we fail sometimes to keep certain *mitzvot,* we will not drop the whole of observance, but rather pick ourselves up and try again. We may erect higher barriers to protect our observance if we have to; but in the end, we will likely maintain observance, because desire maintains our resolve even if we lack discipline. Thus, the *yetzer hara* may have its moments, but will usually not have its way.

That is why the emotional connection and beliefs discussed at the outset of this book are so important. When we have positive feelings and strong belief, we *want* Judaism and observance. We have a strong foundation that empowers us to remain committed in the long run, despite great challenges we may face. That foundation closes the door to the *yetzer hara*, making it difficult for the *yetzer hara* to lure us away from observance. If the *yetzer hara* does enter and successfully challenge us, it will likely only do so momentarily or in particular areas of observance that may be difficult for us.

Positive feelings and belief create the *desire* to beat the *yetzer hara*. A strong character gives us the *ability* to beat the *yetzer hara*. With these elements in place, we are likely to win the war with the *yetzer hara*, even if we lose some battles.

Most people who go off the derech today lack these elements. The foundation of feelings and belief is weakened for them so the door is wide open for the *yetzer hara* to enter and lead them off the derech. In most cases therefore, it is inaccurate to say that the *yetzer hara* took someone off the derech. It is more accurate to say that a lack of positive feelings and belief did so.

Cognitive Dissonance

The only exception to that rule is when one's character is so weak that infractions occur over and over again. When a person consistently loses the battle with the *yetzer hara*, which seems to occur only in the minority of cases who go off the derech, the *yetzer hara* can push one away, even if a person has strong feelings and belief. How exactly does this work?

When actions are repeated often enough, patterns are created. The moments of infraction become the rule, not the exception. That is what happened with Daniel. He gave in to his *yetzer hara*, we might say. He did not intend to stop being observant. It was not a conscious choice as much as it was a progression that crept up on him.

When we behave a certain way long enough, it becomes who we are. When the moments of sin become pervasive, they begin to define our characters, our soul, and ultimately our belief system, as well. As the Talmud tells us, the first time a man sins, it is a sin. The second time, it becomes permissible. By the third time, it is a *mitzvah*.

It is natural to rationalize or explain away sin. In fact, when we sin often enough, it becomes almost necessary to do so. When our actions contradict our values or desires, we experience an internal conflict, a cognitive dissonance that must be reconciled. Man is not at peace when his actions betray his beliefs and in order to regain that peace, he tends to either change his actions or his beliefs. If he lacks the character and conviction to change his actions, he usually changes his beliefs in order to restore inner harmony.

So if one lacks strength of character to beat the *yetzer hara*, and he consistently loses the battles, he may well lose the war as well. Eventually he is likely to go off the derech. His actions will betray his desire for Judaism and his belief in it, and eventually he is likely to change his beliefs to comport with the new behavior, making it even more difficult to return.

This however is not inevitable. For example, while Daniel consistently "gave in to the *yetzer hara*," and moved farther away from observance, he did not blame others for his behavior or rationalize the conflict away. Instead, he held onto his belief in Torah and suffered dissonance as a result. While his character may not have been strong enough to maintain observance over the years, he did have honesty, integrity, and self-knowledge which enabled him to at least maintain his belief, even if it meant suffering conflict. With his belief intact, he has been able to remain connected to Judaism, respectful, admiring, and desirous of it. This means that for him, the door will always be somewhat open for a return.

Conclusion

Character is essential for properly implementing observant Judaism. And while there is interplay between character and environment — the internal and external forces — character is perhaps more important. It determines whether our choices are active or passive, whether they reflect and express our values or contradict them.

The only remaining obstacle to observance then is our environment. Although the environment cannot ultimately determine our choices, it can make our choices easier or harder. An environment that challenges Judaism too much or too often can eventually break our resolve. So the final way to secure observance is to foster the right kind of environment.

CHAPTER 24

Implementing Observance: The Role of Community

With positive feelings, belief, and character in place, there is one last element needed to secure observance: a proper environment in which to observe. Without this, observance is likely to falter and one might even go off the derech completely.

Consider Ari: He grew up in a Modern Orthodox home, kept Shabbat and *kashrut* and attended an Orthodox day school. He had good relationships with his teachers and parents, who provided him with a happy, healthy home. He had positive feelings toward observance and believed in observant Judaism. Though he had questions regarding rabbinic authority and the role of women in Judaism, he respected Judaism and wanted to live an observant life. For the most part, he succeeded. He remained observant throughout high school, and became more observant after he graduated.

But when I met Ari, a few years after graduating college, he was no longer observant. What happened? Ari said it all began when he left college and moved to the Upper West Side of Manhattan. There he sought a community to join but it wasn't as easy as he thought. He went to *shul* every Shabbat, but he explained that:

> People were not interested in the spiritual component.
> They were there to socialize. It was such a turn off. I came
> home feeling as empty, if not emptier, than when I had
> left… people were just looking at each other or would
> come in at the end and see some friends and come over
> and talk between *aliyot* (the act of being called up to the
> Torah), when you are technically permitted to talk, but
> how can you concentrate if you are talking to people?
> …So why am I there? Saying a bunch of words in Hebrew
> that I don't understand? Maybe I'll get a speech out of it,
> but then half the people are falling asleep…That took me
> a long time to deal with because my year in Israel instilled
> [in me] a powerful urge to pray and since then I had been
> putting on *tefilin* everyday.

Over time, Ari didn't enjoy going to *shul* anymore. He went from
being the first person there to showing up quite late. He explains,
"I moved to the West Side, which is supposed to be the bastion of
Modern Orthodoxy in America, and I stopped going to *shul*. At first I
made the commitment to go on Shabbat morning, even if it was just for
15 minutes, because I wanted to keep the continuum of going to *shul*
and I didn't want to get out of the habit. But then I realized that I was
becoming what I didn't like about *shul*. I was becoming the person
who shows up late to socialize and I wasn't even going in to *daven*."

Rather than doing something *for* him, he felt that *shul* was working
against him. In fact, he experienced a more meaningful *davening* at
home. So he stopped going — a simple action. Not very dramatic it
would seem, after all he was still *davening* and having a meaningful
experience while doing so. But eventually, that one simple action led
him off the derech.

Soon Ari's *davening* lost steam. He went from doing it every day to missing it sometimes and eventually he found that he was not putting on *tefilin* every day anymore. It got to the point where he was traveling in Asia one day and he realized that he had forgotten it was Shabbat. Never had he been so far away and never had he felt as disconnected from the Judaism he loved.

Ironically, it was in that moment that he started to make his return. There in Asia, he began to ask himself what Judaism had ever meant to him in the first place. His response to that question was to take time off and study in Israel, where he slowly reconnected and became observant again.

Today he again lives on the West Side of Manhattan but, unlike before, has found a *shul* where the people really *daven* and enjoy it. He has once again become the first person in *shul*, which he says gives him time to slowly get into the *davening* and realize what he is saying.

Ari's story teaches a number of interesting things. First, sometimes we have to go far away in order to come back home. Ari explains that he had to lose Shabbat in order to know what it meant to have it. Others who have gone off the derech explain that their leaving the path was an important part of acquiring a meaningful observance. Once they returned, they had a deeper appreciation for it, and they ended up with a more meaningful Judaism.

Ari's story also indicates the importance of a good foundation. No doubt his return to observance was possible because at one point it *did* mean something to him. He had something to return *to* which gave him the *desire* to seek answers for his questions.

In addition, Ari's story teaches that, unlike popular perception, adults go off the derech too. In fact, in some ways, maintaining observance can be more challenging for adults than for children. Although adults tend to have more education and stronger, better-developed characters than children, they also tend to have more free choice. Adults are less fettered by negative consequences from family or community.

Adulthood offers many people, for the first time, the freedom to truly live as they desire and independently discover what they want for themselves. In terms of life's stages, therefore, adulthood is a testing ground, the final hurdle for commitment to Judaism.

The Role of Community

Finally, Ari's story teaches how vital community can be in fostering observance. Ari's schools served him well. So did his family. What presented an obstacle to his observance was his community. Because his *shul* was not conducive to spirituality, he removed himself. Once he removed himself, his observance ultimately suffered.

The respondents to the web survey had similar experiences. 78% indicated that negative behaviors in their observant communities contributed to their move away from observance.

Removed from community, observance is destined to wane over time. That is why the *Mishnah* tells us *al tifrosh min hatzibur*[1] — don't separate yourself from the community — because a Jew cannot be properly observant in a vacuum. But what happens when the community *itself* becomes an obstacle to observance? The situation often results in people leaving the community, which is often the first step off the derech.

But why is community so important? Because it creates the context for our observance. It determines *what* battles we fight, *how often* we must fight them, and even whether or not we *want* to fight them.

Communities provide an important tool for implementing Judaism. They are like extended families. They not only support us, embrace us, and help reach our religious potentials, they are also the place where our Judaism is transformed from a singular experience to a communal one; where our observance is strengthened, enforced, and enriched. Observance thrives and comes to life with connection to community; and it withers in its absence.

Communities always strongly affect us, for better or worse, no matter what our age. But there are certain times in particular when community becomes more essential than usual: These are transitional periods of life — for example, when we are teenagers, when we move away from home, get married or divorced. At these times, we are particularly vulnerable both emotionally and Jewishly. We are moving from one stage of life to another. We are not quite as anchored as we had been in the period from which we emerged or the one into which we are headed. As such, we have an increased need for support; without that support, observance can be difficult to maintain.

For example, one woman explained that she went off the derech after her divorce because during that vulnerable time, she needed her friends and she felt they had abandoned her. That feeling created so much disdain for the observant world that she moved toward the non-Jewish world that embraced her at the time, until she joined them completely.

In the modern era, transitional periods occur more frequently, dramatically, and for longer time periods than ever before, and that has created some unexpected challenges to observance. For example, people used to live close to home their entire lives, leaving infrequently for short distances. But with the invention of the airplane, families separate frequently and dramatically. Jewish youth move farther away from home and do so at younger ages. As such, they lose their support system earlier and more dramatically than previous generations.

Today, people marry and have children later, prioritize their careers, work longer hours, and get divorced more often than before. This has eroded the family structure so that some people lose their support system early on while others never have it in the first place.

Without a familial atmosphere, or at least a communal one, Judaism loses its meaningful and joyful context and becomes hard to maintain. That may be why Rabbi Ephraim Buchwald contends that if *baalei teshuva* marry, approximately 90% will remain observant. However, if they don't, the fallout rate is 50% or greater.[2]

Certainly relative to previous generations, people today lack consistent environmental support. This means that communities need to step in, especially during transitional periods, to help people implement Judaism and sometimes compensate for what families should have provided in the first place.

This is especially vital for *baalei teshuva*. When I asked Rabbi Buchwald, whose life's work is with *baalei teshuva,* why they sometimes drop observance, he said it's primarily because they fail to integrate into a community. Community is particularly important for *baalei teshuva* for a number of reasons. First, they are experiencing one of the most important and fundamental transitions of their lives — often without familial support. They can therefore feel alone, displaced and alienated. They need communal support to mitigate those feelings. Second, unlike children who are born into the observant world, *baalei teshuva* have no religious role models from their home. They need the community to demonstrate how to live Judaism on a daily basis.

Community will become even more important for the *baal teshuva* if what drew him to observance in the first place was community, which is often the case. Rabbi Buchwald asserts that "the single most important element in attracting a *baal teshuva* is existential loneliness."[3] Community often addresses that existential loneliness by providing a meaningful way of life and warm environment in which to pursue it. If this is what attracted or created the *baal teshuva*, its absence can break him.

Unfortunately, while *baalei teshuva* need community more than others, they can also have a harder time integrating into it because of their unique circumstances. They have to learn the logistics of living an observant life — how to pray, how to read Hebrew — all things that observant Jews take for granted, but are essential for feeling comfortable within a communal environment. *Baalei teshuva* must struggle to gain mastery in these areas and, until they do, won't likely feel at home in any Jewish community. In addition, their experience in the secular world often means they have to juggle, integrate and resolve issues that Jews from observant homes do not. This can create feelings of confusion, loss and sadness — which can make it hard to emotionally connect. Finally, given their great enthusiasm for Yiddishkeit, *baalei teshuva* often have idealistic and sometimes unrealistic expectations of Jewish communities that can disillusion them more quickly than those born into the observant world. This makes them more vulnerable to shortcomings in the community.

Fortunately, most *baalei teshuva* overcome these challenges and integrate successfully into communities; but the obstacles can jeopardize the process, which for the *baal teshuva* in particular, might result in going off the derech.

Fostering Effective Communities

To work, communities cannot merely *exist*; they must exist as the *right kind* of community. For just as we must like a rebbe to learn from him, we must like a community to join it. We must respect it and want to be part of it. As the Talmud tells us: *Torah lo bashamiyim hi* — the Torah does not exist in heaven. It is here on earth, in our families, our schools and communities, in the kind of Judaism we live. It is about the world we create for each other on earth as much as the world God creates for us in heaven.

The right kind of community therefore will advocate and embody the value system we are trying to actualize. It will embrace us, encourage us, and invite us into its homes; it will inspire connection, and perpetuate Jewish values in a way that is attractive, and makes people want to join it and emulate it. Otherwise it will work against Judaism as it did for Ari, and push us off the derech to greater or lesser extents.

Our Communities

How well are our communities doing in terms of the above objectives? In many ways we are doing exceptionally well. Our communities are emulated and respected by many who know them. Observant Jews are known for their kindness and sensitivity to others. Even statistics support these perceptions. *The Jerusalem Post* reported that observant Jews are among the most giving in the world:

> Orthodox Jews are 50% more likely to volunteer their time than non-Orthodox. Nearly 14% of Orthodox Jews contributed more than $5000 each to a Jewish charity last year versus 2.8% for Conservative Jews and 1% for Reform and non-affiliated Jews. Orthodox Jews were even twice as likely as Reform Jews to contribute more than $5000 to a *secular* charity. These disparities become even more remarkable when one considers that the Orthodox are the least affluent sector of American Jewry, and most large Orthodox families stagger under huge tuition bills.[4]

Observant Jews have a special bond — not only toward themselves, but also to the world at large — that stands out. Even those who have gone off the derech often remark on this. In fact, for many, it is what they miss the most about observance — which speaks volumes for the success of our communities.

On the other hand, there are small but significant ways in which we fail to attract and embrace our children, especially those in transition. All too often, for example, we do not reach out to single people to invite them into our homes for Shabbat. Or we go to *shul* and fail to notice the stranger who may have wandered in alone, trying to find his place in our world or needing a Shabbat table to join.

These issues are fairly easy to address with a little foresight and effort. Others are more difficult — problems that revolve around how attractive our communities are, how effectively they model true Torah values.

In either case, when it comes to these issues, perception is a far more important reality. So to understand the role of community in people's dropping observance, we must examine how our communities are perceived — what people think and feel about them. Those who have gone off the derech usually have very negative perceptions about their communities. This includes people from across the religious spectrum, who have had a wide variety of experiences in the observant Jewish world. Listen to some of the statements made when people told their stories on *offthederech.com*:

> **Baalat Teshuva who dropped Yiddishkeit after a divorce:** It's impossible to share any of your personal *tsures* (troubles) with Orthodox people because they simply don't want to know your trouble. They have their own troubles, especially the married ones, especially the women...the Orthodox world castigates people who go to the beach, who go to certain kinds of movies, who watch certain kinds of TV. There is no freedom of conscience....you are not allowed freedom of speech and to top it off if you have no money, you are considered a goy...One rabbi told me that he was disgusted that so-called *baalei teshuva* could just one day decide to put on a black hat and consider themselves as good as he who had been *frum* from birth.

> **A currently observant convert:** I am an observant convert who is thinking of becoming less observant and who fantasizes about dropping it altogether, although I could probably never do that. Despite my love of Yiddishkeit, my experience with the leaders of the community has been so negative. Not the lay people, but the rabbis. I see the whole *shtick* (attitude) as being about how much money you have, and an extreme amount of racism against converts from all sectors of the community. I don't know how much longer my family can take it. And even if we could,

why would we want to? We're becoming almost like cryp-
to Jews, preferring to practice in our home and stay away
from *shul.*

Formerly Modern Orthodox Manhattan Jew: I grew
up as part of the Upper West Side Modern Orthodox community. I went to Ramaz, spent a year in Israel at a *yeshiva*
but was seriously turned off by the hypocrisy, back-stab-
bing, and narrow mindedness there...Add to that the total
disrespect for other Jews and types of Judaism and I decided that I wasn't interested in being a part of that kind
of community.

Formerly observant female teen: ...Mom thinks I'm
sleeping around...well, so does the rest of the community! All anyone is caring about is their reputation not mine
because if they cared about me, then they would ask me,
not spread the **** about me, and that's why I really dislike
the "*frum* community."

Formerly observant male teen: You can't leave your
community. I want to leave so badly!! But I can't — nowhere to go, nowhere to run, nowhere to hide, nowhere
to live if I move out... I live in a community that talks.
I've been told by "adults" that I shouldn't talk to someone
because their friend is friends with this "not nice guy."
Ummm. Excuse me? Who are you to tell me who to be
friends with? I can't pick my family, why can't I pick my
friends? ...please help...I really dislike my community.

Whether or not we sympathize with these passionately negative
perceptions, it is important to consider them closely. No matter how
angry or frustrated, accurate or inaccurate, these remarks teach us how

strongly our behavior affects others, how detrimental seemingly innocent behavior can be, and how significant our communities are. These statements indicate how effective we are at inspiring connection, commitment, and emulation. If we look behind the *tone* of their expressions to examine the *content* objectively, openly, and without judgment, we will learn what we need to do to resolve the problems.

We might be inclined to dismiss these comments because they sound so extreme. But it is essential to remember who these people are — formerly observant teens, who were born into our world, open to all we had to offer; converts who no doubt joined our world with enthusiasm and conviction, and at great cost, who still struggle to maintain their connection despite the difficulty. Such people deserve to be heard and understood. They have every reason to respect and admire our communities and yet they feel dismayed.

If we listen to them, we can learn why they left and how to keep them connected. We can understand what they want and need. We can recognize our strengths and weaknesses and improve ourselves. This can help us not only to keep them connected, but also to achieve our goals of *kiddush Hashem* and *tikun olam*. For if we cannot inspire our own people to emulate us, how can we do so with the rest of the world? But if we can manage to do so with them, we will be on our way to doing so with the rest of the world.

— CHAPTER 25 —
Gaining Respect

Being attractive and fostering respect are the most important components for creating a successful community. These are essential for helping people implement Judaism, keeping them in the fold, and modeling Torah the way it is meant to be lived.

But how do religious communities become attractive to others? In large part by fostering good marriages, happy families, and warm, safe, healthy environments.[1] These are powerful attributes because they are basic things that people in all societies want and are attracted to.

Earning respect requires a little more — behaving a cut above, exhibiting outstanding character and exemplary behavior that causes people not only to want to join us, but also to follow in our ways.

Needless to say, achieving these levels of behavior is challenging. Communal character, like individual character, is defined by action and sometimes just a few "bad apples" can ruin things for an entire community. If those negative behaviors become more prevalent and are exhibited by significant numbers of people, things get even worse. People perceive the problems as inherent to the community, as an integral part of it and they become even more repelled.

This has been the case for numerous formerly observant Jews, such as the ones mentioned in the previous chapter. They often echo the refrain that observant communities are unappealing and unrespectable. These perceptions, they say, caused them to remove themselves from the community, which contributed to their going off the derech.

Although people are offended by a variety of negative behaviors, there are a few in particular that they mention more frequently and passionately than others, behaviors which compromise their respect the most.

Hypocrisy

The first is hypocrisy, which Rav Saadiah Gaon identifies as one of the main reasons people drop observance.[2] 62% of those surveyed said that they had been "turned off" by the hypocritical behavior of "many" observant Jews.

Experts who work with kids at risk, like Avi Rothenberg, say they often hear children complaining about hypocrisy. For example, when "a rabbi talks about Torah, Torah, Torah, and says that money isn't worth anything and then honors a guy who isn't *frum* because he's got money. That's one part of hypocrisy. Another one is when a parent says, go to *yeshiva*, go to *yeshiva*, go to *yeshiva*, but the father is more interested in making money than learning."[3]

The behaviors most likely to be noted hypocritical seem to be infractions between man and man, when observant Jews fail to exhibit fundamental decent behavior toward their fellow human beings. For example, when an observant Jew walks down the street and bumps somebody without saying 'I'm sorry.' He is likely to be condemned and labeled a hypocrite whereas the same behavior from a nonobservant person might result in annoyance, but not nearly the same level of repulsion.

People seem to feel that if observant Jews are meant to be better and observe God's will, they should at least demonstrate the common decency and respect that even non-God fearing people would show to each other. If they fail to do so, these Jews, as well as the Torah they represent, are seen as greater failures than their nonobservant counterparts. So behavior that might go unnoticed if exhibited by another person easily becomes a *chilul Hashem* when exhibited by an observant Jew.

By donning a *kippah* and appearing observant, we send the message that we are representatives of God. We become His emissaries, whether or not we want to be. This means that others expect a higher standard for our behavior than for everyone else. They expect our behavior to correspond to the values represented by the *kippot* we wear. They expect our outside appearance to reflect an internal reality, one of a more refined soul. When we look observant, people expect us to *be* observant especially in terms of *mitzvot bain adam lechavairo*.

We can argue that such infractions are not in fact hypocritical, that as long as someone is *trying* to observe God's will, his failures should be considered human — the simple inability of every man to live up to ideal standards, especially when the standards are so high. Nonetheless, the reality is that such behaviors are *perceived* as hypocrisy and that perception is what counts. Perception determines the extent to which people respect us, regardless of the reality; so our arguments, valid or not, make little difference in terms of people's respect.

Arrogance

What compounds the problem of hypocrisy is perceived arrogance on the part of the observant world. When we perceive people as being humble, we tend to be far more forgiving of their faults. In fact, humility itself fosters great respect, which mitigates the sting of hypocrisy or any other infractions. When, however, people perceive us to be arrogant, they feel justified in pointing the finger at us and will be far less tolerant of our infractions.

People perceive us to be arrogant when we behave as though we feel we are better; when we allow ourselves to judge or reject others, when we condemn them, or ostracize them for not living up to *our* standards. In truth, such behaviors are somewhat arrogant and they certainly make others far more likely to judge us in turn.

Unfortunately for the observant world, simply *being observant* can make others feel that you are arrogant and judgmental. Wearing a *kippah* in and of itself seems to silently condemn. It somehow sends the message that you are doing God's will; that you know what is right and wrong; that you are right and anyone who doesn't behave as you do is wrong. Thus the mere existence of the *kippah* seems to silently condemn by saying, "I am better than you." Therefore, the observant Jew has to go out of his way *not to* be perceived as arrogant.

Humility

Since arrogance exacerbates every other infraction and makes others likely to condemn us, the best place to start in order to foster respect would be with humility.

A poll conducted a number of years ago asked Americans what they considered the most admirable character trait. They answered "humility." Humility earns respect in a way other qualities don't. The humble man, no matter what his faith, inspires admiration, respect, and honor. He speaks without speaking, teaches by modeling, and inspires others to follow his ways. He leads by being, by knowing who he is in a way that respects others, and thereby promotes *kiddush Hashem*. Humility draws people near and fosters awe. That may be why, when God chose the leader of the Jewish people, he looked for the man who was most humble, for with this trait, Moses could lead others most effectively. Like Moses, we too are meant to be spiritual leaders, so it becomes all the more important that as a people, we exhibit the humility that enables leadership and inspires awe.

Humility also tempers mistakes, such that others are more tolerant

285

and forgiving of a humble person. Since it is difficult to eradicate our infractions, we can at least try to acquire humility, which can counter-act potentially negative perceptions and soften the blow of our short-comings.

Beyond that, achieving a higher level of humility may be necessary for achieving all other spiritual goals as well. In her book on Torah parenting, Sara Radcliff points out that "the presence of great humility is a prerequisite to spiritual development. Our Sages tell us that 'the Divine Presence will rest only upon a humble individual.'"[4] So achiev-ing humility will not only foster respect and forgiveness; it can also lay the foundation for general spirituality.

How do we achieve humility? In part, by avoiding the most prob-lematic behaviors such as judgment, intolerance, or disdain for others. This can be achieved in part by internalizing two seemingly contradic-tory messages of the Torah — to believe that the whole world was created for us while believing that we are nothing more than dust. This involves recognizing that we are not valued merely for *having* a role, but for the extent to which we *fulfill* it. It involves recognizing that since we never really know how well we are fulfilling it, we can never feel too proud.

For the same reason, it involves judging others as favorably as pos-sible. Judging others favorably is an essential trait of humility. Sara Radcliff explains that "Those who pass judgment on others do so out of a false sense of superiority,"[5] so an important part of achieving hu-mility is adopting a perspective that minimizes negative judgment and maximizes favorable judgment.

Mitzvot Bain Adam Lechavairo

In conjunction with this, it would help to improve in our *mitzvot bain adam lechavairo*. This area more than others seems to compromise people's respect and admiration for us. People can forgive us if we fail to *daven* with *kavanah* (feeling) or observe the Shabbat with enough joy.

But they seem less willing to forgive infractions toward our fellow men.

These *mitzvot* are perceived as fundamental. They are things that *all* men value — with or without religion — and therefore, when they are missing, draw reactions of the greatest shock and disdain. In addition, these *mitzvot* are the foundation for those between man and God, for if we cannot be good to our friends on earth, how can we be good to our ultimate Friend in heaven whom we cannot see or touch.

Even God Himself seems to prioritize these fundamentals, expecting us to treat each other with respect, kindness, and honesty even before we do so toward Him. For what, after all, did He punish Sodom and Gemorah, destroy the world with flood, and banish us from our temples in Jerusalem? For *mitzvot* between man and man, which seem to be the basis for everything else.

Again, we can argue that this is not the way it should be, that both kinds of *mitzvot* are equally important. But the fact remains that when it comes to people's perception of us, *mitzvot bain adam lechavairo* have a much greater impact. We are perceived far more negatively when we fail in this area, so if we want to foster respect and admiration, we must focus on this. The good news is that when we do, we can make perhaps the greatest impact.

Avi, who was mentioned in a previous chapter, demonstrates this well. Though he went off the derech years ago and has no intention of becoming observant again, he yearns for the communal life he experienced when he was *frum*. Years after leaving the observant world, he continues to speak of it with respect and admiration. Why so? He explains,

> I think that a lot of people in that community live with a genuine sense of brotherhood. People really help each other. There is a lot of kindness there... When I say that someone is my friend in the *frum* world, do you know what it means? It means that I can go to his house any time

287

of day, any day of the week, and I've done that. People feel connected to each other in that world; friendship is more real. It's not always that way, but my feeling is that in the *frum* community they have a sense of loyalty and really being connected to the other person....So I can't say that some guy who is living on Wall Street making millions is better than them. These people sit and study *gemorah* and they are not going to get degrees and they are probably not going to get famous from it. They're not going to publish books. They just do it. They just sit in the corner and nobody knows who they are. They just study and don't have much; it's quite beautiful; their life is nice. I see humane qualities to it. I see good values to it. Even if I don't believe in anything that he believes, look what he lives for. He's relatively unselfish. He's devoted to his family, God, study. He doesn't think too much about money and status. When I think of the *frum* people I know, many of them have souls, you know. They have souls.

What stands out in Avi's mind when he thinks about the *frum* world is its great kindness and the quality of its interpersonal relationships; the humility, integrity and sincerity with which its members learn and dedicate themselves to Torah; the quality of their souls — which easily exceeds the quality of those he has met in the secular world. The admiration he felt meant that, even years later, he is still connected to the *frum* world and respectful of it, which tempers his movement away from Yiddishkeit.

Conclusion

Communities that succeed in *mitzvot bain adam lechavairo,* that manage to do so with humility and without hypocrisy, not only succeed in creating more loving, warm, honest, committed, safe, secure and happy communities, but also inspire others and foster respect and admiration. As a result, those born into our communities will likely stay — for the day-to-day experience of living in a Jewish world will be positive, perhaps more so than any alternative. And those outside our communities may also be drawn to Torah, for we will have achieved what they, too, value. Such has been the case with many *baalei teshuva* whose first exposure to Torah was not the Torah itself, but its lifestyle; not the books, but the people. Their respect and admiration for the people in turn led them to Torah and a Torah way of life.

This may be why, when the prophet Micah asks the question: "And what does God require of you?" He answers with the following: "To act justly, and love mercy, and to walk humbly with your God."[6] If we follow this simple formula — observing the *mitzvot bain adam lechavairo* with honesty, respect, warmth and kindness, and then to walk humbly with God in every moment — we will successfully achieve *kiddush Hashem* and foster respect, which will not only keep observant Jews within our world but also draw others in.

— CHAPTER 26 —

Fostering Spirituality

Being humble and excelling at the *mitzvot bain adam lechaviro* will help make our communities attractive and respectable. But a proper Jewish community must go beyond that. Once it succeeds in fostering respect, it must foster a spiritual environment — for ultimately, Judaism is not only about improving relationships between men, but also about creating one with God. Beyond this, achieving spirituality actually fulfills an important emotional need, namely to achieve meaning and self-actualization.

To achieve Jewish spirituality and proper observance, we need a spiritual environment. A spiritual community is particularly important for observant Jews because, although we can achieve spirituality in solitary moments, true spirituality requires moments shared with others — not only in the privacy of our homes, but also in our engagement with the world outside that home. We must experience spirituality not only as individuals, but also as communities. Those who lack this, as Ari did, are likely to either move away from their community in search of spirituality or lose spirituality altogether.

Many of those surveyed indicated that they considered a lack of spirituality to be a problem in observant communities. 46% did not feel that their communities fostered spirituality, and over one third felt that their communities did not even value it.

More than any other arena, we tend to experience communal spirituality in our *shuls*. It is in our *shuls* where spirituality is transformed from the solitary to the communal; where it is experienced in the warm company of other Jews; where we serve God together, united despite our differences.

What a beautiful moment it must be for God to observe his people — men and women, young and old — all from a variety of social, economic and cultural backgrounds — using the same words at the same time for the same purpose. It is here, in our *shuls*, that the communal expression of spirituality exists. And it is here where we can experience one of the most potentially spiritual experiences possible, communicating with our Creator. Therefore, our *shuls* may be one of the most important gages of how we express and affect spirituality.

So what are our *shuls* really like? Do they foster spirituality or hinder it? Unfortunately the answers to these questions are sometimes not as positive as we might hope. Many *shuls* today are merely places where we wear our finest clothes to impress our neighbors or attract members of the opposite sex. Some are places where we come not to pray but to talk. Others are places where the prayer, although serious, happens so quickly that one can hardly follow the *davening* or find meaning in it.

These realities can dramatically affect an individual's spirituality and potentially push him away from his community, which may be the first step away from observance.

Unfortunately, the lack of spirituality in our *shuls* does not exist in a vacuum. It reflects a greater problem that can be seen in many areas of observant life: observance becoming a hollow ritual, devoid of meaning and spirituality.

But why have we lost our spirituality? The short answer to this question is that we focus on externals at the expense of internals. Rather than focus on who we are, where we are going, how we feel, and what we think, we tend to focus on the external expressions of these things: how we act, how we dress, and how we speak. Rabbi Shimon Kessin, author and psychotherapist for the *frum* community in Brooklyn, explains,

> There are too many Orthodox Jews who define their religiosity through their external behavior. Orthodoxy is moving ever more to the right. But that movement is usually nothing more than a greater accumulation of *chumras* (stringencies of Jewish law). The more *chumras* you adopt, the more *frum* you can say you are. The internal Jew on the other hand, where *yiras shamayim* (fear of heaven) actually resides, is neglected or is given second-class treatment.

So rather than focus on our souls and our connection with God, we focus on the deed, which is more superficial. And ultimately, people become uncomfortable with inner experiences and growth, as Rabbi Kessin continues:

> [Why] do so many people talk in *shul*? Because many people are uncomfortable with fervent prayer, because prayer is largely an inner experience. An undeveloped inner spiritual core is uncomfortable with a religious experience that addresses his states of consciousness....
>
> Why is there such a powerful need to conform and look religiously perfect? When a person ignores his inner experience and his inner growth, he basically abandons his individuality and personal uniqueness. Since he must define himself somehow, he then uses the opinions of others to validate his self worth. Since most of his associ-

ates judge themselves in external terms, he must adopt their external values to get their approval and feel good about himself.....

Why is there so much controversy and *lashon hara* amongst Orthodox Jews? A religious outlook based on primarily external behaviors is inherently frustrating. People having this view really know deep inside themselves that something is wrong, much as they will deny it to others. To maintain this posture, however, they must find some form of compensation and satisfaction. There is no greater satisfaction than the opportunity to feed the ego. The result then is to convince oneself that because of his religious behaviors, he is superior, more holy and a member of the spiritual elite. This powerful sense of self-importance then becomes a distinct reward for adopting what is basically a frustrating experience.[1]

So focusing on externals instead of internals not only undermines spirituality, but also fosters attitudes such as arrogance that undermines people's respect of us.

Ritual and Spirituality

One of the primary ways in which we focus on externals is prioritizing rituals over spirituality. We seem to have forgotten that the rituals of Judaism, whether going to *shul*, observing Shabbat, lighting candles, or saying *kaddish* (the prayer for the dead), are not only about the deeds; they are also about the *feelings* those deeds are meant to inspire. *Halachah*, the letter of the law, is a vehicle for expressing and creating a spiritual reality. But the heart of the experience is not in its physical expression, but rather in its emotional and spiritual cause and effect.

This is not to say the deed is unimportant, that *halachah* takes a

293

secondary role to the values and feelings it is meant to inspire. Rather, without connection to the internal, without expressing and fostering spirituality, it loses the heart and becomes nothing more than an empty shell that fails to inspire and transform the soul. As it is said — *Tefilah beli cavanah hi kegoof beli neshama — prayer without concentration on meaning is like a body without a soul.*[2] So it is with all *mitzvot* that lose their connection to spirituality.

Judaism is about the way our deeds *express* and *create* a refined soul and connect us to God and people in holiness. In this sense, it is not the *doing* that is the essence, but the process of b*ecoming* as a result of what we do. Rabbi Cardozo explains:

> Part of the religious world today has fallen victim to a kind of religious behaviorism, the belief that Judaism glorifies the deed without proper motivation and inspiration…The failure to understand this matter will ultimately lead to the vulgarization of Judaism… without constantly emphasizing the fact that all observance is ultimately for the sake of transformation of the whole man, Judaism will not be a beloved friend of the religious child and student.[3]

What modern man lacks most and what he seeks is connection to something greater than himself. Judaism at its best addresses this need most effectively, for every *mitzvah* is an opportunity to connect with God and experience spirituality. But a Judaism that focuses only on *external* expressions without *internal* meaning cannot address that need at all. It is likely to alienate us and threaten observance, to devalue the greatness of Torah, and divert us from its most meaningful parts. According to Rabbi Menachem Schneerson, this is precisely the conflict that occurred at *akaidat* Yitzchak (the binding of Isaac).[4]

He explains that Isaac represented Judaism. He was the son through which Judaism would continue; so if Isaac died, so would Abraham's faith. When God commanded Abraham to kill Isaac, he was really telling him to kill the religion that was meant to come forth from him. He made Abraham choose between his religion as embodied by Isaac and the will of his God, which was now contradicting it.

The *akaida* was a test to see which Abraham would put first. "Would Abraham show that he was religiously inclined because he loved doctrine, theology and ritual or because he loved God? Would Abraham destroy the faith he fathered if God commanded him to do so?" In choosing to sacrifice Isaac, Abraham showed that he loved God more than he loved doctrine, and thus he became worthy of fathering the Jewish nation, for only a nation who puts God first can truly represent His will in the long run.

The resolution of the *akaida* demonstrates that true Judaism is about achieving spirituality by putting God first, which requires shifting our focus from the external to the inner experience of observance — not at the expense of *halachah*, but in conjunction with it.

Materialism

An alternative expression of over-emphasizing the external is materialism. Materialism focuses on the external, material objects rather than the internal meaning they are meant to express and create. When we focus on things like *bar mitzvah* parties, beautiful homes and quality clothing, we undermine the more important internal experiences of life.

This is not to say there is something wrong with such things. There is nothing particularly religious about depriving ourselves of beauty or physical pleasures. But our material possessions are good only in so far as they do not compete with our spirituality or come at the expense of it. Once material things are prioritized over spiritual experiences, once they become necessary for our happiness, they become problematic. They are likely to compromise our spirituality along with our children's respect for us, our communities, and Judaism.

Professional Choices

Professional choices are another manifestation of this principle. A profession is an external expression that may say very little about our soul, *middot* and values. If it does say something about us, it is often hard to know exactly *what* it says. Yet, we seem to overemphasize what people do over who they are. We often place far more emphasis on whether our children become doctors, lawyers, and successful businessmen than whether they become generous, honest, and God-fearing. But fostering spiritual environments requires focusing less on what you *do* for a living, and more on who you *are*, what your values are, and how you prioritize your values.

Judging Based on Externals

The problem of focusing on externals is compounded when we use externals as the basis for judging others. As discussed, any judgment may reflect arrogance and create a negative perception of observant Jews; but judgment that is based on externals tends to incur the greatest hurt, alienation, rejection, and bitterness.

Often this kind of judgment focuses on the way people dress. Remember Chani, who got in trouble at school for tying her shirt in a knot. She says, "You are immediately rejected when you start dressing like that — immediately. And that rejection is like the wall. Finished! You are out."

Another man who went off the derech says, "What is Orthodoxy? My brother goes to a *shiur* every morning. He is very smart and totally *halachic*. But every night when he goes to *maariv* (evening prayer), people are squeamish to let him join in because he doesn't wear a black hat. He has strength of character so he still goes, but the hat is crazy…people are discriminated against for something that inherently has no value…At **** [*yeshiva*], I was treated like a *kiruv* case because I didn't wear a white shirt."

Why is this kind of judgment so alienating? Because when externals become the basis of evaluating a person's worth and acceptability, we fail to recognize his true essence, the *tzelem elokim* inside which makes him valuable, loveable, and respectable. Since we all need to be known, loved and respected for who we are, this kind of judgment undermines a fundamental emotional need. Since it is often religious standards that form the basis of it, and since it is observant people who are doing the judging, observant life and its people become associated with pain, something to be avoided at any cost.

It is important to realize that while ideally, external dress would reflect an internal reality, often it does not. This is true in both directions. Sometimes those who dress very piously are not religious or observant at all; and sometimes those who dress very immodestly can be connected to God, and observant of things we never see.

It is true that sometimes dress does accurately reflect an internal reality. But even when it does, it can be hard to know exactly *what* it says about a person. Remembering this is especially important in the case of those who have gone off the derech. They may dress differently for a variety of reasons. But even when their dress accurately reflects a troubling internal reality, judgment or rejection will not help matters. The best solution in these cases is not to focus on the externals, but rather to focus on the internal even more — to look even more closely at who the person really is, what they are expressing, and why. It would be wiser to examine the behavior in an open, loving way. This can help a person feel that at least if the community judges, it does so based on more significant things.

Focusing on internals can also foster the spiritual environment necessary to develop a real connection with God. It can increase children's desire to be part of our community and conform to its standards, which would ultimately create the kind of observance we truly want — where the external dress is a true expression of one's choosing Judaism's values, respecting the community, and wanting to join it.

This is the approach taken by many schools that deal with kids at risk. The more successful ones, like Tzofiah, for girls at risk, focus almost entirely on the internal experience of Yiddishkeit. As Rabbi Raviv Shaked, founder and director of the school, explains, "we try to introduce Judaism in a non-threatening way. We talk more about spiritual matters than about *halachah*."[5]

The school's attitude expresses itself not only in the curriculum, but also in its approach to the students. The school does not judge or reject anyone based on dress, language or other external expression of self. Rather it allows the girls relatively free expression in these areas and emphasizes their soul, growth, self-knowledge, commitment to character development, and attitude toward Yiddishkeit. Once their internal self develops, the external dress naturally changes. The school's tolerant approach has resulted in the girls' gaining respect for the Judaism they once shunned, with most of them voluntarily changing their mode of dress, becoming more committed to *halachah*, and attending mainstream *yeshivas* after graduation.

Basy and Raviv Shaked, the founders of Tzofiah, expect the return to Yiddishkeit to be long and time-consuming, if at all. But they know that it can only come with a deep, meaningful, spiritual experience with Torah, one that is ultimately about growth, the process of transforming the soul. Their attitude that Judaism is about *who you are*, not *what you wear* has met with tremendous success.

Conclusion and Source of the Problem

If focusing on internals is so important, why don't we do it? One major reason is that it's easier not to. *Doing* something is easier than *feeling* it. Going to *shul* is easier than concentrating on the words. Throwing a party is easier than making a *bar mitzvah* meaningful. Succumbing to desire for a beautiful home and communal respect is easier than balancing these desires with our need for spirituality. Judging religiosity based on dress is far easier than getting to know a person. Clothing fits into neat categories; who we are does not. That takes time and patience to discover.

Alternatively, this might also be a reaction to the outside world, particularly Christianity. Christianity de-emphasized the deed. For Christians, religion is mostly about belief and feeling, the internal experience. One's behavior, his external expression, seems far less important. Our emphasizing external factors at the expense of the internal may well be a reaction to their minimizing the external.

Having said all this, there are good reasons for focusing on externals. After all, Jewish values live through our actions. We believe that the external not only *expresses* the soul but *also modifies* it. Eventually actions become internalized and affect who we are. That is why it has been said, *be careful what you think, for your thoughts become your words. Be careful what you say, for your words become your actions. Be careful what you do, for your actions become your character.* And character is everything. It determines what you choose, the essence of your life and soul. Your character is your destiny.

But it seems we have moved too far in concentrating on external behavior. A successful Judaism requires balancing the external and internal. Just like ritual without *emunah* and love fails to transform the soul, *emunah* and love without ritual is an expressionless feeling that fails to transform the soul. Bringing the two together is an important way of regaining spirituality and helping to foster life-long Jewish observance.[6]

CHAPTER 27

Conformity and Its Consequences

So far, we have seen how fostering respect and spirituality are essential for drawing people toward community and helping them implement observance. But there is one final component for creating effective environments — enabling people to express and actualize themselves. Numerous people have gone off the derech because they felt unable to actualize or express themselves within their observant world.

Why would this be so? As previously discussed, self-actualization is at the pinnacle of our needs. To be ultimately happy and healthy, we must not only feel safe, loved and important, we must also reach our potentials. At the heart of doing so is our unique self that is different from all others. We are all given personalities with unique strengths, weaknesses, inclinations, and desires. In order to feel happy and become emotionally healthy, we must be able to express our unique attributes.

Stifling self-actualization sabotages the fulfillment of fundamental emotional needs and undermines the importance of our unique self, the *tzelem elokim* which is the Godliest part of our being. This compromises the ability to fulfill our individual missions and sends the message that we are not valuable in and of ourselves, but rather to the extent that we conform, which makes us nothing more than a means to an end.[1]

This may be why the Torah tells us, *chanoch lana'ar al pi darcho, teach a child according to his way*.[2] The Torah acknowledges that each child has his particular way — a way in which he will learn best and feel best, an environment in which he will feel most comfortable. That "way" must be recognized, respected, and addressed if he is to learn, reach his potential, and observe Judaism effectively. In fact, we are supposed to know a child's way *before* we begin educating him to ensure the education will be effective.

Recognizing a person's way enables him to develop and express the "I" at the heart of his observance and relationship with God. It enables him to bring his self to observance, to connect to it personally, and find personal meaning in it. This makes connection stronger, makes it easier to internalize Judaism and make it an integral part of his being. As a result, he is more likely to feel good about Yiddishkeit, to experience it as a source of joy, and remain committed to it.

It is interesting to note the end of that statement which is often omitted — *gam ki yakin lo yasoor mimenah* — also when he grows, he will not stray from it. It is as if the Torah tells us that to ensure he does not stray, teach him according to his way.

Conformity

There are a number of attitudes in our communities that directly undermine self-actualization. One of the most detrimental is insistence on conformity. Paul Shaviv, headmaster of the Community Hebrew Academy of Toronto, identifies the pressure to conform as a main cause for children going off the derech.

> From observation, it seems to me that the greatest pressure in contemporary Orthodox society is the pressure to

conform. Orthodox groups seem not to be able to tolerate the slightest nonconformity — even in matters that are irrelevant to belief. An example can be found in the recent "Jewish Observer" comment on wearing blue shirts rather than white shirts ("Well, there's nothing really wrong, but on the other hand, it's a danger signal.") The lack of tolerance of any individualism — however slight and however innocuous — is the common thread that turns kids "off the derech." Everything else is just a consequence.

While every community has its standards for behavior, observant Jewish communities seem to define more rigid standards and respond more intensely to deviation from the norm. Whether the standards are *halachic* or societal, legitimate or not, when they stifle self-expression, they can push people away from our communities and from observance itself.

That is what happened in Jonathan's case. Jonathan wanted to be a filmmaker. He was creative and talented and felt that filmmaking would enable him to express his unique talents and make an important impact on the world. But his choice was met with disdain, disapproval, and rejection. He felt that he had to choose between his familial/communal expectations — which meant conforming to standards he was not comfortable with — and developing his potential.

Had this been the first time he felt he had to make that choice, or had that choice concerned a less significant issue for him, the outcome might have been less severe. But as it stood, he felt his only real choice was his desired profession. So he left the community, went off the derech, and eventually came to lose respect for the observant world. As he explains,

> In most other systems, in secular systems, there's room
> for growth. You can grow up a certain way and leave
> your small town and move to a big city and no one is go-

302

ing to tear their hair out. I have a friend who grew up in Boulder, Colorado. His father was a shoe salesman. He's from a small-minded community, and he is a filmmaker of experimental films. His family is proud as hell of him. In the Orthodox world you have to leave that world to do that. If you want to become a rabbi, then there's room for growth. But if you don't choose to grow within their little definition, then they ask you to leave. They don't want you living in the community.

Jonathan says that when he was young, he would debate and rebel against the conformity and superficiality he faced. Now he says, he "votes with his feet."

The observant Jewish world has numerous requirements for proper behavior. Those requirements become particularly problematic when a child cannot conform, when our reaction to deviation is extreme, or when the expectations involve external, superficial realities rather than internal, meaningful ones. All these situations make our expectations seem unjustified and can confine self-expression. They can also undermine our fundamental need for unconditional love. As one child quoted in the *Jewish Observer* said, "a teacher...shouldn't make you feel as though if you don't wear a hat and jacket, you're the scum of the earth."[3]

Particularly problematic is when our expectations seem to move away from God and spirituality. For example, one *baal teshuva* couple was chastised by members of their community for abstaining from sugar and meat. As reported in the *Baltimore Jewish Times*, "their preference for herbal and naturopathic healing was, they were told, akin to idol worship. Because their new neighbors and friends were extremely conventional, they felt compelled to hide basic facts about their old bohemian ways. Most telling of all, Ed gave up playing guitar as irrelevantly secular and *goyish* (not Jewish)."[4] Surely, becoming observant was difficult enough. But these social expectations which seemed to have little to do with spirituality were too much for them to bear. Eventually, they chose to leave observance.

This kind of situation seems to be more prevalent and problematic than we think. When survey respondents were asked about conformity to external standards of dress, speech, and behavior, 66% indicated that their communities pressured them to conform to external standards. 22% felt somewhat pressured to do so. And 63% felt negative about the pressure to conform.

Stifles Religious Actualization

Ultimately, forcing conformity goes beyond compromising general self-actualization; it also compromises religious actualization. It does so in two ways in particular. First, by stifling free will. For example, there are communities in Israel that have established "*tzniut* police" who safeguard modest dress. They identify women who wear the wrong colors, short skirts, or who walk down the street with men other than their husbands. Sometimes they contact husbands and sometimes they confront the women directly. While every community has a right to define its own standards and to respectfully *request* adherence, when they *enforce* conformity and respond strongly to deviation, they undermine the very Torah they are trying to protect. They then compromise personal, individual actualization as well as religious actualization.

How so? Because dramatic negative consequences for non-conformity — whether for *mitzvot* or societal standards — stifle our free will. They cause us to act from fear rather than love, from impure motives rather than pure ones. These negative consequences may be precisely why God does not strike us with lightening for not conforming to His standards. Delaying punishment preserves free will. And when communities enforce conformity with severe reactions, they destroy the vital free will that God Himself strives to protect.

Ultimately, this type of behavior also undermines religious growth.

We all grow at different paces in different ways, and we need the integrity of that process to be respected if we are to grow successfully. In fact, real commitment to Torah requires it. As Debbie Greenblatt explains, "We have created a climate where a misstep is falling off a mountain....we should teach kids that it is not a question of standing on top of the mountain but climbing and learning how to enjoy and how to recover if you step back."[5] This means making mistakes, sometimes not fitting into the mold or living up to others' expectations of us.[6] Forcing conformity compromises that process and undermines that message.

Consider Sara for example. She was a Bais Yaacov girl from a Chassidic family in Monsey who had no feeling for or commitment to Yiddishkeit whatsoever. She broke Shabbat, wore bikinis and did it all behind her parents' back. When she went to school in Israel, things started to change. She gained a more positive attitude to observance, and identified some of the issues that had led her away from it. She wanted to stay for a second year but her parents refused. Her father wanted her to return home and get married. She explained that she wanted to stay for her *ruchniyut* (spirituality), that she felt a certain "lacking" which Israel was addressing. But her father insisted she return. As Sara explained to the administrators, "We are not allowed to feel that lacking."

Perhaps had her father known that she was no longer observant, he might have let her stay — but she would never tell him. Sara had seen what happened to her older sister who had gone off the derech. Her father had cut her off. Sara felt she could not withstand that kind of rejection. She needed his approval. So she remained silent and compromised her spiritual development to gain it, even if it was based on a lie. The need to conform had created an unsafe environment that encouraged dishonesty. In such an environment, the fear and reality of rejection was too great to face.

So instead of telling her father the truth, Sara asked the family rav to call him. Finally, her father relented and agreed to let her return to Israel. But when she went home for the summer, he wouldn't let her go. "But you said!" she pleaded. "I was lying," he responded. Desperate and overwhelmed, Sara got as close to telling the truth as she could: "But Daddy, you don't get it. I just don't feel like a good Jew."

His response to that was even worse. "Get with it, honey," he replied. "Most of us are not good Jews. We just have to do it. You think I like *frumkeit* (religiosity)? Who *likes* being *frum*? You just have to do it."

Among other things, Sara's story indicates that sometimes, even though we *can* conform to expectations, we should not. For Sara, conformity would have been devastating. It would have meant sacrificing her emotional and religious growth, and, if she would have married a nice, *frum* boy as her father wanted her to, potentially ruining her life as well as someone else's.

We all need to grow and explore our world, and as children, we are most inclined to do so in the context of our own homes — the *frum* Jewish world. But the pressure to conform can deny us that process and send the message that growth can occur only *outside* of our world. Those with stronger personalities may then leave our communities in order to grow. And those with weaker ones may remain but cease to grow religiously.

Hurts Our Communities

In the long run, our children are not the only ones who suffer the consequences of conformity. Our communities also suffer as a result. Communities are groups of individuals whose unique talents and abilities make them the colorful, properly functioning places they are. To coalesce successfully, the individuals need to share some common values and goals. But the diversity in their personalities, cultures, ages and perspectives all help the community to function. When we stifle the uniqueness of individual members, we lose the very parts that make us whole, special, and vital. To be our best as communities, we must allow every individual to be his unique best.

It is interesting that God chose to reveal himself to Moses directly after one of his sheep straggled away from the flock and Moses abandoned the flock to retrieve the sheep. Rabbi Shmuley Boteach notes that Moses returned for the "smallest and weakest" of the sheep, not because he hoped it would grow big and strong like the others, but rather because he recognized that even this small sheep was an indispensable part of the flock. Without it, the whole flock was deficient. "In other words," Rabbi Boteach explains, "Moses did not return for the sake of the straggler, but for the sake of the flock."[7]

So a *frumkeit* that does not acknowledge the value of the self destroys not only the individual but also the very fabric of its own society. If we value community, the best way to promote it is by valuing the individual who is at the heart of that community.

This is not to say that the individual should come at the expense of community. Judaism is not individualism. But neither is Judaism about the needs of community coming before the individual's. Judaism is about balancing both the individual who serves the greater good and the community which protects the individual.

Doing so requires recognizing differences and respecting them, which in itself is a Godly endeavor. Think of the world God created, so different and varied: There are over 250,000 kinds of plants in the world; more than two million species of animals. Why so many differences? Why so many colors and climates? Why so many planets and solar systems? Would not one million species of animals have sufficed?

Our one universe has so much diversity, so many different kinds of life residing together in harmony. Our communities are best served by being a microcosm of God's own world, by respecting diverse personalities and addressing their various needs.

This does not mean that all differences are acceptable or that individuals are never stifled. Existing in community means making some sacrifices. But those sacrifices should exist in individual *moments* rather than define an entire *way of life*. And when individuals cannot or do not conform to our standards, we should still meet them with warmth and respect. The extent to which we succeed in this will largely determine how positive our communal environments will be and how well they foster observance.

*　　*　　*

Every community has its standards and enforces them to some extent or another. Right wing communities might enforce adherence to modes of dress, while Modern Orthodox communities may focus on choice of profession. In either case, the pressure to conform can create problems. Even when it seems to result in observant behavior, that observance is often hollow — not done out of real belief or love for Yiddishkeit, but rather the desire to please. In the worst cases, it can create bitterness and resentment. So while, at best, the pressure to conform fosters short-term observance, it often sabotages what is necessary for long-term commitment — internal connection, joy, and belief.

Some people feel that conformity does not play a real role when people go off the derech. They point to the low numbers of kids who go off the derech from communities in Meah Shearim or very Chassidic homes. Or they point to the kids who go off the derech from Modern Orthodox homes where there is more flexibility.

There are clearly many factors at play. However, the low numbers of defectors from very restrictive communities does not mean that conformity is not an issue. After all, problems do not necessarily manifest themselves in the dropping of observance. They sometimes prompt only internal suffering, a weakened connection to Yiddishkeit or to the community. Since this is internal, it is difficult to ascertain. It may only manifest itself in the next generation.

In addition, the fewer cases of people going off the derech in more religious communities may say less about children's belief than their need to be accepted and loved. When non-conformity can mean losing everyone and everything you value, the price may be too high to pay. In such circumstances, many will choose to conform in order to gain acceptance, love, and respect. As such, the few numbers who go off the derech in those communities do not necessarily indicate successful Judaism. They may simply reflect how powerful the human need for love and acceptance is. When the price for nonconformity becomes too high, as it sometimes does in more restrictive communities, it is difficult to know exactly what conformity indicates.

Some people argue that kids who go off the derech also subject themselves to peer groups with strict social expectations to which they must conform. But there is a difference between conforming to a peer group and conforming to the Jewish community. First, the child is choosing to join the peer group of his own free will, which makes him less likely to feel restricted by the peer group than he would by the Jewish community. Second, the standards of such groups, although strict, are far less defining than Yiddishkeit is. Yiddishkeit defines correct behavior in every area of life. These groups tend to define it only in a few, which makes it easier to conform. So when given the choice, children will more easily conform to the standards of peer groups than to the standards of the *frum* world.

Conclusion

Conformity will work some times to some extent with some people. But it will not work with everyone all the time. Since we are all different and have different needs and challenges in terms of Yiddishkeit, we all require different methods for meeting those challenges and maintaining observance. Some will need to marry later or sooner. Some may be interested in developing careers or spending time in Israel, or traveling to other parts of the world. Some will merely need the room to dress a little differently while other, more adventurous personalities may need to jump out of airplanes or read controversial books.

As Rabbi Shaya Cohen says, "One size fits none...The reality is that the more potential a teenager has, the more likely he's not going to fit the mold....because someone who is a thinker, an independent spirit, strives for this sense of growth and accomplishment; he can't be just pushed around."[8]

Children need room to express and develop themselves, and forcing conformity can backfire terribly. So rather than try to create them in our image, we would be better served to provide them with as much room as possible to express themselves and their Yiddishkeit.

CHAPTER 28

Narrow Definitions of Being Observant

P art of what makes conformity so problematic is our narrow definitions of *frumkeit*. Being properly observant today involves meeting a very narrow and well-defined criterion that involves not only *halachah*, but also a host of other requirements regarding beliefs, dress, conduct, and other things that inherently have nothing to do with religiosity.

Perhaps this is because we believe that, since we are already *frum*, our children's challenge is to be more *frum*. They were already given Shabbat so their challenge is to build upon that — to make Shabbat more meaningful, more beautiful. We already *daven*, so their challenge is to *daven* with more *cavanah*. We assume they will *daven*! The only question is how hard. We assume they will keep Shabbat, wear a black hat, and attend *yeshiva*; the only question is with how much joy, at how prestigious a *yeshiva*.

This perspective means that we add many requirements to being observant, which compounds the problem of conformity. The narrower our definitions for proper observance, the narrower the path and the harder it is to stay on the derech. The narrower the path, the less room there is for the self. The less room there is to move, make mistakes, or express varying parts of the personality, the more likely a person will fall off the derech.

One formerly observant Jew told me that when he was growing up, bowling was considered 'evil.' People reacted to bowling as strongly as they did to breaking Shabbat. When he went bowling, he was labeled a 'bum.' At first he hid his bowling from others, but eventually came to resent the community for it. If he couldn't even bowl in his community and he had to feel like a bum for wanting to, he couldn't be part of it. As soon as he was old enough, he moved away and left observance. For him the road was simply too narrow, and the reaction to stepping off it so severe that he could no longer feel good about observance and observant people.

Chaim Potok, author of the famed book *The Chosen*, had a similar experience in a different area. Raised in a Chassidic home, he went to *yeshiva* all his life but "he didn't quite fit the mold. As a child, he painted, but his father disapproved of painting, thinking it a 'gentile enterprise.'"[1] No doubt, Mr. Potok was a creative man and highly talented. But the artistic talent that so greatly defined his unique character was deemed *treif* by his father. In all probability, for his father, being a good Jew meant much more than being *halachic;* it meant abstaining from creative endeavors such as painting as well. This narrow definition of proper Jewish behavior may have created an unrealistic expectation for Mr. Potok. And if conformity to that expectation was the prerequisite of acceptance, it may have been too high a price to pay. Whatever the case, today, Mr. Potok is a Conservative rabbi and considers himself "a practicing Conservative Jew." He is also "angry at the ultra-Orthodox Jews for accusing others Jews of being less than Jewish."[2]

Narrow Definitions Blur the Understanding of *Frumkeit*

In addition to potentially sabotaging self-actualization, narrow definitions of proper observance blur the understanding of proper observance. All things become equated until we lose all sense of priority. Non-*halachic* requirements seem the same as *halachic* ones, for breaches in both areas are met with the same condemnation. Our children then begin to equate smaller infractions with more significant ones. Wearing a black hat becomes equated with keeping Shabbat. Wearing a white shirt becomes equated with keeping *kashrut*. They then lose their understanding of observance along with the ability to feel good about themselves for what they *can* accomplish. It has gotten to the point where some children don't even know what it means to be *frum* anymore. One educator told me that a twelfth grade Bais Yaacov girl from a well-known family approached him after a lecture saying,

> "I don't know if I am really *frum*."
>
> "Why not?" he asked her.
>
> "I listen to *goyishe* music and I love it" she said. "And I put lipstick on, on Shabbas. I am *mechalel* Shabbas."

In a sense, it's wonderful that she should care so much about her observance. In another sense, it's very sad. Imagine how hard she has worked to be who she is, especially as a teenager in our modern world. The question alone may reveal how *frum* she really is. But she does not feel that. She cannot feel that. She doesn't know what it means to be *frum* anymore. She speaks about listening to *goyishe* music in the same breath as putting on lipstick, in the same breath as breaking Shabbas. The meaning of the word *frum* is lost to her. The consequence is that she cannot take pride in how *frum* she really is. She cannot even take pride in her desire to grow, which is profoundly religious.

These kinds of expectations make children feel off the derech, even when they are not. And once they psychologically associate themselves with the nonobservant, it's a small leap to join them. For example, hypothetically, if Chaim Potok's father equated painting with being a bad Jew, it would cause Chaim to see himself as a bad Jew for painting. Once he perceived himself as "out," as somewhat off the derech, it would become very easy and perhaps even necessary to drop the whole thing. If you are a bad Jew anyway, what difference does it make? You may as well be free and have a good time. And since a bad Jew does not keep Shabbat, he should not be keeping Shabbat. In order to make the label true, one might be compelled to drop *halachah* altogether.

An All or Nothing Attitude

In these instances, what our children learn is that being observant means being observant *all the way*, not only by adhering to *halachic* standards, but also to stringencies and communal standards. They can feel that if they are not observant all the way, it is as though they are not observant at all. An all or nothing attitude is created and as soon as they go bowling or play the guitar, they feel as though they are off the derech.

Our children get this message not only from our definitions, but the vigor with which we pressure them to conform. They feel it not only through our words, but also our actions — how we talk about people who do not conform, whether or not we associate with them, respect them, and embrace them. We may not send that message directly in our classrooms, but we do so indirectly through our behavior.

The all or nothing message puts our kids in a precarious situation. Reuven is a case in point. Reuven grew up in an observant home. His mother covered her hair, his father learned. They were sincere and committed. They expected that Reuven would follow in their footsteps and he did. Although he moved away from home, he managed to remain *halachically* observant even though he did go to bars sometimes and behave in other imperfect ways.

One Friday afternoon after work, he went to a bar with a couple of friends. They started drinking and having a good time, so much so that they didn't notice the sun was going down. By the time Reuven looked at his watch, it was already Shabbat. He had broken Shabbat for the first time without even realizing it. What now? He was far away from home and he would have to take a cab or a subway to get there.

Oh well, he thought. I already broke Shabbat. I may as well stay and have a good time. So he did. The night passed and eventually he left the bar. Walking down the street, he passed the golden arches — McDonald's. What observant child in America has not thought about a Big Mac or smelled the rich aroma of McDonald's fries?! He had always wanted to taste those fries and now he was hungry and a little intoxicated.

He had already broken Shabbat, he thought, so what difference would it make. He entered the McDonald's, and ordered some fries. In one afternoon, he had managed to not only break Shabbat but also to eat *treif*. That was the beginning of the end of his observance.

Why did he eat the fries? Why did he stay at the bar to have another drink? Why did he not go straight home? Very simply — because he thought, if I've already crossed the line, what difference does it make? His Judaism had become all or nothing. If he couldn't do it all, and do it properly, he might as well do nothing.

What in Reuven's case applied to observance in general, works for others in terms of individual *mitzvot*. For example, I have friends — from across the religious spectrum — who stopped keeping Shabbat in college. When they broke one part of it, they dropped it altogether because they had been taught that keeping Shabbat means keeping it totally or not at all.

Others, who were raised to believe that you do what you can, had a very different experience. Although they, too, struggled with Yiddishkeit, when they failed to keep Shabbat completely, they kept what they could. Their behavior *looked* inconsistent and potentially hypocritical, and it may have been hard for others to understand or respect it. They would smoke, but not watch TV; or watch TV, but not get in cars. But their imperfect observance kept them connected.

315

Technically, their *behavior* might have been as un-*halachic* as the first group. But their *experience* of it was completely different. Experientially, they had a better quality connection to observance. Rather than give them permission to drop Shabbat, the broader, more flexible approach made them adhere to whatever they could. It gave them permission to see themselves as good Jews, even if they were not doing it all. That more positive perception maintained a connection and made it easier for some to return in the future.

Debbie Greenblatt alluded to this when she recounted a story about a Chassidic girl brought to her by a frustrated, distraught mother. Her entire family was up in arms over her Yiddishkeit. She had been kicked out of two schools. She was "going off the derech." Something had to be done. After about a half hour of speaking to this girl, Ms. Greenblatt asked her if she was *frum*. The girl said she didn't know.

> "Do you keep Shabbat?" Ms. Greenblatt asked.
> "Yes."
> "Do you eat only kosher food?"
> "Yes."
> "Do you keep the holidays?"
> "Yes."
> "Then you are *frum*," Ms. Greenblatt told her.

"You should have heard her sigh of relief," Ms. Greenblatt says. "Why did she think she might not be *frum*? Because her socks were down and her skirt was a little high. I am not in favor of that, but we can't have kids think that there is no room. We need to broaden the top of the mountain. When you equate these things with desecrating Shabbat, what happens next is chilul Shabbat. There has to be a difference."[3]

Narrow Definitions Displace God and Torah

Finally, this is particularly problematic when our definitions of proper observance have more to do with our own expectations than God's.

When our definitions move outside of the realm of *halachah*, as they often do, they have the added undesired effect of replacing God and His Torah as the measure of what is right with ourselves.

When communal standards become the measure of *frumkeit* rather than the Torah's, observance starts to become more about what people think, and people then aim to please each other rather than God. In a sense, this creates the same reality as the Enlightenment did — man becomes the measure of what is right rather than God. Of course, this is never intended. But the more we focus on extra-*halachic* require-ments, the greater the possibility that we neglect or forget about the Torah itself.

Conclusion

Forcing conformity undermines basic emotional needs as well as self and religious actualization. It can prompt children to lie and to leave their communities, which can lead them off the derech. Narrow defi-nitions take matters one step further. They make the road sometimes too narrow to walk; they create an all or nothing attitude, blur the real meaning of what it means to be *frum*, and displace God as the mea-sure of proper behavior. This makes it all too easy to go off the derech — or rather to *fall* off of it.

Why then do we persist in these attitudes? Partly because we feel our children can and should observe more than basic *halachah*; we feel they should be able to move beyond basic requirements since they are born into *frum* families. We also feel that the tighter the reigns and the stronger our reactions to deviation, the more likely they will stay on the derech; at least if they fall, they will not fall too far away. But when the self is stifled too much, the opposite occurs. Ultimately, dif-ferentiating between *halachah* and *chumra* and broadening the road as much as possible can help keep children on the derech.

317

CHAPTER 29

Our Attitudes Toward Other Communities: There is One Right Way to be *Frum*

If you do nothing but condemn, certainly people are not going to listen to you...everything by us in the Ashkenazi world is judgmental...Yeshiva University is no good, Chassidim are no good, Mitnagdim are no good, Agudah is no good, Degel HaTorah is no good. In such a world, it is very hard to find yourself.[1]
— Rabbi Berel Wein

Our narrow definitions of proper observance also translate into our attitude toward other observant communities. They sometimes lead us to believe that there is one right way to be *frum* — namely *our* way — and that anything else is 'off the derech.'

As one woman wrote, "years ago, straight out of a *charedi* women's seminary in Boro Park, Brooklyn, I used to think that only those who wore the right outfits, and had the proper wigs and beards, had the keys to the kingdom of heaven; and why not? That's what we were taught. That and that all the other kinds of Jews were mistaken, misguided; even dangerous."[2]

The belief in our own *derech* as the *only derech* does not exist only in Chassidic communities. It exists across the spectrum of the Jewish world. It seems that no matter where we are on the religious spectrum, we tend to brand everything to the right or left of ourselves as unacceptable and inauthentic. In fact, 59% of those surveyed felt that their communities had negative and rejecting attitudes toward Jews who were more, or less, observant than themselves. Of the remaining respondents, 37% felt their communities' attitudes were neutral and only 3% felt they were mixed. *No one* indicated that their communities had a positive attitude toward other Jews. More significantly, when asked whether or not those negative attitudes caused them to respect their own communities less, 76% indicated that it did. And even more telling, 76% indicated that the negative attitudes caused them to move away from their communities.

Sometimes we minimize, marginalize, and discount other observant communities. But sometimes we go beyond that and openly disparage them. Listen to this rav's description of the Modern Orthodox world:

> ...There are communities that believe that *shomer negiah* (the *mitzvah* of unmarried men and women not touching) is optional. Although you can always find individuals with messed up ideas, as communities, you will only find this among the Modern Orthodox; and such communities, and others who have similarly twisted the Torah, are intolerable, and are guilty of a terrible sin of changing the Torah...I am referring to the bungalow colony that advertised as a "Modern Orthodox" colony, and when...asked what that means...they said 'it means we have mixed swimming.' They are changing the Torah. I am referring to those Orthodox high schools that some of my friends' wives went to that used to sponsor proms with mixed dancing. They have changed the Torah.

This rav surely has good intentions and may even have legitimate points to make. But the tone of his remarks is so condemning that it can negatively affect those who hear it. It can certainly cause them to lose respect for him and his brand of Yiddishkeit.

Even worse, it can stifle their self-actualization and religious growth. Why so? Because *our* way may not be the right one for our children. And if that is the case, they will need other legitimate options in the observant world. When we have branded every path other than our own as inauthentic — or worse as akin to not being observant — they will be more likely to go off the derech completely rather than join another community. The more condemning our attitude, the more likely they are to go off the derech rather than join an alternative community.

As Rabbi Moshe Prager of Neve Tzion explains, "a big part of the *hashkafic* problem today is that you're black or nothing."[3] Children feel that anything but the *yeshivish* way is akin to not being observant at all. So if they ever have a problem with the black hat world or its *hashkafa*, there is no alternative.

Children who find the *yeshivish* world too confining, who are not cut out for learning, who have an interest in secular learning, or are drawn to the Modern Orthodox *hashkafa*, become stuck. They can remain in the *yeshivish* world but they may never be happy or reach their religious potential, and their observance will not be as strong and joyful as it would have been had they found a community that better spoke to their "way." Alternatively, they may go off the derech completely, for we will have taught them that other options are akin to not being *frum* at all.

The same is true for children in Modern Orthodox communities. Some of them may not value engagement with the secular world; they may believe more strongly in the *yeshivish* approach. They may find the *yeshivish* approach more meaningful or they may be more inspired by it. Whatever the reason, the community would be gravely mistaken to teach them that Modern Orthodoxy is the only legitimate path. If the community intentionally or inadvertently condemns, shuns or undermines the *yeshivish* world, this would leave the child no viable option.

In that case, he will either remain Modern Orthodox unhappily or he may leave observance altogether. On the off chance that he has the strength of character and objectivity to join the *yeshivish* world anyway, he may suffer a blow to his self-esteem, or develop resentment for his original community.

We intuitively understand that people have different needs. But we don't always apply this to our children or their observance. Rabbi Shlomo Wolbe explains that parents often assume that "his way means their way. Others recognize that their child has a unique way but don't respect it. They think that the child should abandon his way and adopt their way instead."⁴

Psychologist Dr. Lob explains that there are "kids who go through their whole life feeling out of step with Orthodox Judaism when in fact they were just out of step with the brand of Orthodox Judaism that they were in."⁵ Such children would benefit from legitimate alternatives. They would be much less likely to believe that they have to go off the derech in order to actualize themselves. If they were taught that commitment to *halachah*, regardless of *hashkafa* or style, is what makes one observant, they would have permission to see other communities as authentic Torah options. This could greatly help them find their place in the observant world and flourish within it. It could help them find the path that best speaks to them and expresses their individuality. As Rabbi Kook explains, a *tzadik* lives in *his* faith, according to his particular *derech* — not *a derech* or *our derech,* but the one that naturally works with his own.

Failure to provide alternative paths for our children can go beyond pushing them off the derech to creating anger and resentment toward Torah and *frum* Jews. That was the case with Naomi who went to a black hat seminary, which espoused one approach to Judaism, dismissing all others as unauthentic. Her rav went so far as to tell her that if "she were ever to reach her potential in honesty and intelligence, she would see that a black hat life was the only one that was right for her."

He tried to get her to associate with the more *frum* girls in the school and denigrated her less observant friends. This stifled Naomi's growth and personality and stirred anger within her. One day, she found herself writing:

> A black hat life is the ONLY one that is right for me? There are no other options? That's the worst thing — to forget that there were and are other options, to forget that it's an active choice where you go. For me the active choice is essential — never to feel that I've simply been blindly led by others who forgot the other options, unless I make a conscious, independent choice to forget them.
>
> I want to roll along the tracks and remember the destination and cause. Otherwise, I will become like a train going on the same path at the same speed, headed to the same destination every five minutes, with no change, no life — a limp, dead robot with no growth, and no consideration for the value of happiness and ability to use what God gave us. That's what I'm most scared of — becoming a "me" I would hate without realizing it, a "me" that is antithetical to all I am and stand for, a "me" that forgets the options, the destination, the why, the opportunity and gift of happiness.
>
> Being told that a "Black Hat" life is all you are good for, that anything else would be selling yourself short, that your honesty and intelligence would not exist truly or would be deprived if you didn't live that lifestyle, is being told to forget the options. It is seeing one way, one track, and ironically can almost make you feel guilty for not getting on the train when it's dangerous for you to buy the ticket.
>
> He wants me to join them. It's safe. It's secure. It's Truth. It is no option and no need for option, no choices

and no need to choose. I will not have no option and cannot jump into all that security and realness, for the reality is too cold, too true, too confined, too static, too deathly. It's just too black; it's just too grave. To simply jump in would mean committing suicide. It would deceptively appear like creating ideals, but it would be destroying mine. It would seem like aspiring to new dreams, but it would be killing mine. It would seem limitless, and in fact is for those who have chosen to know only the coffin. But their limitless is my lifelessness, and they cannot and will not drag me into that death — the death of my own heart and mind, the death of my own personality, the end of me.

No one knew the girl felt this way, not even she. But since there was no alternative except for one that didn't work, she felt trapped. Her emotional and religious needs to actualize and find her *derech* were compromised. And the more the seminary tried to impose their way, the less room there was for her self and for her free choice. Her means to achieving emotional health, happiness and religious meaning were sabotaged, leaving only anger and resentment toward those who sabotaged it.

Interestingly, Naomi did become observant according to her *yeshiva's* standards—for a while. But it didn't stick. A few years later she went off the derech. Had there been another alternative, she might have found a path that was better suited for her, which might have helped her stay on the derech. But with only one choice that didn't work well for her personality, her observance was undermined from the start.

It is important to realize that we need not be directly condemning to create this kind of situation. We can do so simply by presenting our own perspectives as if the others don't exist or subtly demeaning other *hashkafot*. The point here is not who is right or wrong. The point is that such an attitude is not helpful for our children who might need alternative approaches to Yiddishkeit.

Rejects and Undermines National Unity

Rejecting other communities and their *hashkafot* also undermines the vision of national life and national unity which we need to create a meaningful Judaism. This is especially problematic for those whose personalities may be more inspired by the national component. For example: after fifteen years in the Orthodox world, Susan Levine, a *baalat teshuva,* said that she "cared only for the *halachic* system and felt no connection to Jewish peoplehood." Ed Rosenblatt, another *baal teshuva,* explains that "The one thing I never had, didn't gain, and still don't have is a feeling for the Jewish people."[6] Both of them went off the derech after years of being observant. A national vision and feeling can connect people to observance; a lack of it can push some people away. And while it is hard to know how great a role this played in the process of these people dropping observance, it is noteworthy that the issue arose at all in their discussion of it.

Jewish issues today are deep and complex. When the ghetto walls came crashing down, and Jews were faced with modernity, a challenging conflict ensued. New issues arose. Some, like Samson Raphael Hirsch, addressed the conflict by claiming the holy and secular could work together, that the secular could advance the holy. Others like the Chatam Sofer contended that Judaism could only survive if it were protected and separated from the secular.

There are good reasons for these varying approaches, and strong arguments on all sides. The important thing is to acknowledge them respectfully, for the existence of these different perspectives might well have helped to keep Judaism alive and thriving in our modern world. And to keep it thriving into the future, we may need more of the same.

Attitude Toward the Nonobservant: Obstruction of Truth

Condemnation toward the nonobservant can be equally problematic. 71% of survey respondents said they feel that their community's attitude toward nonobservant Jews was negative and rejecting and *no one* felt that it was positive. Again, this caused most respondents not only to lose respect for our own communities, but also to move away from them.

On the national level, this can create *chilul Hashem* and undermine our ability to serve as a light and inspire respect. Rejecting the nonobservant can also cause them to reject us in turn, as was the case with Chaim Potok. Years after leaving his Chassidic world, he is "angry at the ultra-Orthodox Jews for accusing others Jews of being less than Jewish. He asserts "that language, that rhetoric, is the most dismaying aspect of divisiveness, and they have brought that language into Jewish life. The onus is on them to do away with it."[7]

Our negative attitudes to nonobservant Jews have other somewhat surprising repercussions. Listen to what one formerly observant teen said when asked how she felt about the first time she stopped keeping Shabbat:

> Well, when I decided to do it, I figured I would feel like a bum, because that's the only thing they taught us in school about being religious — that those who don't are bums, basically. But after I did it, I didn't feel like a bum. I felt like me!! So obviously there's no difference between someone who keeps Shabbas and who doesn't except one is religious and one is not. So why should I be religious, I figured? Like what's the point?

Many formerly observant Jews have noted similar feelings. One of them remarked that he felt our attitude toward the nonobservant is such that if Sodom and Gemorah were happening today, rather than beg God for their salvation the way Abraham did, we'd be saying,

"Sodom and Gemorah! Hurry up and kill them already!"

We feel it is justifiable to condemn nonobservance; after all non-observant Jews really are off the derech. And we feel on some level that the more harshly we condemn them, the clearer we make to our children that their way is wrong. This, we believe, will help keep our children *frum*. But often, it backfires.

The girl above, for example, heard the message that those who are not observant are bums. When she became nonobservant, she didn't feel like a bum so, she reasoned, her community was wrong and there was therefore nothing wrong with being nonobservant.

Like Eve in the Garden of Eden, sometimes when we condemn what we should not, we end up losing the very thing we are trying to protect. Eve condemned the act of touching the tree in order to protect the eating from it. But her distortion of the truth unwittingly opened the door for the serpent to enter and tempt her to sin. So when we make the nonobservant out to be worse than they are — when we send the message that they are bums, ignoramuses, or that they must be unhappy and unfulfilled — especially when we do so to keep children religious — we create the wrong foundation for children's observance. We prompt them to observe out of disdain for the other rather than love of the self, which is negatively, rather than positively, based. And if their disdain ever disappears, their basis for observance can go with it, and the condemnation, which was meant to protect them, will backfire, leading them off the derech.

If we have done the job of properly establishing Yiddishkeit emotionally and intellectually, we will not need to knock the alternative in order to strengthen ourselves. Everything else will naturally and clearly pale in comparison without our condemnation. And if we have failed in making a strong case and laying a proper foundation for observance, condemnation of the alternative will not work. At best it may create a negatively based belief and at worst it may distort the truth and thereby lead our kids off the derech.

This is not to say that we should be advocating nonobservance as an alternative to observant life. But neither should we be condemning it as strongly as we do. As the organization, Nefesh, explains in its guide for children in crisis:

> ...youth going through this transition period are conflicted in their belief in God....These youth feel abandoned and disaffected by their parents, by their *rabbaim* and by God...yet at the same time, it is their belief in God, their interest in remaining part of a community, their wanting to be heard and loved that keeps them "inside the fold" albeit at arms length...these kids should be taught that God accepts all forms of service to Him even when it is displayed in the most nominal form.[8]

God accepts "all forms," not just the "right" ones or the ones that correspond with ours. This perspective can be particularly helpful for *baalei teshuva*. *Baalei teshuva* have families that are often largely not observant. Those non-*frum* people are a part of them, an essential part. As one former *baal teshuva* mentioned, "Somebody is telling you that your uncle is not *frum*, but he is part of the family. How do you just get rid of him?"

If the *baal teshuva* is to maintain healthy relationships with his family, and serve as a *kiddush Hashem*, he will need permission to accept his family on their own terms. If he does not, he may have to emotionally amputate an important part of his life, which may be too difficult or painful to bear. Or he may display a superiority or arrogance that turns his family off to Yiddishkeit and creates *chilul Hashem*. This can forever taint his family's perception of observance and make them less likely to support his decision, which will only make his observance more difficult.

Conclusion

It is natural to believe that what we do is right and, by extension, that those who don't do the same thing are wrong, especially if Torah is truth with a capital T. But no matter how natural our negative attitudes may be, or how good our intentions, when they result in the belief that there is only one right way to be *frum,* or in condemnation of other ways, they are counterproductive. They may box our children into a way that is ill-suited for their personality, or may push them off the derech altogether.

A more understanding and respectful attitude of others is far more productive and may in fact be the only perspective that truly reflects the greatness of Torah, for Torah is unique and impressive precisely, in part, because it makes room for every kind of person, every personality from every culture and every profession. It embraces many ways of life as long as there is a core commitment to *halachah.* It recognizes that there are alternative *hashkafot* within Yiddishkeit for coming close to God. It allows truth to be expressed in a variety of ways that can speak to different people according to their particular needs. We say there are *shivim panim leTorah — seventy faces of Torah —* each being authentic while looking and feeling quite different from each other.

As Rabbi Steinsaltz notes when explaining the Talmud's exploration of a variety of answers for any given question, "If you have some mathematical training, even a small one, you know that any equation of the second degree has two right answers that mostly are different. If there's an equation of a higher order, it may have three or four or six right answers. All these answers are right. They have to be applied in different places differently, but basically... [there are] many right answers to the same question.[9]"

Judaism is an equation of the highest order, and it therefore surely offers more than one answer for how to properly live an observant way of life. Validating various paths allows Judaism to shine in its full splendor, more truthfully than one simple perspective would. There are many types of observant Jews today who live different observant lives. And, while each emphasizes his own perspective, they all have something beautiful to add to the colorful picture of our Jewish world.

The Modern Orthodox world may lack fervent or consistent *halachic* observance, but it excels in striving to balance the religious world with involvement in the secular one. This enables them to bring Torah ideals to the outside world and to bring secular knowledge to the observant world in ways other communities cannot.

The *yeshiva* world may lack interest in the outside world and the ability to contribute to it directly, but it excels in the *mitzvah* of Torah learning, in creating impassioned educators for our day schools and strong communities which are extraordinary in the modern world.

The Chassidic world may force insularity but their children posses a rare purity of soul. Chabad excels in emphasizing the importance of joy in observance and embracing all Jews, while religious Zionists excel in love for the land of Israel, reminding us how precious the national part of Torah is.

Each of these communities is like the twelve tribes, all committed to a common goal while possessing unique strengths and weaknesses. The variety modeled by the twelve tribes and the way they worked together to strengthen the Jewish people is a good model for us to follow. After all, as Rabbi Sacks put it:

> Am I supposed to live with a Judaism that is only as big as one particular group? Judaism is bigger than Boro Park. It is bigger than B'nai Brak. It is bigger than Stanford Hill. It is huge. Go and stand at the Kotel and you will see people who have come together to Israel from 103 different countries, speaking 82 different languages. You will see the walls of Jerusalem which have been destroyed so many times and rebuilt by the next conqueror. You will see they are all higgledy-piggledy…sitting next to each

other are stones from all sorts of periods all jumbled together. We live in that kind of time....Judaism is big...and
our kids want something that is big, that gives them room
to grow.[10]

Judaism is broad enough to fit every personality, at every age, in
every generation. That is its strength. That is its beauty. That, in part,
is what has helped it survive and thrive through the ages. And that is
what we need to teach and live if we are to enable our children to find
their place within the Jewish world.

CHAPTER 30

Our Attitude Toward the Outside World

In the previous chapters, we saw how negative attitudes within the Jewish world affect observance; how conformity — narrow definitions of what it means to be *frum*, and the idea that there is one right way to be *frum* — can compromise observance. These issues can turn people off, which may ultimately cause them to separate from us. Whether or not they have anywhere else to go then will result in large part from whether or not we have given them permission to see alternative paths or communities as legitimate.

Similarly, our attitudes toward the outside world and secular education, whether positive or negative, can affect our children's observance for better or worse. These attitudes will usually not be as influential as our attitudes toward the Jewish world, but they are important to consider nonetheless.

Is Engagement Desirable?

Before continuing, it is worth addressing the question: Is engagement in the modern, non-Jewish world desirable at all? It is important at the outset to understand both sides of the answers to this question. Rabbi

Ephraim Buchwald sums them up nicely:

> Let's say you suddenly have an epidemic: what is the
> right attitude for the doctor to take? Do we quarantine the
> healthy people and keep them strong so that, when this
> epidemic is over, we will have a strong sample of people
> who are going to be able to regenerate? Or do we take
> these healthy people out to help those sick people, so that
> some of those sick people can survive? That is the philo-
> sophical debate that is taking place today between Modern
> Orthodoxy and Ultra-Orthodoxy. The Ultra-Orthodox say:
> we are in an epidemic. We're losing masses of people.
> Let's keep ourselves on the side, strengthen ourselves as
> much as we can, take our antibiotics, so that the next
> generation can go out and work. The Modern Orthodox
> say: no. We have to go out there and teach our Torah to
> the world.

The question really is: Is now the time? Are we in a position where
we are strong enough to resist the epidemic or not? That's the debate.
Is it a time to assert ourselves or to strengthen ourselves internally?

Whatever approach we take, it is important to recognize how it
can affect our children's observance. So what exactly are our attitudes?
What messages do we send about the outside world and how can that
affect our children's observance?

Our attitude toward the outside world generally involves two areas: the
first is our attitude toward people; next is our attitude toward ideas. When
our attitudes move to an extreme in either area, they create problems.

Overly Positive Attitudes

An overly positive attitude toward the outside world, one that is totally open and undiscriminating, creates problems because the more
open we are to something, the more likely it is to affect our behavior

and influence us. Engagement with the non-Jewish or secular world — especially in today's age where that world is defined less by objective morality and more by subjective morality — can be a slippery slope. The more open we become to outside influences that contradict Jewish values, the more likely they are to affect us.

There is such a thing as being too open. This occurs when distinctions between Jewish ways of life and alternative ways disappear, thus destroying the foundation of Jewish life. Not everything is kosher. We do not believe that all actions or ways of life are equally good. For the Jew, the Jewish way of life is better. And acting in a way that sends an alternative message damages observance.

To engage with the outside world, a Jew must first know who he is, why he is here, how he is different, and how to live that difference meaningfully in a challenging world without losing his identity. No doubt this means that his identity must be very strong. It must have not only a strong basis in belief, but also very positive feelings that would not easily falter in the face of alternative values. An overly positive or open attitude is often incompatible with developing that strong emotional/intellectual foundation and can undermine pride in the beauty and joy of our heritage.

In such cases, even a little engagement can cause problems. A poor foundation will open the door wide to the outside world and let it in, which can significantly challenge Judaism. With a weak arsenal, we may not be able to fight and may not even want to.

That is why Rabbi Buchwald asserts that "given the blandishments of outside, the forces are so great, that if you want to wind up moderate then you really have to aim to be passionate, extreme, and almost fanatical. If you aim to be fanatical in this world, then you wind up moderate. If you aim to be moderate, you wind up wishy-washy. If you aim to be wishy-washy, you wind up with Episcopalian grandchildren."

Negative Attitudes

The great majority of formerly observant people who mention the outside world as a contributing factor in their move away from observance, speak of our negative attitudes rather than positive ones. They seem to have experienced everything from mildly negative attitudes to extremely negative ones, all of which pushed them away from observance.

The mildest observations involved an indifference to the non-Jewish world. Dennis Prager, for example, experienced a trivializing of non-Jews in the observant world. "Non-Jews became more of an abstraction than real people created in the image of God... In the *yeshiva*, non-Jews — the people who comprise 99.8 percent of humanity — were rarely mentioned. Their significance lay only in their ability to hurt or help Jews. 'All I ask of the goyim is that they leave us alone,' is the way one rebbe put it. That was the entirety of his concern with the rest of the world."[1]

Others were taught to see non-Jews and their world as a threat. As one man from a Hasidic background recalls, his family's major concern "was to insulate us children and to protect us from the threat of others' ideas and lives." This person was not taught to be indifferent to non-Jews and their world, but to fear and avoid them.

Others were raised to believe that non-Jews and their world were to be disdained and looked down upon. Nathan, a Modern Orthodox Jew, was raised to believe that non-Jews are *am hadomeh lachamor, a nation which is similar to the donkey.* Raised by Eastern European parents, he was taught to spit when he passed a church.

Numerous formerly observant Jews from more right wing communities say that their communities' attitudes to the outside world were outright racist. And survey respondents seemed to agree. 65% of them classified "many" to "most" observant Jews as exhibiting racist behavior.

One formerly observant teenage girl summarized these perspectives on a chat board. She posted a note saying that "we're supposed to be a light unto the nations, showing them the right way, but we have no right to look down on them. They are equal to us; we just have more responsibilities and a higher purpose." Another girl responded with the following: "Not true. Goyim are trash according to the Torah."

Given the reality of the outside world today and the centuries of persecution and exile by the nations of the world, it is not surprising that we would have a negative attitude. Nonetheless, it is important to realize that these negative attitudes can create real obstacles to observance.

Self-Actualization

The greatest obstacle they cause is undermining self-actualization, as was the case for Jonathan. Jonathan's community looked down upon non-Jews and rejected secular knowledge. This created conflict for him because although he was very interested in learning *gemorah*, he was also interested in playing sports and exploring other intellectual pursuits. In high school, he was interested in reading the newspaper and knowing what was happening in the outside world. But his parents wanted him to attend right wing *yeshivas*, the kind that left no room for such endeavors. Jonathan would go on interviews for these *yeshivas*, and when he had the chance, he would ask if he would be allowed to read the paper. More often than not, the *Rosh Yeshiva* responded that "real *bachrim* don't read the paper." Needless to say, his parents failed to get him to attend. He didn't want the schools and the schools didn't want him.

Eventually, a rift developed between Jonathan and his Judaism, and ultimately he went off the derech. Why so? Because his community's insularity and rejection of secular learning left no room to pursue the interests that formed an integral part of his personality. He could only be himself, therefore, if he dropped observance and left his world.

In part, this occurred because his community's insularity affected his perception of himself. After all, if real *bachrim* don't read the paper

335

and he reads the paper or wants to, he cannot be a real *bachur*. And if he wasn't a real *bachur*, what was he? Where did he fit in? The answer was nowhere. The community's rejection of these things made him feel like an outsider. Once he felt like an outsider, he was emotionally distanced from his *frum* environment. And once he was distanced, it was just a small step to go off the derech. Dropping observance externally and behaviorally merely expressed what had already happened internally years before.

In the end, Jonathan became ashamed of his community even though he feels pride in the Jewish people as a whole. He views the *yeshiva* world negatively, saying "they have their heads in the sand" and "they wear blinders all the time." He explains,

> I taught in a high school for a year, and kids there would love making fun of *shfartzahs*. But the *shfartzahs* that they were making fun of knew more about stuff than they did. These *yeshiva bachrim* didn't speak proper English. They spoke the same level of slang that inner city black kids spoke. They didn't take the Regents; they were taking ACT's, which is exactly what's going on in the inner city. So they're ignorant.

It has been said that there are people in different times and moments in the *galut* (exile) that feel a restriction that puts a lid on their Jewish creativity. Because they can't change that reality, they search for foreign soil and other environments in which to express their creativity.[2] This occurs if they feel that addressing their needs is not compatible with living an observant life. When they feel that Torah and engagement with the outside world are mutually exclusive, they will feel they have to choose one or the other and may abandon observance to fulfill what seems more fundamental.

Undermines Universal Vision and National Character

Negative attitudes toward the outside world do more than stifle self-actualization. They also undermine our universal vision. For how can we be a light unto the nations when we condemn the very nations we are meant to inspire? How could we help a world we disdain, and why would we want to?

To serve as moral beacons and to do so humbly requires that we remember the words of Rav Kook: "Just as there is a purpose to every individual life, there is a purpose to every nation. Every people and country has its own international role, its unique contribution to the world as whole…and through the nation of Israel all of the contributions of the nations are uplifted to their proper place in the divine harmony of existence."[3] So when we condemn the outside world, we undermine Judaism's inspiring universal vision.

That vision, and the positive attitude it requires, is particularly important today, as Rabbi Cardozo explains, "there is no longer a sense of mission, and young people today feel they need to do something for mankind."[4]

Negative attitudes toward the outside world can be especially problematic for those who are attracted to Judaism *because* of its universal vision. For example Ari, who pulled himself away from the community when his *shul* was not spiritually conducive, also felt disturbed about derogatory attitudes toward non-Jews. He explains:

> I think that Judaism is all about being a light to the world, not just to each other. I could never be someone who participates in a secluded form of Judaism that practices everything but does it in a way that doesn't relate to the rest of the world. Because I think that's what Judaism is all about — showing that we affect the entire world, that there's a lot that we can do and that there's also a lot that we can learn.

When people are drawn to observant life precisely because it promotes universal values and *tikun olam,* our negative attitude toward non-Jews can be particularly problematic. That was the case with Susan Levine. She grew up in a Conservative home and became observant in her teens because Jewish law seemed like "a system aimed at making a better world." Her commitment to observance was genuine and long lasting. But after 15 years, she dropped it. Why? She explains that she lost "her long inner struggle with Orthodoxy's attitude toward non-Jews." And while she feels strange in the secular world, she also feels that "other options seem superior to Judaism for making a better world."[5]

For people like Susan, a negative attitude to the outside world undermines the very thing that drew them to *Yiddishkeit* in the first place. When that element is gone, so is the foundation of their observance.

Particularly Problematic for *Baalei Teshuva*/Converts

A negative attitude can also create specific problems for *baalei teshuva* and converts. These people have experience in the secular world and know how true or false our attitudes are. So when our attitudes do not accurately reflect the world they left behind, anger and frustration can ensue. As one convert notes:

> I have early memories of participating in picket lines and marching in civil rights demonstrations. I lived and worked with blacks and Hispanics as one of two whites in a merchant ship. I hung out in mixed crowds in the Bronx as a teenager. I mingled with all kinds of people regularly when trucking. I simply do not have the luxury of retreating to racial stereotypes and I never have lost the view...
> [that] a common humanity binds us more than the very real, cultural and religious differences that separate us.

Although he is still observant, this man is hanging on by a thread. He says that he finds it "harder and harder to dismiss as an unfortunate

quirk the almost pervasive racism" he finds in the black hat community. He is less and less amused at being teased for being a *"feshtunkena*
liberal," less and less willing to listen to *shfatrza* comments without
giving a sharp retort. He says that he is fatigued by the *charedi* world's
"rejection of everything in the outside world as *trief* — tired of the
ethics in the *charedishe velt* (ultra-Orthodox world) when it comes to
dealing with the outside world." And he finds something amiss with
the "self-proclaimed identity of Torah-True *Yidden* (Jews)."

This man converted to Judaism. Surely he joined our world with
great enthusiasm, having found the truth. But our attitudes to the secular world have caused him to lose respect for Judaism and want to
leave the observant community. He still wears a black hat and externally looks as committed as anyone else, but he has already started to
eat *trief* and skip *davening* now and then, and he says he "fantasizes"
about leaving completely.

Our negative attitudes to the outside world create one more problem for *baalei teshuva*: part of their challenge is to integrate two lives
— the former one, steeped in the secular world, and the new one,
which is distinctly Jewish and *frum*. The more successfully they can integrate and harmonize the two, the easier it is to maintain observance.
When we reject the secular world, it becomes harder for *baalei teshuva*
to reconcile their past and present, which makes it harder to feel at
home in our world. This is especially true if they value their experiences in the secular world. In that case, joining the observant world
may mean losing important parts of one's self.

One *baal teshuva* explained that he went off the derech because he
loved secular learning and wanted to continue it after he became *frum*.
But his environment at a major *yeshiva* condemned his interest. He tried
to comply for a while, but his desire was too great and eventually he
enrolled in university while attending the *yeshiva*, which at the time, he
explained, was taboo, akin to "selling arms to the Palestinians." At one
point, he felt that he would be physically accosted if anyone found out.

Secular learning was a part of him, and every time the *frum* world denigrated the non-Jewish world and its knowledge, they denigrated a part of who he was. This made it difficult for him to integrate. Eventually, he began to lose respect for his *rabbaim* at the *yeshiva*. He viewed them as lacking "psychological, emotional, and inter-personal sophistication." He saw them as "naïve." And ultimately, he felt he had to choose between two worlds. The diminished respect for the observant world combined with his appreciation for secular pursuits eventually led him off the derech completely.

When Engagement Causes Abandonment

Given our history of persecution among the nations, it is not surprising that we should have negative, cynical attitudes toward them. And given how many Jews have left our world for theirs, it is not surprising that we aim to erect strong barriers in the hope that they will help our children remain observant. But no matter how legitimate our concern, denigrating the outside world works against observance. Every condemnation of the outside world can undermine our own. For those who have a strong desire to engage with the outside world, it would be far more productive to provide space to do so within the context of observant life rather than denigrate such engagement.

Unfortunately, we often feel this is too risky. We fear a more positive attitude will threaten the very Judaism we are trying to protect. But based on my research, this is not the case. Engagement with the outside world does not in and of itself seem to cause one to go off the derech. Rather it leads to a *complete* abandonment of observance *only* when the foundations of emotion, intellect, and implementation — in the home, school and community — are not properly established. When these foundations are weak, the outside world can compromise observance. But when they are strong, it seems not to.

Why? Because exposure to the outside world opens the door to an alternative way of life. But whether or not someone walks through the door has less to do with the outside world than the Jewish world. When a Jew's experiences have been positive and fulfilling, and when he believes, he will have no desire to leave. His Jewish world will be more attractive and meaningful than the alternative. If he lacks that positive foundation, however, he will seek the alternative. He will walk through the door in hopes of finding something better.

As with the *yetzer hara,* when a person has a strong connection to Judaism the outside world may win momentary battles but it will not win the war. A person may falter, but if he loves Judaism and believes in it, if he has the basic tools to implement it, he will usually not abandon Judaism altogether for the alternative. He will want to perpetuate observance and do whatever it takes to stay committed.

That is not to say that the soul remains unaffected. Every exposure to impurity can damage the soul, and we would be justified in asserting that engagement is simply not worth that risk. Chassidim, for example, maintain a closed attitude to the outside world and thereby achieve a degree of purity unknown among communities that allow exposure. Just as the *Kohanim* (Jews of the priestly class) were commanded to live more sheltered lives in Jerusalem than the average Jew, focusing on spiritual matters and their relationship with God, so the Jewish people today needs its *'Kohanim.'* But it is important to remember that *Kohanim* always represented a minority in the Jewish world, and they, more than any other group, mingled with *all* the people.

The point here is not to prescribe one approach or the other, but rather to guide either approach toward fostering observance rather than undermining it. Engaging in the outside world will always require careful discrimination between good and bad, holy and profane. The point is that lines should not be drawn indiscriminately. They should be varied according to the needs and personality of each individual. For children who need more exposure, we should find a way to provide an outlet — if not within our own community then within another — so they don't feel they have to go off the derech to meet their needs.

341

There are a number of ways we can do this. For example, we might distinguish between secular knowledge and secular activities. Secular knowledge is not inherently negative or unholy. In fact, our sages say *yaish chachma bagoyim,* there is wisdom among the nations. Rashi also contends that he who truly values wisdom will seek it wherever it can be found and that a person who refuses to learn from someone because he dislikes or disapproves of him places his feelings over his pursuit of knowledge. This is why our Sages instituted a special blessing to be said upon meeting a great non-Jewish scholar.[6]

*   *   *

However we choose to address the issue, it is perhaps most important to do so from a position of strength and not weakness. We should act out of pride in Judaism rather than fear of the alternative. We should realize that if we have done the job of transmitting Yiddishkeit properly, we will not need negativity to protect Judaism. And if we have not, our negative attitudes will not really work.

A Yiddishkeit based on fear of the other is a negatively defined one. It binds us to each other, our tradition, and God through weakness, not strength. That kind of identity fails to inspire pride and it cannot endure, as Lucy Davidowitz, the great Holocaust scholar, wrote, "If we're a people that gets murdered, the young will flee from us. We have something more than that."[7] Focusing on the hatred of others, employing the world's negativity to bolster ourselves, undermines national pride and self-esteem, which can very easily result in children being ashamed of their Yiddishkeit.

Rabbi Steinsaltz explains this as follows: There are two kinds of animals in the world: those with exoskeletons and those with endoskeletons. Animals with exoskeletons, such as shellfish, are defined and protected by hard exterior shells, walls that protect them from a potentially threatening environment. Animals with endoskeletons have backbones; they are defined by internal structures that strengthen and protect them. So too, there are two kinds of Jews: Those whose Judaism is protected by shells (or walls) — their identity stays intact by virtue of barriers to the outside world — and those who have endoskeletons, who are internally strong, whose internal being forms their identity and protects them from potential threats from the outside world.

It is interesting to note that animals with exoskeletons came first. But they were not the more advanced kind. The more advanced creatures of the earth, including humans, have endoskeletons. They are strengthened and bolstered internally. It is also interesting to note that animals with exoskeletons are not kosher to us; only those with endoskeletons are permissible.

This teaches us an important lesson: that 'kosher' religiosity, the more advanced kind, is not defined by putting up barriers. It is not based on fear of the outside world, but rather on a love for Yiddishkeit. It is not defined by the evils of the outside world that keep us in, but by the inside truths that draw us near. It can and probably should be *assisted* by some barriers, but it is not *created* by them. And even when it puts up barriers, it does so out of strength, not weakness; out of a love for Yiddishkeit, not hatred for the outside world. It does so not because it *needs* barriers to maintain identity, but rather because it *wants* them in order to foster holiness. It does not say that the ways of the world are evil and ours is good, but rather that the ways of the world are often good, but ours is better. As one Entebbe survivor put it:

> Today I am part of that chain of believing Jews who recite every morning, 'Blessed art thou God, our Lord, King of the Universe, who did not make me a gentile.' When I do so, I think not of a drunken peasant, but of the most elevated gentile — Goethe or Mozart. No matter how great the achievement of non-Jews may be, the greatest privilege is to have been born into this tiny, despised people, who received His Law and whose every moment is filled with purpose.[8]

This is Jewish pride, the kind of Judaism we should be striving for; one that looks upon the world and knows that no matter how great its riches, ours are better; the kind that stands convicted and able to face any challenge the world can pose. This is far more inspiring and productive, and can allow exposure to the outside world to work for us rather than against us.

CHAPTER 31

Conclusion

I n order for belief in and positive feelings about Judaism to translate into living an observant way of life, they must be accompa-
nied by the ability to implement Judaism. This is the third leg
upon which observance stands, the final element that enables us
to remain committed to observance.

This ability to implement comes from two places — one internal,
one external. The internal place is our own character: our strength, discipline, and knowledge of our strengths and weaknesses. The external
one is our communities — the degree to which they engender respect,
foster spirituality, and allow their members to actualize their unique
souls and personalities.

Our communities become obstacles to observance in a variety of
ways, all of which are integrally related to each other. Problems begin
with our narrow definitions of observance and our belief that there
is one right way to express observance. This can lead to arrogance,
judgmental behavior, and ostracism of others. Within our communities,
it leads us to enforce conformity and sends an all or nothing message,
which stifles growth and individuality. In terms of other communities

and the outside world, it fosters an intolerant, rejecting attitude, which limits even further our children's growth and religious alternatives. And ultimately, when our standards are based on external factors instead of internal, spiritual ones, all these issues become exacerbated, further undermining spirituality.

Solving these problems requires that we return to spirituality and connection to God, that we re-prioritize the internal life of *mitzvot* — not at the expense of the external expressions, but rather in conjunction with them. In addition, it requires broadening our definition of 'properly *frum*,' that we create 'something' between the 'all' and 'nothing' we provide today.

This does not mean compromising *halachah*. It does mean closely evaluating what it means to be *frum*. This is not an easy question to answer, but it is an important one to ask. I asked a number of prominent educators: What does it mean to be *frum?* Listen to what they said:

> *Rabbi Yaakov Shapiro: Frum* doesn't mean anything… There is no such thing as *frum*; there is no such thing as Orthodox….*Frum* is a Yiddish word — there are no objective criteria….*Frum* should be defined as "someone who is committed to doing their best."[1]

> *Rabbi Ephraim Buchwald:* I don't like the term "*frum*." I think a good Jew is a person who is in a growth mode…I don't care whether he is Orthodox, Reform, Conservative or Reconstructionist — that's a good Jew. The term "Orthodox Jew" means nothing to me. The fact that he puts on *tefilin* and *talit* doesn't mean a thing to me. The basic question is: Is he still growing? Is he climbing up the ladder to be closer to God? If he is still growing, then he is a good Jew. [2]

Debbie Greenblatt: I would say it means essentially there is a deep and internal commitment to having a relationship with God and expressing that through the Torah's observance in a growth-full manner.[3]

Rabbi Jonathan Sacks: That's not a relevant characterization to me. I look at all sorts of different things. Jews are great in different ways. There are people who act so as to be a *kiddush Hashem.* There are those who act so as to implant in their children a love of *Yiddishkeit.* There are those who teach all of us how not to be intimidated by the pressures of the secular culture. I am not sure '*frum*' is a word that appears in the Chumash or the Tanach or the *Mishnah* or the *Gemorah* or the *Medrash* or Rashi. I am not sure how significant a word that is.[4]

Rabbi Norman Lamm: Chassidim say that Jews should not be *frum.*....A priest should be *frum* — Jews should be *ehrlich. Ehrlich* in Yiddish has a dual connotation. It means observant, and it means honorable...It's got to be *noach labriot* and *noach lamakom* (pleasant to people *and* pleasant to God) or the person does not qualify as pious...so *ehrlich* means the ability to integrate both sides.[5]

Leah Kohn: The minimum definition of being *frum* is Shabbas, *kashrus,* and family purity....There is no *halachic* definition. It's what we call it. Being a Jew the way a Jew should be is being committed to *halachah.* But that's not even all because it's developing a relationship with *Hashem* and growing. That's what being a Jew is all about. You can be very *frum* and not a *tzadik.* And you can be a big *tzadik* and not *frum.* A *tzadik* is one who utilizes his potential and the tools he was given to the best of his ability.[6]

The interesting thing about these definitions is that they are far broader than one would have anticipated. Judging from our behavior, the way we educate our children, and the extent to which we pressure them to conform to our communal standards, one would have thought the definitions would be much narrower and more externally defined. But even when they do use *halachic* observance as the criterion, as did Mrs. Kohn, they use only the most minimum standards of Shabbat and *kashrut*. And most do not even use a *halachic* standard. They focus on growth toward Torah, the internal process of self-improvement, and coming closer to God rather than external behavior. They define *frumkeit* by the very elements we have identified as the most productive in creating respectful, spiritual communities that help people implement observance.

Such definitions would broaden the path for our children, provide them with a middle ground, and help them to see themselves as on the derech even if they are off ours. This, in turn, would help them to remain psychologically and emotionally connected to us, which can prevent complete defection or facilitate return. It can also help us remain more positive toward other communities, so that our children will be likely to find *some derech* even if it is not *ours*. In the least, it can help them maintain self-esteem and a positive attitude to observant life and its people.

This is not to say we should not have standards. We should have standards. But they should be broad enough and flexible enough to make room for mistakes, for differences, and for the variety of personalities in our *frum* world. Even if we used the entire body of *halachah* as our minimum standard, it would be broader than our standards today.

It is true there may be advantages to remaining narrow and creating an all or nothing situation. Many, when faced with an all or nothing choice will chose all. But we want them to choose all because they want to and believe it is right — not because they had no options or because we would ostracize them if they didn't. If they choose "all" for fear of the rejection, lack of self-esteem, and ostracism that would result, they will likely never live the kind of Judaism we hope they will.

If we have done the job of enabling our children to feel good about and believe in the Torah and *mitzvot*, we will not need narrow definitions to keep them *frum*. They will be *frum* of their own accord, for positive reasons, from strength of belief and not weakness. They may not be *frum* our way, it is true, but they will choose another way, one that works better for them.

Whatever the case, one thing is clear: God cannot be confined to the narrow path we walk. His Torah cannot be confined and neither can his people. God is broad, His Torah is broad, and His people are tremendously diverse. The more room there is for us, the more reflective of God's greatness, the more true to His Torah, and the more beneficial for His people.

IV
Conclusion

CHAPTER 32

Putting it All Together: Causes

U nderstanding why people go off the derech is not a simple matter. It is as complicated as each of us is. The reasons vary from person to person, and there are usually a host of reasons that work together to determine the outcome.

Of all contributing factors, emotional issues — the extent to which a person feels positive or negative about observance — are the most influential. They are determined primarily by one's family and tend to start very early on in life, as soon as a child is old enough to keep any *mitzvot* at all. People's feelings about observance will be determined by whether or not observance was a source of joy for them; whether or not it enabled them to feel safe, loved, accepted and worthy; and whether or not it enabled them to self-actualize, express and develop their particular character and needs. How observance was modeled plays an important part in this process as well. If parents and other authority figures love observance and feel joyful about it, children will be more likely to maintain observance more than if parents felt only neutral toward it.

But emotional factors do not work on their own. Next comes belief, which is primarily developed in the school and secondarily at home. The influence of belief on observance begins a bit later in life, usually in early adolescence when children develop intellectual abilities. They will then need to establish an intellectual foundation for commitment based on belief that the Torah is true, divinely given, and properly applied throughout the generations. They will need to believe that it is a meaningful way of life — one with individual, national, and universal goals that can best be achieved through the *mitzvot*.

The last piece of the puzzle is the ability to implement those feelings and beliefs. On a personal level people need discipline, self-knowledge, and the willingness to work hard. On an environmental level, they need a spiritual community that they respect enough to join and that allows them to develop their unique emotional and religious potential. These issues primarily involve the community and often arise later in life, when we have reached adulthood and seek to find our own place in the Jewish world.

These emotional, intellectual, and implementation issues all work together to determine whether or not someone will remain observant. To simplify we could say:

Observance =
Positive Feelings + Belief + Ability to Implement
(in that order).

A graph might illustrate these issues more clearly. Those circles closest to the self are most influential for observance:

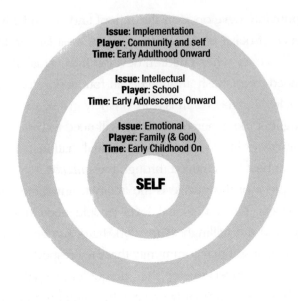

Issue: Implementation
Player: Community and self
Time: Early Adulthood Onward

Issue: Intellectual
Player: School
Time: Early Adolescence Onward

Issue: Emotional
Player: Family (& God)
Time: Early Childhood On

SELF

If we had to summarize the process, it would be accurate to say the following:

> *People go off the derech to the extent that their relationships with family, school, and community have failed to fulfill their emotional, intellectual and implementation needs.*

The Individual Self

But understanding each one of these areas does not adequately answer the question. It only clarifies *what* the issues are and how they relate to *each other.* To properly understand the phenomenon, we need to look further — to know not only what the issues are and how they relate to each other, but also how they relate *to each individual.* We need to ascertain not only the extent to which Yiddishkeit addresses *general* emotional, intellectual, and implementation needs, but also the extent to which it addresses *unique, individual* needs.

People do not go off the derech only in relation to how well their general needs are met, but also in relation to how well their *unique* needs are met. At the heart of all experience is the individual self. The family, school, and community are the players that influence a person and his observance. But how exactly he is influenced will be determined by who he is.

Two people can have the exact same experience with Yiddishkeit. One will end up dropping observance and one will remain. There are observant families who manage to raise six children who are strongly committed and one goes off the derech. How are we to understand this? The answer lies in the child's particular character. Each of these factors — feelings, beliefs, and the ability to implement — will apply differently to each child according to who he is.

For example, everyone needs love — but not everyone needs it the same way or in the same amount. Everyone needs to believe — but not everyone will have the same questions, or rely on the intellect as much as the other. Everyone needs a supportive environment, but the kind of environment will vary from person to person. It is the *interplay* between the elements and our individual character that determines the extent to which Yiddishkeit is transmitted. The more our unique needs are met, the more likely we are to remain observant. Since our needs are met primarily through relationships with others, it is relationships that most strongly affect the process.

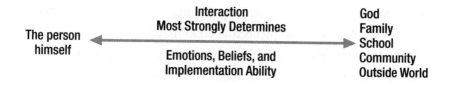

| The person himself | Interaction
Most Strongly Determines

Emotions, Beliefs, and
Implementation Ability | God
Family
School
Community
Outside World |

So the emotional, intellectual, and implementation issues do not work in a vacuum — they work in connection with the person. They are general categories that need to be applied in specific ways according to the person's unique character and needs. (See footnote for examples).[1]

So to remain observant, everyone needs to feel good about Yiddishkeit. Everyone needs belief, strength of character, and a supportive environment. But the extent to which we need one versus the other depends on personality. Our unique personalities determine *how* and *how much* these things affect us.

The child who thrives on security is particularly hurt by rejection. The child who thrives on freedom of expression is particularly wounded by being forced to conform. The child who is intellectually oriented is more likely than another to drop observance if he doesn't get the answers he needs. The child who is particularly idealistic has a greater need for an inspiring universal vision in order to feel good about Judaism, whereas one who is down-to-earth is more likely to need concrete details about *mitzvah* observance and how they affect his life today.

This enables us to understand how two children in the same family with the same experiences can end up in different religious places. Two children are deprived of answers to their questions. One is more intellectual in nature than his brother. The intellectual child may respond to deprivation of answers by moving away from observance by 10 or 15% while the less intellectual child may move away only 5%.

So while the emotional, intellectual, and implementation needs are general rules, they will affect a person differently according to personality. To guarantee observance, we could say that the emotional, intellectual, and practical factors must all add up to 100% on the positive side. But we cannot say exactly how each experience will contribute to that 100%. We know that the emotional almost *always* plays the greatest role in determining observance. But whether it plays a 50%

role or a 70% role will depend on whether one is more emotional or intellectual in nature.

Finally, everyone's threshold for choosing observance will vary. For example, one person may need 70% good feelings in order to choose observance. Another may need only 50%.

So the most important piece of information for effectively transmitting Torah to an individual may be knowing his unique personality and realizing that, just as we cannot change our genes, we cannot change our nature. We can improve it and modify the way we express it. But we cannot change its fundamental inclination, as Rabbi Wolbe explains when quoting the Vilna Gaon: "there are certain things that can't be changed in a man. His nature is one of them. He has no free will in this area. He only has free will in what he *does* with that nature."[2] The most important thing is to recognize that different solutions work differently for different people. But *every* nature is completely compatible with a Torah way of life, and if we work with it instead of against it, we can harness even weaknesses and transform them into strengths.

How can we know what a child's natural way is? In analyzing the statement *chinuch lenaar al pi darcho*, the Malbim explains that we know a child's particular nature when we give the child space and observe his character carefully.[3] What does he like to do with his free time when there is no influence from others? What does he lean toward and enjoy? What makes him laugh? What makes him feel proud? Giving our children the space to be free and express themselves may be hard; but it is essential. As the Malbim explains: *chinuch* is the art of finding a person's nature and developing it. This requires building on who the person is, not who we would *like* him to be. His fate, his destiny, his happiness, and future observance all depend upon the extent to which we can identify his personality and address it according to his way. The better we do so, the higher the quality of our relationship with him, and the more likely he will remain observant.

Free Will

But what about free will? When it comes to our moral choices, Judaism does not believe that anything is determined. The Talmud tells us that *hakol beyadi shamayim chutz miyirat shamayim* — *all is in the hands of heaven except for fear of heaven.*[4] This is the one area in which we are given free choice and the meaning of our entire lives. This is our challenge. This is within our power, and this is our uniqueness. We can always choose the good on some level, no matter what the circumstances. We can go against the tide of our environment no matter how detrimental it may be.

To sum up by saying that children's lack of observance depends on their environment would form an incomplete picture and ignore the value of free will.

So what is the role of free will? We can think of it this way: When a person is born, he is neutral when it comes to his feelings and beliefs about Yiddishkeit. He is like an empty vessel waiting to be filled with experiences that will move him toward one end of the spectrum or another. At birth, he can go in either direction. He has total free choice. There is a 50/50 chance he will remain observant or go off the derech. In essence his situation looks like this.

100% Negative Experiences =	Born	100% Positive Experiences =
	Free Will	
Not Frum	50/50	Frum

As he grows, his *bechira* (choice) level changes, as Rav Dessler explains in his treatise, *Mechtav Me'eliyahu* (Strive for Truth). Our *bechira* levels change according to our choices.[5] The more we choose good, the more likely we are to choose good again.

Just as our choices can affect our *bechira* level, so can our experiences. Our experiences and environment affect the direction our free will takes. As soon as we encounter the Jewish world, our location on the spectrum begins to move. Positive experiences move us along the spectrum toward observance while negative experiences push us away. And where our *bechira* point falls at the end of the day, where we end up after all our experiences are taken into account, will determine how easy or difficult it will be for us to choose observance.

So a person always has free will, but it is not always a 50/50 choice. Negative experiences can harden our hearts like Pharoah's. Unfulfilled needs can stack the deck so much that choosing observance becomes nearly impossible. A person for example who has suffered in every area — who never felt good about Yiddishkeit, was never taught to believe, never developed strength of character or found a supportive environment — may have only a 1% chance of being *frum*. He can still choose observance, it is true. But under those circumstances, it would be unrealistic to expect him to do so.

So we could summarize the entire process as follows:

1) Observance is (in large part) determined by the extent to which relationships with family, school, and community fulfill our general *and* particular emotional, intellectual, and implementation needs.

2) The extent to which our needs are met determines where along the spectrum of free choice we end up and how easy or difficult it is for us to choose observance. Fulfilled needs make it easier; unfulfilled needs make it more difficult.

To illustrate:

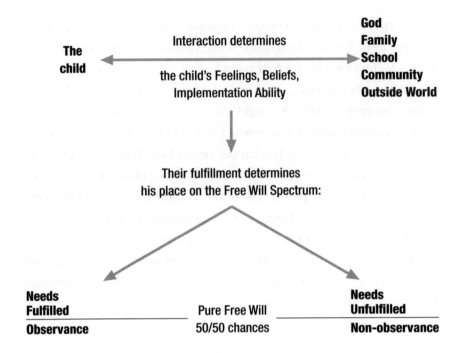

Compensation

Having said all this, there is one last element to understand. Just as the emotional, intellectual, and implementation issues work in connection with an individual person, they also work in conjunction with each other. There is a relationship between them and, to an extent, they can compensate for each other. For example, a strong intellectual foundation can compensate for negative emotional experiences. A strong spiritual environment can compensate for a weak intellectual foundation. Given the respective roles of feelings and belief in influencing behavior, it is probably safe to say that positive feelings compensate more than belief, and that belief compensates more than community.

In general, the more success there is in one area, the less there needs to be in another. And the less success there is in one area, the more there needs to be in another. So for example, if we feel extremely joyful about observance to an 80 or 90% level, we may need only a little belief. If we have tremendous belief in the truth of observance, we may need only a little joy. If we have the strength of character to put belief into practice, we may not need a highly supportive environment.

Theoretically, to *guarantee* observance, the three factors must total 100% positivism. But how they do so does not really matter as long as they get to the 100% level. So the different areas can compensate for each other. The problem is that, because personality plays such an important role and because each of the factors strongly affects observance, we can never know the extent to which one factor will compensate for the other and whether or not the compensation will be enough to guarantee observance.

As a result, perhaps the wisest thing we can do to help ensure our children's observance is to build as strong an arsenal as possible by striving to meet their general and specific needs in all three areas — emotional, intellectual, and practical. And since all relationships within the Jewish world play a role in meeting those needs, we are best served by playing a vital role in the process. Parents, educators, and communal leaders all affect the free choice decisions our people make, and so should work together, accept responsibility, meet the challenge, and create the kind of environments our children need to feel good about Yiddishkeit, believe in it, and put it into practice.

CHAPTER 33

Those Who Return Again

O ur exploration of emotional, intellectual, and implementation issues explains why people leave observance. But why is it that some return while others never look back? What is the difference between these two groups?

The key to those who return is that they resolve the *cause* of their break from observance. If they left because of negative feelings, they resolve those feelings and replace them with positive ones. If they left because they failed to believe, they address their questions and establish belief. If they were simply unable to implement observance, they strengthen themselves or change their environment.

Resolving the causes of defection does not necessarily guarantee return. But without resolution, return seems impossible. This seems to be the case with everyone who returns to observance, no matter how long the lapse or what the cause. A return becomes possible only when the issue that caused the break is addressed and resolved. It is important to realize that the more fundamental the issue, the harder it is to resolve; and the less fundamental, the easier to resolve. But whatever the issue, resolution opens the door to return.

Of all groups, those who go off the derech because of negative feelings or experiences have the hardest time returning. That's because emotional issues are hardest to address. Feelings are harder to define, and they lay much deeper than our thoughts and beliefs. Emotional issues can create scars that take years to heal.

Those who went off the derech because of emotional issues must address the source of their negative feelings if they are to return. If their negative feelings stemmed directly from negative experiences with *frum* people, then positive experiences with *frum* people may be all it takes to turn things around. For example, if they were rejected by *frum* people for not conforming to religious standards, then being accepted by *frum* people despite non-conformity can heal the wounds.

Those whose negative feelings stem from more fundamentally damaging experiences face a bigger challenge. Simply creating positive relationships with *frum* people will likely not suffice. They will also have to deal with the source of their trauma if they are ever to return. For example, a child who was abused by a *frum* parent or teacher will likely never feel good about observance until he deals with the abuse itself, separates the trauma from observance, and addresses his need for safety.

Those who left for intellectual reasons usually have an easier time returning than the first group. They may return once their questions are answered or once they establish a meaningful vision for Judaism. What makes things challenging for this group is that since most have already experienced a lifetime of Jewish education, they are likely to be cynical about the possibility of learning anything new. Why would they now seek answers if their lifetime of education failed to provide any? Many lose the desire to search, become convinced there are no answers, or search elsewhere. Some, whose beliefs are entrenched with age, simply close themselves off to the possibility.

Nonetheless, sometimes such people meet an exceptional rebbe, read an exceptional book, or take a course in other philosophies that reveals some strengths of Jewish perspectives. Or they may be faced with new and challenging life-circumstances and may turn to Judaism in search of guidance. Any of these can prompt renewed questioning and help establish belief where there was none, which enables a return.

The last group, the smallest — those who leave because of implementation issues — seem to have the easiest time returning. Their issues involve character traits and environmental circumstances rather than deep internal realities and thus seem easiest to resolve. Sometimes all it takes to affect a return is a change in their circumstances, a modified behavior or supportive environment.

This may explain why we find many people return to observance when they get married. Marriage often creates a supportive environment, integration within a community, and new perspectives on the importance of observance and transmitting those values to children. The fact that these people return to observance so quickly and easily when there is an environmental change indicates that they probably went off the derech because of implementation issues rather than negative feelings or beliefs.

Our Role in the Return

No matter how fundamental the issue or how difficult to resolve, it is always possible to heal. The most important thing for us as parents, teachers, and communal leaders to realize is that we can do a lot to help the process, particularly by maintaining positive relationships with those who have gone off the derech.

Since most people go off the derech because of negative relationships and feelings regarding observance, the simple *existence* of positive relationships can make a significant difference. Positive relationships can help resolve issues, create positive feelings toward observance, provide answers to unanswered questions, or generate a spiritual, respectable environment that attracts people back. They can shatter negative perceptions and help to create new, positive associations with Yiddishkeit. They can also create a warm, attractive place worth returning to.

If the positive relationships also respect the person who has gone off the derech on his own terms and appreciates him for who he *is* rather than what we *want* him to be, it may even heal old wounds. Just one positive relationship that inspires or fulfills our emotional needs, that accepts us despite our differences and without an agenda, can make all the difference in the world. At the very least, positive relationships can challenge negative perceptions of the observant world and thus begin the process of return.

It is important to realize that maintaining a positive connection does not mean condoning the behavior. In any case, after living in our homes, our children know quite well what we believe. But acceptance of them does mean maintaining a positive, warm, loving and kind attitude toward them as people.

Love can inspire the greatest of changes and may be the most powerful motivator in every area of life. Sparking a return for those who have gone off the derech is no different. Consider this: up to 3% of observant Jews intermarry, which means that people committed to Yiddishkeit are willing to drop their entire way of life because they fall in love with someone. If love is powerful enough to draw them from *halachic* observance all the way to intermarriage, then surely it can take our children from nonobservance to observance. One child who went off the derech expressed this poignantly in the *Jewish Observer:*

> I wish I could speak and be listened to.
> I cannot speak because I am too young.
> I cannot speak for it's too late for me.
> I cannot speak because I've lost the desire to keep fighting. It's too hard... too painful...
> I don't want to try, have no more tears to cry. My emo-

tions have bled out; I am left an empty shell. I am in your school, your *shul*, on your block. You don't want your kids hanging out with me. You won't let me play with your son. You won't let your daughter sleep over at my house. I try not to dream...

But I'll speak anyways, because I've made it. I am not better or more intelligent than my friends. I am not more personable or loveable. I am no warmer or deeper than my friends, and my insides hide no secrets of beauty or potential.

There were just some people, a handful or less, who gave me a penny, a tiny lift. Sometimes they lied to me, saying how well I did. But the little love that came with it was perfect and genuine....

You can help us. You don't have to think. There's no magic system. Don't change or fight the system. Don't change the formula. Don't change at all, except for one thing: your heart.[1]

The Talmud tells us that what comes from the heart goes to the heart. Real love goes to our hearts. It embraces us, heals us, and can recreate us. It addresses our most fundamental needs as people, especially when it comes unconditionally and accepts us for the *tzelem elokim* within.

Providing this is a matter of perspective. It is like the story of the Chassidic rebbe and his friend who see Jews smoking outside a *shul* on Yom Kippur. The friend says: "How terrible that these people desecrate Yom Kippur right outside the *shul*." The rebbe responds: "How wonderful that even as they desecrate Yom Kippur, they still come to *shul*." It is a matter of perspective.

How can we achieve this perspective, especially when our children have rejected the very thing most important to us? We can do so in a number of ways:

First, we can try not to take it personally. Although we may have made mistakes, it is hard to know truly why someone has left observance. And no matter what the reason, they always have free choice. As adults, their choices are their own and we cannot take responsibility for their ultimate decisions. That is their job, and between them and God.

Second, we can remember that we can never truly judge where someone is or where someone is meant to be in God's eyes. As Leah Kohn explains, "In *objective* terms he is not where he is supposed to be. But in *subjective* terms, he might be where he is *able* to be and we cannot judge. In objective terms we say every Jew should keep Torah. But is this person doing what he can even though he doesn't do anything? Only *Hashem* can judge."[2] Perhaps in God's eyes he is doing better than in our eyes.

Third, we can realize that sometimes the break itself can cause a return. Especially people who have negative feelings about observance, who have been scarred by practitioners of Judaism, may need to remove themselves from the source of pain in order to resolve it. Doing so may be the only possible way to return.

Sometimes, to appreciate something, we have to lose it. It is said that we had to be slaves before we received the Torah, otherwise we could never have appreciated what it meant for God to save us, give us the Torah and help us attain freedom in its truest sense.

What we have or are given, we tend to take for granted. What we lose and gain again or have to work for, we cherish more passionately.[3] So losing observance may be the first step to appreciating it properly. And the proof is that those who return often do so with greater resolve, strength, passion, and optimism than they ever had before.

Finally, it may help to remember that those who drop observance often maintain strong Jewish identities and values. This is because it is far more difficult to drop values than behavior. Behavior is an external expression but values live deep inside. They are harder to change and often remain long after observance has gone. Those who go off the derech often respect Jewish values and strive for some kind of relationship with God.

Consider the following story. In an apartment in New York, filled with twenty college students who had all gone off the derech, a debate was raging. They had spent the evening smoking marijuana and wanted to buy more. They searched the corners of the room for money, dug out the ends of their pockets, swept away the breadcrumbs from between the couch cushions, and managed to come up with nine dollars, one dollar short. Just then, Michael reached into his wallet and found one dollar. It was the rebbe's dollar. He had received it when he went to visit him the year before. Thus the debate began. Should they use the rebbe's dollar to buy the pot? Did the dollar have inherent spiritual value? Would it be sacrilegious to spend it on marijuana? It was the kind of debate that could only happen in a group of formerly observant Jews. And it ended with the kind of conclusion only possible in such a group. They decided that, as badly as they wanted more pot, it was simply wrong to use the rebbe's dollar to buy it.

As disturbing as this story is on one level, it indicates dramatically how values remain long after behavior is gone. Their lifetime of experience in the Jewish world had touched them in a place marijuana couldn't. They had stopped keeping Shabbat but they hadn't stopped caring. They *couldn't* stop caring. Their lifestyles had changed, but their values remained and that connection alone was valuable. It could help them return in the future or help their children to return.

As long as they internally respect and connect to Judaism and its values, there is a good chance they will give their children respect for Torah as well. Their children may then take that positive attitude one step further to *halachic* observance.

Unfortunately, as communities, it is hard to maintain a positive outlook on the issue. Instead we seem to feel great shame for those who go off the derech. For example, one mother who wrote to the *Jewish Observer* withheld her name "for obvious reasons," saying that her family was traumatized by a wayward child whose debasing lifestyle had put the family in turmoil. Words like *traumatized, debasing,* and *turmoil,* and the fact that it is "obvious" why she would not reveal her name, express just how much shame and negativity is associated with these matters and how far we have to go to properly address the issue.

A sense of shame greatly hinders the possibility of return. For the child, it removes the warmth and acceptance he may need to resolve his problems. It may further fuel his anger and justify his negative perception of the observant world. And it can mean that even one who wants to return will find a very hostile environment to return to that can hinder his doing so. He may feel that shame will follow him wherever he goes, a reality that may be too frightening to confront, which can close the door and sabotage any hope for return.

This often occurs with girls. While boys can rebel and return finding acceptance years later, girls often feel continued rejection, judgment, and ostracism. They fear they will never be accepted and that no amount of repentance will remove the blemishes of their past. This makes them far less likely to return than their male counterparts.[4]

David Mandel, CEO of Ohel, explains that "many of those victims/survivors need the *hechsher* (rabbinical approval) and support from the community as part of the healing process and as long as we continue to see them as damaged goods and as the person with the problems, we are delaying their ability to completely heal."[5]

But our sense of shame goes beyond hurting those who have left. It hurts us as well. It can blind us to the many positive aspects of our children, deprive us of the ability to enjoy and take pride in them. It can make us loath to share our troubles with others, which means we may fail to glean useful advice from others or that we may feel alone in our pain even though we are not. It can mean that a potentially uniting, strengthening and supporting experience instead becomes an alienating one in which we fear our neighbors' scorn and treat them like enemies rather than supportive friends. We may then fail to understand how prevalent these issues are and fail to learn from each other's experiences. This hurts everyone involved — individuals, communities, our children and ourselves.

*   *   *

If it is true that problems are opportunities in disguise, then the challenge of Jews who leave observance is an opportunity. In the same way that bodily pain tells us something is wrong, the pain of losing children from the path of observance could be God's way of telling us something is wrong. It may well be a call to change — to strengthen our way of life, our families, schools and communities and to create the kind of observant life that inspires our children.

The pain may also be an opportunity to heal wounds *outside* of our observant world so that we can help improve the Jewish world at large.

For generations the Jewish world has been beset with division and discord. This *galut* began because of *sinat chinam* (senseless hatred),[6] and we have been plagued by it throughout the generations. Today, as during the destruction of the Temple, there is disunity, disrespect and sometimes hatred within the Jewish world. Healing this fractionalization has been and remains our greatest challenge. It has plagued us for centuries and continues to do so with no end in sight. But since it caused this *galut*, resolving it may be the only way to end it. So while this may be our hardest challenge, it may also be our most important.

How can we possibly meet such a challenge? How can we create unity between such varying groups? Perhaps this phenomenon can or is meant to play a role in that.

Our children often motivate us to understand and accept what we would never do otherwise. We can debate, argue, and discuss the positives and negatives of alternative Jewish lifestyles. We can try as hard as we might to understand those who are not observant and try to unite with them. But no intellectual argument will impact us as strongly as when we are forced, through our children, to understand the other side.

When our children go off the derech many of us are forced for the first and only time in our lives to understand nonobservance. We may not *want* to, but, when we are confronted with the choice of rejecting our own children or understanding their nonobservance, many of us choose understanding. For the love of our children, we begin to emotionally understand what our minds alone cannot, and we may well become motivated in a way we would never be otherwise to understand the nonobservant.

Interestingly enough, nonobservant Jews experience the same thing in the other direction. The *baal teshuva* phenomenon, which has taken off in the last decades, confronts nonobservant Jews with the same situation. They are forced, when their children join the observant world, to understand observance in a way they never would otherwise — not intellectually, but emotionally. They are often motivated to tolerate in their hearts what they could never do in their minds. They often begin, for the time, to gain respect or understanding for observant people.

It is ironic that children seem to be prompting changes that nothing else has managed to achieve. And it is interesting that it is now happening on both sides of the Jewish world. One cannot help but wonder if this phenomenon may not be God's means of getting us to unite. When both sides incur losses, and those losses prompt understanding more effectively than anything else, it is hard not to wonder if they may not be *meant* as opportunities for us to heal the very wounds that need addressing if our world is to be united and redeemed.

Such an overwhelming task would require an overwhelming counterforce, and is there any force greater in the world than the love of our children? Surely children's going off the derech is one of the most difficult experiences for observant Jews. But it is precisely the most difficult experiences that can be most rewarding. And given our generations of *sinat chinam,* the most rewarding response might be to unite our world. If we could use this challenge as an opportunity to understand

371

the rest of the Jewish world, our greatest pain might achieve our greatest accomplishment.

Like all opportunities, this will be what we make of it. God can only present us with a choice. He does not force the outcome. If we take it to its ultimate place, perhaps we can use this as an opportunity to heal our national wounds. But in the least, we can use it to strengthen our families, schools, and communities and create the kind of observant world that inspires our children to return and, perhaps more importantly, never to leave in the first place.

CHAPTER 34

Putting It All Together: Solutions

Having a positive attitude toward those who leave observance may facilitate their return. But if we have the right attitudes to begin with, we will not need to bring anyone back. Our children will naturally want to be part of our world and perpetuate our values and way of life.

Throughout this book we have addressed many ways to solve some of the causes of defection. Most of them seem to require one thing: becoming more broad and open in our approach. Virtually every issue discussed, whether emotional, intellectual or practical, benefits from broadening our perspectives. In essence, it seems that in many cases we must leave behind narrowness, as we did when we left *Mitzrayim*. The word *Mitzrayim*, the Hebrew word for Egypt, the place we were enslaved, literally means "narrow straits."[1] Interestingly, we became God's nation, a truly free people, only when we were released from our narrow straights; and it seems that perhaps we must do so again if we are to create a more vital observant world.

Emotional issues

In terms of the emotional issues, we need to ensure that observance and relationships with observant people are loving and warm, healthy and affirming, positive and joyful. While openness or broadness will not necessarily help to create *shalom bayit*, it can help ensure that we do not force observance on our children, but rather give them room to make mistakes and find their own way. It can help us to be open to their differences from us and place their emotional needs first to ensure that observance never compromises their health and happiness.

An open attitude can also help us prevent problems. It can help us to consider our own role in shaping our children's attitudes, and to improve our characters, relationships, and observance. If we fail to prevent defection, openness could help us consider options like therapy and help us recognize that Judaism is not a cure for all wounds, but rather ideally the pinnacle of an emotionally healthy foundation. All this can be achieved with an open attitude that is willing to listen and learn.

Education

This same openness can go a long way in solving our educational and communal problems as well. To establish strong belief, we need to encourage our children to explore their beliefs, ask questions, and challenge the status quo. We need to consider the most challenging questions as marks of pride rather than shame, as healthy religiosity rather than heresy. Openness to this kind of exploration can help our children discover the truths of Judaism we want to impart and help them establish strong belief.

Along with a more open attitude toward *how* we teach, we need greater broadness in *what* we teach. Our current educational curricula focus on truth and fear at the expense of love, understanding, and meaning. We focus on the *mitzvot* between ourselves and God but often neglect the *mitzvot* between man and man. We narrow our focus onto technical *halachic* observance rather than some of its more inspiring elements.

But Judaism is about more than *halachah*. It is also about a philosophy, a culture, a people, a nation, a land. It is about all of these things — the old and the new, the future and the past, the *mitzvot bain adam lemakom* and *bain adam lechavairo* — the ritual and the ethical. It is about what you do *and* what you feel, the letter *and* the spirit. It is about the outside world as well as the inside one.

Judaism works best when we acknowledge all these aspects and are broad enough to bring them together. The alternative is like having an arm without a leg. The body can work with only one, but not as well. It can accomplish some tasks, but not all. It can meet some challenges but cannot meet them all. It can speak to some people, but will not inspire *all* of them. A narrow Judaism is simply less effective than a broader one, for it fails to be true to the greatness of Judaism and reveal it in all its inspiring aspects.

Broadness can help our children appreciate and connect with Judaism. Those who cannot relate to learning can take pride in their *chessed;* those who cannot find meaning in the Diaspora can take pride in moving to Israel; those who cannot relate to ritual can take pride in excelling at other *mitzvot.* The more broad our Jewish education, and the more numerous the avenues for connecting to it, the greater the chance that every Jew from every culture at every stage of life with every kind of personality will find something that speaks to him, inspires him, and keeps him connected.

What we do in our classrooms, we need to do in our behavior as well — broaden our appreciation for the numerous facets of Torah and focus on some of its neglected elements. Currently our families and communities tend to focus on certain categories of *mitzvot,* or even individual *mitzvot* that become the whole of our Judaism.

For example: the Conservative, Reform and secular value interpersonal *mitzvot,* often at the expense of the rest of the Torah. These are their *mitzvot* and their entire Judaism is defined by it. The observant world focuses instead on *mitzvot* between man and God and makes that the whole of their Torah.

Communities within the observant world also have their focuses, each concentrating on a narrow part of Judaism that becomes the whole essence. For the Modern Orthodox, it's about balancing secular and Torah educations and engaging in the outside world. For the *yeshiva* world, it's about learning. For the Chassidishe world, it's about holiness in seclusion. And for the religious Zionists, it's about Israel.

Each is right and each is wrong in its approach, for Judaism is not any one of these elements, but rather all of them. It is wonderful and natural to focus on our strengths and excel at certain *mitzvot*. But when our focus becomes too narrow, when we value one element at the expense of others, we deny the rich tapestry of elements that God carefully created for us. We deny the very thing that makes us strong and unique. When we remove one thread, or focus on one at the expense of the other, the garment starts to unravel and the broad foundation God intended for observance, the kind that draws all personalities to our religion and demonstrates its beauty and greatness, becomes lost.

If we could do in our communal behavior what we should do in our classrooms — broaden our appreciation for the varying parts of Judaism — we could help all kinds of people to connect, find a place, and take pride in the *mitzvot* that speak to their particular being.

Implementation

This is also essential for addressing implementation needs. In order to do so effectively, we must broaden our focus from external expressions of observance to internal spiritual matters, and we must broaden our definition of the right way to be *frum* so our children can find their own way.

Broadening our vision and concept of the right *derech* can provide our children with an alternative choice between the all and nothing that currently nudges them off the derech at times. The parents whose children *all* stay on the derech are often the ones who implement this approach. They recognize the differences among their children and provide room for each to flourish according to his needs. In a sense, they do not believe in "a *derech*." They believe in the *derech* that works best for their child. They do not denigrate other observant communities but rather try to find strengths in them all.

Their children may each dress differently and align themselves with different communities. But rather than consider that a point of failure, the parents take pride in it. Their children may not be on *their parents' derech* but they are still within the fold, committed, and dedicated to observance. They remain committed because their parents' Judaism was not a one-lane highway with limited options, but rather a broad open road, a multi-lane highway with enough room for each child to find his path.

These parents ensure that *chinuch lenaar al pi darcho* does not remain an empty saying, meaningless in its application, but rather a living lesson.

We can all benefit from such success if we take pride in our communal differences and regard them as legitimate alternatives to our own. We need not undermine *halachah* or denigrate our own *derech* to do so. We need only to value the idea of *shivim panim* with faith that, when we have done our jobs, the question will not be whether our children stay on the derech, but rather which *derech* they will choose.

Of course, becoming more broad and open in these ways can be frightening. It is natural, understandable and, to some extent necessary, to establish walls to protect our children's observance.

But walls cannot take the place of internal strength. It is internal strength that fosters pride and joy in Judaism. Condemning the alternatives in order to foster observance may work on some level. But it often simply pressures our children to be *frum* and creates a shallow Judaism that we cannot detect until our grandchildren go off the derech.

Far more effective than social walls or verbal condemnation is a strengthening of our own Jewish world. Those with a strong identity, with a love, respect and belief in Judaism, as well as the tools to implement it, have little to fear. They will not need external walls as much as others do, for they will have internal strength. They will not want any alternative, for Judaism will clearly be better.

The key is in recognizing that broadness and narrowness each have their place — broadness works well, but only after narrowness has established identity and internal strength. The birth of our nation indicates this well. To become God's people and serve Him properly, we needed the narrow straits of Egypt to help us coalesce into a nation and develop our unique identity, culture, language, and history that would bind us and serve as the foundation for our future.

Narrowness had to come first, as it seems to do in many cases. Many things are born in narrowness. The creation of the world began that way — we are told that in order to create the world God constricted Himself. Our souls are born that way; they can only exist and enter this world when confined to a body. Our bodies are born that way; they develop in the confinement of the womb that protects and nurtures them. And we must enter the world through a narrow canal if we are to grow into something greater. Finally, once born we can only survive and grow into adults within the confines of a nurturing and caring family unit.

So, too, with our children's observance, we should start by being narrow in order to create and strengthen their Jewish identity. Protected environments will help us meet their emotional, intellectual and implementation needs and a narrow focus on their Judaism will help develop and establish their identity.

But, while we begin in confinement, we can't end there. Once we established our identity and nationhood, God liberated us from slavery and broadened our narrow straits. The Jewish nation had to leave *Mitzrayim* to become the people of God. Likewise, a body must leave the womb to enter the world; a person must eventually leave his family to grow and his create his own; and a soul must eventually leave the narrow confines of the physical body to reunite with its Creator.

So what requires narrowness in birth requires broadness to fully actualize. As in these other areas, so it is with our observant children. They need the narrow focus of our small protective world to develop identity and commitment to Torah. But they need broadness to develop and grow beyond.

If we have done our jobs, when our children were in our grasp, to bring joy, strong belief, and practical tools to observance, we need not fear later that broadness will compromise observance. We will have strengthened them internally and given them a true, meaningful, and joyful way of life that outshines any alternative.

If we have done our jobs, our broad and open approach will exist for them within a *halachic* framework for we will have maximized the advantages of being both narrow and broad, providing each in its own time.

This may be especially important today for, in the modern world, Judaism competes in a free marketplace of ideas and lifestyles. The alternatives to observant Judaism are attractive and enticing, certainly more broad, open and accepting than our own — and will likely accept them no matter who they are or want to be.

In such a world, narrowness alone is a liability. When not balanced or graduated with a broader approach, it forces our children into a world of black and white when all that surrounds them is in full vibrant color. It provides them with too few options when a stroll down a supermarket aisle gives them at least fifteen different options for soup or cream cheese. In this world — a world of color, a world of choice — narrow options pale in comparison. They will not be good enough, not nearly accommodating enough, and not attractive enough to be better than the alternative.

Today's observant Judaism must recognize this new reality, not by compromising itself or the beauty and strength of the Torah. But rather by making more room *within* the system, wherever possible. By recognizing our differences and providing us with options to be who we are and need to be.

If we can succeed in giving our children positive feelings, strong belief, and a supportive environment to express them, they will likely choose *halachah* while also gaining the freedom to reach their potential and connect with observance in their own way. In that case, no riches of the world would undermine their commitment. They will face the outside world armed with pride and conviction. Their question will not be *whether* or not to be *frum*, but rather *how* to be *frum*. Their question will not be whether to join the *outside* world, but rather which *Jewish* community to join.

Since they are born into our homes, schools, and communities, since they are born neutral, ready to absorb what we give them, much is up to us. We play a significant role in creating their Judaism and defining their perception of it. It is frightening and exhilarating to realize how much influence we have — that we hold the keys to shaping their observance; that *we* are the Judaism our children experience; that *we* give them the joy or the pain, the knowledge or the ignorance, the pride or the shame.

It is easier to blame the lures of the outside world and it is far more difficult to take responsibility ourselves. But we must do so for, like most things in life, the answers lay not out there, but in here with us — with who we are, how much we love Judaism, how accommodating we make it. That is the heart of the challenge. That is what will make the difference. That is what will determine whether or not Judaism can compete and how much of a threat the outside world really is.

Let us not look to the world with fear, but look to ourselves with strength. Let us recognize that, whatever we face, God has created the challenge and given us the tools. Our journey has lasted through thousands of years, and throughout it all, we have found the strength to meet each challenge, recreate our lives, speak new languages and adapt to the world without losing our Jewish identities.

We can do so again. We can make our children proud of the legacy we leave them if only we lead them with strength, with pride, with vision and the courage to change and be the best of who we are. We need only to look at ourselves with honesty and integrity, to assess what we lack and what we possess; to live Torah joyfully, to teach it broadly, and be open to the variety of ways of expressing it; to have faith in ourselves, in our children, and our Torah to know that, with a little more effort, the beauty of our Torah will clearly shine.

All we have to do is come home again to the Judaism that speaks without shouting, that leads without pressuring, and inspires without condemning. We need only for Judaism to be better than the alternatives, attractive and warm, true to its roots and broad in its application. For we are God's chosen people and as He chose us, we chose Him. And our children would easily do so again if we model a kind, attractive, joyful, meaningful Judaism that inspires. As long as we are truly His people, He will be our God and we will achieve our mission to serve as a light — not only for the rest of the world, but also for our own.

Highlights of Web Survey Results

Respondents were asked to participate in the survey if:
1) They were raised in an observant home OR if they became observant on their own

AND

2) If they stopped being observant either temporarily or permanently.

Terms were defined as follows:

Observant — observing at least Shabbat and *kashrut* according to Orthodox Judaism

Modern Orthodox — observing primarily only Shabbat and *kashrut* according to Orthodox Judaism

Halachic — observing *halachah* strictly, but living modern lifestyle with exposure to secular world/education

Black Hat/Yeshivish — *halachic* observance with little value for or openness toward the secular

Of 466 valid respondents, upbringing was classified as follows:

Secular — 2%[1]

Traditional — 30%

Modern Orthodox — 38%

Halachic — 7%

Black Hat/Yeshivish — 12%

Chassidic — 12%

They classified their high schools as follows:

Secular — 28%

Modern Orthodox — 41%

Black/Yeshivish — 20%

Chassidic — 10%

74% attended *yeshiva* after high school.

General Information

If you had to attribute your not being observant to one thing, what would it be?

Observant People — 44%

Judaism Itself — 26%

Life Circumstances — 27%

God — 2%

Emotional Issues

Did you ever feel rejected because you were not observant enough?

Yes — 75%

No — 25%

By Whom?

Parents — 44%

Friends — 53%

Teachers — 66%

Community — 91%

Growing up did you feel that observance was imposed upon you?

Yes — 66%

No — 34%

Did you feel your parents' love was conditional on your being observant?

Yes — 24%

Somewhat — 27%

No — 49%

Were you physically or verbally abused by someone observant?

Yes — 51%

Somewhat — 4%

No — 45%

How did your parents feel about observance?

Mother		Father	
Hated/Resented It	7%	Hated/Resented It	12%
Indifferent	4%	Indifferent	36%
Mixed Feelings	27%	Mixed Feelings	0%
Loved it	61%	Loved it	50%

Intellectual Issues

Do you believe that God gave the Torah?

No — 32%

Not Sure — 7%

Yes — 61%

Do you believe that Talmudic rabbis had the authority to apply the Torah/make rules?

No — 25%

Not Sure — 7%

Yes — 69%

Do you believe that rabbis today have the authority to make rules or apply the Torah?

No — 32%

Not Sure — 7%

Yes — 61%

Do you believe that Judaism expresses what God wants?

No — 50%

Not Sure — 9%

Yes — 42%

Do you believe that Orthodox Judaism promotes happiness and fulfillment?

Strongly Disagree	14%	
Disagree	14%	**54%**
Not sure	26%	
Agree	17%	
Strongly Agree	29%	

Were you taught the benefits/reasons for individual *mitzvot* (other than God told you to)?

No — 23%

Somewhat — 26%

Yes — 51%

385

Were you taught to see the *mitzvot* as deep and beautiful?

No — 22%

Somewhat — 31%

Yes — 47%

Were you able to question these (intellectual) issues in class?

No — 51%

Sometimes — 6%

Yes — 43%

Did you feel you were answered satisfactorily?

No — 64%

Sometimes — 6%

Yes — 31%

If you had to guess, to what extent would you say you have experienced the following in your Jewish education?

Poor Mentors:			Teachers who were not well educated:		
Most	14%		Most	8%	
More than Half	12%	**53%**	More than Half	7%	**41%**
Half	8%		Half	8%	
Many	19%		Many	18%	
A few	22%		A few	30%	
None	26%		None	28%	

Teachers who were dishonest:		
Most	4%	
More than Half	5%	**22%**
Half	3%	
Many	10%	
A few	38%	
None	40%	

Hypocritical Teachers:		
Most	10%	
More than Half	8%	**36%**
Half	3%	
Many	15%	
A few	34%	
None	30%	

Teachers who chided you too often or were overly dogmatic regarding observance:		
Most	7%	
More than Half	9%	**45%**
Half	5%	
Many	14%	
A few	23%	
None	26%	

Teachers who could not relate to you:		
Most	21%	
More than Half	12%	**56%**
Half	3%	
Many	20%	
A few	17%	
None	27%	

Teachers who could not answer your questions:		
Most	20%	
More than Half	9%	**54%**
Half	4%	
Many	21%	
A few	25%	
None	21%	

Do you believe that these relationships/experiences contributed in any way to your move away from observance?

Yes — 72%

No — 28%

Implementation/Community Issues

Do you consider yourself a hard-working/disciplined person?

Yes — 73%

Somewhat 19%

No — 8%

Do you generally live the values you preach/believe in?

Yes — 81%

Somewhat — 19%

No — 5%

Do you believe that Orthodox Judaism IS practiced properly today?

Strongly Disagree	14%	
Disagree	24%	**60%**
Not Sure	22%	
Agree	13%	
Strongly Agree	27%	

Have you ever been turned off by any of the following in the Orthodox community?

People who were smug or displayed an attitude of superiority?			People who were hypocritical?		
Most	19%		Most	20%	
More than Half	12%	**62%**	More than Half	11%	**62%**
Half	4%		Half	7%	
Many	27%		Many	24%	
A few	15%		A few	16%	
None	23%		None	22%	

People who committed *chilul Hashem?*			People who berated or marginalized other observant communities?		
Most	12%	**51%**	Most	26%	**63%**
More than Half	6%		More than Half	7%	
Half	4%		Half	5%	
Many	29%		Many	25%	
A few	24%		A few	16%	
None	25%		None	21%	

People who were intolerant of difference or nonobservance?			People who were racist?		
Most	26%	**68%**	Most	24%	**65%**
More than Half	14%		More than Half	10%	
Half	5%		Half	5%	
Many	23%		Many	26%	
A few	9%		A few	11%	
None	22%		None	24%	

Do you believe these relationships/experiences contributed to your move away from observance?

Yes — 78%

No — 22%

Do you respect the community you were raised in?

No — 23%

Somewhat — 31%

Yes — 46%

Do you believe Orthodox Judaism will make you a better person?

Strongly Disagree	16%	
Disagree	17%	**60%**
Not Sure	27%	
Agree	11%	
Strongly Agree	29%	

Do you feel your observant community valued spirituality?

No — 36%

Somewhat — 34%

Yes — 31%

Did your community foster spirituality?

No — 46%

Somewhat — 31%

Yes — 24%

Do you believe that Orthodox Judaism will make you more spiritual?

Strongly Disagree	16%	
Disagree	17%	**56%**
Not Sure	23%	
Agree	15%	
Strongly Agree	30%	

Was your experience of observant Judaism meaningful?

No — 20%

Somewhat — 33%

Yes — 48%

Was your experience of observant Judaism fulfilling?

No — 35%

Somewhat — 32%

Yes — 34%

Did your community pressure you to conform to external standards of dress, speech etc…?

Yes — 66%

Somewhat — 22%

No — 12%

If so, how did you feel about that?

Negative — 63%

Neutral — 17%

Positive — 19%

Other — 2%

Do you believe that Orthodox Judaism:

Allows you to be whatever kind of person you want to be?		Allows you to choose any kind of profession (barring illegal ones)?	
Strongly Disagree	34%	Strongly Disagree	34%
Disagree	29% **71%**	Disagree	29% **71%**
Not Sure	8%	Not Sure	8%
Agree	5%	Agree	5%
Strongly Agree	24%	Strongly Agree	24%

What was your community's attitude to the following:

Jews who were more or less observant than your community?		Jews who were not observant:	
Negative and Rejecting	59%	Negative and Rejecting	71%
Neutral	37%	Neutral	27%
Mixed	3%	Mixed	1%
Positive	0%	Positive	0%

Non-Jews and the outside world:		Secular learning and knowledge:	
Negative and Rejecting	59%	Negative and Rejecting	49%
Neutral	29%	Neutral	45%
Mixed	2%	Mixed	3%
Positive	10%	Positive	0%

If their attitudes were negative, did that cause you to *respect* your community less?

Yes — 75%

Somewhat — 18%

No — 8%

If their attitudes were negative, did that cause you to move *away* from your community more?

Yes — 76%

Somewhat — 14%

No — 10%

If so, their attitude toward what?

Other Observant Jews — 65%

Nonobservant Jews — 57%

Non-Jews and the Secular World — 86%

Secular Learning and Knowledge — 59%

Getting Help for Struggling Adolescents

Sometimes no matter what a parent does, nothing will work. Solutions can seem like putting a band-aid on a broken arm and the best of efforts can fall short of desired results.

In such cases, parents should not be afraid to seek help whether formally or informally. One way they can do so is by speaking with other parents who may have had similar experiences. This can provide perspective, support, and solutions. It can help parents realize that the problems are more common than they think and can help struggling parents feel less alone, which is helpful in and of itself.

On the more formal level, there are a variety of programs and schools — more and more every year — which attend to the spectrum of kids from those who are mildly off the derech to kids who are completely at risk. Some are more successful than others and success with some children does not necessarily make a program right for a particular child. In seeking the help of programs or alternative schools, it is vital to take note of both a general track record and the individual strengths of the program in terms of a child's particular needs. Particularly instructive is hearing what the children themselves have to say of these schools and programs when not in the presence of their authority figures. If the children respect their authority figures and seem to develop positive attitudes toward themselves and Yiddishkeit, the school or program may be a good choice.

A family rav can also be an important resource. A rav who is trusted and respected by his community will have gained exposure to many kinds of problems within many kinds of families. If he knows a particular family and child well, he may be uniquely equipped to determine how to deal with specific issues as they arise. A good indicator of success would be if a rav has healthy relationships with his own children or other youth.

A rav's ability to help might be limited, however, when it comes to resolving fundamental emotional issues. Addressing those issues can be complex and hard to uncover. Resolving the issues can require not only a lot of time and objectivity, but also a thorough understanding of emotional processes, relationships, and personality. Therapists are properly equipped to deal with such issues. Unlike *rabbanim*, they have time at their disposal and are specifically trained in identifying and resolving emotional issues. Since they exist outside of the context of a child's daily life, therapists can be perceived as less threatening, making it easier to establish trusting relationships. In addition, the process of therapy itself is unique. It is not about passively receiving advice, but actively engaging in understanding and improving one's self. It is about discovering and uncovering the self through communication and the help of objective guidance. In the process of therapy, a person takes an active role in examining his life and relationships, identifying his strengths and weaknesses, and hopefully gaining the insight and tools to address them effectively. This active participation and patient exploration of self is unique and can be greatly beneficial in dealing with a rebellious adolescent.

Some observant parents have an aversion to therapy, dismissing it as unproductive or considering it shameful. But virtually all *gedo-*

lim and experts who have worked with kids who have gone off the derech agree that therapy can be an essential tool. And it should be far from shameful to pursue a process which, even in the case of healthy people, fosters growth and introspection, essential tools for achieving emotional health, improving relationships with people, and coming closer to God. A growth-oriented society should consider anything that fosters these kinds of results a *mitzvah*. And those who are truly interested in helping struggling adolescents cannot afford the luxury of dismissing it.

The only real question is which therapist to seek. Observant therapists tend to know the issues best, although sometimes a child's anger toward Orthodoxy may be so great that he cannot trust an observant therapist. In that case, a therapist who knows and respects the Orthodox world can be a good alternative. The only problematic therapist is a bad one. An inexperienced or untalented therapist can do tremendous damage, so it is vital to do research and obtain referrals.

For more information, go to *www.offthederech.com*

Endnotes

Introduction

1   Adin Steinsaltz, Lecture: "The State of the Nation." King David Hotel. Jerusalem. 7 April 1996. http://www.judaica.ru/english/articles/state.html.

2   Jonathan Sacks. *A Letter in the Scroll: Understanding Our Jewish Identity and Exploring the Legacy of the World's Oldest Religion.* New York: The Free Press, Simon & Schuster Inc, 2000, p. 213.

3   *Sifri,* Deuteronomy 346, from Adin Steinsaltz, Lecture: "The State of the Nation."

4   Steinsaltz, Lecture: "The State of the Nation."

5   Jonathan Sacks. *A Letter in the Scroll: Understanding Our Jewish Identity and Exploring the Legacy of the World's Oldest Religion,* p. 178.

Chapter 1

1   Yohanan Danziger. Personal Interview. 2001.

2   Moshe Schapiro. "Ohr Samayach Addresses the Teen-Dropout Issue." *Yated Ne'eman* 16 April 1999.

3   Chanan Tigay. "Dope Yomi: Drug Abuse Rises Among Orthodox Teens." *Jewish Sentinel* 23 — 28 March 2001: 12-13.

4   Yohanan Danziger, under contract with The Metropolitan New York Coordinating Council on Jewish Poverty. *Report to the City of New York Department of Youth and Community Development on the Incidence of At-Risk Youth in the Orthodox Jewish Community of Brooklyn, NY.* New York: The Metropolitan Coordinating Council on Jewish Poverty, 1999-2000, p. 13.

5   Danziger, p. 14.

6   Danziger, p. 13.

7   Berel Wein. Personal Interview. 28 August, 2000 and 8 January, 2001.

8   Mareleyn Schneider based on Alvin Schiff and Mareleyn Schneider, "Fortifying and Restoring Jewish Behavior: The Interaction of Home and School." New York, David H. Azrieli Graduate Institute, Report 3, 1994. These figures are perhaps the most accurate on the subject I have seen for the study defined "Orthodox" by *halachic* observance of Shabbat and *kashrut*; it differentiated between those raised with one or two observant parents as well the level of Jewish education; and the data was gathered years after graduation when the observant children had presumably made independent religious choices.

9   This data corresponds with another study conducted in Israel by the Religious Education Authority which found that 8.2% of 1999 *yeshiva* high graduates were no longer religious and 14.4% of those who graduated state religious high schools no longer kept Shabbat. Abigail Radoszkowicz. "Not So Many Youths Throwing Off Their Crocheted Kippot, Studies Show." *The Jerusalem Post*. 15 August 2003.

10   David Berger. Personal Interview: 17 March, 2003.

11   Berel Wein, Personal Interview.

12   Daniel Mechanic. Personal Interview. 12 September, 2000. Some of the increase is due to the fact people are more willing to talk about the issue. But some of those numbers are new cases.

13   Yaakov Shapiro, Project Rejewvenation. In addition, he expects that in the next two years, there will be greater problems among the female population whose percentage of at risk behavior is growing at a faster rate than boys. According to Rabbi Shapiro's research, if in 1990, 70% of at risk cases were boys and 30% were girls, those numbers have steadily shifted to where in 2000, 55% were girls and 45% were boys.

14   Rabbi Berel Wein asserts that "Ezra rebuilt the Temple and launched the Second Commonwealth with only 42,000 Jews..." Also it is estimated that at the time of the great biblical commentator Rashi (11th Century France), there were probably no more than a million Jews in the world. Even by the time of the 17th century Chmielnicki pogroms in Eastern Europe, there were hardly two million." *The Jerusalem Post*, Up Front Magazine. 23 January 2004, pp. 32-33.

Chapter 2

1   Berel Wein, Personal Interview. 28 August, 2000 and 8 January, 2001.

2   Wein, Personal Interview and Chaim Dov Rabinowitz. *The History of the Jewish People: From Nehemia to the Present. Vol. II*. New York / Jerusalem: Moznaim Publishing Corporation, 1998, p. 304-306.

3   Ephraim Buchwald, Personal Interview, 22 August 2000. See also Rabinowitz, p. 306, who estimates that during the 19th century alone, 200,000 Jews converted.

4   Jonathan Sacks, *Arguments for the Sake of Heaven*. Northvale NJ: Jason Aronson, 1995, 1991, p. 87.

5   Yaffa Eliach. *There Once Was a World*. Boston / New York / London: Little, Brown, and Company. p. 468. Also, Wein, Personal Interview.

6   Buchwald, Personal Interview.

7   Buchwald, Personal Interview. Also Rabinowitz, chapters 106-107, 132-133. Eliach, p. 149-150, 171-173.

8   To make matters worse, most European Jews lived in poverty, suffering high infant mortalities and high unemployment rates. They experienced their Jewishness as a problem rather than as a matter of pride. Berel Wein, Personal Interview. 28 August, 2000 and 8 January, 2001. See also Rabinowitz, chapters 92-93.

9   Buchwald, Personal Interview.

10 Yaakov Shapiro, Personal Interview. 8 August 2000.

11 Jonathan Sacks, Personal Interview. 23 April 2001.

12 Norman Lamm, Personal Interview. 16 November, 2000.

13 Tehilim 119:45.

14 Jonathan Sacks, *A Letter in the Scroll: Understanding Our Jewish Identity and Exploring the Legacy of the World's Oldest Religion*. New York: The Free Press, Simon & Schuster Inc, 2000. p. 176.

15 Harav Yehuda Amital. Lecture on Parshat Vayechi, "Commitment vs. Connecting — the Current Crisis of our Youth." http://www.vbm-Torah.org/archive/sichot61/12vayechi.htm.

16 Leah Kohn, Personal Interview. 7 and 21 September, 2000, and 16 and 26 October, 2000.

17 Kohn, Personal Interview.

18 Bamidbar, 15:39.

19 Jonathan Rosenblum, "Not God's Scorekeeper." *The Jerusalem Post* 15 June 2001.

20 Rosenblum, "Not God's Scorekeeper."

Chapter 3

1   David Margolis, "Going Away Again." *Baltimore Jewish Times*. 23 December 1988, p. 31.

2   This commentary is attributed to Rabbi Bunam of P'shis'cha.

Chapter 4

1   Sanhedrin 107b quoted from Natan Lopez Cardozo. "Thoughts to Ponder 27: Concerning the Millennium, A Jewish Child and a Hand Wave." 22 December 1999. http://www.cardozoschool.org/thoughts27.htm.

2   Sanhedrin 99b, quoted from Cardozo, "Thoughts to Ponder 27."

3   Natan Lopez Cardozo. "Thoughts to Ponder 39: The Birth of Amalek, the Making of an Enemy." 15 March 2000. http://www.cardozoschool.org/thoughts39.htm.

4   Chapter 13.5, quoted from Cardozo, "Thoughts to Ponder 27."

5   As Rabbi Shapiro says, "You can't make them a *mitzvah*. They can't be your lulav or etrog." Yaacov Shapiro. Personal Interview. 8 August 2000.

6   *Pirkei Avot* 3:14, *Yalkut Me'am Lo'ez* on *Avot* #90:1. There is a very strong statement about this in *Da'at Chochmah U'Mussar* by Rabbi Yerucham Levovitz, p. 67.

7   See *Outside Inside* by Gila Manolson, *A Hedge of Roses* by Dr. Norman Lamm, and *Total Immersion* by Rivka Slonim.

8   Interestingly enough, rejection may also actually diminish intelligence. Subjects

in a recent study were given IQ tests, then made to feel rejected by a group they thought they were going to be part of. When they took the IQ test again after being rejected, their scores plummeted by about 25%, with a 30% drop in analytical reading scores. The detrimental effects were relatively short lived, however no one knows how repeated rejection can damage not only the heart, but the mind as well. Jimmie Briggs. *Popular Science*, August 2002, p. 42.

9   Shapiro, Personal Interview.

10 Maslow's Hierarchy of Needs 17 May 2001. http://web.utk.edu/~gwynne/maslow.HTM and http://www.connect.net/georgen/maslow.htm.

11 AH Maslow, "A Theory of Human Motivation" (1943). Originally published in *Psychological Review*, 50, 370-396. Quoted from http://psychclassics.yorku.ca/Maslow/Motivation.htm.

Chapter 5

1   Yaakov Shapiro. "What a Parent Can Do" and "Straight Talk." *Jewish Action.* Summer 1999: p. 49.

2   AH Maslow, "A Theory of Human Motivation" (1943) Originally Published in *Psychological Review*, 50, 370-396. Quoted from http://psychclassics.yorku.ca/Maslow/motivation.htm.

3   Dennis Prager. *Happiness is a Serious Problem.* New York: Regan Books. 1998, p. 32.

4   See Abraham Isaac Kook in *Chachmat Hakadosh.*

5   Shraga Fisherman. *Noar HaKippot Zerukot.* Elkana, Israel, Introduction translated by Nancy and Maurice Benyaer.

6   Rabbi Ephraim Buchwald says, "It is interesting to note that the *medrash* says that none of the people converted by Abraham and Sara ever made it into Egypt. They fell out; they were lost. I think there is even an oblique criticism of Abraham that he would offer charity to people but he would say 'who gave you this food?' and they would say 'you did.' And he would say 'No. God did. You have to make a *bracha*." And by hard tactics, his people didn't really gain an appreciation of God and maybe that was one of the reasons that they fell out. It is not very clear why these souls that he made in Charan never joined the Jewish people. It is interesting though that the ancient rabbis thought you should have a soft touch when it comes to spiritualizing a person." Ephraim Buchwald. Personal Interview. 22 August 2000.

7   Yechezkel 18:23, see Vayikra Rabbah 17; commentary of the Or Hachayim to Devarim 32:11.

8   Devarim 30:15-19.

9   Moshe Chayim Luzatto, *Derech Hashem* I:3:1.

10 Shabbat 108a; Yerushalmi Shabbat 6.

11 Natan Lopez Cardozo. "Thoughts to Ponder 152: The Waters of Strife, Religious Coercion or Gentle Persuasion." 10 July 2003. http://www.cardozoschool.org.thoughts152.htm.

12 Maharal Gur Aryeh, Shemos (4:19) quoted from Yaakov Shapiro. "What a Parent Can Do" and "Straight Talk." *Jewish Action.* Summer 1999: p. 49.

13 Yaakov Shapiro, "What a Parent Can Do" and "Straight Talk." *Jewish Action.* Summer 1999: p. 45.

Chapter 6

1   Rabbi Sacks also notes that "We know from all recent research that the single greatest influence on whether we will have Jewish grandchildren is religious observance in the home: our British data suggest that this outweighs any other influence by a factor of at least five to one." Jonathan Sacks. "Love, Hate and Jewish Identity." *First Things: The Journal of Religion and Public Life*. 24 August 2000 http://firsththings.com/ftissues/ft9711/articles/sacks.html.

2   Meir Wikler, Personal Interview. 28 August, 2000.

3   Shlomo Riskin, Personal Interview. 7 and 10 January 2001.

4   Yaacov Horowitz, "Report from Ground Zero." *Jewish Observer*. November 1999: p. 51.

5   Horowitz, "Report from Ground Zero."

6   Moshe Prager. Personal interview. June 2001.

7   Chazal, Devarim 21:11 as quoted by Yaacov Shapiro, "Torah Advice for Raising Teenagers Part I" February 1995, http://www.shemayisrael.co.il/orgs/rejew/advice1.htm.

8   Wikler, Personal Interview.

9   Devorah Greenblatt, Personal Interview. 26 October, 2000.

10 Wikler, Personal Interview.

Chapter 7

1   A friend of mine, Tzvi Bing, likes to say that to be observant, you need to see Torah, live Torah, and learn Torah.

2   Shlomo Wolbe, "Basic Principles of Parenting." *Jewish Observer*. November 1999: p. 16.

3   Yaacov Shapiro, "Torah Advice for Raising Teenagers Part II," February 1995. http://www.shemayisrael.co.il/orgs/rejew/advice2.htm.

4   Naftali Weinberg, "Crucial Elements in Parenting." *Jewish Observer* March 2000: p.44.

5   Wolbe, p. 15-16.

Chapter 8

1   Jerry Lob, Personal Interview. 14 September 2000.

2   Lob, Personal Interview.

3   Rabbi Yabrov, "The Chazon Ish on the Educator's responsibility to the Weak and Wayward Student: Principles and Vignettes." *Jewish Observer*. November 1999: p. 12. Based on *Avot* 1:2. A similar idea is found in the writings of the Chazon Ish, *Emunah U'Bitachon* 4:16.

4   Jonathan Sacks. *A Letter in the Scroll: Understanding Our Jewish Identity and Exploring the Legacy of the World's Oldest Religion*. New York: The Free Press, Simon & Schuster Inc, 2000. p. 218.

5   Yabrov, p. 12.

6   Devarim 6:7, see Sifri there. Yevamot 62b; Sanhedrin 19b; on honoring one's students: Avot 4:12.

Chapter 9

1   Shlomo Wolbe, *Planting and Building: Raising a Jewish Child*. Jerusalem, Israel: Feldheim Publishers, 2000, p. 22.

2   Wolbe, p. 34.

3   Shlomo Wolbe, "Basic Principles of Parenting." *Jewish Observer*. November 1999: p. 21.

4   Yehuda Mendelson. "Basic Principles of Parenting: Postscript." *Jewish Observer*. March 2000, p.9 and Schwab, Shimon. "On Being a Trusted Friend to Your Children: Traditional Chinuch in Modern Times." *Jewish Observer* March 2000: p.16.

5   Sarah Chana Radcliffe, *The Delicate Balance: Love and Authority in Torah Parenting*. Jerusalem, Israel: Targum Press, 1989 p. 38.

6   Radcliffe, p. 38.

7   As Shloime Mandel says, "Not only must words be laced with love, they must be based on love, and resonate with love." In "Where Responsibility and Love Intersect: A Rosh Yeshiva's View of Kids at Risk." *Jewish Observer*. November 1999: p. 29.

8   Aberbach, Avrohom. "A Menahel's Suggestions." *Jewish Observer* March 2000: p. 25.

9   In addition, they enable humility which is a prerequisite to spiritual development as our sages state that, 'the Divine Presence will rest only upon a humble individual.'" Radcliffe, p. 265.

10 "Criticism and love cannot coexist...[they] go together like hot water and ice cubes; three cups of hot water and two cubes results in a bucket of hot water and no ice at all. Just as hot water melts ice, words of criticism melt messages of love." Radcliffe, p. 75.

11 Radcliffe, p. 41.

12 Moshe Speiser, "A Safety Net of Telephone Lines." *Jewish Observer* March 2000: p. 59.

13 Speiser, p. 56.

14 Shapiro, Yaakov. "Torah Advice for Raising Teenagers Part II." February 1995 http://www.shemayisrael.co.il/orgs/rejew/yonah.htm.

15 Yohanan Danziger, Personal Interview.

16 Meir Wickler, Personal Interview. 28 August, 2000.

17 Radcliffe, p. 128.

18 Mandel, Shloime. "Where Responsibility and Love Intersect: A Rosh Yeshiva's View of Kids at Risk." *Jewish Observer*. November 1999, p. 29-30.

19 Radcliffe, p. 141.

20 Shimon Schwab, "On Being a Trusted Friend to Your Children: Traditional Chinuch in Modern Times." *Jewish Observer* March 2000: p. 12 his quote continues — "The parents who preserve a child' self respect can hope to reap a rich harvest."

21 Basy Shaked, Personal Interview. 15 August, 2000 and 11 January, 2001.

22 Radcliffe, p. 136.

23 Wolbe, "Basic Principles of Parenting." p. 15.

24 Wolbe, "Basic Principles of Parenting." p. 15.

25 Radcliffe, p. 141.

26 Yaakov Shapiro, "What a Parent Can Do" and "Straight Talk." *Jewish Action.* Summer 1999: 44-48 from Bamidbar 11:12.

27 Noach Orlowek, "How to Raise a Mensch." November 1999. http://www.aish.com/family/mensch/disciplining_kids_effectively.asp. p. 1.

Chapter 10

1 Meir Wikler, Personal Interview. 28 August, 2000.

2 Wikler, Personal Interview.

3 Wikler, Personal Interview.

4 Wikler, Personal Interview.

5 Sanhedrin 108a; See Rabbi Samson Rafael Hirsch's commentary on Bereishit 6:11.

6 Dennis Prager, Personal Interview. 16 October, 2000.

7 In general, one is not permitted to invite someone to their home when he knows the person would desecrate the Sabbath to come. However, there are exceptions to that rule; for example, when it comes to someone who was raised in a nonobservant home. In that case, an exception can be made in the hopes that exposure to Shabbat may bring the person closer to Judaism and observance.

    In general, those who have gone off the derech seem not to warrant an exception to the general rule. However, one wonders if *rabbanim* who allow for flexibility in the case of the nonobservant would also allow for flexibility when it comes to those who have gone off the derech. There can be a good case made for doing so since often the very reason a person may have gone off the derech is feeling rejected by observant people for not being observant enough. In that case, not inviting him for Shabbat because he is not observant can fuel the fire and push him further away from observance. Whereas, inviting him despite his lack of observance may demonstrate acceptance, the very antidote he needs to move closer. Given this reality, extending an invitation to one who was formerly observant may have a greater chance of *mekareving* him (bringing him closer) than anything else and would create the same basis for an exception used in the case of the person raised without observance.

8 Wikler, Personal Interview.

9 Yevamot 65b. It is clear however, that one must always do whatever one can to minimize falsehood to whatever degree possible. Other situations in which we are allowed to "lie" or equivocate the truth include for privacy, maintaining our humility, and preventing someone from being taken advantage of. Bava Metzia 23b and Bava Kama 114a.

10 Phrase means literally, *we will do and then we will listen,* taken to mean that first Jews should observe and in doing so will come to understand the meaning and purpose of *mitzvot.*

11 Norman Lamm, Personal Interview. 16 November, 2000.

12 Wikler, Personal Interview.

13 Shira Berkovitz. "Accepting Punishment When it Comes with Love," *Jewish Observer,* March 2000, p. 39.

14 Yaakov Shapiro, "Torah Advice for Raising Teenagers: A Speech Given by Jonah 17 at a Project Rejewvenation Dinner." February 1995. http://www.shemayisrael.co.il/orgs/rejew/yonah.htm.

15 Yaakov Shapiro, "What a Parent Can Do" and "Straight Talk," *Jewish Action.* Summer 1999: p. 46.

16 Moshe Prager. Personal Interview. June 2001.

17 Judy Young, Personal Interview. 8 November, 2000.

18 See *Medrash Shmuel* on *Pirkei Avot* 2:5. For a profound explanation of this idea, see *Likutei Moharan* I:1:14.

19 Leah Kohn, Personal Interview. 7, 21 September, 2000, and 16, 26 October, 2000.

Chapter 11
1 Devarim, 28:15.

2 Devarim, 28:46.

3 Devarim 28:41.

4 Natan Lopez Cardozo, "Thoughts to Ponder 56: There is No Mashiach Without a Song." 9 August 2000. http://www.cardozoschool.org/thoughts47.htm.

5 An expression of his found in his work Shirath Yisrael, p. 157.

6 Pirush Alseich, "Torat Moshe" on Deuteronomy 6:5-7.

7 Natan Lopez Cardozo, "Thoughts to Ponder 21: Educating Towards Enjoyment." November 1999. http://www.cardozoschool.org/thoughts21.htm.

8 Yerushalmi Kiddushin 4.

9 Leah Kohn, Personal Interview. 7, 21 September, 2000, and 16, 2 October, 2000.

10 Natan Lopez Cardozo, "Thoughts to Ponder 21."

11 Chief Rabbi Mordechai Eliyahu, Personal Interview. June, 2001.

Chapter 12
1 Berachot 33.

2 Debbie Greenblatt, Personal Interview. 26 October, 2000.

Chapter 13
1 Nachum Braverman, "Falling in Love with Judaism." 1 August 2000. http://aish.com/spirituality/odesseys/Falling_in_Love_With_Judaism.asp, p. 4 of 7.

2 This has been attributed to Rav Elya Lopian.

Chapter 14
1 Adin Steinsaltz, Personal Interview. 8 November 2000 and 5 January 2001.

2   Jonathan Sacks, *Will We Have Jewish Grandchildren: Jewish Continuity and How to Achieve it.* London: Ballentine Mitchell, 1995 p. 119.

3   Leah Kohn, Personal Interview. 7, 21 September, 2000, and 16, 26 October, 2000.

4   Daniel Mechanic, Personal Interview. 12 September, 2000.

5   Shaya Cohen, Personal Interview. 11 October, 2000.

6   Devorah Greenblatt, Personal Interview. 26 October, 2000.

7   Literally "measure for measure"; the process by which God gives a person what his/her actions merit.

Chapter 15

1   Ahron Kaufman, "Of Growth and Belonging." *Jewish Observer.* November 1999: 35-38.

2   Sacks, Jonathan. Personal Interview. 23 April 2001.

3   Rabbi Abraham Isaac Kook, *Midot HaRe'iyah,* "Ahava," subsections 5, 10. Jerusalem: Mossad HaRav Kook, 1985.

4   Rabbi Sacks discusses a famous survey conducted in Los Angeles in 1988, " …in answer to the questions, which qualities do you consider most important to your Jewish identity, 59% replied "a commitment to social equality." A mere 17 % chose "religious observant." From Jonathan Sacks, "Love, Hate and Jewish Identity." *First Things: The Journal of Religion and Public Life.* 24 August 2000 http://firsththings.com/ftissues/ft9711/articles/sacks.html, p. 8 of 13.

5   Heschel, Susannah. "What Do American Jews Believe? A Symposium." *Commentary.* August 1996. http://www.commentarymagazine.com/9608/sym1.html, p. 6 of 20.

Chapter 16

1   Pesach Woliki, "Shavuot: The Purpose of Freedom." 16 May 2002. Email from rabbipesach@yahoo.com.

2   Natan Lopez Cardozo, Personal Interview. 31 October, 2000.

3   Yaacov Shapiro, "What a Parent Can Do" and "Straight Talk." *Jewish Action.* Summer 1999: 44-48.

4   Ahron Kaufman, "Of Growth and Belonging." *Jewish Observer.* November 1999: p. 37.

5   Berel Wein, Personal Interview. 28 August, 2000 and 8 January, 2001.

Chapter 17

1   Richard John Neuhaus, "What Dennis Prager Did, and Didn't, Learn in *Yeshiva.*" *The Public Square: A Continuing Survey of Religion and Public Life.* 24 August 2000. http://firstthings.com/ftissues/ft9510/public.html.

2   Sample Student Responses to Project Chazon Seminars. Provided by Rabbi Daniel Mechanic.

3   http://www.pbs.org/faithandreason/gengloss/enlight-body.html.

4   Amy Dockser Marcus,. "A Young Man Flees Orthodoxy, Taking Others With Him." *Wall Street Journal.* 15 November 1991.

5   Shaya Cohen, Personal Interview. 11 October, 2000.

6   Relly Sa'ar, "Religious Graduates Becoming More Secular." *Ha'aretz News.* 4 May 2001. Ha'aretz Daily Newspaper — English Internet Edition. 10 May 2001.

7   Natan Lopez Cardozo, Personal Interview. 31 October, 2000.

8   Norman Lamm, Personal Interview. 16 November, 2000.

Chapter 18

1   Elihu Katz, and Mordechai Rimor, *Jewish Involvement in the Baby Boom Generation: Interrogating the 1990 National Jewish Population Survey.* Jerusalem, Israel: The Louis Guttman Israel Institute of Applied Social Research, November 1993, p. 22.

2   Anthony Gordon and Richard Horowitz, "Will Your Grandchildren Be Jewish?" 1997.

3   A.I. Schiff and M. Schneider, "Fortifying and Restoring Jewish Behavior: The Interaction of Home and School." New York, David H. Azrieli Graduate Institute, Report 3, 1994.

4   In an article entitled *Judaism or Jewishness (First Things: The Journal of Religion and Public Life.* 24 August 2000) Elliot Abrams writes that Judaism is more vulnerable to modernity than Christianity because Judaism emphasizes ritual and habit and has traditionally spent little time providing a doctrine to fall back on. Eastern European Jews for example, tended to concentrate far more on ritual than on doctrine. Those who came to America were usually not the most devout people in their communities. In Europe, they may have "performed the rituals for there was parental and social pressure to do so and it was easier to live as a Jew than to violate community norms. But in New York, the reverse was true. There was pressure to grab a sandwich, to work on the Shabbat, to skip a prayer here and there. And as the ritual pillars began to collapse, they brought down with them the whole structure of faith..." If the pillars were *hashkafic*, on the other hand, even if the rituals were to become challenged, there would still be a belief system to appeal to. And with that belief system underpinning the ritual and providing it with meaning, it would be harder to drop.

5   Moshe Schapiro, "Ohr Samayach Addresses the Teen-Dropout Issue." *Yated Ne'eman* 16 April 1999.

6   Eliyahu Bergstein, "Time to Learn to Trust the Menahelim of Our Schools." *Jewish Observer* March 2000, p. 21.

7   Ephraim Buchwald, Personal Interview. 22 August 2000.

8   Rabbi Nathan Lopez Cardozo relates an interesting comparison made in the Talmud which sheds light on this. The Talmud compares Edom to a pig and Babylonia to a camel, a strange comparison. Why these two countries? Why these two animals? What is the Talmud trying to tell us? Rabbi Cardozo says that these two animals each bear one of two signs that renders it kosher. The pig has split hooves but does not chew its cud. The camel chews its cud but does not have split hooves.

What is the connection to the countries? Edom is ancient Rome and Western civilization — cultures that are essentially forward-looking in their approach. Their spirit lies not in the past, but in the future. For example, the United States reveres the future, progress; it seeks the new rather than the old, the young rather than the aged. Babylonia, on the other hand, and today's Middle East is the opposite. They are past-oriented rather than future oriented. They revere the ancient and the old, their elders, tradition and history.

The animals correspond to the countries in the same way. The pig, like Edom, is future-oriented so to speak. Its split hooves function to propel it forward, into the future. The camel, like Babylonia, is past-oriented. Its nourishment comes from chewing its cud; returning to the past for sustenance.

This sheds interesting insight into the signs that make an animal kosher. For an animal to be kosher, it must bear two signs. It must chew its cud and have split hooves. One is insufficient. And the same can be said for our Judaism. A kosher Judaism needs two approaches simultaneously: one that looks to the past and one that looks to the future.

9   Mishnah Yoma 6:1.Also see the Torah Temimah on "veahavta et Hashem Elokecha."

10 *Kitzur Shulchan Aruch* 131:4, and the comments of the *Kuntres Acharon* of the *Sha'arim Metzuyanim Bi'Halachah* there.

11 Shlomo Riskin, Personal Interview. 7 and 10 January 2001.

12 Joseph Telushkin, Personal Interview. 16 October, 2000.

13 Riskin, Personal Interview.

Chapter 19

1   Sarah Chana Radcliffe, *The Delicate Balance: Love and Authority in Torah Parenting.* Jerusalem, Israel: Targum Press, 1989, p. 18.

2   Rambam, *Laws of the Foundations of Torah* (Hilchot Yesodei HaTorah), Chapter 2 Laws 1, 2.

3   Leah Kohn, Personal Interview. 7, 21 September, 2000, and 16, 26 October, 2000.

4   Shlomo Wolbe, *Planting and Building: Raising a Jewish Child.* Jerusalem, Israel: Feldheim Publishers, 2000. p. 56.

5   Natan Lopez Cardozo, "Thoughts to Ponder 58: Surround Yourself with Art and Beauty." 13 September 2000. http://www.cardozoschool.org/thoughts58.htm.

6   Berachot 57B as quoted by Natan Lopez Cardozo, "Thoughts to Ponder 58: Surround Yourself with Art and Beauty." 13 September 2000 http://www.cardozoschool.org/thoughts58.htm.

7   Some things are more interesting than others and we can try to incorporate these more exciting things in our daily education. Most importantly, we can hire teachers who themselves are inspired for passion is contagious and a passionate teacher more than anything else can infect our children with a love for Torah. *Baalei teshuva* can be a wonderful resource in this respect. Even if they lack as much information as some other teachers, they have passion. Children from observant homes can be greatly inspired by their stories, experiences, and love for Yiddishkeit.

Finally, the methods of teaching themselves can become more exciting. Our black and white texts are competing with a world of color — with animated computers, television, advertisements, music and magazines. All are exciting.

All bombard the senses with images and sounds that are stimulating and interesting. Simple things like pictures, varied fonts, or colorful paper can and should make our books and benchers more exciting and interesting.

In the least, we can strive to make learning more fun through games and field trips as Rabbi Dovid Brezak does. The educator managed to keep 120-150 children awake until four o'clock in the morning learning on Shavuot night. He said that when everyone else was falling asleep, these kids were "screaming their heads off." Why? Because he made it fun for them. He turned it into a game, a contest, with prizes. It stimulated them, made it interesting, and inspirational and they wanted as much of it as they could get.

Such techniques could easily extend to outside of the classroom as did Judy Young's *parsha* clues baked into her challahs, which creates a meaningful and enjoyable game at the Shabbat table.

Chapter 20

1   Jonathan Sacks, *A Letter in the Scroll: Understanding Our Jewish Identity and Exploring the Legacy of the World's Oldest Religion.* New York: The Free Press, Simon & Schuster Inc, 2000 p. 169.

2   Norman Lamm, "The Uncivil War." *Los Angeles Jewish Times* 9-15 July 1999.

3   Shlomo Riskin. "The Need to Debate." *Los Angeles Jewish Times* 9-15 July 1999. The Talmud says "For three years the Academy of Hillel disputed with the Academy of Shamai, until a voice (bat kol) descended from the heaven declaring, 'These and those are both the words of the living God, and the Law is like the Academy of Hillel.'" Why did the law go the way of the Academy of Hillel? Because, the Talmud tells us, they were much more accommodating and accepting of insults, and whenever they were asked a question, they first presented the opposing view.

4   Meir Wikler, Personal Interview. 28 August, 2000.

5   Shlomo Riskin, "The Need to Debate."

6   Natan Lopez Cardozo, "Thoughts to Ponder 44: Tolerance and Dialogue." 11 May 2000. http://www.cardozoschool.org/thoughts44.htm.

7   Judaism has never really believed in blind faith anyway. There is no real phrase for blind faith in Judaism. The closest term we have is *emunah peshuta, a simple faith,* one that is uncomplicated and untarnished by the turmoil of the world and conflict in the soul. Today this faith can only be achieved with the help of reason, which aids us when facing doubt and arms us when facing a contradictory world.

8   Rabbi Lamm notes that the *gemorah* explains that his prophecy differed from all other prophets — they saw God as a vague image, as if through a smoky glass, but Moses saw through a looking glass that was perfectly clear. What does that mean? Rashi explains that the others thought they saw, but they did not see. Moses knew that he didn't see, which is what made his perception of God so much clearer. Humility and acknowledgement of limitations are essential character traits for ultimate teaching and true leadership. Norman Lamm, Personal Interview. 16 November, 2000.

Chapter 21

1   William Symonds, "How to Fix America's Schools." *Business Week*. 19 March 2001: 67-80, p.69.

2   Dr. David Lazerson, "Space, Place and Pace: Keeping Jewish Teens in Jewish Schools." *Jewish Action*. Winter 1998. Also from http://www.ou.org/publications/ja/5758/spring98/lazerson.htm.

3   Nefesh, the International Network of Orthodox Mental Health Professionals. Russel, Shimon and Blumenthal, Dr. Norman Editors. *Children in Crisis Detection and Intervention: A Practical Guide for Educators, Parents, and Mental Health Professionals*. New York: Nefesh, October 2000, p. 34.

4   For example, dyslexic children tend to see things others don't see; they tend to be visionaries who think out of the box, bringing new and insightful perspectives to problems. They often graphically visualize solutions to problems without being able to explain how they arrived there. But they do this so effectively, that some of the most successful entrepreneurs of our day have been dyslexic. Consider these interesting facts:

   "Kinko's founder Paul Orfalea failed the second grade and spent part of third grade in a class of mentally retarded children. He could not learn to read. One educator told his mother to enroll him in trade school, suggesting that he could become a carpet layer.

   "Charles Schwab, who virtually created the discount brokerage business, failed remedial English and came perilously close to flunking out of college. He was very strong in math, science and sports...but he couldn't listen to a lecture...couldn't memorize four words in a row.

   "Richard Branson who developed Virgin Records and Virgin Atlantic Airways was spanked by his teacher for bad grades and a poor attitude. He dropped out of school at 16. He says, "If I'd had been any good at math, I probably never would have started an airline."

   Other dyslexics include John chambers, CEO of Cisco; billionaire Craig McCaw, who pioneered the cellular industry; and John Reed, who led Citibank to the top of banking — from Betsy Morris, "Overcoming Dyslexia." *Fortune Magazine*. May 13, 2002. pp. 56-62.

5   Gail Lichtman, "Where Dropouts Drop In" *The Jerusalem Post*. April 21, 2002, Programs such as the Jacob's Ladder Center have been established to train teachers and therapists to work with children with ADHD/ADD and learning disabilities. More than 1000 Israeli teachers and therapists have attended these seminars.

6   Yaakov Shapiro, "Program Director: Manage Thyself!"

7   Shapiro, "Program Director: Manage Thyself." p. 8.

8   Shaya Cohen, Personal Interview. 11 October, 2000.

9   Chaim Eisen. "Pluralism: Rx for Orthodox Intolerance." *Jewish Action*. http://www.ou.org/publications/ja/pluralismeisen.html.

10 Nefesh with Shimon and Blumenthal, p. 17.

11 According to Ann Julian, director of the Jewish Association for ADD. Betsy Morris, "Overcoming Dyslexia." *Fortune Magazine*. May 13, 2002. p.56 Statistics show that approximately 5% of children in America's public schools have been

diagnosed with a learning disability. Of these, approximately 80% are dyslexia related. Some studies indicate, that as much as 20% of the general population have some degree of dyslexia.

12 Jerry Lob, Personal Interview. 14 September, 2000.

13 Dr. David Pelcovitz, and Shimon Russel, "The At Risk Child: Early Identification and Intervention." *Jewish Observer*. November 1999: p. 46.

14 Rabbi Yabrov, "The Chazon Ish on the Educator's responsibility to the Weak and Wayward Student: Principles and Vignettes." *Jewish Observer*. November 1999: 12-14, p. 13-14.

15 Lichtman, "Where Dropouts Drop In" *The Jerusalem Post*. April 21, 2002.

16 William Symonds, "How To Fix America's Schools." *Business Week*. 19 March 2001: p. 69.

Chapter 22

1 Leah Kohn, Personal Interview. 7, 21 September, 2000, and 16, 26 October, 2000.

Chapter 23

1 Richard John Neuhaus, "What Dennis Prager Did, and Didn't, Learn in Yeshiva." *The Public Square: A Continuing Survey of Religion and Public Life*. 24 August 2000. http://firstthings.com/ftissues/ft9510/public.html.

2 Chief Rabbi Mordechai Eliyahu, Personal Interview. He explains that what is expressed as idealism is sometimes rooted in laziness which creates an ideal in order to justify, rationalize and mask a less noble inclination.

3 Dennis Prager, Lecture: "Obstacles to Achieving Goodness." University of Judaism. Los Angeles. 5 September 2000 http://www.dennisprager.net/indexp25.html.

4 Bereishit 3:19 and Sanhedrin 37.

5 Rabbi Zvi Yabrov. "The Chazon Ish on the Educator's Responsibility to the Weak and Wayward Student: Principles and Vignettes." *Jewish Observer*. November 1999: p. 12.

6 Jonathan Sacks, *Celebrating Life*. London: Fount, Harper Collins, 2000, p. 164.

7 Neuhaus, "What Dennis Prager Did, and Didn't, Learn in Yeshiva."

Chapter 24

1 Avot 2:5.

2 Ephraim Buchwald, Personal Interview. 22 August 2000.

3 Buchwald, Personal Interview.

4 Jonathan Rosenblum quoting Raymond Legge Jr, on the basis of a 1999 survey of giving patterns of American Jews, Jonathan Rosenblum "Who are the Real Givers." *The Jerusalem Post*. 15 November 2002.

Chapter 25

1 Shlomo Riskin, Personal Interview. 7 and 10 January 2001.

2 Debbie Greenblatt, Personal Interview. 26 October, 2000.

3 Avi Rothenberg, Personal Interview. 2001.

4   Nedarim 31A, Sarah Chana Radcliffe, *The Delicate Balance: Love and Authority in Torah Parenting*. Jerusalem, Israel: Targum Press, 1989, p 265.

5   Radcliffe, *The Delicate Balance: Love and Authority in Torah Parenting*, p. 266.

6   Micah 6:7-8.

Chapter 26

1   Shimon Kessin, "Healing the Orthodox Community: A Time for Reexamination." *Country Yossi Family Magazine*. September 1998. http://www.countryyossi.com/sept98/Torah.htm.

2   Found in the Ramak's commentary on the second chapter of Sefer Yetzirah. *Ohr Yakar*, 15:3.

3   Natan Lopez Cardozo, "Thoughts to Ponder 57: When Times Change, Jewish Education Changes." 7 September 2000. http://www.cardozoschool.org/thoughts57.htm.

4   Rabbi Menachem Mendel Schneerson, *Likutei Sichot, Parshat Vayeira,* and Shmuley Boteach, *Judaism for Everyone: Renewing Your Life Through the Vibrant Lessons of the Jewish Faith*. New York: Basic Books, 2002, p. 113-114.

5   Miriam Shaviv, "She's a Rebel." *The Jerusalem Post Online*. April 9, 2002. http://cgis.jpost.com/cgi-bin/General/printarti...Features.46565.htm.

6   That is why Shamai would not let anyone into the *beit medrash* whose inside didn't match his outside.

Chapter 27

1   When we understand the importance of self-actualization, we can better understand women who complain about their role in observant Judaism. Some women surely complain about traditional Judaism from impure motives, but, without passing judgment one way or another, we can understand why gender issues would be of concern in the first place. Gender is one of the most fundamental and defining parts of our being; it therefore requires expression and development. Those who are observant will seek that expression and development within observance itself. A woman who, rightly or wrongly, feels that Judaism does not allow for this experiences a lack of fulfillment and feels unable to actualize one of the most vital parts of her self. As such, she may abandon observance as a whole.

2   Mishlei 22:6.

3   Yaakov Shapiro. "Rebels Without a Cause." http://www.shemayisrael.co.il/orgs/rejew/j-week.htm

4   David Margolis, "Going Away Again." *Baltimore Jewish Times*. 23 December 1988: 58-63.

5   Debbie Greenblatt, Personal Interview. 26 October, 2000.

6   It might help to remember what the Kotsker Rebbe said when he was asked who is higher on a ladder: the person on top or the person on the bottom. He responded that it depended which direction they were going. If the person on the top was on his way down, and the person on the bottom was on his way up, then the person on the bottom was higher than the one on top.

7   Shmuley Boteach, *Judaism for Everyone: Renewing Your Life Through the*

Vibrant Lessons of the Jewish Faith. New York: Basic Books, 2002, p. 279.

8   Larry Gordon, "One Size Fits None," *Five Towns Jewish Times*. 1 March 2002. www.priority-1.org/articles/osnf.asp.

Chapter 28

1   "Hassidic Man In Full." *Atlanta Jewish Times Internet Edition*. 22 October 1999. http://www.atljewishtimes.com/102299cs.htm, p. 2 of 7.

2   "Hassidic Man In Full," p. 5 of 7.

3   Debbie Greenblatt, Personal Interview. 26 October, 2000.

Chapter 29

1   Berel Wein, Personal Interview. 28 August, 2000 and 8 January, 2001.

2   Naomi Ragen, "The System Needs an Overhaul." *Los Angeles Jewish Times* 9 July, 1999.

3   Moshe Prager, Personal Interview. June 2001.

4   Shlomo Wolbe, *Planting and Building: Raising a Jewish Child*. Jerusalem, Israel: Feldheim Publishers, 2000, p. 43.

5   Jerry Lob, Personal Interview. 14 September, 2000.

6   David Margolis, "Going Away Again." *Baltimore Jewish Times*. 23 December 1988: 58-63.

7   "Hassidic Man In Full." *Atlanta Jewish Times Internet Edition*. 22 October 1999. http://www.atljewishtimes.com/102299cs.htm.

8   Dr. Norman Blumenthal and Shimon Russell, CSW editors, *Children in Crisis Detection and Intervention: A Practical Guide for Educators, Parents, and Mental Health Professionals*. New York: Nefesh, October 2000, p. 46.

9   Adin Steinsaltz, Interview with Robert Siegel: "Rabbi Steinsaltz Discusses His Completion of a Translation of the Talmud into English" for All Things Considered, National Public Radio. 14 April 2000.

10 Jonathan Sacks, Personal Interview. 23 April 2001.

Chapter 30

1   Richard John Neuhaus, "What Dennis Prager Did, and Didn't, Learn in Yeshiva." *The Public Square: A Continuing Survey of Religion and Public Life*. 24 August 2000. http://firstthings.com/ftissues/ft9510/public.html.

2   I have heard this in the name of Rav Meir Simcha.

3   David Samson and Tzvi Fishman, *Lights on Orot*. Jerusalem: Torat Erertz Yisrael Publications. 5756, p. 125.

4   Natan Lopez Cardozo. Personal Interview. 31 October, 2000.

5   David Margolis, "Going Away Again." *Baltimore Jewish Times*. 23 December 1988: 58-63.

6   Jonathan Sacks, *Will We Have Jewish Grandchildren: Jewish Continuity and How to Achieve it*. London: Ballentine Mitchell, 1995, p. 77-79.

7   Jonathan Sacks, *Arguments for the Sake of Heaven*. Northvale NJ: Jason Aronson. 1991, p. 102.

8   Jonathan Rosenblum, "Think Again: Grateful for Being Chosen." *The Jerusalem Post.* 6 June 2002.

Chapter 31
1   Yaakov Shapiro, Personal Interview. 8 August 2000. (93).

2   Ephraim Buchwald, Personal Interview. 22 August 2000.

3   Debbie Greenblatt, Personal Interview. 26 October, 2000.

4   Jonathan Sacks, Personal Interview. 23 April 2001.

5   Normann Lamm, Personal Interview. 16 November, 2000.

6   Leah Kohn, Personal Interview. 7, 21 September, 2000, and 16, 26 October, 2000.

Chapter 32
1   It is interesting to note that what is true emotionally, socially, and religiously is also true biologically. For example, each person has his own particular DNA that determines how he responds to various stimuli. One person takes a drug and he is cured; another is not cured; yet another dies. One person eats a high fat diet of butter and steak and lives until the age of ninety. Another person watches his diet, and dies at a young age with high cholesterol. It is not our genes that determine our destiny, nor our environment, but the interplay between them.

Psychologists have spent a lot of time trying to understand personality. There are so many complex elements that affect us, and so much interplay between nature and nurture, that it is difficult to isolate and define personality types. Nonetheless, examining one or two models might help shed light on why people go off the derech.

For example, musicians and artists — the Artisan personality type — seek sensation, variety and excitement. They are daring in nature and tend to be playful. They need stimulation of various sorts and need room, in the classroom and in life, to be creative and explore bold ideas.

Unlike a student who can learn Torah all day, for example, those with artistic personalities may need to study a variety of subjects and creatively explore and apply ideas. Unlike the person who can pursue a technically oriented profession, the artist needs something that allows for creativity or he will not be as happy as he could be.

If the artist and his brother, who is different in nature, both learn *gemorah*, the brother may thrive while the artist gets bored. Though he may learn all the "right things," they may not penetrate if not taught according to *his way*, addressing his particular learning style. As a result, he may not enjoy or internalize his learning. Because his needs are not met he may fail to believe, while his brother who learned the same information may end up believing strongly.

Some children do not seek sensation or variety, but rather security. These personalities are called "Guardians." They tend to rely on the tried and true rather than venture into unpredictable territory. They respect authority and follow procedure. They hunger for membership in groups and tend to conform to expectations in order to earn that membership. Just as they need communal acceptance more than the average person, so they suffer more if deprived of it.

So for example, rejection would make them more likely than others to go off the derech, and acceptance into community would more likely motivate them toward observance than the average person.

2   Shlomo Wolbe, *Planting and Building: Raising a Jewish Child.* Jerusalem, Israel: Feldheim Publishers, 2000. p. 26.

3   Malbim and Gra on Mishlei 22:6. This idea is also given as the reason for the Chassidic custom to cut a child's hair for the first time at the age of three. Three is the age of education, when we begin to shape a child's character. But before we do so, we should see what his natural way is for that is the foundation of good education.

4   Berachot 33.

5   Michtav Me'Eliyahu vol. II, second part of Kuntress HaBechirah titled, "Nekudat Ha'Bechirah."

Chapter 33

1   Anonymous. *Jewish Observer.* March 2000. p. 38.

2   Leah Kohn, Personal Interview. 7, 21 September, 2000, and 16, 26 October, 2000.

3   Jonathan Sacks, *A Letter in the Scroll: Understanding Our Jewish Identity and Exploring the Legacy of the World's Oldest Religion.* New York: The Free Press, Simon & Schuster Inc, 2000, p. 111-113.

4   Debbie Greenblatt. Personal Interview. 26 October, 2000.

5   David Mandel, "Teamwork." *Jewish Observer* March 2000: 46-49.

6   Educator, Tzipora Heller explains that "Hatred is senseless when there is no desire to improve the relationship between oneself and another person. The fact that they are not you is enough of a threat to first fear them and then to hate them. The more different they are, the greater the threat." It occurs when we fail to see the "common bond of goodness that binds us together," when we "focus on the limitations that separate us." Tzipporah Heller, "Feeling the Loss: Tisha B'Av and the Three Weeks." 24 June 2002. http://www.aish.com/tishabav/tishavbavdefault/Feeling_the_Loss.asp.

Chapter 34

1   David Samson, and Tzvi Fishman, *Lights on Orot.* Jerusalem: Torat Erertz Yisrael Publications. 5756. p. 129.

Web Survey

1   All numbers have been rounded. Percentages may not equal 100%.

Bibliography

Aaron, Joseph. "The Only Thing Jews Should Fear is Fear." *Los Angeles Jewish Times* 7-13 August, 1998.

Aberbach, Avrohom. "A Menahel's Suggestions." *Jewish Observer* March 2000: 22-25.

Abrams, Elliot. "Judaism or Jewishness." *First Things: The Journal of Religion and Public Life*. 24 August 2000. http://www.firstthings.com/ftissues/ft9706/articles/abrams.html

Amital, Yehuda. Lecture on Parshat Vayechi, "Commitment vs. Connecting — the Current Crisis of our Youth." http://www.vbm-torah.org/archive/sichot61/12vayechi.htm

Anonymous, Interviews with formerly observant Jews. January 2000-June 2001.

— "Hereby Resolved: A Father's Kabbalos." *Jewish Observer*. November 1999: 74-75.

— *Jewish Observer*. March 2000: 38.

— "Thoughts of a Mother." *Jewish Observer*. November 1999: 9-10.

Ain, Stuart. "Teen Crisis' Detailed in Orthodox Brooklyn." *Jewish Week* 10 Dec. 1999. http://www.thejewishweek.com/jwcurr.exe?9912102

A Speech Given by Jonah 17 at a Project Rejewvenation Dinner." February 1995. http://www.shemayisrael.co.il/orgs/rejew/yonah.htm

414

Becher, Mordechai. Lecture: "Why Do Bad Things Happen to Good People." Jewish Enrichment Center. New York. 2000.

Belsky, Hillel. "Guidance For Parents-at-Risk." *Jewish Observer* March 2000: 49.

Berger, David. Personal Interview: March 17, 2003.

Bergstein, Eliyahu. "Time to Learn to Trust the Menahelim of Our Schools." *Jewish Observer* March 2000: 19-22.

Berkovitz, Eliezer. *Essential Essays on Judaism*. Jerusalem, Israel: Shalem Press, 2002: 235-247.

Berkovitz, Shira. "Accepting Punishment When it Comes with Love," *Jewish Observer,* March 2000: 39.

Birnbaum, M. "Raising the Standards for Parents and Educators." *Jewish Observer* March 2000: 26.

Blum, Robert, Regarding the National Longitudinal Study of at-Risk Behaviors. Aired on C-SPAN, 9 March 2001. 2:45 pm.

Blumenthal, David R. "What Do American Jews Believe? A Symposium." *Commentary.* August 1996. http://www.commentarymagazine.com/9608/sym1.html

Boteach, Shmuley. *Judaism for Everyone: Renewing Your Life Through the Vibrant Lessons of the Jewish Faith*. New York: Basic Books, 2002.

Braverman, Nachum. "Falling in Love with Judaism." 1 August 2000. http://aish.com/spirituality/odesseys/Falling_in_Love_With_Judaism.asp

Briggs, Jimmie. *Popular Science*. August 2002: 42.

Brody, Aaron. "Better Late Than Never." *Jewish Observer* March 2000: 61-62.

Buchwald, Ephraim. Personal Interview. 22 August 2000.

Cardozo, Natan Lopez. Personal Interview. 31 October, 2000.

— *Judaism on Trial: An Unconventional Discussion about Jews, Judaism and the State of Israel*. Urim Publications, Dec 15, 2000.

— "Thoughts to Ponder 21: Educating Towards Enjoyment." November 1999. http://www.cardozoschool.org/thoughts21.htm

— "Thoughts to Ponder 22: Chumrot — Religious Stringencies: Good or Bad." 18 November 1999. http://www.cardozoschool.org/thoughts22.htm

— "Thoughts to Ponder 23: Mitzvoth, Minhagim and Their Dangers."
25 November 1999.
http://www.cardozoschool.org/thoughts23.htm

— "Thoughts to Ponder 27: Concerning the Millennium, A Jewish
Child and a Hand Wave." 22 December 1999.
http://www.cardozoschool.org/thoughts27.htm

— "Thoughts to Ponder 39: The Birth of Amalek, the Making of an
Enemy." 15 March 2000.
http://www.cardozoschool.org/thoughts39.htm

— "Thoughts to Ponder 44: Tolerance and Dialogue." 11 May 2000.
http://www.cardozoschool.org/thoughts44.htm

— "Thoughts to Ponder 47: Alan M. Dershowitz, Klotz Kashes and
the Chozrim B'she'ela Movement." 1 June 2000.
http://www.cardozoschool.org/thoughts47.htm

— "Thoughts to Ponder 56: There is No Mashiach Without a Song." 9
August 2000. http://www.cardozoschool.org/thoughts47.htm

— "Thoughts to Ponder 57: When Times Change, Jewish Education
Changes." 7 September 2000.
http://www.cardozoschool.org/thoughts57.htm

— "Thoughts to Ponder 58: Surround Yourself with Art and Beauty."
13 September 2000.
http://www.cardozoschool.org/thoughts58.htm

— "Thoughts to Ponder 83: The Destructionist Synagogues: The
Ceremonial Hall, the Nostalgia Center and the Davening Club." 7
June 2001. http://www.cardozoschool.org/thoughts83.htm

— "Thoughts to Ponder 152: The Waters of Strife, Religious Coercion
or Gentle Persuasion." 10 July 2003.
http://www.cardozoschool.org.thoughts152.htm.

Cattan, Nacha. "Orthodox Rehab Programs: Too Much of a Good
Thing?" *Forward.* August 17, 2001: Front Page.

Cohen, Shaya. Personal Interview. 11 October, 2000.

Council of Jewish Federations. *Highlights of the CJF National Jewish
Population Survey.* New York: Council of Jewish Federations,
1990.

Dalin, David. "What Do American Jews Believe? A Symposium."
Commentary. August 1996.
http://www.commentarymagazine.com/9608/sym1.html

Danziger, Yohanan. Personal Interview. 2001.

Danziger, Yohanan under contract with The Metropolitan New York Coordinating Council on Jewish Poverty. *Report to the City of New York Department of Youth and Community Development on the Incidence of At-Risk Youth in the Orthodox Jewish Community of Brooklyn, NY.* New York: The Metropolitan Coordinating Council on Jewish Poverty, 1999-2000.

Deckelman, Paul. "Frum Kids on the Street: Saving the Yeshiva Children of the Night." *Country Yossi Family Magazine.* March 1994. http://www.shemayisrael.co.il/orgs/rejew/yossi.htm

DellaPergola, Sergio and Uzi Rebun. "American Orthodox Jews: Demographic Trends and Scenarios." *Jewish Action.* Fall 1998.

Eisen, Chaim. "Pluralism: Rx for Orthodox Intolerance." *Jewish Action.* http://www.ou.org/publications/ja/pluralismeisen.html

Eizenstat, Stuart. Keynote Address to the JCC Association Leadership Conference: "The American Jewish Community at the Crossroads." *JCC Circle.* June 1991.

Eliyahu, Chief Rabbi Mordechai. Personal Interview. June 2001.

Ellenson, David. "What Do American Jews Believe? A Symposium." *Commentary.* August 1996. http://www.commentarymagazine.com/9608/sym1.html

Fertel, Morty. "The Garden of Jewish Education." *Isralite Quarterly Newsletter.* February 2001: 7.

Fisherman, Shraga. *Noar HaKippot Zerukot.* Elkana, Israel. 1999.

Frankel, Rochel. "A Teacher's List of Do's (Not Don't's)" *Jewish Observer.* November 1999: 31.

Gordon, Anthony and Richard Horowitz. "Will Your Grandchildren Be Jewish?" CA: Self commissioned research study, 1997.

Gordon, Larry. "One Size Fits None," *Five Towns Jewish Times.* 1 March 2002. www.priority-1.org/articles/osnf.asp

Greenblatt, Devorah. Personal Interview. 26 October, 2000.

— "Making our 'Bayis' a Mobil Home." *Jewish Observer.* November 1999: 49-50

Gross, Netty C. "Questions to Ponder." *The Jerusalem Report.* 28 May 2000. http://jrep.com/UpFront/Article-0.html

Grossman, Heshy. "The Happy, Well Adjusted Orthodox Dropout" *Jewish Action* Fall 2000.

"Hassidic Man In Full." *Atlanta Jewish Times Internet Edition.* 22 October 1999. http://www.atljewishtimes.com/102299cs.htm

Heller, Chana. "How to Raise a Mensch." November 1999. http://www.aish.com.

Heller, Tzipporah. "Feeling the Loss: Tisha B'Av and the Three Weeks." 24 June 2002. http://www.aish.com/tishabav/tishavbavdefault/Feeling_the_Loss.asp

Heschel, Susannah. "What Do American Jews Believe? A Symposium." *Commentary.* August 1996. http://www.commentarymagazine.com/9608/sym1.html

Horowitz, Yaacov. "Report from Ground Zero." *Jewish Observer.* November 1999: 51-54.

The Jerusalem Post, Up Front Magazine. 23 January 2004: 32-33.

Jewish Observer: Children on the Fringe and Beyond. November 1999.

Jewish Observer: The Readers Respond. March 2000.

Kamenetsky, Shmuel. "Dealing with the Dilemmas of Kids-at-Risk." *Jewish Observer.* November 1999: 25-26.

Katz, Elihu and Mordechai Rimor. *Jewish Involvement in the Baby Boom Generation: Interrogating the 1990 National Jewish Population Survey.* Jerusalem, Israel: The Louis Guttman Israel Institute of Applied Social Research, November 1993.

Kaufman, Ahron. "Of Growth and Belonging." *Jewish Observer.* November 1999: 35-38.

— "Consequential Conversations…Without Being Confrontational." *Jewish Observer* March 2000: 64-68.

Kessin, Shimon. "Healing the Orthodox Community: A Time for Reexamination." *Country Yossi Family Magazine.* September 1998. http://www.countryyossi.com/sept98/torah.htm.

Keirsey, David. "The Four Temperaments" *Personality: Character and Temperament.* 15 December 2000. http://www.keirsey.com/

— "Parenting and Temperament" excepted from *Please Understand Me II,* 1988. 21 May 2001. http://keirsey.com/parent.html

Kohn, Leah. Personal Interview. 7, 21 September, 2000, and 16, 26 October, 2000.

Kook, Rabbi Avraham. *Midot HaRe'iyah,* "Ahava," Subsections 5, 10. Jerusalem: Mossad HaRav Kook, 1985.

— *Lights on Orot, War and Peace: The Teachings of HaRav Avraham Yitzhak HaCohen Kook.* Jerusalem: Torat Eretz Yisrael Publications, 5757.

Klugman, Eliyahu Meir. "Children on the Fringe and Beyond: Intro" *Jewish Observer.* November 1999: 6.

Lachman, Zalman MSW. "When Conventional Parenting is Not Enough: Dealing with a New American Crisis." *Jewish Observer.* November 1999: 62-64.

Lamm, Norman. Personal Interview. 16 November, 2000.

— "The Uncivil War." *Los Angeles Jewish Times* 9-15 July 1999.

Lazerson, David Dr. "Space, Place and Pace: Keeping Jewish Teens in Jewish Schools." *Jewish Action.* Winter 1998.

Levy, Michoel. "Buying Time." *Jewish Observer.* November 1999: 66-67.

Lichtman, Gail. "Where Dropouts Drop In" *The Jerusalem Post.* April 21, 2002.

Lieblich, Julia. "High Holy Days; Showing Spiritual Simplicity." Associated Press, *Dayton Daily News.* 11 September 1999.

Lob, Jerry. Personal Interview. 14 September, 2000.

Lopiansky, Ahron. "Why a Joy-Filled Sukkot?" 16 October 2000. Email from Aish.com Holiday Series.

Mandel, David. Personal Interview. 6 September 2000.

— "Teamwork." *Jewish Observer* March 2000: 46- 49.

Mandel, Shloime. "Where Responsibility and Love Intersect: A Rosh Yeshiva's View of Kids at Risk." *Jewish Observer.* November 1999: 29-30.

Marcus, Amy Dockser. "A Young Man Flees Orthodoxy, Taking Others With Him." *Wall Street Journal.* 15 November 1991.

Margolis, David. "Going Away Again." *Baltimore Jewish Times.* 23 December 1988: 58-63.

"Maslow's Hierarchy of Needs." 17 May 2001. http://web.utk.edu/~gwynne/maslow.HTM and http://www.connect.net/georgen/maslow.htm

AH Maslow, "A Theory of Human Motivation" (1943). Originally published in *Psychological Review,* 50, 370-396. Quoted from http://psychclassics.yorku.ca/Maslow/Motivation.htm

Mechanic, Daniel. Personal Interview. 12 September, 2000.

Mendelson, Yehuda. "Basic Principles of Parenting: Postscript." *Jewish Observer.* March 2000.

Miller, Stephen. "Confessions of a Rootless Cosmopolitan Jew." *First Things: The Journal of Religion and Public Life.* 24 August 2000. http://firstthings.com/ftissues/ft9202/opinion/miller.html.

Mitnick, Yitchok. "An Unorthodox Approach for the Orthodox Teen." *Jewish Observer.* November 1999: 69-72.

Morris, Betsy. "Overcoming Dyslexia." *Fortune.* May 13, 2002: 55-70.

Myers-Briggs Personality Type on the Web. 26 March 2001. http://mbtypeguide.com/Type/types.html

Nefesh, The International Network of Orthodox Mental Health Professionals. Russel, Shimon and Dr. Norman Blumenthal, Editors. *Children in Crisis Detection and Intervention: A Practical Guide for Educators, Parents, and Mental Health Professionals.* New York: Nefesh, October 2000.

Neuhaus, Richard John. "What Dennis Prager Did, and Didn't, Learn in Yeshiva." *The Public Square: A Continuing Survey of Religion and Public Life.* 24 August 2000. http://firstthings.com/ftissues/ft9510/public.html

Newman, David. "Losing the Religious Zionist Plot." *The Jerusalem Post, Internet Edition.* 9 May 2001. http://www.jpost.com/Editions/2001/05/09/Opinion/ Opinion25816.html

"The November 1996 issue of Buzz Magazine listed Dennis Prager as one of the 'Ten Most Powerful People in LA.'" http://www.dennisprager.net/indexp12.html

Orlowek, Noach. "How to Raise a Mensch." November 1999. http://www.aish.com/family/mensch/disciplining_kids_effectively. asp.

Pelcovitz, David PhD and Shimon Russel, LCSW. "The At Risk Child: Early Identification and Intervention." *Jewish Observer.* November 1999: 43-46.

Personality Parlour. 26 March 2001. http://www.geocities.com/Athens/Atrium/8202/pp/pphome.html

Potash, David. "Prevention Through Informed Faith." *Jewish Observer.* March 2000.

Prager, Dennis. Personal Interview. 16 October, 2000.

— *Happiness is a Serious Problem*. New York: Regan Books. 1998.

— Lecture: "Obstacles to Achieving Goodness." University of Judaism. Los Angeles. 5 September 2000 http://www.dennisprager.net/indexp25.html

Prager, Moshe. Personal Interview. June, 2001.

Radcliffe, Sarah Chana. *The Delicate Balance: Love and Authority in Torah Parenting*. Jerusalem, Israel: Targum Press, 1989.

Radoszkowicz, Abigail. "Not So Many Youths Throwing Off Their Crocheted Kippot Studies Show." *The Jerusalem Post*. 15 August 2003.

Ragen, Naomi. "The System Needs an Overhaul." *Los Angeles Jewish Times* 9 July, 1999.

Riskin, Shlomo. Personal Interview. 7 and 10 January 2001.

— "The Need to Debate." *Los Angeles Jewish Times* 9-15 July 1999.

Rosenblatt, Gary. "Moderation Leads to Success, Say Local Rabbis." *Baltimore Jewish Times*. 23 December 1988: 60-61.

Rosenblum, Jonathan. "Not God's Scorekeeper." *The Jerusalem Post* 15 June 2001.

— "Think Again: Grateful for Being Chosen." *The Jerusalem Post*. 6 June 2002.

— "Who are the Real Givers." *The Jerusalem Post*. 15 November 2002.

Rothenberg, Avi. Personal Interview. 2001.

Sa'ar, Relly. "Religious Graduates Becoming More Secular." *Ha'aretz News*. 4 May 2001. Ha'aretz Daily Newspaper — English Internet Edition. 10 May 2001. http://www3haaretz.co.il/eng/scripts/article.asp?id=118734&wordd=bar+ilan+university.../0.

Sacks, Jonathan. Personal Interview. 23 April 2001.

— *Arguments for the Sake of Heaven*. Northvale NJ: Jason Aronson. 1991.

— *Celebrating Life*. London: Fount, Harper Collins, 2000.

— *A Letter in the Scroll: Understanding Our Jewish Identity and Exploring the Legacy of the World's Oldest Religion*. New York: The Free Press, Simon & Schuster Inc, 2000.

— "Love, Hate and Jewish Identity." *First Things: The Journal of Religion and Public Life*. 24 August 2000 http://firsththings.com/ftissues/ft9711/articles/sacks.html

— "On Pluralism" *Los Angeles Jewish Times*. 20-26 February 1998.

— *Will We Have Jewish Grandchildren: Jewish Continuity and How to Achieve it.* London: Ballentine Mitchell, 1995.

Samson, David and Tzvi Fishman. *Lights on Orot.* Jerusalem: Torat Erertz Yisrael Publications. 5756.

Sarna, Jonathan D. "The Future of American Orthodoxy." *Sh'ma*. February 2001: 1-3.

Schapiro, Moshe. "Ohr Samayach Addresses the Teen-Dropout Issue." *Yated Ne'eman* 16 April 1999.

— "Drawing Lines in a Moving Field: Lessons to Be Gleaned From the Israeli At-Risk Scene." *Jewish Observer* March 2000: 52-54.

Schiff, A.I. and M. Schneider, "Fortifying and Restoring Jewish Behavior: The Interaction of Home and School." New York, David H. Azrieli Graduate Institute, Report 3, 1994.

Schwab, Shimon. "On Being a Trusted Friend to Your Children: Traditional Chinuch in Modern Times." *Jewish Observer* March 2000: 10-15.

Seidler-Feller, Chaim. "Freedom to Doubt." Olam. May 10, 2002. www.olam.org/magazine/issue6

Shaked, Basy. Personal Interview. 15 August, 2000 and 11 January, 2001.

Shapiro, Yaakov. Personal Interview. 8 August 2000.

— "Changing the System." http://www.shemayisrael.co.il/orgs/rejew/system.htm

— "Choosing a High School for Your Daughter." http://www.shemayisrael.co.il/orgs/rejew/choosing.htm

— "Help, I've Lost my Child: Why Some of Our Children Lose Faith." http://www.shemayisrael.co.il/orgs/rejew/bpvoice.htm

— "Program Director: Manage Thyself!"

— "Rebels Without a Cause. http://www.shemayisrael.co.il/orgs/rejew/j-week.htm

— "Torah Advice for Raising Teenagers. February 1995. http://www.shemayisrael.co.il/orgs/rejew/advice1.htm

— "Torah Advice for Raising Teenagers Part II." February 1995 http://www.shemayisrael.co.il/orgs/rejew/advice2.htm

— "What a Parent Can Do" and "Straight Talk." *Jewish Action.* Summer 1999: 44-48.

Shaviv, Miriam. "She's a Rebel." *The Jerusalem Post Internet Edition.* April 9, 2002. http://cgis.jpost.com/cgi-bin/General/printarti...Features.46565.htm

Shellenbarger, Sue. "Parents of Teenagers Demand, and Get, More Outside Support." *Wall Street Journal* 28 June 2000: B1

Siegal, Nate. Personal Interview. November or December 2001.

Sorotzkin, Benzion. "Begin the Healing Process." *Jewish Action.* Fall 2001.

Speiser, Moshe. "A Safety Net of Telephone Lines." *Jewish Observer* March 2000: 55-59.

Steinsaltz, Adin. Personal Interview. 8 November, 2000 and 5 January, 2001.

— Lecture: "The State of the Nation." King David Hotel. Jerusalem. 7 April 1996. http://www.judaica.ru/english/articles/state.html

— "The Strife of the Spirit." The Institute for Jewish Studies. 16 October 2000. http://www.judaica.ru/english/articles/strife.html

— "Diaspora as a Dream." Interview for Magisterium. 16 October 2000. http://judaica.ru/english/articles/diaspora.html

— Interview with Robert Siegel: "Rabbi Steinsaltz Discusses His Completion of a Translation of the Talmud into English" for All Things Considered, National Public Radio. 14 April 2000.

Symonds, William. "How To Fix America's Schools." *Business Week.* 19 March 2001: 67-80.

Telushkin, Joseph. Personal Interview. 16 October, 2000.

Tigay, Chanan. "Dope Yomi: Drug Abuse Rises Among Orthodox Teens." *Jewish Sentinel* 23 — 28 March 2001: 12-13.

Twerski, Avraham J. MD. "Preventing Teen Drop-Outs: A Matter of Attitude." *Jewish Observer.* November 1999: 68, 79.

— "Tackling a Shonde." *Jewish Action.* 12 December 1999. http://www.ou.org/publications/ja/shondeh/htm

Twerski, Benzion Dr. "Orthodox Youth and Substance Abuse: Shattering the Myths." *Jewish Action.* 12 December 1999.

TypeLogic. 26 March 2001. http://typelogic.com

US News and World Report, 2 Aug. 1999: 11.

Various Authors, 2 August 2000. Online Posting from various forums on Anything You Want to Know About Judaism but Have Nobody to Ask. http://bbs.shemayisrael.com/anything/default.asp

Wein, Berel. Personal Interview. 28 August, 2000 and 8 January, 2001.

Weinberg, Naftali. "Crucial Elements in Parenting." *Jewish Observer* March 2000: 44.

Weinberg, Noah. "Jewish Secrets of Success." 13 September 2000. http://www.aish.com/spirituality/foundations/Jewish_Secrets_of_Success.asp

Wikler, Meir. Personal Interview. 28 August, 2000.

— "Israeli Group Glorifies Adolescent Rebellion." *Wall Street Journal: Letters to the Editor.* 6 December 1991: A15.

Wolbe, Shlomo. "Basic Principles of Parenting." *Jewish Observer.* November 1999: 15-23

— *Planting and Building: Raising a Jewish Child.* Jerusalem, Israel: Feldheim Publishers, 2000.

Woliki, Pesach. "Shavuot: The Purpose of Freedom." 16 May 2002. Email from rabbipesach@yahoo.com.

Wolpin, Yisroel. "Some Kids on the Brink Can be Saved." *Jewish Observer* March 2000: 18.

Young, Judy. Personal Interview. 8 November, 2000.

Yabrov, Zvi Rabbi. "The Chazon Ish on the Educator's responsibility to the Weak and Wayward Student: Principles and Vignettes." *Jewish Observer.* November 1999: 12-14.

Zakutinsky, Yehuda. Personal Interview. 2001.

Glossary

aliyot   the honor of being called up to the Torah

am haaretz   simple person or ignoramus

apikores   apostate

aseret hadibrot   the 10 Commandments

baal musar   a person who knows how to behave

baal(ei) teshuva   returnee(s) to observant Judaism

bachur(im)   student(s)

bechira   choice

beit   second letter of Hebrew alphabet

Bereishit   Genesis

blatt gemorah   a page of the Talmud

blech   hot plate or metal tray used atop the stove to keep food heated on Shabbat

bracha, brachot   blessing(s)

bubbe   grandmother

charedi   ultra-Orthodox

charedishe velt   the world of the ultra-Orthodox

Chasidishe   Chasidic

cheder   class

cherem   excommunication

chessed kindness

chilul Hashem profaning God's name

chinuch education

chiyuv requirement

Chumash the Pentateuch

chumras stringencies of Jewish law

chutzpadik insolent

daven pray

dayan a Jewish judge

derech eretz Jewish ethical behavior

Devarim Deuteronomy

emunah belief

frum observant

frumkeit religiosity

gadol great leader

gadol hador a rabbinical leader of his generation

galut exile

Gan Eden the Garden of Eden

Gehenom Hell

goy non-Jew

goyish not Jewish

halacha Jewish Law

halachically according to Jewish Law

halachot Jewish laws

hamotzi the blessing for bread

Har Sinai Mt. Sinai

Hashem God

hashkafa, hashkafic intellectual or philosophical approach toward
  or understanding of Judaism

hechsher rabbinical approval

kaddish the prayer for the dead

karet capital punishment from God

kashrut kosher

kavanah feeling

kiddushei Hashem   those who sanctify God's name

kippah   skullcap

kiruv   bringing people closer to Judaism

kohanim   people of the Jewish priestly class

kollel   yeshiva for post Talmudic studies

lashon hara   negative speech about someone, tongue-wagging

maariv   evening prayer

maasim   deeds

mashgiach   supervisor

mashiach   the messiah

mechalel Shabbat   profaning the Shabbat

mechallelei Shabbat   those who profane the Shabbat

mechanech   religious teacher, usually for young children

mechitzah   physical separation between men and women

mensch   a moral/ethical person

mezuzah   fixture on door post containing scripture

midah keneged midah   literally "measure for measure"; the process
   by which God gives a person what his/her actions merit

middot   character traits

minchah   afternoon prayer

minhagim   customs

minyan   a quorum of 10 males

Mishnah   first section of the Talmud

mitzvah, mitzvot   commandment(s)

mitzvot bain adam lechavairo   commandments between man and
   man

mitzvot bain adam lemakom   commandments between man and
   God

naaseh venishma   we will do and we will hear

nachas   joy

navi   prophet

negiah   the prohibition of touching a woman

nigunim   tunes

nisyanot   tests from God

olam haba the next world

parsha chapter/section

payas sidelocks

rabbaim, rabbanim rabbis

rasha merusha truly evil

rebbe, rebbeim rabbi(s)

rebetzin the rabbi's wife

ribono shel olam Master of the Universe

Rosh Yeshiva the rabbinic head of the yeshiva

ruchniyut spirituality

sefirah the days between the second night of Passover and Shavuot
which are counted every night

semichah rabbinic ordination

Shabbas, Shabbat Sabbath

shalom bayit family harmony

shaygitz, shkutz a derogatory term for a non-Jew

shidduch(im) matche(s) for marriage

shiur, shiurim class(es)

shivim panim 70 faces (usually refers to the Torah)

shomer negiah men and women who are careful not to touch
each other

shtick attitude (usually in a negative vein)

shul synagogue

shvartza a derogatory term for an Afro-American

sinat chinam senseless hatred

taharat mishpachah family purity

talmid, talmidim student(s)

tefilin phylacteries

tikun fixing, changing

tikun olam fixing or improving the world

treif not kosher

tsniustically modestly dressed

tsures trouble

tzadik(im) righteous person(s)

tzedakah   charity

tzelem elokim   the image of God

tzitzis   four cornered garment with fringes

tzniut   modesty (usually in dress)

yarmulke   skullcap

yeshiva   religious day school or institute of higher learning

yeshivish   relating to the yeshiva world

yetzer hara   the evil inclination

Yidden   Jews

Yiddishkeit   Judaism or Jewish Observance

yiras shamayim   fear of God

zaide   grandfather